SOCIAL SECURITY LE
SUPPLEMENT 2023/24

General Editor
Nick Wikeley, M.A. (Cantab)

Commentary by
Ian Hooker, LL.B.
Formerly Lecturer in Law, University of Nottingham
Formerly Chairman, Social Security Appeal Tribunals

John Mesher, B.A., B.C.L. (Oxon), LL.M. (Yale)
Retired Judge of the Upper Tribunal
Emeritus Professor of Law, University of Sheffield

Edward Mitchell, LL.B.
Judge of the Upper Tribunal

Will Rolt, LL.B.
Judge of the First-tier Tribunal

Tom Royston, M.A. (Cantab)
Barrister

Christopher Ward, M.A. (Cantab)
Judge of the Upper Tribunal

Nick Wikeley, M.A. (Cantab)
Judge of the Upper Tribunal,
Emeritus Professor of Law, University of Southampton

Consultant Editor
Child Poverty Action Group

SWEET & MAXWELL

THOMSON REUTERS

Published in 2024 by Thomson Reuters,
trading as Sweet & Maxwell.
Registered in England & Wales. Company No. 1679046.
Registered office and address for service: 5 Canada Square, Canary
Wharf, London, E14 5AQ.

For further information on our products and services, visit
http://www.sweetandmaxwell.co.uk.

Typeset by Cheshire Typesetting Ltd, Cuddington, Cheshire
Printed and bound by CPI Group (UK) Ltd, Croydon, CR0 4YY

A CIP catalogue record for this book is
available from the British Library.

ISBN (print): 978-0-41411-915-4
ISBN (e-book): 978-0-41411-918-5
ISBN (print and e-book): 978-0-41411-917-8

FSC
www.fsc.org
MIX
Paper | Supporting
responsible forestry
FSC® C013604

PREFACE

This is the Supplement to the 2023/24 edition of *Social Security Legislation*, which was published in September 2023 in four volumes. Part I of this Supplement contains new legislation, presented in the same format as in the main volumes. Parts II, III, IV and V contain the standard updating material—a separate Part for each volume of the main work—which amends the legislative text and key aspects of the commentary, drawing attention to important recent case law, so as to be up to date as at December 4, 2023 (although we have squeezed in some more recent case law developments thanks to the generous understanding of our publishers Sweet & Maxwell). Part VI comprises the cumulative updating material for Volume V, *Income Support and the Legacy Benefits*, which was last published in the 2021/22 edition. Finally, Part VII gives some notice of changes forthcoming between December 2023 and the date to which the main work (2024/25 edition) will be up to date (mid-April 2024), along with the April 2024 benefit rates.

The updating changes in this Supplement include a multitude of amendments to both the primary and secondary legislation governing social security provision. There is detailed analysis of the developing case law on universal credit, now the main means-tested benefit. There have in addition been a myriad of amendments to devolved social security provision in Scotland.

Finally, we have great pleasure in welcoming District Tribunal Judge Will Rolt to our expert team of authors and look forward to working with him on many future editions of these Volumes.

As always, we welcome comments from those who use this Supplement. Please address these to the General Editor, Nick Wikeley, c/o School of Law, The University of Southampton, Highfield, Southampton SO17 1BJ (njw@soton.ac.uk).

Ian Hooker
John Mesher
Edward Mitchell
Will Rolt
Tom Royston
Christopher Ward
Nick Wikeley

February 3, 2024

CONTENTS

USING THE UPDATING MATERIAL IN
THIS SUPPLEMENT

The amendments and updating material contained in Parts II–VI of this Supplement are keyed to the page numbers of the relevant main volume of *Social Security Legislation 2023/24*. Where there have been a significant number of changes to a provision, the whole section, subsection, paragraph or regulation, as amended will tend to be reproduced. Other changes may be noted by an instruction to insert or substitute new material or to delete part of the existing text. The date the change takes effect is also noted. Where explanation is needed of the change, or there is updating relating to existing annotations but no change to the legislation, you will also find commentary in this Supplement. The updating material explains new statutory material, takes on board Upper Tribunal or court decisions, or gives prominence to points which now seem to warrant more detailed attention.

For the most part any relevant new legislation since the main volumes were published is contained in Part I, while amendments to existing legislative provisions are contained in Parts II–VI respectively, together with commentary on new case law. This Supplement amends the text of the main volumes of *Social Security Legislation 2023/24* to be up-to-date as at December 4, 2023.

Nick Wikeley
General Editor

PAGES OF MAIN VOLUMES AFFECTED BY MATERIAL IN THIS SUPPLEMENT

VOLUME III

VOLUME IV

Pages of Main Volumes Affected by Material in this Supplement

Pages of Main Volumes Affected by Material in this Supplement

Main volume page
affected

Relevant paragraph
in supplement

VOLUME V

TABLE OF ABBREVIATIONS USED IN THIS SERIES

1975 Act	Social Security Act 1975
1977 Act	Marriage (Scotland) Act 1977
1979 Act	Pneumoconiosis (Workers' Compensation) Act 1979
1986 Act	Social Security Act 1986
1996 Act	Employment Rights Act 1996
1998 Act	Social Security Act 1998
2002 Act	Tax Credits Act 2002
2004 Act	Gender Recognition Act 2004
2006 Act	Armed Forces Act 2006
2008 Act	Child Maintenance and Other Payments Act 2008
2013 Act	Marriage (Same Sex Couples) Act 2013
2014 Act	Marriage and Civil Partnership (Scotland) Act 2014
2018 Act	Social Security (Scotland) Act 2018
A1P1	Art.1 of Protocol 1 to the European Convention on Human Rights
AA	Attendance Allowance
AA 1992	Attendance Allowance Act 1992
AAC	Administrative Appeals Chamber
AACR	Administrative Appeals Chamber Reports
A.C.	Law Reports, Appeal Cases
A.C.D.	Administrative Court Digest
Admin	Administrative Court
Admin L.R.	Administrative Law Reports
Administration Act	Social Security Administration Act 1992
Administration Regulations	Statutory Paternity Pay and Statutory Adoption Pay (Administration) Regulations 2002
AIP	assessed income period
All E.R.	All England Reports
All E.R. (E.C.)	All England Reports (European Cases)
AMA	Adjudicating Medical Authorities
AO	Adjudication Officer
AOG	*Adjudication Officers Guide*
art.	article
Art.	Article
ASD	Autistic Spectrum Disorder
ASPP	Additional Statutory Paternity Pay
A.T.C.	Annotated Tax Cases

Attendance Allowance Regulations	Social Security (Attendance Allowance) Regulations 1991
AWT	All Work Test
BA	Benefits Agency
Benefits Act	Social Security Contributions and Benefits Act 1992
B.H.R.C.	Butterworths Human Rights Cases
B.L.G.R.	Butterworths Local Government Reports
Blue Books	*The Law Relating to Social Security*, Vols 1–11
B.P.I.R.	Bankruptcy and Personal Insolvency Reports
B.T.C.	British Tax Cases
BTEC	Business and Technology Education Council
B.V.C.	British Value Added Tax Reporter
B.W.C.C.	Butterworths Workmen's Compensation Cases
c.	chapter
C	Commissioner's decision
C&BA 1992	Social Security Contributions and Benefits Act 1992
CAA 2001	Capital Allowances Act 2001
CAB	Citizens Advice Bureau
CAO	Chief Adjudication Officer
CB	Child Benefit
CBA 1975	Child Benefit Act 1975
CBJSA	Contribution-Based Jobseeker's Allowance
C.C.L. Rep.	Community Care Law Reports
CCM	HMRC *New Tax Credits Claimant Compliance Manual*
C.E.C.	European Community Cases
CERA	cortical evoked response audiogram
CESA	Contribution-based Employment and Support Allowance
CFS	chronic fatigue syndrome
Ch.	Chancery Division Law Reports; Chapter
Charter	Charter of Fundamental Rights of the European Union
Citizenship Directive	Directive 2004/38/EC of the European Parliament and of the Council of April 29, 2004
CJEC	Court of Justice of the European Communities
CJEU	Court of Justice of the European Union
Claims and Payments Regulations	Social Security (Claims and Payments) Regulations 1987
Claims and Payments Regulations 1979	Social Security (Claims and Payments) Regulations 1979
Claims and Payments Regulations 2013	Universal Credit, Personal Independence Payment, Jobseeker's Allowance and Employment and Support Allowance (Claims and Payments) Regulations 2013
CM	Case Manager
CMA	Chief Medical Adviser
CMEC	Child Maintenance and Enforcement Commission

C.M.L.R.	Common Market Law Reports
C.O.D.	Crown Office Digest
COLL	*Collective Investment Schemes Sourcebook*
Community, The	European Community
Computation of Earnings Regulations	Social Security Benefit (Computation of Earnings) Regulations 1978
Computation of Earnings Regulations 1996	Social Security Benefit (Computation of Earnings) Regulations 1996
Consequential Provisions Act	Social Security (Consequential Provisions) Act 1992
Contributions and Benefits Act	Social Security Contributions and Benefits Act 1992
Contributions Regulations	Social Security (Contributions) Regulations 2001
COPD	chronic obstructive pulmonary disease
CP	Carer Premium; Chamber President
CPAG	Child Poverty Action Group
CPR	Civil Procedure Rules
Cr. App. R.	Criminal Appeal Reports
CRCA 2005	Commissioners for Revenue and Customs Act 2005
Credits Regulations 1974	Social Security (Credits) Regulations 1974
Credits Regulations 1975	Social Security (Credits) Regulations 1975
Crim. L.R.	Criminal Law Review
CRU	Compensation Recovery Unit
CSA 1995	Children (Scotland) Act 1995
CSIH	Inner House of the Court of Session (Scotland)
CSM	Child Support Maintenance
CS(NI)O 1995	Child Support (Northern Ireland) Order 1995
CSOH	Outer House of the Court of Session (Scotland)
CSPSSA 2000	Child Support, Pensions and Social Security Act 2000
CTA	Common Travel Area
CTA 2009	Corporation Tax Act 2009
CTA 2010	Corporation Tax Act 2010
CTB	Council Tax Benefit
CTC	Child Tax Credit
CTC Regulations	Child Tax Credit Regulations 2002
CTF	child trust fund
CTS	Carpal Tunnel Syndrome
DAC	Directive 2011/16/ EU (Directive on administrative co-operation in the field of taxation)
DAT	Disability Appeal Tribunal
dB	decibels
DCA	Department for Constitutional Affairs
DCP	Disabled Child Premium
Decisions and Appeals Regulations 1999	Social Security Contributions (Decisions and Appeals) Regulations 1999

Dependency Regulations	Social Security Benefit (Dependency) Regulations 1977
DfEE	Department for Education and Employment
DHSS	Department of Health and Social Security
Disability Living Allowance Regulations	Social Security (Disability Living Allowance) Regulations
DIY	do it yourself
DLA	Disability Living Allowance
DLA Regs 1991	Social Security (Disability Living Allowance) Regulations 1991
DLAAB	Disability Living Allowance Advisory Board
DLADWAA 1991	Disability Living Allowance and Disability Working Allowance Act 1991
DM	Decision Maker
DMA	Decision-making and Appeals
DMG	*Decision Makers' Guide*
DMP	Delegated Medical Practitioner
DP	Disability Premium
DPT	diffuse pleural thickening
DPTC	Disabled Person's Tax Credit
DRO	Debt Relief Order
DSD	Department for Social Development (Northern Ireland)
DSM IV; DSM-5	Diagnostic and Statistical Manual of Mental Disorders of the American Psychiatric Association
DSS	Department of Social Security
DTI	Department of Trade and Industry
DWA	Disability Working Allowance
DWP	Department for Work and Pensions
DWPMS	Department for Work and Pensions Medical Service
EAA	Extrinsic Allergic Alveolitis
EAT	Employment Appeal Tribunal
EC	European Community
ECHR	European Convention on Human Rights
ECJ	European Court of Justice
E.C.R.	European Court Reports
ECSC	European Coal and Steel Community
ECSMA	European Convention on Social and Medical Assistance
EEA	European Economic Area
EEA EFTA Separation Agreement	Agreement on arrangements between Iceland, the Principality of Liechtenstein, the Kingdom of Norway and the United Kingdom of Great Britain and Northern Ireland following the withdrawal of the United Kingdom from the European Union, the EEA Agreement and other agreements applicable between the United Kingdom and the EEA EFTA States by virtue of the United Kingdom's membership of the European Union

EEA Regulations 2016	Immigration (European Economic Area) Regulations 2016
EEC	European Economic Community
EESSI	Electronic Exchange of Social Security Information
E.G.	Estates Gazette
E.G.L.R.	Estates Gazette Law Reports
EHC plan	education, health and care plan
EHIC	European Health Insurance Card
EHRC	European Human Rights Commission
E.H.R.R.	European Human Rights Reports
EL	employers' liability
E.L.R	Education Law Reports
EMA	Education Maintenance Allowance
EMP	Examining Medical Practitioner
Employment and Support Allowance Regulations	Employment and Support Allowance Regulations 2008
EPS	extended period of sickness
Eq. L.R.	Equality Law Reports
ERA	evoked response audiometry
ERA scheme	Employment, Retention and Advancement scheme
ES	Employment Service
ESA	Employment and Support Allowance
ESA Regs 2013	Employment and Support Allowance Regulations 2013
ESA Regulations	Employment and Support Allowance Regulations 2008
ESA WCAt	Employment and Support Allowance Work Capability Assessment
ESC	employer supported childcare
ESE Scheme	Employment, Skills and Enterprise Scheme
ESE Regulations	Jobseeker's Allowance (Employment, Skills and Enterprise Scheme) Regulations 2011
ESES Regulations	Jobseeker's Allowance (Employment, Skills and Enterprise Scheme) Regulations 2011
ETA 1973	Employment and Training Act 1973
ETA(NI) 1950	Employment and Training Act (Northern Ireland) 1950
ETS	European Treaty Series
EU	European Union
Eu.L.R.	European Law Reports
EWCA Civ	Civil Division of the Court of Appeal (England and Wales)
EWHC Admin	Administrative Court, part of the High Court (England and Wales)
FA 1993	Finance Act 1993
FA 1996	Finance Act 1996
FA 2004	Finance Act 2004
Fam. Law	Family Law

FAS	Financial Assistance Scheme
F.C.R.	Family Court Reporter
FEV	forced expiratory volume
FIS	Family Income Supplement
FISMA 2000	Financial Services and Markets Act 2000
F.L.R.	Family Law Reports
FME	further medical evidence
F(No.2)A 2005	Finance (No.2) Act 2005
FOTRA	Free of Tax to Residents Abroad
FRAA	flat rate accrual amount
FRS Act 2004	Fire and Rescue Services Act 2004
FSCS	Financial Services Compensation Scheme
FTT	First-tier Tribunal
General Benefit Regulations 1982	Social Security (General Benefit) Regulations 1982
General Regulations	Statutory Shared Parental Pay (General) Regulations 2014
GMCA	Greater Manchester Combined Authority
GMFRA	Greater Manchester Fire and Rescue Authority
GMP	Guaranteed Minimum Pension
GMWDA	Greater Manchester Waste Disposal Authority
GNVQ	General National Vocational Qualification
GP	General Practitioner
GRA	Gender Recognition Act 2004
GRB	Graduated Retirement Benefit
GRP	Graduated Retirement Pension
HB	Housing Benefit
HB (WSP) R (NI) 2017	Housing Benefit (Welfare Social Payment) Regulations (Northern Ireland) 2017
HBRB	Housing Benefit Review Board
HCA	Homes and Communities Agency
HCD	House of Commons Debates
HCP	healthcare professional
HCV	Hepatitis C virus
Health Service Act	National Health Service Act 2006
Health Service (Wales) Act	National Health Service (Wales) Act 2006
HIV	Human Immunodeficiency Virus
HL	House of Lords
H.L.R.	Housing Law Reports
HMIT	Her Majesty's Inspector of Taxes
HMRC	Her Majesty's Revenue and Customs
HMSO	Her Majesty's Stationery Office
Hospital In-Patients Regulations 1975	Social Security (Hospital In-Patients) Regulations 1975
Housing Benefit Regulations	Housing Benefit Regulations 2006
HP	Health Professional
HPP	Higher Pensioner Premium
HRA 1998	Human Rights Act 1998

Table of Abbreviations used in this Series

H.R.L.R.	Human Rights Law Reports
HRP	Home Responsibilities Protection
HSE	Health and Safety Executive
IAC	Immigration and Asylum Chamber
IAP	Intensive Activity Period
IB	Incapacity Benefit
IB PCA	Incapacity Benefit Personal Capability Assessment
IB Regs	Social Security (Incapacity Benefit) Regulations 1994
IB Regulations	Social Security (Incapacity Benefit) Regulations 1994
IB/IS/SDA	Incapacity Benefits Regime
IBJSA	Income-Based Jobseeker's Allowance
IBS	Irritable Bowel Syndrome
ICA	Invalid Care Allowance
I.C.R.	Industrial Cases Reports
ICTA 1988	Income and Corporation Taxes Act 1988
IFW Regulations	Incapacity for Work (General) Regulations 1995
IH	Inner House of the Court of Session
I.I.	Industrial Injuries
IIAC	Industrial Injuries Advisory Council
IIDB	Industrial Injuries Disablement Benefit
ILO	International Labour Organization
Imm. A.R.	Immigration Appeal Reports
Incapacity for Work Regulations	Social Security (Incapacity for Work) (General) Regulations 1995
Income Support General Regulations	Income Support (General) Regulations 1987
IND	Immigration and Nationality Directorate of the Home Office
I.N.L.R.	Immigration and Nationality Law Reports
I.O.	Insurance Officer
IPPR	Institute of Public Policy Research
IRESA	Income-Related Employment and Support Allowance
I.R.L.R.	Industrial Relations Law Reports
IS	Income Support
IS Regs	Income Support Regulations
IS Regulations	Income Support (General) Regulations 1987
ISA	Individual Savings Account
ISBN	International Standard Book Number
ITA 2007	Income Tax Act 2007
ITEPA 2003	Income Tax, Earnings and Pensions Act 2003
I.T.L. Rep.	International Tax Law Reports
I.T.R.	Industrial Tribunals Reports
ITS	Independent Tribunal Service
ITTOIA 2005	Income Tax (Trading and Other Income) Act 2005

IVB	Invalidity Benefit
IW (General) Regs	Social Security (Incapacity for Work) (General) Regulations 1995
IW (Transitional) Regs	Incapacity for Work (Transitional) Regulations
Jobseeker's Allowance Regulations	Jobseeker's Allowance Regulations 1996
Jobseeker's Regulations 1996	Jobseeker's Allowance Regulations 1996
JSA	Jobseeker's Allowance
JSA 1995	Jobseekers Act 1995
JSA (NI) Regulations	Jobseeker's Allowance (Northern Ireland) Regulations 1996
JSA (Transitional) Regulations	Jobseeker's Allowance (Transitional) Regulations 1996
JSA Regs 1996	Jobseeker's Allowance Regulations 1996
JSA Regs 2013	Jobseeker's Allowance Regulations 2013
JS(NI)O 1995	Jobseekers (Northern Ireland) Order 1995
J.S.S.L.	Journal of Social Security Law
J.S.W.L.	Journal of Social Welfare Law
K.B.	Law Reports, King's Bench
L.& T.R.	Landlord and Tenant Reports
LCW	limited capability for work
LCWA	Limited Capability for Work Assessment
LCWRA	limited capability for work-related activity
LDEDC Act 2009	Local Democracy, Economic Development and Construction Act 2009
LEA	local education authority
LEL	Lower Earnings Limit
LET	low earnings threshold
LGA 2003	Local Government Act 2003
L.G. Rev.	Local Government Review
L.G.L.R.	Local Government Reports
L.J.R.	Law Journal Reports
LRP	liable relative payment
L.S.G.	Law Society Gazette
Luxembourg Court	Court of Justice of the European Union (also referred to as CJEC and ECJ)
MA	Maternity Allowance
MAF	Medical Assessment Framework
Maternity Allowance Regulations	Social Security (Maternity Allowance) Regulations 1987
MDC	Mayoral development corporation
ME	myalgic encephalomyelitis
Medical Evidence Regulations	Social Security (Medical Evidence) Regulations 1976
MEN	Mandatory Employment Notification
Mesher and Wood	*Income Support, the Social Fund and Family Credit: the Legislation* (1996)
M.H.L.R.	Mental Health Law Reports
MHP	mental health problems
MIF	minimum income floor

MIG	minimum income guarantee
Migration Regulations	Employment and Support Allowance (Transitional Provisions, Housing Benefit and Council Tax Benefit (Existing Awards) (No.2) Regulations 2010
MP	Member of Parliament
MRSA	methicillin-resistant Staphylococcus aureus
MS	Medical Services
MWA Regulations	Jobseeker's Allowance (Mandatory Work Activity Scheme) Regulations 2011
MWAS Regulations	Jobseeker's Allowance (Mandatory Work Activity Scheme) Regulations 2011
NCB	National Coal Board
NDPD	Notes on the Diagnosis of Prescribed Diseases
NHS	National Health Service
NI	National Insurance
N.I..	Northern Ireland Law Reports
NICA	Northern Ireland Court of Appeal
NICom	Northern Ireland Commissioner
NICs	National Insurance Contributions
NINO	National Insurance Number
NIRS 2	National Insurance Recording System
N.L.J.	New Law Journal
NMC	Nursing and Midwifery Council
Northern Ireland Contributions and Benefits Act	Social Security Contributions and Benefits (Northern Ireland) Act 1992
N.P.C.	New Property Cases
NRCGT	non-resident capital gains tax
NTC Manual	Clerical procedures manual on tax credits
NUM	National Union of Mineworkers
NUS	National Union of Students
OCD	obsessive compulsive disorder
Ogus, Barendt and Wikeley	A. Ogus, E. Barendt and N. Wikeley, *The Law of Social Security* (1995)
Old Cases Act	Industrial Injuries and Diseases (Old Cases) Act 1975
OPB	One Parent Benefit
O.P.L.R.	Occupational Pensions Law Reports
OPSSAT	Office of the President of Social Security Appeal Tribunals
Overlapping Benefits Regulations	Social Security (Overlapping Benefits) Regulations 1975
P	retirement pension case
P. & C.R.	Property and Compensation Reports
para.	paragraph
Pay Regulations	Statutory Paternity Pay and Statutory Adoption Pay (General) Regulations 2002; Statutory Shared Parental Pay (General) Regulations 2014
PAYE	Pay As You Earn

PC	Privy Council
PCA	Personal Capability Assessment
PCC	Police and Crime Commissioner
PD	Practice Direction; prescribed disease
Pens. L.R.	Pensions Law Reports
Pensions Act	Pension Schemes Act 1993
PEP	Personal Equity Plan
Persons Abroad Regulations	Social Security Benefit (Persons Abroad) Regulations 1975
Persons Residing Together Regulations	Social Security Benefit (Persons Residing Together) Regulations 1977
PIE	Period of Interruption of Employment
PILON	pay in lieu of notice
Pilot Scheme Regulations	Universal Credit (Work-Related Requirements) In Work Pilot Scheme and Amendment Regulations 2015
PIP	Personal Independence Payment
P.I.Q.R.	Personal Injuries and Quantum Reports
Polygamous Marriages Regulations	Social Security and Family Allowances (Polygamous Marriages) Regulations 1975
PPF	Pension Protection Fund
Prescribed Diseases Regulations	Social Security (Industrial Injuries) (Prescribed Diseases) Regulations 1985
PSCS	Pension Service Computer System
Pt	Part
PTA	pure tone audiometry
P.T.S.R.	Public and Third Sector Law Reports
PTWR 2000	Part-time Workers (Prevention of Less Favourable Treatment) Regulations 2000
PVS	private and voluntary sectors
Q.B.	Queen's Bench Law Reports
QBD	Queen's Bench Division
QCS Board	Quality Contract Scheme Board
QEF	qualifying earnings factor
QYP	qualifying young person
r.	rule
R	Reported Decision
R.C.	Rules of the Court of Session
REA	Reduced Earnings Allowance
Reciprocal Agreement with Ireland	Convention on Social Security between the Government of the United Kingdom and Northern Ireland and the Government of Ireland
reg.	regulation
RIPA	Regulation of Investigatory Powers Act 2000
RMO	Responsible Medical Officer
rr.	rules
RR	reference rate
RSI	repetitive strain injury
RTI	Real Time Information

R.V.R.	Rating & Valuation Reporter
s.	section
S	Scottish Decision
SAP	Statutory Adoption Pay
SAPOE Regulations	Jobseeker's Allowance (Schemes for Assisting Persons to Obtain Employment) Regulations 2013
SAWS	Seasonal Agricultural Work Scheme
SAYE	Save As You Earn
SB	Supplementary Benefit
SBAT	Supplementary Benefit Appeal Tribunal
SBC	Supplementary Benefits Commission
S.C.	Session Cases
S.C. (H.L.)	Session Cases (House of Lords)
S.C. (P.C.)	Session Cases (Privy Council)
S.C.C.R.	Scottish Criminal Case Reports
S.C.L.R.	Scottish Civil Law Reports
Sch.	Schedule
SDA	Severe Disablement Allowance
SDP	Severe Disability Premium
SEC	Social Entitlement Chamber
SEN	special educational needs
SERPS	State Earnings Related Pension Scheme
ShPP	statutory shared parental pay
ShPP Regulations	Statutory Shared Parental Pay (General) Regulations 2014
SI	Statutory Instrument
SIP	Share Incentive Plan
S.J.	Solicitors Journal
S.J.L.B.	Solicitors Journal Law Brief
SLAN	statement like an award notice
S.L.T.	Scots Law Times
SMP	Statutory Maternity Pay
SMP (General) Regulations 1986	Statutory Maternity Pay (General) Regulations 1986
Social Security Directive	Council Directive 79/7/EEC of 19 December 1978 on the progressive implementation of the principle of equal treatment for men and women in matters of social security
SPC	State Pension Credit
SPC Regulations	State Pension Credit Regulations 2002
SPCA 2002	State Pension Credit Act 2002
SPL Regulations	Shared Parental Leave Regulations 2014
SPP	Statutory Paternity Pay
ss.	sections
SS (No.2) A 1980	Social Security (No.2) Act 1980
SSA 1975	Social Security Act 1975
SSA 1977	Social Security Act 1977
SSA 1978	Social Security Act 1978

Table of Abbreviations used in this Series

SSA 1979	Social Security Act 1979
SSA 1981	Social Security Act 1981
SSA 1986	Social Security Act 1986
SSA 1988	Social Security Act 1988
SSA 1989	Social Security Act 1989
SSA 1990	Social Security Act 1990
SSA 1998	Social Security Act 1998
SSAA 1992	Social Security Administration Act 1992
SSAC	Social Security Advisory Committee
SSAT	Social Security Appeal Tribunal
SSCBA 1992	Social Security Contributions and Benefits Act 1992
SSCB(NI)A 1992	Social Security Contributions and Benefits (Northern Ireland) Act 1992
SSCPA 1992	Social Security (Consequential Provisions) Act 1992
SSD	Secretary of State for Defence
SSHBA 1982	Social Security and Housing Benefits Act 1982
SSHD	Secretary of State for the Home Department
SSI	Scottish Statutory Instrument
SS(MP)A 1977	Social Security (Miscellaneous Provisions) Act 1977
SSP	Statutory Sick Pay
SSP (General) Regulations	Statutory Sick Pay (General) Regulations 1982
SSPA 1975	Social Security Pensions Act 1975
SSPP	statutory shared parental pay
SS(S)A 2018	Social Security (Scotland) Act 2018
SSWP	Secretary of State for Work and Pensions
State Pension Credit Regulations	State Pension Credit Regulations 2002
S.T.C.	Simon's Tax Cases
S.T.C. (S.C.D.)	Simon's Tax Cases: Special Commissioners' Decisions
S.T.I.	Simon's Tax Intelligence
STIB	Short-Term Incapacity Benefit
subpara.	subparagraph
subs.	subsection
Swiss Citizens' Rights Agreement	Agreement between the United Kingdom of Great Britain and Northern Ireland and the Swiss Confederation on citizens' rights following the withdrawal of the United Kingdom from the European Union and the Free Movement of Persons Agreement
T	Tribunal of Commissioners' Decision
T.C.	Tax Cases
TCA 1999	Tax Credits Act 1999
TCA 2002	Tax Credits Act 2002
TCC	Technology and Construction Court
TCEA 2007	Tribunals, Courts and Enforcement Act 2007

TCGA 1992	Taxation of Chargeable Gains Act 2002
TCTM	*Tax Credits Technical Manual*
TEC	Treaty Establishing the European Community
TENS	transcutaneous electrical nerve stimulation
TEU	Treaty on European Union
TFC	tax-free childcare
TFEU	Treaty on the Functioning of the European Union
TIOPA 2010	Taxation (International and Other Provisions) Act 2010
TMA 1970	Taxes Management Act 1970
T.R.	Taxation Reports
Transfer of Functions Act	Social Security Contributions (Transfer of Functions etc.) Act 1999
Tribunal Procedure Rules	Tribunal Procedure (First-tier Tribunal)(Social Entitlement Chamber) Rules 2008
UB	Unemployment Benefit
UC	Universal Credit
UC Regs 2013	Universal Credit Regulations 2013
UCB	Unacceptable Customer Behaviour
UCITS	Undertakings for Collective Investments in Transferable Securities
UKAIT	UK Asylum and Immigration Tribunal
UKBA	UK Border Agency of the Home Office
UKCC	United Kingdom Central Council for Nursing, Midwifery and Health Visiting
UKFTT	United Kingdom First-tier Tribunal Tax Chamber
UKHL	United Kingdom House of Lords
U.K.H.R.R.	United Kingdom Human Rights Reports
UKSC	United Kingdom Supreme Court
UKUT	United Kingdom Upper Tribunal
UN	United Nations
Universal Credit Regulations	Universal Credit Regulations 2013
URL	uniform resource locator
USI Regs	Social Security (Unemployment, Sickness and Invalidity Benefit) Regulations 1983
USI Regulations	Social Security (Unemployment, Sickness and Invalidity Benefit) Regulations 1983
UT	Upper Tribunal
VAT	Value Added Tax
VCM	vinyl chloride monomer
Vol.	Volume
VWF	Vibration White Finger
W	Welsh Decision
WCA	Work Capability Assessment
WCAt	limited capability for work assessment
WFHRAt	Work-Focused Health-Related Assessment
WFI	work-focused interview
WFTC	Working Families Tax Credit

Wikeley, Annotations	N. Wikeley, "Annotations to Jobseekers Act 1995 (c.18)" in *Current Law Statutes Annotated* (1995)
Wikeley, Ogus and Barendt	Wikeley, Ogus and Barendt, *The Law of Social Security* (2002)
Withdrawal Agreement	Agreement on the Withdrawal of the United Kingdom of Great Britain and Northern Ireland from the European Union and the European Atomic Energy Community 2019
W.L.R.	Weekly Law Reports
WLUK	Westlaw UK
Workmen's Compensation Acts	Workmen's Compensation Acts 1925 to 1945
WP	Widow's Pension
WPS	War Pensions Scheme
WRA 2007	Welfare Reform Act 2007
WRA 2009	Welfare Reform Act 2009
WRA 2012	Welfare Reform Act 2012
W-RA Regulations	Employment and Support Allowance (Work-Related Activity) Regulations 2011
WRAAt	Work-Related Activity Assessment
WRPA 1999	Welfare Reform and Pensions Act 1999
WRP(NI)O 1999	Welfare Reform and Pensions (Northern Ireland) Order 1999
WRWA 2016	Welfare Reform and Work Act 2016
WSP (LCP) R (NI) 2016	Welfare Supplementary Payment (Loss of Carer Payments) Regulations (Northern Ireland) 2016
WSP (LDRP) R (NI) 2016	Welfare Supplementary Payment (Loss of Disability-Related Premiums) Regulations (Northern Ireland) 2016
WSPR (NI) 2016	Welfare Supplementary Payment Regulations (Northern Ireland) 2016
WTC	Working Tax Credit
WTC Regulations	Working Tax Credit (Entitlement and Maximum Rate) Regulations 2002

TABLE OF CASES

Table of Cases

TABLE OF COMMISSIONERS' DECISIONS

TABLE OF EUROPEAN LEGISLATION

TABLE OF STATUTES

TABLE OF STATUTORY INSTRUMENTS

PART I

NEW LEGISLATION

NEW STATUTES

Neonatal Care (Leave and Pay) Act 2023

(2023 c.20)

Neonatal care leave and pay

1. In the Schedule— 1.001
(a) Part 1 creates a statutory entitlement to neonatal care leave,
(b) Part 2 creates a statutory entitlement to neonatal care pay, and
(c) Part 3 contains related amendments.

Power to make consequential provision

2. *[not yet in force]* 1.002

Extent, commencement and short title

3.—(1) An amendment or repeal made by the Schedule has the same 1.003
extent as the provision to which it relates.

(2) Otherwise, this Act extends to England and Wales, Scotland and
Northern Ireland.

(3) Section 1, section 2 and the Schedule come into force on such day
as the Secretary of State may by regulations made by statutory instrument
appoint; and different days may be appointed for different purposes.

(4) This section comes into force on the day on which this Act is passed.

(5) This Act may be cited as the Neonatal Care (Leave and Pay) Act
2023.

SCHEDULE – *[not yet in force]*

GENERAL NOTE

This Act will amend or insert a number of provisions into the Employment Rights 1.004
Act 1996 and the Social Security Contributions and Benefits Act 1992. These
provide powers to make regulations to create an entitlement to Neonatal Care Leave
and Pay for eligible employees with parental or other relevant personal relationship
with a child who is receiving, or has received, neonatal care. In particular, the Act's
powers allow provision to be made for Neonatal Care Leave—a right for employed
parents to be absent from work for a prescribed period (to be set at a minimum of
one week) in respect of a child who is receiving, or has received, neonatal care (with
associated employment protections). All employees who meet the eligibility conditions will be entitled to this leave, regardless of how long they have worked for their
employer. The leave must be taken before the end of a period of at least 68 weeks
beginning with the date of the child's birth. In addition, the Act's powers allow provision to be made for Neonatal Care Pay—a right for those eligible parents who meet
minimum requirements relating to continuity of employment (at least 26 weeks with
their current employer) and earnings to be paid during that leave at a prescribed
rate. In line with other entitlements to paid statutory leave, the Act enables provision
to be made for employers to reclaim payments from the Government. It is antici-
pated that the new provisions will be in force as from April 2025.

Retained EU Law (Revocation and Reform) Act 2023

(2023 c.28)

ARRANGEMENT OF SECTIONS REPRODUCED

Schedules are not reproduced. While Sch.1 contains a lengthy list of legislative provisions which are subject to the "sunset" effected by s.1, none of them addresses matters which are the subject of the present volume.

Sunset of EU-derived subordinate legislation and retained direct EU legislation

1.005   **1.**—(1) Legislation listed in Schedule 1 is revoked at the end of 2023, to the extent specified there.

(2) In that Schedule—

(a) Part 1 lists subordinate legislation;

(b) Part 2 lists retained direct EU legislation.

(3) The revocation of an instrument, or a provision of an instrument, by subsection (1) does not affect an amendment made by the instrument or provision to any other enactment.

(4) Subsection (1) does not apply to anything specified in regulations made by a relevant national authority.

(5) No regulations may be made under subsection (4) after 31 October 2023.

GENERAL NOTE

1.006   Regulations under subs.(4) are the Retained EU Law (Revocation and Reform) Act 2023 (Revocation and Sunset Disapplication) Regulations 2023 (SI 2023/1143). As no social security measure is within the sunset, there is no relevant question of disapplication for the purposes of this Supplement.

Sunset of retained EU rights, powers, liabilities et

1.007   **2.**—(1) Section 4 of the European Union (Withdrawal) Act 2018 (saving for rights, powers, liabilities etc under section 2(1) of the European Communities Act 1972) is repealed at the end of 2023.

(2) Accordingly, anything which, immediately before the end of 2023, is retained EU law by virtue of that section is not recognised or available in domestic law at or after that time (and, accordingly, is not to be enforced, allowed or followed).

"Assimilated law"

5.—(1) As regards all times after the end of 2023, the things listed in the left-hand column are to be known by the names in the right-hand column.

1.008

At or before the end of 2023	After the end of 2023
Retained EU law	Assimilated law
Retained case law	Assimilated case law
Retained direct EU legislation	Assimilated direct legislation
Retained direct minor EU legislation	Assimilated direct minor legislation
Retained direct principal EU legislation	Assimilated direct principal legislation
Retained domestic case law	Assimilated domestic case law
Retained EU case law	Assimilated EU case law
Retained EU obligation	Assimilated obligation
Retained EU law governing the CAP direct payment schemes	Assimilated law governing the CAP direct payment schemes
Retained direct EU CAP legislation	Assimilated direct CAP legislation

(2) Accordingly, as regards all times at or before the end of 2023, the things listed in the right-hand column continue to be known by the names in the left-hand column.

(3) *[not in force]*.

(4) A reference in an enactment to a thing in the left-hand column of the table in subsection (1) is to be read, as regards all times after the end of 2023, as a reference to the thing by its name in the right-hand column.

(5) Subsection (4) does not apply to any title of an enactment (including any provision about how an enactment may be cited) or any reference to a title of an enactment.

(6) The provision that may be made by regulations under section 19 (power to make consequential provision) in consequence of subsection (1) of this section includes, in particular—

(a) provision adding entries to the table in subsection (1) for things which relate to the things for which there are entries in the table (and adding definitions for those things to subsection (7));

(b) provision amending an enactment in consequence of the name of a thing being changed by subsection (1) (including by virtue of regulations under section 19).

(7) In this section—

"retained case law", "retained domestic case law" and "retained EU case law" have the meaning given by section 6(7) of the European Union (Withdrawal) Act 2018 (as it has effect on the day on which this Act is passed);

"retained EU law", "retained direct EU legislation", "retained direct minor EU legislation", "retained direct principal EU legislation" and "retained EU obligation" have the meaning given by Schedule 1 to the Interpretation Act 1978 (as it has effect on the day on which this Act is passed);

... [*omitted*].

Compatibility

1.009   **7.**—(1) A relevant national authority may by regulations provide that subsection (2) applies (and section 5(A2) of the European Union (Withdrawal) Act 2018 does not apply) to the relationship between—

(a) any domestic enactment specified in the regulations, and

(b) any provision of retained direct EU legislation so specified.

(2) Where this subsection applies, the domestic enactment specified under subsection (1)(a)—

(a) must, so far as possible, be read and given effect in a way which is compatible with the provision of retained direct EU legislation specified under subsection (1)(b), and

(b) is subject to that provision of retained direct EU legislation so far as it is incompatible with it.

(3) Regulations under subsection (1) may make provision by modifying any enactment.

(4) No regulations may be made under subsection (1) after 23 June 2026.

(5) In this section "domestic enactment" has the same meaning as in section 5 of the European Union (Withdrawal) Act 2018.

Sections 9 and 10 make extensive modifications to Sch. 8 to the European Union (Withdrawal) Act 2018, in particular as to the scope of regulation-making powers, but do not amend the selected provisions of Sch. 8 in the main volume. An amendment made to s. 7(5) of the 2018 Act is noted separately.

Power to restate retained EU law

1.010   **11.**—(1) A relevant national authority may by regulations restate, to any extent, any secondary retained EU law.

(2) In this Act "secondary retained EU law" means—

(a) any retained EU law that is not primary legislation;

(b) any retained EU law that is primary legislation the text of which was inserted by subordinate legislation.

(3) A restatement is not retained EU law.

(4) Any effect which is produced in relation to the thing being restated by virtue of the retained EU law mentioned in subsection (5) does not apply in relation to the restatement.

(5) The retained EU law referred to in subsection (4) is—

(a) the principle of the supremacy of EU law,

(b) retained general principles of EU law, and

(c) anything which is retained EU law by virtue of section or 6(3) or (6) of the European Union (Withdrawal) Act 2018.

(6) But a restatement may, if the relevant authority considers it appropriate, itself produce an effect that is equivalent to an effect referred to in subsection (4).

(7) No regulations may be made under this section after the end of 2023.

(8) In this section—

"restatement": references to restatement, in relation to anything which is retained EU law by virtue of section 4 or 6(3) or (6) of the European Union (Withdrawal) Act 2018, include codification;

"retained general principles of EU law" the meaning given by section 6(7) of the European Union (Withdrawal) Act 2018.

Power to restate assimilated law or reproduce sunsetted retained EU rights, powers, liabilities etc

12.—(1) A relevant national authority may by regulations restate, to any extent, any secondary assimilated law.

1.011

(2) In this Act "secondary assimilated law" means—

(a) any assimilated law that is not primary legislation;

(b) any assimilated law that is primary legislation the text of which was inserted by subordinate legislation.

(3) A restatement is not assimilated law.

(4) Any effect which is produced in relation to the thing being restated by virtue of anything that is assimilated law by virtue of section 6(3) or (6) of the European Union (Withdrawal) Act 2018 does not apply in relation to the restatement.

(5) But a restatement may, if the relevant national authority considers it appropriate, itself produce an effect that is equivalent to an effect referred to in subsection (4).

(6) A restatement may also, if the relevant national authority considers it appropriate, produce an effect that is equivalent to an effect within subsection (7).

(7) An effect is within this subsection if it would, but for sections 2 to 4, be produced in relation to the thing being restated by virtue of—

(a) the principle of the supremacy of EU law,

(b) retained general principles of EU law, or

(c) anything which was retained EU law by virtue of section 4 of the European Union (Withdrawal) Act 2018.

(8) A relevant national authority may by regulations reproduce, to any extent, the effect that anything which was retained EU law by virtue of section 4 or 6(3) or (6) of European Union (Withdrawal) Act 2018 would have, but for sections 2 to 4 of this Act.

(9) No regulations may be made under this section after 23 June 2026.

(10) In this section—

"restatement": references to restatement, in relation to anything which is assimilated law by virtue of section 6(3) or (6) of the European Union (Withdrawal) Act 2018, include codification;

"retained general principles of EU law" has the meaning that was given by section 6(7) of the European Union (Withdrawal) Act 2018 immediately before the end of 2023.

Powers to restate or reproduce: general

1.012

13.—(1) This section applies for the purposes of sections 11 and 12.

(2) A restatement may use words or concepts that are different from those used in the law being restated.

(3) A restatement may make any change which the relevant national authority considers appropriate for one or more of the following purposes—

(a) resolving ambiguities;

(b) removing doubts or anomalies;

(c) facilitating improvement in the clarity or accessibility of the law (including by omitting anything which is legally unnecessary).

(4) Regulations under section 11 or 12—

(a) may make provision about the relationship between what is restated and a relevant enactment specified in the regulations, but

(b) subject to that, may not make express provision about the relationship between what is restated and other enactments.

(5) Regulations under section 11 or 12 may not codify or reproduce the principle of the supremacy of EU law or a retained general principle of EU law.

(6) Nothing in subsection (5)—

(a) prevents regulations under section 11 or 12 from codifying or reproducing, in relation to a particular enactment, an effect equivalent to an effect which is produced, or would but for sections 2 to 4 be produced, in relation to the enactment by virtue of the principle of supremacy of EU law or retained general principles of EU law, or

(b) prevents regulations under section 11 or 12 which codify or reproduce anything which is or was retained EU law by virtue of section 4 of the European Union (Withdrawal) Act 2018 from producing an effect equivalent to an effect which is produced, or would but for sections 2 to 4 be produced, in relation to that thing by virtue of the principle of supremacy of EU law or retained general principles of EU law.

(7) The provision that may be made by regulations under section 11 or 12 may be made by modifying any enactment.

(8) In sections 11 and 12, references to producing an effect that is equivalent to another effect are to doing so by express provision or otherwise.

(9) In subsection (4)(a) "relevant enactment" means—

(a) if the provision made by the regulations is made by modifying retained direct EU legislation, any retained direct EU legislation;

(b) otherwise, any domestic enactment (as defined by section 5 of the European Union (Withdrawal) Act 2018).

(10) In subsections (5) and (6) "retained general principles of EU law" has the same meaning as in section 11 or 12 (as the case may be).

(11) In this section "restatement"—

(a) in relation to section 11, has the same meaning as in that section;

(b) in relation to section 12, has the same meaning as in that section but also includes reproduction;

and similar references are to be read accordingly.

Powers to revoke or replace

1.013

14.—(1) A relevant national authority may by regulations revoke any secondary retained EU law without replacing it.

(2) A relevant national authority may by regulations revoke any secondary retained EU law and replace it with such provision as the relevant national authority considers to be appropriate and to achieve the same or similar objectives.

(3) A relevant national authority may by regulations revoke any secondary retained EU law and make such alternative provision as the relevant national authority considers appropriate.

(4) Regulations under subsection (2) or (3)—

(a) may confer a power to make subordinate legislation that corresponds or is similar to a power to make subordinate legislation conferred by secondary retained EU law revoked by the regulations (and may not otherwise confer a power to make subordinate legislation);

(b) subject to that, may confer functions (including discretions) on any person;

(c) may create a criminal offence that corresponds or is similar to a criminal offence created by secondary retained EU law revoked by the regulations (and may not otherwise create a criminal offence);

(d) may provide for the imposition of monetary penalties in cases that correspond or are similar to cases in which secondary retained EU law revoked by the regulations enables monetary penalties to be imposed (and may not otherwise provide for the imposition of monetary penalties);

(e) may provide for the charging of fees;

(f) may not—
  (i) impose taxation;
  (ii) establish a public authority.

(5) No provision may be made by a relevant national authority under this section in relation to a particular subject area unless the relevant national authority considers that the overall effect of the changes made by it under this section (including changes made previously) in relation to that subject area does not increase the regulatory burden.

(6) For the purposes of subsection (5), the creation of a voluntary scheme is not to be regarded as increasing the regulatory burden.

(7) The provision that may be made by regulations under this section may be made by modifying any secondary retained EU law.

(8) Any provision made by virtue of this section is not retained EU law.

(9) No regulations may be made under this section after 23 June 2026.

(10) In this section—

"burden" includes (among other things)—

(a) a financial cost;

(b) an administrative inconvenience;

(c) an obstacle to trade or innovation;

(d) an obstacle to efficiency, productivity or profitability;

(e) a sanction (criminal or otherwise) which affects the carrying on of any lawful activity;

"revoke"—

(a) includes repeal, and

(b) in relation to anything which is retained EU law by virtue of section 4 of the European Union (Withdrawal) Act 2018, means provide that it is not recognised or available in domestic law (and, accordingly, not to be enforced, allowed or followed);

"secondary retained EU law": references to secondary retained EU law are to be read after the end of 2023 as references to secondary assimilated law.

(11) In subsection (8) the reference to retained EU law is to be read after the end of 2023 as a reference to assimilated law.

GENERAL NOTE

1.014 Regulations under subs.(4) are the Retained EU Law (Revocation and Reform) Act 2023 (Revocation and Sunset Disapplication) Regulations 2023 (SI 2023/1143). The Regulations, seemingly by way of tidying up, revoke the Immigration (European Economic Area) and Accession (Amendment) Regulations 2004 (SI 2004/1236), the Accession (Immigration and Worker Authorisation) (Amendment) Regulations 2007 (SI 2007/475) and the Accession (Worker Authorisation and Worker Registration) (Amendment) Regulations 2009 (SI 2009/2426).

Power to update

1.015 **15.**—(1) A relevant national authority may by regulations make such modifications of any secondary retained EU law, or of any provision made by virtue of section 11, 12 or 14, as the relevant national authority considers appropriate to take account of—

(a) changes in technology, or

(b) developments in scientific understanding.

(2) In subsection (1), the reference to secondary retained EU law is to be read after the end of 2023 as a reference to secondary assimilated law.

Consequential provision

1.016 **19.**—(1) A relevant national authority may by regulations make such provision as the relevant national authority considers appropriate in consequence of this Act.

(2) The provision referred to in subsection (1) includes provision modifying any enactment, including this Act.

Regulations: general

1.017 **20.**—(1) A power to make regulations under this Act includes power to make—

(a) different provision for different purposes or areas;

(b) supplementary, incidental, consequential, transitional, transitory or saving provision (including provision modifying any enactment, including this Act).

(2) Schedule 4 contains restrictions on the powers of devolved authorities to make regulations under this Act.

(3) Schedule 5 contains provision about the procedure for making regulations under this Act.

(4) A prohibition in this Act on making regulations after any particular time does not affect the continuation in force of regulations made before that time.

(5) ... *[omitted].*

[Schedules 4 and 5 are not reproduced for reasons of space.]

Interpretation

21.—(1) In this Act— 1.018

"assimilated law" has the meaning given by section 5(1);

"devolved authority" means—

(a) the Scottish Ministers,

(b) the Welsh Ministers, or

(c) a Northern Ireland department;

"domestic law" means the law of England and Wales, Scotland or Northern Ireland;

"enactment" means—

(a) an enactment (whenever passed or made) contained in, or in an instrument made under, any primary legislation, or

(b) any retained direct EU legislation;

"Minister of the Crown" has the same meaning as in the Ministers of the Crown Act 1975 and also includes the Commissioners for His Majesty's Revenue and Customs;

"modify" includes amend, repeal or revoke (and related expressions are to be read accordingly);

"Northern Ireland devolved authority" means—

(a) the First Minister and deputy First Minister acting jointly,

(b) a Northern Ireland Minister, or

(c) a Northern Ireland department;

"primary legislation" means—

(a) an Act of Parliament,

(b) an Act of the Scottish Parliament,

(c) an Act or Measure of Senedd Cymru, or

(d) Northern Ireland legislation;

"relevant national authority" means—

(a) a Minister of the Crown,

(b) a devolved authority, or

(c) a Minister of the Crown acting jointly with one or more devolved authorities;

"secondary assimilated law" has the meaning given by section 12(2);

"secondary retained EU law" has the meaning given by section 11(2);

"subordinate legislation" means—

(a) an instrument (other than an instrument that is Northern Ireland legislation) made under any primary legislation, or

(b) an instrument made on or after IP completion day under any retained direct EU legislation.

(2) In this Act—

(a) references to an instrument made under an Act include in particular any Order in Council, order, rules, regulations, scheme, warrant or byelaw made under an Act;

(b) references to an instrument made under any retained direct EU legislation include in particular any Order in Council, order, rules, regulations, scheme, warrant or byelaw made under any retained direct EU legislation.

(3) In this Act references to anything which is retained EU law by virtue of section 4 of the European Union (Withdrawal) Act 2018 include references to any modifications, made on or after IP completion day, of the rights, powers, liabilities, obligations, restrictions, remedies or procedures concerned.

Commencement, transitional and savings

1.019   **22.**—(1) The following provisions come into force on the day on which this Act is passed—

(a) sections 1 and 2;

(b) section 5(1), (2) and (4) to (7);

(c) section 7;

(d) sections 9 to 17 and Schedule 3;

(e) sections 19 to 21, this section, section 23 and Schedules 4 and 5.

(2) Section 18 comes into force at the end of the period of two months beginning with the day on which this Act is passed.

(3) The other provisions of this Act come into force on such day as a Minister of the Crown may by regulations appoint.

(4) A relevant national authority may by regulations make such transitional, transitory or saving provision as the relevant national authority considers appropriate in connection with—

(a) the coming into force of any provision of this Act,

(b) the revocation of anything by section 1, or

(c) anything ceasing to be recognised or available in domestic law (and, accordingly, ceasing to be enforced, allowed or followed) as a result of section 2.

(5) Sections 2, 3 and 4 do not apply in relation to anything occurring before the end of 2023.

(6) The amendments made by Schedule 2 do not apply as regards any time at or before the end of 2023.

Extent and short title

1.020   **23.**—(1) Subject to subsection (2), this Act extends to England and Wales, Scotland and Northern Ireland.

(2) Any amendment, repeal or revocation made by this Act has the same extent within the United Kingdom as the provision to which it relates.

(3) This Act may be cited as the Retained EU Law (Revocation and Reform) Act 2023.

NEW REGULATIONS

NEW SCOTTISH STATUTORY INSTRUMENTS

Carer's Assistance (Carer Support Payment) (Scotland) Regulations 2023

(SSI 2023/302)

Made   *25th October 2023*
Coming into force in accordance with regulation 1

The Scottish Ministers make the following Regulations in exercise of the powers conferred by sections 28(2), 41(4)(a), 43(5), 51(1), 52, 81(8) and 95 of the Social Security (Scotland) Act 2018 and all other powers enabling them to do so.

In accordance with section 96(2) of that Act, a draft of these Regulations has been laid before and approved by resolution of the Scottish Parliament.

In accordance with section 97(2) of that Act, the Scottish Ministers have informed the Scottish Commission on Social Security of their proposals, notified the Scottish Parliament that they have done so and made their proposals publicly available by such means as they consider appropriate.

PART 1

INTRODUCTORY AND INTERPRETATION

PART 2

CARER SUPPORT PAYMENT

PART 3

ELIGIBILITY

PART 4

MAKING OF APPLICATIONS AND PAYMENTS AND DURATION OF ELIGIBILITY

PART 5

SUSPENSIONS

PART 6

RE-CONSIDERATION OF ENTITLEMENT TO CARER SUPPORT PAYMENT:
DETERMINATION WITHOUT APPLICATION

PART 7

BREAKS IN CARE

PART 8

MOVEMENT OF INDIVIDUALS BETWEEN SCOTLAND AND
THE REST OF THE UNITED KINGDOM

PART 9

PERIODS IN RESPECT OF A RE-DETERMINATION REQUEST

PART 10

TRANSFER FROM CARER'S ALLOWANCE TO CARER SUPPORT PAYMENT

PART 11

INITIAL PERIOD FOR APPLICATIONS

PART 12

TRANSITORY PROVISION

PART 13

CONSEQUENTIAL AMENDMENTS

48.   Consequential amendments

SCHEDULE 1

SCHEDULE 2 Calculation of earnings

PART 1

INTRODUCTORY AND INTERPRETATION

Citation and commencement

1.021   **1.**—(1) These Regulations may be cited as the Carer's Assistance (Carer Support Payment) (Scotland) Regulations 2023.

(2) Subject to paragraph (3), these Regulations come into force on 19 November 2023.

(3) Regulation 13(2) and (3) come into force on 1 October 2024.

Interpretation

1.022   **2.** In these Regulations—

"the 2018 Act" means the Social Security (Scotland) Act 2018,

"the 1992 Act" means the Social Security Contributions and Benefits Act 1992,

"Adult Disability Payment" means disability assistance for adults given in accordance with the Disability Assistance for Working Age People (Scotland) Regulations 2022,

"Armed Forces Independence Payment" means a payment under the Armed Forces and Reserve Forces (Compensation Scheme) Order 2011,

"Attendance Allowance" means an attendance allowance under—

(a) section 64 of the 1992 Act, or

(b) the Social Security (Attendance Allowance) Regulations (Northern Ireland) 1992,

"award week" means a period of 7 days beginning on a Sunday and ending on a Saturday,

"cared for person" is a person described in regulation 5(1),

"carer element of Universal Credit" means the amount awarded by virtue of—

(a) section 12(2)(c) of the Welfare Reform Act 2012, or

(b) article 17(2)(c) of the Welfare Reform (Northern Ireland) Order 2015,

"Carer's Allowance" means a benefit for carers given under—

(a) section 70 (carer's allowance) of the 1992 Act, or

(b) section 70 (carer's allowance) of the Social Security Contributions and Benefits (Northern Ireland) Act 1992,

"Carer Support Payment" means carer's assistance given in accordance with these Regulations,

"Child Disability Payment" means disability assistance for children and young people given in accordance with the Disability Assistance for Children and Young People (Scotland) Regulations 2021,

"Constant Attendance Allowance" means an allowance under—

(a) section 104 of the 1992 Act, or

(b) article 8 of the Naval, Military and Air Forces Etc. (Disablement and Death) Service Pensions Order 2006,

"couple" has the meaning given by section 39 of the Welfare Reform Act 2012,

"determination" or "determination of entitlement" has the meaning in section 25 of the 2018 Act,

"Disability Living Allowance" means a disability living allowance under—

(a) section 71 of the 1992 Act, or

(b) section 71 of the Social Security Contributions and Benefits (Northern Ireland) Act 1992,

"EEA state" means—

(a) any member state of the European Union, or

(b) any other state that is party to the Agreement on the European Economic Area signed at Oporto on 2 May 1992, together with the Protocol adjusting that Agreement signed at Brussels on 17 March 1993, as modified or supplemented from time to time,

"Industrial Injuries Disablement Benefit" means a benefit payable under Part V and section 103 of the 1992 Act,

"legal detention" means detention in legal custody within the meaning of section 295 of the Criminal Procedure (Scotland) Act 1995,

"Personal Independence Payment" means personal independence payment under—

(a) Part 4 of the Welfare Reform Act 2012, or

(b) Article 82 of the Welfare Reform (Northern Ireland) Order 2015,

"qualifying disability benefit" means—

(a) the daily living component of Adult Disability Payment at the standard or enhanced rate,

(b) the daily living component of Personal Independence Payment,

(c) the care component of Child Disability Payment at the middle or highest rate,

(d) the care component of Disability Living Allowance at the middle or highest rate,

(e) Attendance Allowance,

(f) Armed Forces Independence Payment, or

(g) Constant Attendance Allowance—

  (i) at or above the normal maximum rate with Industrial Injuries Disablement Benefit, or

  (ii) at the basic (full day) rate with a War Disablement Pension,

"relevant EU Regulation" means—

   (a) one of the following Regulations—
      (i) Council Regulation (EC) No 1408/71 of 14 June 1971 on the application of social security schemes to employed persons, to self-employed persons and to members of their families moving within the Community,
      (ii) Regulation (EC) No 883/2004 of the European Parliament and of the Council of 29 April 2004 on the coordination of social security systems, or
   (b) in relation to an individual to whom the agreement constituted by the exchange of letters set out in the schedule of the Family Allowances, National Insurance and Industrial Injuries (Gibraltar) Order 1974 applies, a Regulation mentioned in paragraph (a) of this definition as it forms part of domestic law by virtue of section 3 of the European Union (Withdrawal) Act 2018,

"War Disablement Pension" means—
   (a) any retired pay, pension or allowance granted in respect of disablement under powers conferred by or under the Air Force (Constitution) Act 1917, the Personal Injuries (Emergency Provisions) Act 1939, the Pensions (Navy, Army, Air Force and Mercantile Marine) Act 1939, the Polish Resettlement Act 1947, or Part VII or section 151 of the Reserve Forces Act 1980,
   (b) without prejudice to paragraph (a) of this definition, any retired pay or pension to which any of paragraphs (a) to (f) of section 641(1) of the Income Tax (Earnings and Pensions) Act 2003 applies, and

"Young Carer Grant" means a grant paid under the Carer's Assistance (Young Carer Grants) (Scotland) Regulations 2019.

PART 2

CARER SUPPORT PAYMENT

Overview

1.023   **3.** An individual is entitled to Carer Support Payment in accordance with these Regulations if they meet the eligibility rules in—
   (a) regulation 4 (age criteria),
   (b) regulation 5 (provision of care to a cared for person),
   (c) regulations 6 to 11 (residence and presence conditions),
   (d) regulation 12 (entitlement to other benefits),
   (e) regulation 13 (individuals in education),
   (f) regulation 14 (earnings limit).

PART 3

ELIGIBILITY

Age criteria

4.—(1) Carer Support Payment may only be paid in respect of an indi-   1.024
vidual who is 16 years of age or older.

(2) Where an individual was born on 29 February, the individual's birth-
day is to be taken to fall on 28 February in a year which is not a leap year.

Provision of care to a cared for person

5.—(1) Carer Support Payment may only be paid to an individual in   1.025
respect of a period during which that individual provides regular and substantial care to a person to whom a qualifying disability benefit is normally
payable (a "cared for person").

(2) For the purposes of paragraph (1), an individual shall only be treated
as being regularly and substantially engaged in caring for a cared for person
on every day in a week if they are, or are likely to be, regularly engaged for
at least 35 hours in an award week in caring for that cared for person.

(3) No individual can be entitled to Carer Support Payment in respect of
a cared for person where another individual is entitled to—

(a) Carer Support Payment,

(b) Carer's Allowance, or

(c) the carer element of Universal Credit,

in respect of that cared for person.

(4) The care must not be provided by an individual—

(a) under or by virtue of a contract, unless the contract is of a kind
specified by regulations made under section 1(3)(a) of the Carers
(Scotland) Act 2016 as not to be regarded as a contract for the purposes of that Act, or

(b) as voluntary work done for a charity or other not-for-profit organisation for which no payment is received other than reasonable
expenses.

(5) No individual can be entitled to more than one Carer Support
Payment in respect of the same period.

(6) No individual can be entitled to Carer Support Payment in respect of
a period during which they are in legal detention.

(7) For the avoidance of doubt, an individual may be entitled to Carer
Support Payment in respect of a cared for person where another individual
is entitled to Young Carer Grant for that cared for person.

Residence and presence conditions

6.—(1) An individual satisfies the residence and presence conditions   1.026
where on any day that individual—

(a) is ordinarily resident in Scotland,

(b) is habitually resident in the common travel area,

(c) is not a person subject to immigration control within the meaning of
section 115(9) of the Immigration and Asylum Act 1999,

19

(d) is present in the common travel area, and

(e) has been present in the common travel area for a period of, or for periods amounting in the aggregate to, not less than 26 weeks of the 52 weeks immediately preceding that day.

(2) In this Part, "common travel area" has the meaning given in section 1(3) of the Immigration Act 1971.

(3) The residence condition set out in paragraph (1)(a) does not apply where on any day the individual—

(a) is habitually resident in Ireland,

(b) has a genuine and sufficient link to Scotland, and

(c) is an individual—

    (i) to whom the Convention on Social Security between the Government of the United Kingdom of Great Britain and Northern Ireland and the Government of Ireland signed at Dublin on 1 February 2019, as modified from time to time in accordance with any provision of it, applies, and

    (ii) in respect of whom the United Kingdom is, as a result, competent for the payment of long term care benefits.

(4) The reference in paragraph (3)(b) to an individual's link to Scotland being sufficient is to it being sufficiently close that if the individual were not entitled to Carer Support Payment, paragraph (3) would be incompatible with the Convention on Social Security between the Government of the United Kingdom of Great Britain and Northern Ireland and the Government of Ireland signed at Dublin on 1 February 2019.

(5) Paragraph (1)(c) does not apply to a person subject to immigration control within the meaning of section 115(9) of the Immigration and Asylum Act 1999 where the person—

(a) is lawfully working in the United Kingdom and is a national of a state with which the United Kingdom has concluded an agreement which replaces in whole or in part an agreement under Article 217 of the Treaty on the Functioning of the European Union which has ceased to apply to, and in, the United Kingdom, providing, in the field of social security, for the equal treatment of workers who are nationals of the signatory state and their families,

(b) is a member of the family of, and living with, a person specified in sub-paragraph (a), or

(c) has been given leave to enter, or remain in, the United Kingdom by the Secretary of State upon an undertaking by another person or persons pursuant to the immigration rules, to be responsible for their maintenance and accommodation.

(6) The past presence condition in paragraph (1)(e) does not apply where an individual—

(a) has a terminal illness, or

(b) cares for a cared for person who—

    (i) has a terminal illness,

    (ii) is in receipt of Armed Forces Independence Payment or Constant Attendance Allowance at or above the normal maximum rate with Industrial Injuries Disablement Benefit, or at the basic (full day) rate with a War Disablement Pension, or

    (iii) is not required to meet a past presence condition by virtue of an exception set out in—

     (aa) regulation 2A(1) or 2C(1) of the Social Security (Attendance Allowance) Regulations 1991,

     (bb) regulation 2A(1) or 2C(1) of the Social Security (Disability Living Allowance) Regulations 1991,

     (cc) regulation 2A(1), 2B, 2C(1) or paragraph 5 of Schedule 2 of the Social Security (Disability Living Allowance) Regulations (Northern Ireland) 1992,

     (dd) regulation 22 or 23A(1) of the Social Security (Personal Independence Payment) Regulations 2013,

     (ee) regulation 5(8), (10)(b), 5(10A) or 8 of the Disability Assistance for Children and Young People (Scotland) Regulations 2021, or

     (ff) regulation 15(7), 17(2), 18 or 19 of the Disability Assistance for Working Age People (Scotland) Regulations 2022.

(7) For the purposes of paragraph (6), an individual or a cared for person has a terminal illness where they are entitled to—

(a) Disability Living Allowance by virtue of regulation 2(4) of the Social Security (Disability Living Allowance) Regulations 1991,

(b) Disability Living Allowance by virtue of regulation 2(3) of the Social Security (Disability Living Allowance) Regulations (Northern Ireland) 1992,

(c) Attendance Allowance by virtue of section 66 of the 1992 Act,

(d) Attendance Allowance by virtue of regulation 2(3) of the Social Security (Attendance Allowance) Regulations (Northern Ireland) 1992,

(e) Personal Independence Payment by virtue of regulation 21 of the Social Security (Personal Independence Payment) Regulations 2013,

(f) Universal Credit by virtue of regulations 16(2), 28(5)(a) or 40(5) read with paragraph 1 of Schedule 9 of the Universal Credit Regulations 2013,

(g) Employment and Support Allowance by virtue of regulations 7(1)(a), 16(1)(a), 31(1)(a), 45(2) or 85(2)(b) of the Employment and Support Allowance Regulations 2013,

(h) Personal Independence Payment by virtue of regulation 21 of the Personal Independence Payment Regulations (Northern Ireland) 2016,

(i) Child Disability Payment by virtue of regulation 15 of the Disability Assistance for Children and Young People (Scotland) Regulations 2021,

(j) Adult Disability Payment by virtue of regulation 26 of the Disability Assistance for Working Age People (Scotland) Regulations 2022.

(8) The habitual residence condition in paragraph (1)(b) and the past presence condition in paragraph (1)(e) do not apply where an individual is a person who—

(a) has leave to enter or remain in the United Kingdom granted under the immigration rules by virtue of—

     (i) the Afghan Relocations and Assistance Policy, or

     (ii) the previous scheme for locally-employed staff in Afghanistan (sometimes referred to as the ex-gratia scheme),

(b) has been granted discretionary leave outside the immigration rules as a dependant of a person referred to in sub-paragraph (a),

    (c) has leave granted under the Afghan Citizens Resettlement Scheme,

    (d) has been granted refugee status or humanitarian protection under the immigration rules,

    (e) has leave to enter or remain in the United Kingdom as the dependant of a person referred to in sub-paragraph (d),

    (f) has leave to enter or remain in the United Kingdom granted under or outside the immigration rules, has a right of abode in the United Kingdom within the meaning given in section 2 of the Immigration Act 1971 or does not require leave to enter or remain in the United Kingdom in accordance with section 3ZA of that Act, where the individual—

        (i) was residing in Ukraine immediately before 1 January 2022, and

        (ii) left Ukraine in connection with the Russian invasion which took place on 24 February 2022, [1 ...]

    (g) has leave to enter or remain in the United Kingdom granted under or outside the immigration rules, has a right of abode in the United Kingdom within the meaning given in section 2 of the Immigration Act 1971 or does not require leave to enter or remain in the United Kingdom in accordance with section 3ZA of that Act, where the individual—

        (i) was residing in Sudan before 15 April 2023, and

        (ii) left Sudan in connection with the violence which rapidly escalated on 15 April 2023 in Khartoum and across Sudan[1, or

    (h) has leave to enter or remain in the United Kingdom granted under or outside the immigration rules, a right of abode in the United Kingdom within the meaning given in section 2 of the Immigration Act 1971 or does not require leave to enter or remain in the United Kingdom in accordance with section 3ZA of that Act, where the individual—

        (i) was residing in Israel, the West Bank, the Gaza Strip, East Jerusalem, the Golan Heights or Lebanon immediately before 7 October 2023, and

        (ii) left Israel, the West Bank, the Gaza Strip, East Jerusalem, the Golan Heights or Lebanon in connection with the Hamas terrorist attack in Israel on 7 October 2023 or the violence which rapidly escalated in the region following the attack.]

    (9) For the purposes of this regulation—

    (a) "immigration rules" means the rules laid before Parliament under section 3(2) of the Immigration Act 1971,

    (b) "the Afghan Citizens Resettlement Scheme" means the scheme announced by the United Kingdom Government on 18 August 2021.

AMENDMENT

1. Social Security (Residence and Presence Requirements) (Israel, the West Bank, the Gaza Strip, East Jerusalem, the Golan Heights and Lebanon) (Scotland) Regulations 2023 (SSI 2023/309) reg.11(2) (October 26, 2023 at 5:38pm).

Temporary absence from the common travel area

1.027   **7.**—(1) Where an individual is temporarily absent from the common travel area, the individual is to be treated as present in the common travel area during the first—

(a) 4 weeks of any period of absence,

(b) 13 weeks of any period of absence where that period of absence, or any extension to that period of absence, is for the specific purpose of caring for a cared for person who is also absent from the common travel area and where that cared for person is paid a qualifying disability benefit during that period, or

(c) 26 weeks of any period of absence where—

   (i) that period of absence, or any extension to that period of absence, is for the specific purpose of caring for a cared for person and is in connection with arrangements made for the medical treatment of the cared for person for a disease or bodily or mental disablement which commenced before leaving the common travel area and where that cared for person is paid a qualifying disability benefit during that period, and

   (ii) the arrangements relate to medical treatment—

      (aa) outside the common travel area,

      (bb) during the period when the cared for person is temporarily absent from the common travel area, and

      (cc) by, or under the supervision of, a person appropriately qualified to carry out that treatment.

(2) For the purposes of paragraph (1)—

(a) an individual is "temporarily absent" if, at the beginning of the period of absence, that absence is unlikely to exceed 52 weeks, and

(b) "medical treatment" means medical, surgical, psychological or rehabilitative treatment (including any course or diet regimen).

Serving members of His Majesty's forces, civil servants and their family members

8.—(1) A relevant individual is to be treated as meeting the residence and presence conditions set out in regulations 6(1)(a), (b) and (d) where on any day that individual is outside the common travel area—   1.028

(a) by reason of their capacity mentioned in paragraph (3)(a) provided that the individual satisfied the residence and presence conditions set out in regulation 6(1)(a), (b) and (d) immediately prior to the start of their employment mentioned in paragraph (3)(a), or

(b) by reason of being a person mentioned in paragraph (3)(b) living with an individual to whom paragraph (3)(a) applies.

(2) The past presence condition set out in regulation 6(1)(e) does not apply to a relevant individual.

(3) A "relevant individual" in paragraph (1) and (2) means an individual who is—

(a) outside of the common travel area in their capacity as a—

   (i) serving member of His Majesty's forces, or

   (ii) civil servant, or

(b) living with a person mentioned in sub-paragraph (a) and—

   (i) is the child, step-child or child in care of that person,

   (ii) is the parent, step-parent or parent-in-law of that person, or

   (iii) is married to or in a civil partnership with that person, or is living together with that person as if they were married or in a civil partnership.

(4) In this regulation—

"child in care" means—

(a) under the law of Scotland, a child in respect of whom a relevant individual listed in paragraph (3)(a)—

    (i) is a foster carer within the meaning of regulation 2 of the Looked After Children (Scotland) Regulations 2009,

    (ii) is a kinship carer within the meaning of regulation 2 of the Looked After Children (Scotland) Regulations 2009,

    (iii) has a kinship care order within the meaning of section 72 of the Children and Young People (Scotland) Act 2014, or

(b) under the law of England and Wales and Northern Ireland, a child in respect of whom a person listed in paragraph (3)(a) has a relationship equivalent to those listed under the law of Scotland,

"civil servant" has the meaning given by section 1(4) of the Constitutional Reform and Governance Act 2010, and

"serving member of His Majesty's forces" means a member of a regular force or a reserve force ("M") as defined, in each case, by section 374 (definitions applying for purposes of the whole Act) of the Armed Forces Act 2006, unless—

(a) M is under the age of 16,

(b) M is committing an offence under section 8 of the Armed Forces Act 2006 (desertion),

(c) the force concerned is one of His Majesty's naval forces which M locally entered at an overseas base without—

    (i) previously being an insured person under the National Insurance Act 1965, or

    (ii) paying or having previously paid one or more of the following classes of contributions under the Social Security Act 1975 or the 1992 Act—

        (aa) primary Class 1,

        (bb) Class 2, or

        (cc) Class 3, or

(d) the force concerned is one of His Majesty's military forces or His Majesty's air forces which M entered, or was recruited for, outside the United Kingdom and—

    (i) where that force is one of His Majesty's military forces, the depot for M's unit is outside the United Kingdom, or

    (ii) where that force is one of His Majesty's air forces, M is liable under the terms of M's engagement to serve only in a specified area outside the United Kingdom.

Aircraft workers, mariners and continental shelf operations

1.029

9.—(1) An individual is to be treated as meeting the presence conditions set out in regulation 6(1)(d) and (e) for any period where that individual is—

(a) outside the common travel area in their capacity as an aircraft worker or a mariner, or

(b) in employment prescribed for the purposes of section 120 (employment at sea (continental shelf operations)) of the 1992 Act in connection with continental shelf operations.

(2) In this regulation—

"aircraft worker" means a person who is, or has been, employed under a contract of service either as a pilot, commander, navigator or other member of the crew of any aircraft, or in any other capacity on board any aircraft where—

(a) the employment in that other capacity is for the purposes of the aircraft or its crew or of any passengers or cargo or mail carried on that aircraft, and

(b) the contract is entered into in the United Kingdom with a view to its performance (in whole or in part) while the aircraft is in flight,

but does not include a person so far as that employment is as a serving member His Majesty's forces, and

"mariner" means a person who is, or has been, in employment under a contract of service either as a master or member of the crew of any ship or vessel, or in any other capacity on board any ship or vessel where—

(a) the employment in that other capacity is for the purposes of that ship or vessel or its crew or any passenger or cargo or mail carried by the ship or vessel, and

(b) the contract is entered into in the United Kingdom with a view to its performance (in whole or in part) while the ship or vessel is on voyage,

but does not include a person in so far as that employment is as a serving member of His Majesty's forces.

Persons residing in the United Kingdom to whom a relevant EU regulation applies

10.—(1) The past presence condition set out in regulation 6(1)(e) (residence and presence conditions) does not apply where on any day the individual is—   1.030

(a) ordinarily resident in Scotland,

(b) habitually resident in the United Kingdom,

(c) an individual—

(i) to whom the rules set out in a relevant EU regulation apply by virtue of—

(aa) Title III of Part 2 of the EU withdrawal agreement,

(bb) Part 3 or Article 23(4) of the Swiss citizens' rights agreement (as defined in section 39(1) of the European Union (Withdrawal Agreement) Act 2020 ("the 2020 Act"),

(cc) Title III of the EEA EFTA separation agreement (as defined in section 39(1) of the 2020 Act), or

(dd) the agreement constituted by the exchange of letters set out in the schedule of the Family Allowances, National Insurance and Industrial Injuries (Gibraltar) Order 1974,

(ii) in respect of whom the United Kingdom is, as a result, competent for payment of sickness benefits in cash.

(2) An individual to whom a relevant EU regulation applies is not entitled to Carer Support Payment for a period unless during that period the United Kingdom is competent for payment of sickness benefits in cash to the person for the purposes of the relevant EU regulation in question.

Persons residing outside the United Kingdom to whom a relevant EU regulation applies

1.031   **11.**—(1) The residence and presence conditions set out in regulation 6(1) (residence and presence conditions) do not apply in relation to Carer Support Payment where on any day the individual satisfies the conditions in paragraph (2).

(2) The conditions referred to in paragraph (1) are that the individual must—

    (a) be an individual—

        (i) to whom the rules set out in a relevant EU regulation apply by virtue of—

            (aa) Title III of Part 2 of the EU withdrawal agreement,

            (bb) Part 3 or Article 23(4) of the Swiss citizens' rights agreement (as defined in section 39(1) of the European Union (Withdrawal Agreement) Act 2020 ("the 2020 Act")),

            (cc) Title III of the EEA EFTA separation agreement (as defined in section 39(1) of the 2020 Act), or

            (dd) the agreement constituted by the exchange of letters set out in the schedule of the Family Allowances, National Insurance and Industrial Injuries (Gibraltar) Order 1974, and

        (ii) in respect of whom the United Kingdom is, as a result, competent for payment of sickness benefits in cash,

    (b) be habitually resident in—

        (i) Switzerland,

        (ii) an EEA state, or

        (iii) Gibraltar, and

    (c) have a genuine and sufficient link to Scotland.

(3) The reference in paragraph (2)(c) to an individual's link to Scotland being sufficient is to it being sufficiently close that if the individual were not entitled to Carer Support Payment, paragraph (2) would be incompatible with the applicable agreement mentioned in sub-paragraph (a)(i) of that paragraph.

(4) An individual to whom a relevant EU regulation applies is not entitled to Carer Support Payment for a period unless during that period the United Kingdom is competent for payment of sickness benefits in cash to the person for the purposes of the relevant EU regulation in question.

Entitlement to other benefits

1.032   **12.**—(1) An individual is not entitled to Carer Support Payment in respect of a cared for person for any period that they are entitled to—

    (a) Carer's Allowance,

    (b) the carer element of Universal Credit in respect of a different cared for person, or

    (c) Young Carer Grant.

(2) An individual may be entitled to Carer Support Payment in respect of a cared for person where they have previously been entitled to Young Carer Grant.

Individuals in education

13.—(1) An individual who has not reached the age of 20 will not be
entitled to Carer Support Payment if they are—
  (a) undertaking a course of full-time education, which is not advanced
  education and which is not provided by virtue of their employment
  or any office held by them, or
  (b) being provided with "appropriate full-time education" in England
  within the meaning of section 4 (appropriate full-time education or
  training) of the Education and Skills Act 2008, which is not—
    (i) a course in preparation for a degree, a diploma of higher edu-
    cation, a higher national certificate, a higher national diploma,
    a teaching qualification, any other course which is of a stand-
    ard above ordinary national diploma, a national diploma, or
    national certificate of Edexcel, a general certificate of education
    (advanced level), or Scottish national qualifications at higher or
    advanced higher level,
    (ii) provided by virtue of their employment of any office held by
    them,
  (c) undertaking approved training that is not provided by means of a
  contract of employment.
(2) This regulation does not apply to an individual if they are—
  (a) without parental support,
  (b) entitled to disability living allowance, child disability payment,
  adult disability payment or personal independence payment and,
  on a date before the date on which the individual starts receiving
  education—
    (i) it has been determined that they have limited capability for
    work or limited capability for work and work-related activity on
    the basis of an assessment under Part 5 of the Universal Credit
    Regulations 2013 or under Part 4 or 5 of the Employment and
    Support Allowance Regulations 2013, or
    (ii) they are treated as having limited capability for work under
    schedule 8 of the Universal Credit Regulations 2013 or limited
    capability for work and work-related activity under schedule 9
    of the Universal Credit Regulations 2013,
  (c) responsible for a child or a qualifying young person,
  (d) single and is a foster parent with whom a child is placed,
  (e) a member of a couple—
    (i) and the other member of the couple is not undertaking a course
    of education, or
    (ii) both of whom are receiving education, and the other member
    of the couple falls within one of the exceptions set out in para-
    graph (2)(a) to (d).
(3) For the purposes of paragraph (2)(a), an individual is without parental support if they are not being looked after by a local authority and—
  (a) has no parent,
  (b) cannot live with their parents because—
    (i) the individual is estranged from them, or
    (ii) there is a serious risk to the individual's physical or mental
    health, or that individual would suffer significant harm if the
    individual lived with them,

(c) is living away from their parents, and neither parent is able to support the individual financially because that parent—
    (i) has a physical or mental impairment,
    (ii) is detained in custody pending trial or sentence upon conviction or under a sentence imposed by a court, or
    (iii) is prohibited from entering or re-entering Great Britain.

(4) For the purposes of this regulation—

"advanced education" means full-time education (which is not school education within the meaning of the Education (Scotland) Act 1980) for the purposes of—
(a) a course in preparation for a degree, a diploma of higher education, a higher national certificate, a higher national diploma, or a teaching qualification, or
(b) any other course which is of a standard above ordinary national diploma, a national diploma or national certificate of Edexcel, a general certificate of education (advanced level), or Scottish national qualifications at higher or advanced higher level,

"approved training" means arrangements made by the Government—
(a) in relation to Wales, known as "Traineeships" or "Foundation Apprenticeships",
(b) in relation to Scotland, known as "No One Left Behind", or
(c) in relation to Northern Ireland, known as "PEACE IV Children and Young People 2.1", "Training for Success", or "Skills for Life and Work",

"arrangements made by the Government" means arrangements—
(a) in relation to England and Wales, made by the Secretary of State under section 2 of the Employment and Training Act 1973,
(b) in relation to Scotland, made—
    (i) by the Scottish Ministers under section 2 of the Employment and Training Act 1973,
    (ii) by Scottish Enterprise or Highlands and Islands Enterprise under section 2 of the Enterprise and New Towns (Scotland) Act 1990, or
(c) in relation to Northern Ireland, made by the Department for Communities or the Department for the Economy under sections 1 and 3 of the Employment and Training Act (Northern Ireland) 1950,

"foster parent" means—
(a) under the law of Scotland, a foster carer or kinship carer with whom a child is placed under the Looked After Children (Scotland) Regulations 2009, or
(b) under the law of England and Wales and Northern Ireland, a person with whom a child is placed who has an equivalent relationship with the child to those listed under the law of Scotland,

"full-time education"—
(a) is education undertaken in pursuit of a course, where the average time spent during term time in receiving tuition, engaging in practical work, or supervised study, or taking examinations exceeds 21 hours per week, and
(b) in calculating the time spent in pursuit of the course, no account is taken of time occupied by meal breaks or spent on unsupervised study, and

"qualifying young person" has the same meaning as regulation 5 of the Universal Credit Regulations 2013.

GENERAL NOTE

Note that reg.13(2) and (3) do not come into force until October 1, 2024.   1.034

Earnings limit

14.—(1) An individual is not entitled to Carer Support Payment in any   1.035
award week in which their earnings in respect of that award week exceed
£139.

(2) Earnings are to be calculated in accordance with schedule 2.

PART 4

MAKING OF APPLICATIONS AND PAYMENTS AND
DURATION OF ELIGIBILITY

Making payments

15.—(1) Where Carer Support Payment is payable in respect of an indi-   1.036
vidual, the Scottish Ministers may, where they consider it appropriate, make
the payment to another person to be used for the benefit of the individual.

(2) Where the Scottish Ministers consider, for any reason, that it is no
longer appropriate for a particular person who falls within paragraph (1) to
continue to receive the payment, they may cease making payment to that
person.

Amount and form of Carer Support Payment

16.—(1) Subject to regulation 21 (amount and form of carer support   1.037
payment where payments are backdated), the weekly rate of payment of
Carer Support Payment is £76.75.

(2) For any award week where an individual is entitled to one or more
overlapping benefit, the amount of Carer Support Payment that is to be
given to the individual is to be reduced—

(a) by the amount of the overlapping benefit paid, or

(b) where the amount of the overlapping benefit is equal to or greater
than the amount of Carer Support Payment, the value of Carer
Support Payment that is to be given to the individual is £0.

(3) In this regulation "overlapping benefit" means—

(a) State Pension or Retirement Pension,

(b) Incapacity Benefit,

(c) Severe Disablement Allowance,

(d) Unemployability Supplement that is paid with Industrial Injuries
Disablement benefit or War Pension,

(e) Widow's Allowance or Widow's Benefit or Widowed Parent's
Allowance or Widowed Mother's Allowance or Widow's Pension,
excluding additional pension,

(f) Bereavement Allowance,

(g) War Widow's or Widower's Pension,
(h) Maternity Allowance,
(i) Industrial Death Benefit,
(j) Contribution-based Jobseeker's Allowance,
(k) Contributory Employment and Support Allowance,
(l) Training Allowance.

(4) When the cared for person dies and an individual was entitled to Carer Support Payment in respect of that cared for person immediately before their death, the individual's entitlement to Carer Support Payment will continue to be paid until whichever of the following comes first—

(a) until the first day of the award week following the award week in which the individual ceases to satisfy any of the eligibility requirements set out in regulations 6 to 14, or
(b) for a period of 8 award weeks after the first day of the award week following the award week in which the cared for person died.

(5) Carer Support Payment may only be given as money, except as provided for by—

(a) regulation 17 (abatement in respect of a relevant individual), or
(b) regulation 26 (form of payment – giving Carer Support Payment by way of deduction).

(6) For the purposes of this regulation—

"1914–1918 War Injuries Scheme" means any scheme made under the Injuries in War (Compensation) Act 1914 or under the Injuries in War Compensation Act 1914 (Session 2) or any Government scheme for compensation in respect of persons injured in any merchant ship or fishing vessel as the result of hostilities during the 1914–1918 War,

"Bereavement Allowance" means an allowance referred to in section 39B of the 1992 Act subject to the transitional provisions specified in article 4 of the Pensions Act 2014 (Commencement No.10) Order 2017,

"Contribution-based Jobseeker's Allowance" means an allowance under the Jobseekers Act 1995 as amended by the provisions of Part 1 of Schedule 14 to the Welfare Reform Act 2012 that remove references to an income-based allowance, and a contribution-based allowance under the Jobseekers Act as that Act has effect apart from those provisions,

"Contributory Employment and Support Allowance" means an allowance under Part 1 of the Welfare Reform Act 2007 as amended by the provisions of Schedule 3, and Part 1 of Schedule 14, to the Welfare Reform Act 2012 Act that remove references to an income-related allowance, and a contributory allowance under Part 1 of the Welfare Reform Act 2007 as that Part has effect apart from those provisions,

"Incapacity Benefit" means a benefit referred to in section 30A of the 1992 Act,

"Industrial Death Benefit" means a benefit referred to in Part VI of Schedule 7 to the 1992 Act,

"Maternity Allowance" means an allowance referred to in sections 35 and 35B of the 1992 Act,

"Personal Injuries Scheme" means any scheme made under the Personal Injuries (Emergency Provisions) Act 1939 or under the Pensions (Navy, Army, Air Force and Mercantile Marine) Act 1939,

"Retirement Pension" means a pension payable under Part II and Part III of the 1992 Act, excluding any additional pension or graduated retirement benefit,

"Service Pensions Instrument" means any instrument described in sub-paragraphs (a) or (b) below in so far, but only in so far, as the pensions or other benefits provided by that instrument are not calculated or determined by reference to length of service, namely:—

(a) any instrument made in exercise of powers—

    (i) referred to in section 12(1) of the Social Security (Miscellaneous Provisions) Act 1977 (pensions or other benefits for disablement or death due to service in the armed forces of the Crown); or

    (ii) under section 1 of the Polish Resettlement Act 1947 (pensions and other benefits for disablement or death due to service in certain Polish forces); or

(b) any instrument under which a pension or other benefit may be paid to a person (not being a member of the armed forces of the Crown) out of public funds in respect of death or disablement, wound, injury or disease due to service in any nursing service or other auxiliary service of any of the armed forces of the Crown, or in any other organisation established under the control of the Defence Council or formerly established under the control of the Admiralty, the Army Council or the Air Council,

"Severe Disablement Allowance" means an allowance referred to in sections 68 and 69 of the 1992 Act,

"State Pension" means a pension payable under Part 1 of the Pensions Act 2014,

"Training Allowance" means an allowance (whether by way of periodical grants or otherwise) payable out of public funds by a Government department or by or on behalf of Scottish Enterprise, Highlands and Islands Enterprise, the Secretary of State, the National Assembly for Wales to a person for their maintenance, or in respect of any dependant of theirs, for the period, or part of the period, during which they are following a course of training or instruction provided by, or in pursuance of arrangements made with, that department or approved by that department in relation to them or so provided or approved by or on behalf of the Scottish Enterprise, Highlands and Islands Enterprise, the National Assembly for Wales or the said Commission but it does not include—

(a) an allowance paid by any Government department to or in respect of a person by reason of the fact that they are following a course of full-time education or is training as a teacher, or

(b) a payment made by or on behalf of Scottish Enterprise, Highlands and Islands Enterprise or the Secretary of State to any person by way of training premium or training bonus in consequence of that person's use of facilities for training provided in pursuance of arrangements made under section 2 of the Employment and Training Act 1973 or section 2 of the Enterprise and New Towns (Scotland) Act 1990,

"Unemployability Supplement" includes an increase on account of unemployability under any Personal Injuries Scheme, Service Pensions Instrument or 1914–1918 War Injuries Scheme,

"War Widow's Pension" means any widow's or surviving civil partner's pension or allowance granted in respect of a death due to service or war injury and payable by virtue of any enactment mentioned in paragraph

(a) of the definition of "War Disablement Pension" in regulation 2, or a pension or allowance for a widow or surviving civil partner granted under any scheme mentioned in section 641(1)(e) or (f) of the Income Tax (Earnings and Pensions) Act 2003,

"Widowed Mother's Allowance" means an allowance referred to in section 37 of the 1992 Act,

"Widowed Parent's Allowance" means an allowance referred to in section 39A of the 1992 Act,

"Widow's Pension" means a pension referred to in section 38 of the 1992 Act.

Abatement in respect of a relevant benefit

1.038

17.—(1) This regulation applies where an individual—

(a) makes an application for Carer Support Payment, or

(b) becomes entitled to an increased amount of Carer Support Payment following a determination without application, and

(c) that individual is (or if they are a member of a couple, their partner is) in receipt of a relevant benefit at any time during the abatement period.

(2) Where this regulation applies, Carer Support Payment may be given (in whole or in part) to the Secretary of State in order to meet, or contribute towards meeting, any liability the individual has to the Secretary of State in connection with a relevant benefit, provided that the individual has—

(a) agreed to the assistance being given in that form, or

(b) unreasonably refused to agree to the assistance being given in that form.

(3) The amount of Carer Support Payment that is to be given by way of payment to the Secretary of State in accordance with paragraph (2) is to be the difference between—

(a) the total amount of any relevant benefits the individual or their partner is paid during the abatement period, and

(b) the total amount of any relevant benefits the individual or their partner would have been paid during the abatement period had their entitlement to those relevant benefits been adjusted as a result of their entitlement to Carer Support Payment (which, for the avoidance of doubt, includes any carer premia, carer additions, or carer elements that they would be entitled to receive).

(4) For the purposes of this regulation—

"abatement period" means—

(a) where sub-paragraph (1)(a) applies, a period, as short as reasonably practicable, beginning with the first day of the award week in which the individual's entitlement to Carer Support Payment begins and ending on the day before the first day of the award week in which the individual's first payment of Carer Support Payment is made, or

(b) where sub paragraph (1)(b) applies, a period, as short as reasonably practicable, beginning with the first day of the award week in which the individual's entitlement to Carer Support Payment increases and ending on the day before the first day of the award week in which the individual received the first payment of Carer Support Payment at that increased amount,

"Income Support" means a payment made under section 124 of the 1992 Act,

"Income-based Jobseeker's Allowance" means a jobseeker's allowance entitlement to which is based on the individual's satisfying conditions which include those set out in section 3 of the Jobseeker's Act 1995, or a joint-claim jobseeker's allowance,

"Income-related Employment and Support Allowance" means an income-related allowance under Part 1 of the Welfare Reform Act 2007,

"joint-claim jobseeker's allowance" means a jobseeker's allowance entitlement to which arises by virtue of section 1(2B) of the Jobseeker's Act 1995, and

"Pension Credit" means a pension credit under the State Pension Credit Act 2002, and

"relevant benefit" means—

(a) Income Support,

(b) Income-based Jobseeker's Allowance,

(c) Income-related Employment and Support Allowance, or

(d) Pension Credit.

When an application is to be treated as made and beginning of entitlement to assistance

18.—(1) An application for Carer Support Payment is to be treated as made on the day it is received by the Scottish Ministers.

1.039

(2) Where, on the basis of an application, a determination is made that an individual is entitled to Carer Support Payment, entitlement to assistance is to begin—

(a) on the first day of the award week in which the application is treated as made in accordance with paragraph (1),

(b) where the individual has notified the Scottish Ministers that they wish their entitlement to assistance to begin on a date prior to the day on which their application is treated as made, on the first day of the award week in which that chosen date falls, provided that—

(i) the date chosen by the individual is no more than 13 weeks prior to the day on which their application is treated as made, and

(ii) the individual satisfied the eligibility requirements set out in Part 3 of these Regulations on that chosen date, or

(c) where regulation 19 applies (applications made within 13 weeks of a qualifying disability benefit), a date to be chosen by the Scottish Ministers in accordance with that regulation.

(3) Where the individual does not satisfy the eligibility requirements set out in Part 3 of these Regulations on the chosen date mentioned in paragraph (2)(b), the Scottish Ministers may choose that entitlement to assistance begins on a later date, provided the individual satisfied the eligibility requirements on that later date.

(4) For the purposes of section 38(3) of the 2018 Act, the period covered by an application for Carer Support Payment—

(a) under paragraph (2)(a)—

(i) begins on the day on which the application is treated as having been made, and

(ii) ends on the day on which the determination of entitlement is made,

(b) under paragraph (2)(b) or (c)—

    (i) begins on the date chosen or the later date in accordance with paragraph (3),

    (ii) ends on the day on which the determination of entitlement is made.

Applications made within 13 weeks of a qualifying disability benefit decision

1.040   **19.**—(1) Where an individual makes an application for Carer Support Payment in respect of a cared for person within 13 weeks of a relevant qualifying disability benefit decision, the Scottish Ministers may determine that entitlement to Carer Support Payment begins on the first day of the award week in which, as a result of that relevant qualifying disability benefit decision, entitlement to that benefit begins, provided the individual satisfied the eligibility requirements set out in Part 3 of these Regulations on that date.

(2) Where the individual does not satisfy the eligibility requirements set out in Part 3 of these Regulations on the date on which the relevant qualifying disability benefit decision falls, the Scottish Ministers may determine that entitlement to Carer Support Payment begins on a later date, provided the individual satisfies those eligibility requirements on that later date.

(3) For the purposes of this regulation, "relevant qualifying disability benefit decision" means a decision—

(a) made by the Secretary of State, the Scottish Ministers, or the Department for Communities in Northern Ireland—

    (i) on a claim or an application, or

    (ii) on revision, determination of entitlement, or supersession, or

(b) on appeal whether by the First-tier Tribunal, the First-tier Tribunal for Scotland, the Upper Tribunal, the court, the Northern Ireland Appeal Tribunal or the Northern Ireland Social Security and Child Support Commissioner,

awarding a qualifying disability benefit to the cared for person mentioned in paragraph (1).

Entitlement beginning before the commencement of these Regulations

1.041   **20.** Where the Scottish Ministers make a determination under regulation 19 (applications made within 13 weeks of a qualifying disability benefit decision) the effect of which is that an individual's entitlement to Carer Support Payment would begin on a date before the commencement of these Regulations—

(a) the individual is treated as having made a claim for Carer's Allowance under section 70 of the 1992 Act for the period starting with that date and ending on the day before the date of commencement of these Regulations,

(b) the determination is to be made on the assumption that the individual satisfied the eligibility requirements in section 70 of the 1992 Act, read with the Social Security (Invalid Care Allowance) Regulations 1976 for that period, and

(c) any payments of Carer Support Payment made in respect of that period are to be treated as though they were payments of Carer's Allowance.

Amount and form of Carer Support Payment where payments are backdated

21. Any payment of Carer Support Payment made in respect of a period—   1.042
(a) before the commencement of these Regulations is to be paid at the weekly rate specified in paragraph 4 of Part III of schedule 4 of the 1992 Act, or
(b) after the commencement of these Regulations is to be paid at the weekly rate specified in regulation 16(1) (amount and form of Carer Support Payment),
as it had effect during the period to which that payment relates.

Time of payment

22. Where an award of Carer Support Payment is made, the Scottish   1.043
Ministers are to—
(a) make the first payment of assistance on a date specified in the notice of determination, and
(b) inform the individual that any subsequent payment will be made—
   (i) 4 weekly in arrears, or
   (ii) weekly in advance.

Temporary stop in entitlement

23.—(1) This paragraph applies where the Scottish Ministers have made   1.044
a determination without application under regulation 36 (determination following a change of circumstances etc.) that an individual is no longer entitled to Carer Support Payment in respect of a cared for person because—
(a) the individual's earnings in respect of an award week exceeded the earnings limit set out in regulation 14,
(b) the cared for person has voluntarily relinquished their entitlement to their qualifying disability benefit and the individual therefore no longer satisfies the requirements of regulation 5(1) (provision of care to a cared for person) in respect of an award week, or
(c) subject to regulation 40 (temporary break in care), the individual failed to satisfy the requirements of regulation 5(1) (provision of care to a cared for person) in respect of an award week.
(2) Where paragraph (1) applies, the Scottish Ministers are to make a determination without application of the individual's entitlement to Carer Support Payment if, within 26 weeks of the determination mentioned in paragraph (1), the Scottish Ministers establish that the individual satisfies the eligibility requirements set out in Part 3 of these Regulations.
(3) The duty on the Scottish Ministers to make a determination without application mentioned in paragraph (2) does not apply where another individual has been awarded—
(a) Carer Support Payment,
(b) Carer's Allowance, or
(c) the carer element of Universal Credit,
in respect of the cared for person mentioned in paragraph (1).

(4) This paragraph applies where an individual who has an ongoing entitlement to Carer Support Payment cares for a cared for person whose qualifying disability benefit has been—

(a) reduced to £0,

(b) ended as a result of the cared for person being—
    (i) admitted to a hospital or care home, or
    (ii) in legal detention,

(c) suspended as a result of—
    (i) the circumstances mentioned in—
        (aa) regulation 26A(3)(a) of the Disability Assistance for Children and Young People (Scotland) Regulations 2021, or
        (bb) regulation 38(3)(a) of the Disability Assistance for Working Age People (Scotland) Regulations 2022,
    (ii) a failure to provide information in accordance with—
        (aa) regulation 17 of the Social Security and Child Support (Decisions and Appeals) Regulations 1999,
        (bb) regulation 17 of the Social Security and Child Support (Decisions and Appeals) Regulations (Northern Ireland) 1999,
        (cc) regulation 45 of the Universal Credit, Personal Independence Payment, Jobseeker's Allowance and Employment and Support Allowance (Decisions and Appeals) Regulations 2013, or
        (dd) regulation 44 of the Universal Credit, Personal Independence Payment, Jobseeker's Allowance and Employment and Support Allowance (Decisions and Appeals) Regulations (Northern Ireland) 2016, or
    (iii) the circumstances mentioned in—
        (aa) regulation 16(3)(a)(i) or (ii) of the Social Security and Child Support (Decisions and Appeals) Regulations 1999,
        (bb) regulation 16(3)(a)(i) or (ii) of the Social Security and Child Support (Decisions and Appeals) Regulations (Northern Ireland) 1999,
        (cc) regulation 44(2)(a)(i) or (ii) of the Universal Credit, Personal Independence Payment, Jobseeker's Allowance and Employment and Support Allowance (Decisions and Appeals) Regulations 2013, or
        (dd) regulation 43(2)(a)(i) or (ii) of the Universal Credit, Personal Independence Payment, Jobseeker's Allowance and Employment and Support Allowance (Decisions and Appeals) Regulations (Northern Ireland) 2016.

(5) Where paragraph (4) applies, the Scottish Ministers are to make a determination without receiving an application that the individual is no longer entitled to Carer Support Payment.

(6) Where paragraph (4)(a) or (b) applies, the determination comes into effect on the first day of the award week following the award week in which the cared for person's qualifying disability benefit has been ended or reduced to £0.

(7) Where paragraph (4)(c) applies, the determination comes into effect on the first day of the award week following the day on which the cared for person's qualifying disability benefit has been suspended for 4 weeks.

(8) Where paragraph (5) applies, the Scottish Ministers are to make a determination without application of the individual's entitlement to Carer Support Payment if, within 26 weeks of the determination mentioned in paragraph (5), the Scottish Ministers establish that—

(a) a determination is made that the value of the qualifying disability benefit that is to be given to the cared for person is an amount more than £0, or

(b) the suspension of the cared for person's qualifying disability benefit mentioned in paragraph (4)(c) is ended and the cared for person would have been entitled to the qualifying disability benefit during the period of suspension.

(9) Where paragraph (2) applies, the individual's entitlement to assistance begins—

(a) where the individual notifies the Scottish Ministers that they satisfy the eligibility requirements set out in Part 3 of these Regulations within 13 weeks of that change occurring, on the first day of the award week in which that change occurred,

(b) where the individual notifies the Scottish Ministers that they satisfy the eligibility requirements set out in Part 3 of these Regulations later than 13 weeks of the change occurring, but where the Scottish Ministers consider that the individual has good reason for not notifying the change within 13 weeks, on the first day of the award week in which that change occurred,

(c) where the individual notifies the Scottish Ministers that they satisfy the eligibility requirements set out in Part 3 of these Regulations later than 13 weeks of the change occurring and where the Scottish Ministers do not consider that the individual has good reason for not notifying that change within 13 weeks, on the first day of the award week in which the individual notified that change, or

(d) in any other case, the first day of the award week in which the individual satisfies the eligibility requirements set out in Part 3 of these Regulations.

(10) Where paragraph (8)(a) applies, the individual's entitlement to assistance begins—

(a) where the individual notifies the Scottish Ministers that the cared for person's qualifying disability benefit is paid at an amount more than £0 within 13 weeks of that change occurring, on the first day of the award week in which that change occurred,

(b) where the individual notifies the Scottish Ministers that the cared for person's qualifying disability benefit is paid at an amount more than £0 later than 13 weeks of the change occurring, but where the Scottish Ministers consider that the individual has good reason for not notifying the change within 13 weeks, on the first day of the award week in which that change occurred,

(c) where the individual notifies the Scottish Ministers that the cared for person's qualifying disability benefit is paid at an amount more than £0 later than 13 weeks of the change occurring and where the Scottish Ministers do not consider that the individual has good reason for not notifying that change within 13 weeks, on the first day of the award week in which the individual notified that change, or

(d) in any other case, the first day of the award week in which the cared for person's qualifying disability benefit is paid at an amount more than £0.

(11) Where paragraph (8)(b) applies, the individual's entitlement to assistance begins—

(a) where it is determined that during the period of suspension, the cared for person would have been entitled to a qualifying disability benefit in respect of that period, on the first day of the award week in which the cared for person's entitlement to the qualifying disability benefit begins,

(b) in any other event, on the first day of the award week in which the suspension is ended.

Multiple applications involving the same cared for person

1.045   **24.**—(1) Where the Scottish Ministers receive two or more applications for Carer Support Payment from different individuals in respect of the same cared for person, the Scottish Ministers must determine the application made first before determining any other application.

(2) Where, but for regulation 5(3) (provision of care to a cared for person), two or more individuals would be entitled to Carer Support Payment in respect of the same cared for person for the same period, only one of them may be entitled, being either—

(a) one of them as they may jointly agree in accordance with paragraph (5), or

(b) in absence of such agreement, one of them as may be determined by the Scottish Ministers in accordance with paragraph (6).

(3) Where, but for regulation 5(3) (provision of care to a cared for person), a person ('carer A') would be entitled to Carer's Allowance payable by the Scottish Ministers and another person ('carer B') would be entitled to Carer Support Payment in respect of the same cared for person for the same period, carer B will only be entitled if—

(a) carer A and carer B jointly agree in accordance with paragraph (5) that carer A will not be entitled, or

(b) in absence of such agreement, the Scottish Ministers determine that carer B is or remains entitled to Carer Support Payment in respect of that period.

(4) Where, but for regulation 5(3) (provision of care to a cared for person), a person ('carer A') would have a relevant entitlement and another person ('carer B') would be entitled to Carer Support Payment in respect of the same cared for person for the same period, carer B will only be entitled to Carer Support Payment if—

(a) carer A and carer B jointly agree in accordance with paragraph (5) that carer A will not have a relevant entitlement, or

(b) in absence of such agreement, the Scottish Ministers determine that carer B is or remains entitled to Carer Support Payment in respect of that period, following—

    (i) in a case where the relevant entitlement is to—

        (aa) a Carer's Allowance payable by the Secretary of State under section 70 of the 1992 Act,

        (bb) the carer element of Universal Credit payable by the Secretary of State under section 12(2)(c) of the Welfare Reform Act 2012,

consultation with the Secretary of State,

(ii) in a case where the relevant entitlement is to—

    (aa) a Carer's Allowance payable by the Department for Communities in Northern Ireland under section 70 of the Social Security Contributions and Benefits (Northern Ireland) Act 1992,

    (bb) the carer element of Universal Credit payable by the Department for Communities in Northern Ireland under Article 17(2)(c) of the Welfare Reform (Northern Ireland) Order 2015,

consultation with the Department for Communities in Northern Ireland.

(5) An agreement under paragraph (2)(a), (3)(a) or (4)(a) is to be made by giving the Scottish Ministers a notice in writing signed by the individuals mentioned in paragraph (2), (3) or (4) as the case may be, specifying one of them as the individual to be entitled to assistance.

(6) When making a determination under paragraph (2)(b), (3)(b) or (4)(b), the Scottish Ministers must have regard to factors including but not limited to—

(a) the best interests of the cared for person,

(b) whether any of the individuals mentioned in paragraph (2), (3) or (4)—

    (i) are family members of the cared for person,

    (ii) live with or near the cared for person,

    (iii) receive any benefits on behalf of, or as a result of their responsibility for, the cared for person.

(7) The Scottish Ministers may, having considered the factors set out in paragraph (6), make a determination without application that—

(a) one of the individuals mentioned in paragraph (2) or (3), or

(b) following consultation with the Secretary of State or, as the case may be, the Department for Communities in Northern Ireland, carer B mentioned in paragraph (4),

who has ongoing entitlement to Carer Support Payment, is no longer entitled to Carer Support Payment.

(8) For the purposes of this regulation, an individual has a "relevant entitlement" if the individual is entitled to—

(a) a Carer's Allowance, or

(b) the carer element of universal credit.

(9) Where paragraph (2) applies at the same time as paragraphs (3) or (4), the Scottish Ministers must make a determination under paragraph (2) before making a determination under paragraph (3) or (4).

Continuing eligibility

25.—(1) Subject to paragraphs (3) and (4), a determination that an individual is entitled to Carer Support Payment in respect of a period is to be made on the basis that the individual has an ongoing entitlement to Carer Support Payment after the end of that period, except where paragraph (2) applies.

(2) This paragraph applies where, after the end of the period mentioned in paragraph (1), the individual no longer satisfies the eligibility rules.

(3) A determination of ongoing entitlement is made on the basis that—

    1.046

(a) the individual will continue to be entitled to Carer Support Payment for a fixed or indefinite period as specified in the notice of determination, and

(b) the decision that the individual is entitled to Carer Support Payment for each subsequent 4-week period is to be taken in accordance with these Regulations, on the strength of the assumptions set out in paragraph (4).

(4) The assumptions are that—

(a) the individual continues to satisfy the eligibility criteria which were satisfied to be entitled to Carer Support Payment under the determination mentioned in paragraph (1),

(b) the information on which the determination mentioned in paragraph (1) was made still applies and is relevant in the individual's case, and

(c) there is no change in circumstances of the individual which would require to be notified under section 56 of the 2018 Act.

Form of payment – giving Carer Support Payment by way of deduction

1.047   **26.**—(1) Where an individual has a liability to the Scottish Ministers under section 63 of the 2018 Act, the individual's payment of Carer Support Payment may be given (in whole or in part) by way of deduction, at a reasonable level, from that liability either—

(a) with the agreement of the individual, or

(b) without the individual's agreement, where the individual has unreasonably refused to agree to the assistance being given in that form.

(2) For the purposes of paragraph (1), "reasonable level" means a level that is reasonable having regard to the financial circumstances of the individual.

When a decrease in amount or cessation of entitlement takes effect

1.048   **27.**—(1) Where, as a result of a determination without application, the amount of Carer Support Payment payable in respect of an individual is decreased or their entitlement to Carer Support Payment ceases, the change takes effect—

(a) in the case of a determination without application under regulation 35 (consideration of entitlement after specified period) or 36(a) (determination following change of circumstances etc.), on the first day of the award week following the award week in which—

(i) the individual should have notified the Scottish Ministers of the change, where the individual was required to notify a change under section 56 of the 2018 Act, if the individual—

(aa) knowingly fails to notify a change, or

(bb) fails to notify the change as soon as reasonably practicable after it occurred, or

(ii) in any other case, the Scottish Ministers make the determination,

(b) in the case of an earlier determination which was based on error within the meaning of—

(i) regulation 37 (determination following official error – underpayments), on the first day of the award week in which the earlier determination took effect, or

(ii) regulation 38 (determination following error – overpayments), on the first day of the award week following the award week in which the earlier determination took effect,

(c) in any other case, on the first day of the award week following the award week in which the Scottish Ministers make the determination.

(2) Where the Scottish Ministers consider that in all the circumstances it would be unjust not to do so, they may, when making their determination, set a later date for the purposes of paragraph (1).

When an increase in amount of entitlement takes effect

28.—(1) Where, as a result of a determination without application, the amount of Carer Support Payment payable in respect of an individual is increased, the change takes effect—

   1.049

(a) in the case of an increase pursuant to a determination made under regulation 36(a) or (b) (determination following change of circumstances etc.), on the first day of the award week in which—

   (i) the individual first satisfies the requirements for an increased amount of Carer Support Payment—

   (aa) where the individual reports the change within 13 weeks of the change occurring, or

   (bb) where the individual reports the change more than 13 weeks after the change occurring, but only if the Scottish Ministers consider that the individual has good reason for not reporting the change within 13 weeks, or

   (ii) in any other case, the individual reports the change,

   (iii) where as a result of the Scottish Ministers becoming aware that a determination of an individual's entitlement was made in ignorance of a material fact, the Scottish Ministers make the determination.

(b) in the case of an earlier determination which was based on error within the meaning of—

   (i) regulation 37 (determination following official error – underpayments), on the first day of the award week in which the earlier determination took effect, or

   (ii) regulation 38 (determination following error – overpayments), on the first day of the award week following the award week in which the earlier determination took effect,

(c) in any other case, on the first day of the award week following the award week in which the Scottish Ministers make the determination.

(2) Where the Scottish Ministers consider that in all the circumstances it would be unjust not to do so, they may, when making their determination, set an earlier date for the purposes of paragraph (1).

PART 5

SUSPENSIONS

Circumstances in which assistance may be suspended

1.050

29.—(1) The Scottish Ministers may decide that an individual who has an ongoing entitlement to Carer Support Payment in respect of a period by virtue of regulation 25 (continuing eligibility) is not to become entitled to be given some or all of that assistance at the time at which the individual otherwise would in accordance with that regulation, as read with regulation 22 (time of payment) (referred to in these Regulations as a decision to suspend the individual's Carer Support Payment).

(2) Where such a decision is made in respect of an individual, payments of Carer Support Payment to that individual are to be suspended until such a time as the Scottish Ministers decide that the individual is once again to become entitled to be given Carer Support Payment.

(3) The Scottish Ministers may decide to suspend an individual's Carer Support Payment only in the circumstances where—

(a) section 54(1A) of the 2018 Act applies, or

(b) the Scottish Ministers have made arrangements (whether under section 85B of the 2018 Act or otherwise) for a person to receive Carer Support Payment on the individual's behalf, and the Scottish Ministers consider that it is necessary to suspend the Carer Support Payment—

    (i) in order to protect the individual from the risk of financial abuse, or

    (ii) because the person with whom the Scottish Ministers have made arrangements is unable to continue to receive the Carer Support Payment.

(c) In this regulation "financial abuse" includes—

    (i) having money or other property stolen,

    (ii) being defrauded,

    (iii) being put under pressure in relation to money or other property,

    (iv) having money or other property misused.

Having regard to financial circumstances

1.051

30. The Scottish Ministers must have regard to an individual's financial circumstances prior to making a decision to suspend payment to the individual of some or all of Carer Support Payment.

Information to be given following suspension

1.052

31.—(1) Having made a decision to suspend an individual's Carer Support Payment, the Scottish Ministers must inform the individual of—

(a) their decision to suspend the individual's Carer Support Payment,

(b) the reasons for their decision,

(c) any steps which might be taken by the individual in order for the Scottish Ministers to consider ending the suspension, and

(d) the individual's right under regulation 32 (right to review suspension) to require the Scottish Ministers to review their decision.

(2) The Scottish Ministers must fulfil their duty under paragraph (1) in a way that leaves the individual with a record of the information which the individual can show to, or otherwise share with, others.

Right to review suspension

32.—(1) An individual may require the Scottish Ministers to review a decision to suspend that individual's Carer Support Payment.

(2) The Scottish Ministers must—

(a) complete a review mentioned in paragraph (1) within 31 days beginning with the day on which they received notice from the individual requiring them to review their decision,

(b) inform the individual of the outcome of the review including the reasons for it.

(3) The Scottish Ministers must fulfil their duty under paragraph (2)(b) in a way that leaves the individual with a record of the information which the individual can show to, or otherwise share with, others.

Ending a suspension

33. The Scottish Ministers are to make a decision to end a suspension where—

(a) the individual provides the information requested under section 54(1) of the 2018 Act and the Scottish Ministers consider that they do not require to make a determination without application,

(b) regulation 29(3)(a) (circumstances in which assistance may be suspended) applies and the Scottish Ministers make a determination without application under regulation 35 (consideration of entitlement after specified period), 36 (determination following change of circumstances, etc.), 37 (determination following official error – underpayments), 38 (determination following error – overpayments) or 39 (determination to effect a deduction decision),

(c) the Scottish Ministers make a determination under section 54(2) of the 2018 Act,

(d) the circumstances mentioned in regulation 29(3)(b) (circumstances in which assistance may be suspended) no longer apply, or

(e) the Scottish Ministers consider it appropriate in the circumstances, including having regard to the financial circumstances of the individual.

Effect of suspension ending

34. When—

(a) the suspension of an individual's Carer Support Payment ends, and

(b) under the latest determination of the individual's entitlement to Carer Support Payment relating to the period of the suspension the individual would have become entitled to be given Carer Support Payment during that period,

the individual is immediately to be given the Carer Support Payment that the individual would have become entitled to be given under the determination during the period of suspension.

1.053

1.054

1.055

PART 6

RE-CONSIDERATION OF ENTITLEMENT TO CARER SUPPORT PAYMENT:
DETERMINATION WITHOUT APPLICATION

Consideration of entitlement after specified period

1.056   **35.** The Scottish Ministers must make a determination of an individual's entitlement to Carer Support Payment, without receiving an application, after the end of the period specified (if any) in—
  (a) the individual's notice of determination under section 40 or notice of re-determination under section 44 (as the case may be), or
  (b) a determination made by the First-tier Tribunal for Scotland under section 49,
of the 2018 Act.

Determination following change of circumstances etc.

1.057   **36.** The Scottish Ministers must make a determination of an individual's entitlement to Carer Support Payment, without receiving an application, where the individual has an ongoing entitlement to Carer Support Payment and they become aware—
  (a) of a change of circumstances whether or not notified by the individual in accordance with section 54 or 56 of the 2018 Act,
  (b) that a determination of an individual's entitlement was made in ignorance of a material fact which is likely to result in an alteration to the amount of Carer Support Payment payable to the individual or which is likely to mean that the individual is no longer entitled to Carer Support Payment,
  (c) that the individual has died,
  (d) that the cared for person has died,
  (e) that the individual has notified the Scottish Ministers that they wish for their entitlement to assistance to begin on a date prior to the day on which their application was treated as made, provided that—
    (i) the date chosen by the individual is no more than 13 weeks prior to the day on which their application was treated as made, and
    (ii) the individual satisfied the eligibility requirements set out in Part 3 of these Regulations on that chosen date,
  (f) of an alteration of the award of Carer's Allowance which the individual was entitled to immediately before the date of transfer to Carer Support Payment in accordance with Part 2 of schedule 1, as a result of a decision made pursuant to—
    (i) a revision under regulation 3 of the Social Security and Child Support (Decisions and Appeals) Regulations 1999 ("the 1999 Regulations"),
    (ii) a supersession under regulation 6 of the 1999 Regulations,
    (iii) an appeal under section 12 of the Social Security Act 1998 ("the 1998 Act"),
    (iv) a redetermination under section 13 of the 1998 Act,
    (v) an appeal to the Upper Tribunal under section 14 of the 1998 Act,

    (vi) a revision under article 10 of the Social Security (Northern Ireland) Order 1998 ("the 1998 Order"),

   (vii) a supersession under article 11 of the 1998 Order,

  (viii) an appeal under article 13 of the 1998 Order, or

   (ix) an appeal to the Commissioner under article 15 of the 1998 Order,

(g) of an alteration of the award of Carer's Allowance which the individual was entitled to immediately before moving to Scotland in circumstances in which regulation 41 (individuals in respect of whom Carer's Allowance is paid in another part of the United Kingdom immediately before moving to Scotland) applies, as a result of a decision made pursuant to—

     (i) a revision under regulation 3 of the Social Security and Child Support (Decisions and Appeals) Regulations 1999 ("the 1999 Regulations"),

    (ii) a supersession under regulation 6 of the 1999 Regulations,

   (iii) an appeal under section 12 of the Social Security Act 1998 ("the 1998 Act"),

   (iv) a re-consideration under section 13 of the 1998 Act,

    (v) an appeal to the Upper Tribunal under section 14 of the 1998 Act,

   (vi) a revision under article 10 of the Social Security (Northern Ireland) Order 1998 ("the 1998 Order"),

   (vii) a supersession under article 11 of the 1998 Order,

  (viii) an appeal under article 13 of the 1998 Order, or

   (ix) an appeal to the Commissioner under article 15 of the 1998 Order.

Determination following official error – underpayments

37.—(1) The Scottish Ministers are to make a determination of an individual's entitlement to Carer Support Payment, without receiving an application, where—   1.058

(a) they have previously made a determination of the individual's entitlement to Carer Support Payment ("the original determination"),

(b) they establish that, due to an official error, the original determination was incorrect resulting in the individual—

     (i) not being given an award of Carer Support Payment, or

    (ii) being given a lower award than that,

to which the individual was entitled,

(c) the Scottish Ministers are not considering a request for a re-determination of the individual's entitlement to Carer Support Payment, and

(d) the individual has not appealed to the First-tier Tribunal for Scotland against the Scottish Minister's determination of the individual's entitlement to Carer Support Payment.

(2) In making a determination required by paragraph (1) the Scottish Ministers are to use—

(a) any information—

     (i) provided in the application that led to the original determination,

    (ii) they have obtained in connection with that application, and

(b) any other information they have obtained in connection with the individual's entitlement to Carer Support Payment.

(3) In this regulation "official error" means an error made by someone acting on behalf of the Scottish Ministers or on behalf of a Minister of the Crown that was not materially contributed to by anyone else.

Determination following error – overpayments

1.059
38.—(1) The Scottish Ministers are to make a determination of an individual's entitlement to Carer Support Payment, without receiving an application, where—

(a) they have previously made a determination of the individual's entitlement to Carer Support Payment ("the original determination"),
(b) they establish that, due to an error, the original determination was incorrect resulting in the individual being given—
    (i) an award of Carer Support Payment to which the individual was not entitled, or
    (ii) a higher award than that to which the individual was entitled,
(c) the Scottish Ministers are not considering a request for a re-determination of the individual's entitlement to Carer Support Payment, and
(d) the individual has not made an appeal to the First-tier Tribunal for Scotland or Upper Tribunal against the Scottish Minister's determination of the individual's entitlement to Carer Support Payment, that has not yet been determined.

(2) In making a determination required by paragraph (1) the Scottish Ministers are to use—

(a) any information—
    (i) provided in the application that led to the original determination, and
    (ii) they have obtained in connection with that application,
(b) any other information they have obtained in connection with the individual's entitlement to Carer Support Payment, and
(c) any other information available to them that is relevant to their consideration of whether the individual is entitled to Carer Support Payment.

(3) In this regulation references to an "error" are to—

(a) an error in the performance of a function conferred by these Regulations or the 2018 Act, including a determination being made—
    (i) wrongly, or
    (ii) correctly but on the basis of—
        (aa) incorrect information, or
        (bb) an assumption which proves to be wrong, or
(b) a new determination not being made after an assumption on the basis of which an earlier determination was made has proved to be wrong.

Determination to effect a deduction decision

1.060
39.—(1) The Scottish Ministers are to make a determination of an individual's entitlement to Carer Support Payment, without receiving an application, where the circumstances in paragraphs (2) and (3) apply.

(2) This paragraph applies where—

(a) regulation 26 (form of payment – giving Carer Support Payment by way of deduction) allows Carer Support Payment to be given to the individual by way of deduction, or

(b) Carer Support Payment is being given to the individual by way of deduction, and the Scottish Ministers consider that may no longer be appropriate.

(3) This paragraph applies where the Scottish Ministers have decided to—

(a) vary the amount of Carer Support Payment to be given by way of deduction (including introducing a deduction, where the full amount of Carer Support Payment was previously given as money),

(b) vary any period for which the individual's Carer Support Payment is to be given by way of deduction, that may have been specified in a previous determination of the individual's entitlement, or

(c) cease making deductions, and instead give the individual's Carer Support Payment in the form of money.

(4) The Scottish Ministers are to make a determination, without receiving an application, where an individual who is receiving Carer Support Payment by way of deduction under a previous determination of entitlement notifies the Scottish Ministers that the individual—

(a) withdraws their agreement to their Carer Support Payment being given by way of deduction,

(b) wishes the Scottish Ministers to increase the amount of their Carer Support Payment that is given by way of deduction,

(c) wishes the Scottish Ministers to decrease the amount of their Carer Support Payment that is given by way of deduction (including ceasing the deduction), or

(d) wishes the Scottish Ministers to amend the length of any period referred to in paragraph (3)(b).

PART 7

BREAKS IN CARE

Temporary break in care

40.—(1) An award week in respect of which an individual fails to satisfy 1.061
the requirement of regulation 5(2) (provision of care to a cared for person) is to be treated as an award week in respect of which that individual satisfies that requirement if—

(a) that individual has only temporarily ceased to satisfy it, and

(b) that individual has satisfied it for at least 14 weeks in the period of 26 weeks ending with that award week and would have satisfied it for at least 22 weeks in that period but for the fact that—

(i) that individual was undergoing medical or other treatment as an in-patient in a hospital or similar institution, or

(ii) the cared for person was undergoing medical or other treatment as an in-patient in a hospital or similar institution.

(2) Regulation 14 (earnings limit) does not apply to an individual in respect of an award week mentioned in paragraph (1).

PART 8

MOVEMENT OF INDIVIDUALS BETWEEN SCOTLAND AND THE REST OF THE UNITED KINGDOM

Individuals in respect of whom Carer's Allowance is paid in another part of the United Kingdom immediately before moving to Scotland

1.062   **41.**—(1) Where an individual—
(a) becomes resident in Scotland,
(b) was resident in another part of the United Kingdom, and
(c) was entitled to Carer's Allowance in respect of a cared for person immediately before the date of the move,
the Scottish Ministers are to make a determination without application of the individual's entitlement to Carer Support Payment.

(2) Entitlement to Carer Support Payment under paragraph (1) begins on the day after the day on which the individual's entitlement to Carer's Allowance ends.

(3) In this regulation, "the date of the move" is the date when the individual becomes resident in Scotland, as notified by the individual or otherwise communicated to the Scottish Ministers (whether the notification takes place before or after the date of the move).

Individuals in respect of whom Carer Support Payment is paid at the time of moving to another part of the United Kingdom

1.063   **42.**—(1) Where the Scottish Ministers become aware that an individual who is entitled to Carer Support Payment has moved or is to move to become resident in another part of the United Kingdom, the individual is to be treated as though the individual meets the condition under regulation 6(1)(a) (residence and presence conditions) of being ordinarily resident in Scotland for a period of 13 weeks beginning in accordance with paragraph (4).

(2) Where the Scottish Ministers become aware that an individual has moved or is to move to another part of the United Kingdom mentioned in paragraph (1), they are to make a determination without application at the end of the 13-week period mentioned in paragraph (1) that the individual's entitlement to Carer Support Payment is to terminate.

(3) Where before the end of the 13-week period, the Scottish Ministers become aware that the individual is no longer to move to become resident in another part of the United Kingdom, the duty in paragraph (2) does not apply.

(4) The 13-week period mentioned in paragraph (1) begins on the date the individual ceases to be ordinarily resident in Scotland.

(5) On the day after the 13-week period specified in paragraph (4) ends—
(a) entitlement to Carer Support Payment ceases, and

(b) regulation 38 (determination following error – overpayments) applies to any Carer Support Payment paid to an individual in relation to a period after the end of that 13-week period.

PART 9

PERIODS IN RESPECT OF A RE-DETERMINATION REQUEST

Periods in respect of a re-determination request

43.—(1) The period for requesting a re-determination of entitlement to Carer Support Payment under section 41 of the 2018 Act is 42 days beginning with the day that the individual is informed, in accordance with section 40 of the 2018 Act, of the right to make the request.   1.064

(2) In relation to determining entitlement to Carer Support Payment, the period allowed for re-determination (within the meaning of section 43 of the 2018 Act) is 56 days beginning with—

(a) the day that the request for a re-determination is received by the Scottish Ministers,

(b) in a case where the request for a re-determination is received by the Scottish Ministers outwith the period prescribed in paragraph (1), the day on which it is decided by the Scottish Ministers or (as the case may be) the First-tier Tribunal for Scotland that the individual in question has a good reason for not requesting a re-determination sooner, or

(c) in a case where the Scottish Ministers have informed the individual of their decision that the request for a re-determination was not made in such form as the Scottish Ministers require, the day on which it is subsequently decided by the First-tier Tribunal for Scotland that the individual in question has made the request in such form as the Scottish Ministers require.

PART 10

TRANSFER FROM CARER'S ALLOWANCE TO CARER SUPPORT PAYMENT

Transfer from Carer's Allowance to Carer Support Payment

44. Part 2 of schedule 1 makes provision about transferring from Carer's Allowance to Carer Support Payment.   1.065

PART 11

INITIAL PERIOD FOR APPLICATIONS

Initial period for applications

1.066   **45.** Part 1 of schedule 1 makes provision about the initial period for applications.

PART 12

TRANSITORY PROVISION

Transitory provision – initial period for applications

1.067   **46.**—(1) During the initial period for applications, in addition to satisfying the residence and presence conditions in regulations 6 to 11, an individual must be resident in one of the local authority areas specified in paragraph 2 of Part 1 of schedule 1 on the date their application is received by the Scottish Ministers.

(2) In this regulation and in Part 1 of schedule 1, "initial period for applications" means the period beginning with 19 November 2023 and ending with 30 September 2024.

Exclusion to transitory provision

1.068   **47.**—(1) An individual who has made a claim for Carer's Allowance prior to 19 November 2023 which has not yet been decided is not entitled to be paid Carer Support Payment during the initial period for applications.

(2) In paragraph (1) a claim for Carer's Allowance is decided if it has—

(a) been decided by the Secretary of State under section 70 of the 1992 Act,

(b) been withdrawn in accordance with regulation 5(2) of the Social Security (Claims and Payments) Regulations 1987, or

(c) otherwise is no longer to be decided by the Secretary of State as mentioned in sub-paragraph (a).

PART 13

CONSEQUENTIAL AMENDMENTS

Consequential amendments

1.069   **48.** The amendments specified in Part 3 of schedule 1 have effect.

SCHEDULE 1   Regulations 44, 45 and 48

PART 1

INITIAL PERIOD FOR APPLICATIONS

Initial period for applications

1.—(1) These Regulations apply to an individual who is resident in one of the local authority areas mentioned in paragraph 2 when the individual makes an application for Carer
Support Payment during the initial period for applications.

(2) An individual who is awarded Carer Support Payment pursuant to an application made
during the initial period for applications will continue to be entitled if that individual moves to
another local authority area in Scotland.

1.070

Local authority areas for initial period for applications

2. The local authority areas specified for the purposes of regulation 45 (initial period for
applications) are—

    (a) Perthshire and Kinross,

    (b) City of Dundee, and

    (c) the Western Isles.

PART 2

TRANSFER TO CARER SUPPORT PAYMENT

Interpretation

3. In this Part of the schedule—

"date of transfer" means the date when a transferring individual's entitlement to
    Carer Support Payment begins by virtue of a determination made under paragraph
    5(1),

"relevant individual" means an individual—

    (a) who has an award of Carer's Allowance who appears to the Scottish Ministers to be
        likely to be eligible for Carer Support Payment, and

    (b) who is—

        (i) ordinarily resident in Scotland, or

        (ii) someone to whom regulation 6(3) (residence and presence conditions) or 11(2)
            (persons residing outside the United Kingdom to whom a relevant EU regula-
            tion applies) applies,

"sufficient" means a link to Scotland that is sufficiently close that regulation 6(3) or 11(2)
    would be incompatible with the applicable agreement mentioned in that regulation, if
    the relevant individual were not entitled to Carer Support Payment,

"transfer notice" means the notice required by paragraph 4, and

"transferring individual" means an individual on whom the Scottish Ministers have served
    a notice of intention to transfer in accordance with paragraph 4.

1.071

Notice of intention to transfer to Carer Support Payment

4.—(1) The Scottish Ministers are to notify each relevant individual of their intention
to transfer that individual's entitlement to carer's assistance from an entitlement to Carer's
Allowance to an entitlement to Carer Support Payment.

(2) Notice under sub-paragraph (1) must—

    (a) be given in a way that leaves the relevant individual with a record of the information
        which they can show to, or otherwise share with, others,

    (b) inform the relevant individual that—

        (i) they have been identified as a relevant individual for the purpose of transfer to
            Carer Support Payment,

        (ii) the Scottish Ministers will make a determination without receiving an appli-
            cation to transfer the individual's entitlement to Carer's Allowance to an
            entitlement to Carer Support Payment within a period to be specified in
            the notice (the individual will be notified when the determination is made
            and informed about their award and start date of Carer Support Payment),
            and

        (iii) the individual's award of Carer's Allowance will cease immediately before the
            award of Carer Support Payment begins.

51

(3) Where a notice under sub-paragraph (1) is given—
   (a) to a transferring individual who, before a determination is made under paragraph 5(1)—
      (i) ceases to be ordinarily resident in Scotland, or
      (ii) cares for a cared for person who dies, or
   (b) in error where the individual is neither—
      (i) ordinarily resident in Scotland, nor
      (ii) an individual who is habitually resident in an EEA state, Gibraltar or Switzerland and has a genuine and sufficient link to Scotland,
   the duty on the Scottish Ministers in paragraph 5(1) does not apply.
(4) Where sub-paragraph (3) applies in respect of an individual and a determination under paragraph 5(1) has not been made, the Scottish Ministers are to notify the individual that the duty on the Scottish Ministers in paragraph 5(1) does not apply.

Determination without application of entitlement to Carer Support Payment
   5.—(1) The Scottish Ministers are to make a determination without receiving an application in respect of a transferring individual of that individual's entitlement to Carer Support Payment.
   (2) Entitlement to Carer Support Payment under a determination under sub-paragraph (1) begins on the date specified in the notice of determination given to the transferring individual in accordance with section 40 of the 2018 Act.
   (3) The determination under sub-paragraph (1) is to be made on the basis of—
      (a) such information as the Scottish Ministers have received from the Secretary of State in respect of the transferring individual's entitlement to Carer's Allowance, and
      (b) any other information available to the Scottish Ministers that appears to be relevant.
   (4) A determination under sub-paragraph (1) must be made on the basis that the transferring individual is entitled to the amount of Carer Support Payment that is equivalent to the amount of Carer's Allowance to which the individual was entitled immediately before the date of transfer.
   (5) A determination under sub-paragraph (1)—
      (a) may be made on the assumption that whatever can be discerned about the transferring individual's circumstances from the information mentioned in sub-paragraph (3) remains accurate on the date on which the determination is made,
      (b) notwithstanding the generality of head (a), is to be made on the assumption that the conditions relating to residence and presence set out in regulations 6 to 11 (residence and presence conditions etc.) are satisfied in the individual's case, and
      (c) must be made no later than the period specified in the notice under paragraph 4(1) (notice of intention to transfer to Carer Support Payment) unless the Scottish Ministers have—
         (i) good reason to extend that period,
         (ii) agreed the period for extension with the Secretary of State, and
         (iii) notified the transferring individual of the extension and reason for it.
   (6) Where the Scottish Ministers make a determination under paragraph (1) that a transferring individual is entitled to Carer Support Payment, for the week in which that determination takes place, "award week" means—
      (a) where the individual cares for a cared for person who is in receipt of Constant Attendance Allowance, a period of 4 days, starting on the Wednesday of that week and ending on the following Saturday, or
      (b) in all other cases, a period of 6 days, starting on the Monday of that week and ending on the following Saturday.

Date of cessation of Carer's Allowance
1.072   **6.** Where a determination is made under paragraph 5(1) (determination without application of entitlement to Carer Support Payment) that the transferring individual is entitled to Carer Support Payment, the transferring individual's entitlement to Carer's Allowance will cease on the date their entitlement to Carer Support Payment begins.

Modification of these regulations: transferring individuals
   7. These Regulations apply to a transferring individual on and after the date of transfer with the following modifications—
   In regulation 22, for sub-paragraph (b), substitute—
   "(b) inform the transferring individual that any subsequent payment will be made—
      (i) 4 weekly in arrears,
      (ii) weekly in advance,

   (iii) in respect of an individual who was paid Carer's Allowance one week in advance and 3 weekly in arrears—

     (aa) 4 weekly in arrears, or

     (bb) weekly in advance, provided that the individual has informed the Scottish Ministers that they wish to be paid weekly in advance before the date specified in the notice of intention to transfer given to the individual in accordance with paragraph 4(1) of schedule 1,

   (iv) where the Scottish Ministers consider that it would be unjust not to do so, at such intervals as may be specified in the notice of determination. ".

Appointees

8.—(1) A person appointed by the Secretary of State under regulation 33 (persons unable to act) of the Social Security (Claims and Payments) Regulations 1987 to receive Carer's Allowance on behalf of a transferring individual is to be treated on and after the date of transfer as though appointed by the Scottish Ministers to act on behalf of that transferring individual under section 85B of the 2018 Act.

(2) As soon as reasonably practicable after the date of transfer, the Scottish Ministers must—

 (a) consider whether the conditions for making an appointment in respect of the transferring individual are met (having regard to section 85B(3) of the 2018 Act),

 (b) consider whether to terminate the appointment that is treated as having been made by virtue of sub-paragraph (1) and terminate it if they consider it appropriate, and

 (c) if they have terminated an appointment in pursuance of head (b), appoint under section 85B of the 2018 Act another person to act on the transferring individual's behalf if they consider it appropriate to do so.

(3) The duty in paragraph (2) does not apply to a person in respect of whom the Scottish Ministers have already—

 (a) appointed to act on behalf of that transferring individual under section 85B of the 2018 Act, or

 (b) considered whether the conditions for making an appointment are met in accordance with paragraph 15 (appointees) of Part 3 of schedule 2 of the Disability Assistance for Working Age People (Scotland) Regulations 2022 or paragraph 14 (appointees) of Part 3 of the schedule of the Disability Assistance for Children and Young People (Scotland) Regulations 2021.

PART 3

CONSEQUENTIAL AMENDMENTS

These amendments have been noted in Part V of this Supplement, updating Vol IV of the main volumes. **1.073**

SCHEDULE 2   Regulation 14

CALCULATION OF EARNINGS

Interpretation

1. In this schedule— **1.074**

"basic rate" means the rate of income tax of that name determined in accordance with section 6(2) of the Income Tax Act 2007,

"board and lodging accommodation" means—

 (a) accommodation provided to a person or, if they are a member of a family, to them or any other member of their family, for a charge which includes the provision of that accommodation and at least some cooked or prepared meals (which are provided by a person other than the person to whom the accommodation is provided or a member of their family) and are consumed in that accommodation, or

 (b) accommodation provided to a person in a hotel, guest house, lodging house or some similar establishment,

except accommodation provided by a close relative of theirs or of any other member of their family, or other than on a commercial basis,

"close relative" means a parent, parent-in-law, son, son-in-law, daughter, daughter-in-law, step-parent, step-son, step-daughter, brother, sister, or if any of the preceding persons is one member of a couple, the other member of that couple,

53

"dwelling occupied as the home" means the dwelling together with any garage, garden and outbuildings, normally occupied by the individual as their home including any premises not so occupied which it is impracticable or unreasonable to sell separately, in particular, in Scotland, any croft land on which the dwelling is situated,

"employed earner" means a person who is in gainful employment in Great Britain under a contract of service, or in an office (including elective office) with emoluments chargeable to income tax under schedule E of the Income and Corporation Taxes Act 1988 and includes—

(a) a person in any employment which would be such employment if it were in Great Britain, and

(b) a person in any such employment which, in accordance with the provisions of the 1992 Act and of any regulations made under it, is to be disregarded in relation to liability for contributions,

"employment" includes any trade, business, profession, office or vocation,

"individual" means any person making an application for Carer Support Payment or transferring from Carer's Allowance to Carer Support Payment under these Regulations,

"maximum weekly amount" means the maximum weekly amount which, on the date on which the payment of compensation is made, is specified in section 227(1) of the Employment Rights Act 1996,

"occupational pension scheme" has the same meaning as in section 1 of the Pension Schemes Act 1993,

"pay period" means the period in respect of which an individual is, or expects to be, normally paid by their employer, being a week, a fortnight, 4 weeks, a calendar month, or such other period as the case may be,

"personal pension scheme" has the same meaning as in section 1 of the Pension Schemes Act 1993 and, in the case of a self-employed earner, includes a scheme approved by the Inland Revenue under Chapter IV of Part XIV of the Income and Corporation Taxes Act 1988,

"relevant earnings limit" means the earnings limit set out in regulation 14 of these Regulations,

"retirement annuity contract" means a contract or trust scheme approved under Chapter III of Part XIV of the Income and Corporation Taxes Act 1988,

"Scottish basic rate" means the rate of income tax of that name calculated in accordance with section 6A of the Income Tax Act 2007,

"Scottish taxpayer" has the same meaning as in Chapter 2 of Part 4A of the Scotland Act 1998,

"self-employed earner" means a person who is in gainful employment in Great Britain otherwise than as an employed earner and includes a person in any—

(a) employment which would be such employment if it were in Great Britain, and

(b) such employment which, in accordance with the provisions of the 1992 Act and of any regulations made under it, is to be disregarded in relation to liability for contributions, and

"year of assessment" means, with reference to any income tax, the year for which such tax was granted by any enactment granting income tax.

Calculation of earnings

2.—(1) For the purposes of regulation 14 (earnings limit), the earnings of an individual are to be calculated by determining the weekly amount of their earnings in accordance with this schedule.

(2) The amount of an individual's earnings for any period are the whole of those earnings (including any earnings which they are treated as possessing under paragraph 3 (notional earnings)) except in so far as paragraphs 9 (calculation of net earnings of employed earners) and 12 (calculation of net profit of self-employed earners) provide that certain sums are to be disregarded or deducted.

Notional earnings

1.075

3.—(1) Where an individual's earnings are not ascertainable at the date on which the Scottish Ministers are determining the individual's entitlement to Carer Support Payment or considering whether they are required to make a determination of the individual's entitlement to Carer Support Payment without receiving an application, the individual is treated as possessing such earnings as is reasonable in the circumstances having regard to the number of hours worked and the earnings paid for comparable employment.

(2) Where an individual is treated as possessing any earnings under sub-paragraph (1), this schedule applies for the purposes of calculating the amount of those earnings as if a payment

had actually been made and as if they were actual earnings which that individual does possess, except that paragraph 9(3) (calculation of net earnings of employed earners) does not apply and their net earnings are calculated by taking into account the earnings which they are treated as possessing, less—

(a) an amount in respect of income tax equivalent to an amount calculated by applying to those earnings the basic rate, or in the case of a Scottish taxpayer, the Scottish basic rate, of tax in the year of assessment less only the personal reliefs to which the individual is entitled under Chapters 2, 3 and 3A of Part 3 of the Income Tax Act 2007 as are appropriate to their circumstances; but if the period over which those earnings are to be taken into account is less than a year, the earnings to which the basic rate, or Scottish basic rate, of tax is to be applied and the amount of the personal reliefs deductible under this paragraph are calculated on a pro rata basis,

(b) where the weekly amount of those earnings equals or exceeds the lower earnings limit, an amount representing primary Class 1 contributions under the 1992 Act, calculated by applying to those earnings the initial and main primary percentages in accordance with section 8(1)(a) and (b) of that Act, and

(c) one half of any sum payable by the individual in respect of a pay period by way of a contribution towards an occupational or personal pension scheme,

(d) any care charges to which paragraph 15 (care charges to be deducted in the calculation of earnings) applies up to a maximum deduction, in respect of such care charges incurred by any individual, of 50% of their notional earnings.

Rounding of fractions

4. Where any calculation under this schedule results in a fraction of a penny that fraction is, if it would be to individual's advantage, treated as a penny, otherwise it is disregarded.

Calculation of earnings of employed earners

5.—(1) Earnings derived from employment as an employed earner are calculated or estimated over a period determined in accordance with the following paragraphs and at a weekly amount determined in accordance with paragraph 7 (calculation of weekly amount of earnings).

(2) Subject to sub-paragraphs (3) and (5) to (7), the period over which a payment is to be taken into account—

(a) in a case where it is payable in respect of a period, is a period equal to the total number of award weeks in the period commencing on the date on which the earnings are treated as paid under paragraph 6 (date on which earnings are treated as paid) and ending on the day before the date on which earnings of the same kind (excluding earnings of the kind mentioned in paragraph 8(1)(a) to (j)) and from the same source would, or would if the employment was continuing, next be treated as paid under that paragraph, or

(b) in any other case, and where it would cause the individual's earnings to exceed the relevant earnings limit if it were taken into account only in respect of the period in which it was received, is a period equal to such number of weeks as is equal to the number (less any fraction of a whole number) calculated in accordance with the formula—

$$\frac{P}{Q} + R$$

where—

P is the net earnings,

Q is the amount of the relevant earnings limit plus one penny, and

R is the total of the sums which would fall to be disregarded or deducted as appropriate under paragraph 9(2) (calculation of net earnings of employed earners),

and that period begins on the date on which the payment is treated as paid under paragraph 6 (date on which earnings are treated as paid).

(3) Where earnings not of the same kind are derived from the same source and the periods in respect of which those earnings would, but for this sub-paragraph, fall to be taken into account overlap, wholly or partly, those earnings are taken into account over a period—

(a) equal to the aggregate length of those periods, and

(b) beginning with the earliest date on which any part of those earnings would otherwise be treated as paid under paragraph 6 (date on which earnings are treated as paid).

(4) In a case to which paragraph (3) applies, earnings under paragraph 8 (earnings of employed earners) are taken into account in the following order of priority—

(a) earnings normally derived from the employment,

(b) any payment to which paragraph 8(1)(b) or (c) applies,

(c) any payment to which paragraph 8(1)(i) applies,

(d) any payment to which paragraph 8(1)(d) applies.

(5) Where earnings to which paragraph 8(1)(b) to (d) (earnings of employed earners) applies are paid in respect of a part of a day, those earnings are taken into account over a period equal to a week.

(6) Where earnings to which paragraph 8(1)(i)(i) (earnings of employed earners) applies are paid in respect of or on the termination of any employment which is not part-time employment, the period over which they are taken into account is—

(a) a period of weeks equal to the number of weeks (less any fraction of a whole number) obtained by dividing the net earnings by the maximum weekly amount which, on the date on which the payment of earnings is made, is specified in section 227(1) of the Employment Rights Act 1996, or

(b) a period equal to the length of the specified period,

whichever is the shorter, and that period begins on the date on which the payment is treated as paid under paragraph 6 (date on which earnings are treated as paid).

(7) In this paragraph—

"part-time employment" means—

(a) subject to the provisions of heads (b) to (d) of this definition, employment in which a person is engaged, or, where their hours of work fluctuate, they are engaged on average for less than 16 hours a week, being work for which payment is made or which is done in expectation of payment,

(b) subject to head (c) of this definition, the number of hours for which an individual is engaged in work is determined—

(i) where no recognisable cycle has been established in respect of an individual's work, by reference to the number of hours, or, where those hours are likely to fluctuate, the average of the hours, which they are expected to work in a week,

(ii) where the number of hours for which they are engaged fluctuates, by reference to the average of hours worked over—

(aa) if there is a recognisable cycle of work, the period of one complete cycle (including, where the cycle involves periods in which the individual does not work, those periods but disregarding any other absences),

(bb) in any other case, the period of 5 weeks immediately before the date on which an application for Carer Support Payment is treated as received, or the date on which a determination without application falls to be made, or such other length of time as may, in the particular case, enable the individual's average hours of work to be determined more accurately,

(c) where for the purpose of head (b)(ii)(aa) of this definition, an individual's recognisable cycle of work at a school, other education establishment or other place of employment is one year and includes periods of school holidays or similar vacations during which they do not work, those periods and any other periods not forming part of such holidays or vacations during which they are not required to work is disregarded in establishing the average hours for which they are engaged in work,

(d) for the purposes of heads (a) and (b) of this definition, in determining the number of hours for which an individual is engaged in work, that number includes any time allowed to that individual by their employer for a meal or for refreshment, but only where that individual is, or expects to be, paid earnings in respect of that time,

"specified period" means a period equal to—

(a) a week or such number of weeks (less any fraction of a whole number) as comprise the period of notice which is applicable to an individual, or would have been applicable if it had not been waived, less

(b) any part of that period during which the individual has continued to work in the employment in question or in respect of which they have received any payment in lieu of notice,

and for the purposes of this definition "period of notice" means the period of notice of termination of employment to which an individual is entitled by statute or by contract, whichever is the longer, or, if they are not entitled to such notice, the period of notice which is customary in the employment in question.

Date on which earnings are treated as paid

1.076   **6.** Earnings to which paragraph 5 (calculation of earnings of employed earners) or 10(2) (calculation of earnings of self-employed earners) applies are treated as paid on the first day of the award week in which the payment is received.

Calculation of weekly amount of earnings

7.—(1) For the purposes of paragraph 5 (calculation of earnings of employed earners), subject to sub-paragraphs (2) to (4), where the period in respect of which a payment is made—

(a) does not exceed a week, the weekly amount is the amount of that payment,

(b) exceeds a week, the weekly amount is determined—

    (i) where that period is a month, by multiplying the amount of that payment by 12 and dividing the product by 52,

    (ii) where that period is 3 months, by multiplying the amount of the payment by 4 and dividing the product by 52,

    (iii) where that period is a year, by dividing the amount of the payment by 52,

    (iv) for any other period, by multiplying the amount of the payment by 7 and dividing the product by the number equal to the number of days in the period in respect of which it is made.

(2) Where a payment of earnings from a particular source is or has been paid regularly and that payment falls to be taken into account in the same award week as a payment of the same kind from the same source, the amount of those earnings to be taken into account in any one award week will not exceed the weekly amount determined under sub-paragraph (1)(a) or (b), as the case may be, of the payment which under paragraph 6 (date on which earnings are treated as paid) is treated as paid first.

(3) Where the amount of the individual's net earnings fluctuates and has changed more than once, or an individual's regular pattern of work is such that they do not work every week, the application of sub-paragraphs (1) and (2) may be modified so that the weekly amount of their earnings is determined by reference to their average weekly earnings—

(a) if there is a recognisable cycle of work, over the period of one complete cycle,

(b) if the individual has provided the Scottish Ministers with payslips, over the period to which the payslips relate, up to a maximum period of 26 weeks, or

(c) in any other case, over a period of 5 weeks or such other period as may, in the particular case, enable the individual's average weekly earnings to be determined more accurately.

Earnings of employed earners

8.—(1) Subject to sub-paragraphs (2) and (3), "earnings", in the case of employment as an employed earner means the remuneration or profit derived from the employment and includes—

(a) any bonus or commission,

(b) any payment in lieu of remuneration except any periodic sum paid to an individual on account of the termination of their employment by reason of redundancy,

(c) any payment in lieu of notice,

(d) any holiday pay except where it is payable more than 4 weeks after the termination or interruption of employment,

(e) any payment by way of a retainer,

(f) any payment made by the individual's employer in respect of expenses not wholly, exclusively and necessarily incurred in the performance of the duties of the employment, including any payment made by the employer in respect of—

    (i) travelling expenses incurred by the individual between their home and place of employment,

    (ii) expense incurred by the individual under arrangements made for the care of a member of their family owing to the individual's absence from home,

(g) any award of compensation made under section 112(4) (the remedies: orders and compensation) or 117(3)(a) (enforcement of order and compensation) of the Employment Rights Act 1996 (remedies and compensation),

(h) any such sum as is referred to in section 112(3) of the 1992 Act (certain sums to be earnings for social security purposes),

(i) where—

    (i) a payment of compensation is made in respect of employment which is not part-time employment and that payment is not less than the maximum weekly amount, the amount of the compensation less the deductible remainder, where that is applicable,

    (ii) a payment of compensation is made in respect of employment which is part-time employment, the amount of the compensation,

(j) any remuneration paid by or on behalf of an employer to the individual in respect of a period during which the individual is—

        (i)   on maternity leave or paternity leave,

       (ii)   on adoption leave, or

     (iii)   absent from work because they are ill.

(2) For the purposes of sub-paragraph (1)(i)(i), the "deductible remainder"—

    (a)   applies in cases where dividing the amount of the compensation by the maximum weekly amount produces a whole number plus a fraction, and

    (b)   is equal to the difference between—

        (i)   the amount of the compensation, and

       (ii)   the product of the maximum weekly amount multiplied by the whole number.

(3) "Earnings" do not include any payment in respect of expenses—

    (a)   wholly, exclusively and necessarily incurred in the performance of the duties of the employment, or

    (b)   arising out of the individual participating as a service user.

(4) The reference in sub-paragraph (3)(b) to the individual participating as a service user is to—

    (a)   a person who is being consulted by or on behalf of—

        (i)   a body which has a statutory duty to provide services in the field of health, social care or social housing, or

       (ii)   a body which conducts research or undertakes monitoring for the purpose of planning or improving such services,

    in their capacity as a user, potential user, carer of a user or person otherwise affected by the provision of those services,

    (b)   a person who is being consulted by or on behalf of—

        (i)   the Secretary of State or the Scottish Ministers in relation to any of their functions in the field of social security or child support under section 2 of the Employment and Training Act 1973, or

       (ii)   a body which conducts research or undertakes monitoring for the purpose of planning or improving such functions,

    in their capacity as a person affected or potentially affected by the exercise of those functions or the carer of such a person, or

    (c)   the carer of a person consulted under sub-paragraphs (a) or (b).

(5) In this paragraph—

"adoption leave" means a period of absence from work on ordinary or additional adoption leave under section 75A or 75B of the Employment Rights Act 1996,

"compensation" means any payment made in respect of or on the termination of employment in a case where a person has not received or received only part of a payment in lieu of notice due or which would have been due to them had they not waived their right to receive it, other than—

    (a)   any payment specified in sub-paragraph (1)(a) to (h),

    (b)   any payment specified in sub-paragraph (3)

    (c)   any redundancy payment within the meaning of section 135 of the Employment Rights Act 1996,

    (d)   any refund of contributions to which that person was entitled under an occupational pension scheme,

"maternity leave" means a period during which a person is absent from work because they are pregnant or have given birth to a child, and at the end of which they have the right to return to work either under the terms of their contract or under Part 8 of the Employment Rights Act 1996,

"part-time employment" has the same meaning as in paragraph 5(7) (calculation of earnings of employed earners),

"paternity leave" means a period of absence from work on leave under section 80A (entitlement to paternity leave: birth) or 80B (entitlement to paternity leave: adoption) of the Employment Rights Act 1996.

Calculation of net earnings of employed earners

1.077   **9.**—(1) For the purposes of paragraphs 2 (calculation of earnings) and 5 (calculation of earnings of employed earners) the earnings of an individual derived from employment as an employed earner to be taken into account are, subject to sub-paragraphs (2) and (3), their net earnings.

(2) There is disregarded or deducted as appropriate from an individual's net earnings—

    (a)   any sum, where applicable, specified in paragraph 14 (sums to be disregarded in the calculation of earnings), and

(b) any care charges to which paragraph 15 (care charges to be deducted in the calculation of earnings) applies up to a maximum deduction, in respect of such care charges incurred by any individual, of 50% of their net earnings less those sums, if any, specified in paragraph 14 which are disregarded.

(3) For the purposes of sub-paragraph (1) net earnings are calculated by taking into account the gross earnings of the individual from that employment, less—

(a) any amount deducted by way of—
    (i) income tax,
    (ii) primary Class 1 contributions under the 1992 Act, and
(b) one half of any sum paid by the individual in respect of a pay period by way of a contribution towards an occupational or personal pension scheme.

Calculation of earnings of self-employed earners

10.—(1) Except where paragraph (2) applies, where an individual's earnings consist of earnings from employment as a self-employed earner the weekly amount of their earnings are determined by reference to their average weekly earnings from that employment—

(a) over a period of one year, or
(b) where the individual has been engaged in that employment for less than a year or there has been a change which is likely to affect their normal pattern of earnings, over such other period as may, in any particular case, enable the weekly amount of their earnings to be determined more accurately.

(2) Where the individual's earnings—

(a) consist of royalties or other sums paid as a consideration for the use of, or the right to use, any copyright, design, patent or trade mark, and
(b) the individual is the first owner of the copyright, design, patent or trade mark,

those earnings are taken into account over a period equal to such number of weeks as is equal to the number (less any fraction of a whole number) calculated in accordance with the formula—

$$\frac{S}{T} + U$$

where—
    S is the earnings,
    T is the relevant earnings limit plus one penny, and
    U is the total of the sums which would fall to be disregarded or deducted as appropriate under paragraph 12(2) (calculation of net profit of self-employed earners).

(3) The period mentioned in sub-paragraph (2) begins on the date on which the payment is treated as paid under paragraph 6 (date on which earnings are treated as paid).

Earnings of self-employed earners

11. "Earnings", in the case of employment as a self-employed earner, means the net profits of the employment and includes any allowance paid under section 2 of the Employment and Training Act 1973 or section 2 of the Enterprise and New Towns (Scotland) Act 1990 to the individual for the purpose of assisting them in carrying on their business.

Calculation of net profit of self-employed earners

12.—(1) For the purposes of paragraphs 2 (calculation of earnings) and 10 (calculation of earnings of self-employed earners), the earnings of an individual to be taken into account are, in the case of a self-employed earner—

1.078

(a) who is engaged in employment on their own account, the net profit derived from that employment,
(b) whose employment is carried on in partnership or is that of a share fisherman, their share of the net profit derived from that employment less—
    (i) an amount in respect of income tax and social security contributions payable under the 1992 Act calculated in accordance with paragraph 13 (deduction of tax and contributions for self-employed earners), and
    (ii) one half of any premium paid in the period that is relevant under paragraph 10 in respect of a retirement annuity contract or a personal pension scheme,
(c) in sub-paragraph (b), "share fisherman" means any person who—
    (i) is ordinarily employed in the fishing industry otherwise than under a contract of service, as a master or member of the crew of any fishing boat manned by more than one person, and is remunerated in respect of that employment in whole or in part by a share of profits or gross earnings of the fishing boat, or

    (ii) has ordinarily been so employed, but who by reason of age or infirmity perma-
nently ceases to be so employed and becomes ordinarily engaged in employment ashore in Great Britain, otherwise than under a contract of service,
performing any services ancillary to or in connection with a fishing boat and
is remunerated in respect of that employment in whole or in part by a share
of the profits or gross earnings of that boat and has not ceased to be ordinarily
engaged in that employment.

(2) There is to be disregarded or deducted as appropriate from an individual's net profit—

    (a) any sum, where applicable, specified in paragraph 14 (sums to be disregarded in the
calculation of earnings), and

    (b) any care charge to which paragraph 15 (care charges to be deducted in the calcula-
tion of earnings) applies up to a maximum deduction, in respect of such care charges
incurred by any individual, of 50% of their net profit less those sums, if any, specified
in paragraph 14 which are disregarded.

(3) For the purposes of sub-paragraph (1)(a), the net profit of the employment is, except
where sub-paragraph (9) applies, calculated by taking into account the earnings of the employment over the period determined under paragraph 10 (calculation of earnings of self-employed
earners), less—

    (a) subject to sub-paragraphs (5) to (7), any expenses wholly and exclusively paid in that
period for the purposes of that employment,

    (b) an amount in respect of—

        (i) income tax, and

        (ii) social security contributions payable under the 1992 Act, calculated in accord-
ance with paragraph 13 (deduction of tax and contributions for self-employed
earners), and

    (c) one half of any premium paid in the period that is relevant under paragraph 10 (calcu-
lation of earnings of self-employed earners) in respect of a retirement annuity contract
or a personal pension.

(4) For the purposes of sub-paragraph (1)(b), the net profit of the employment is calculated
by taking into account the earnings of the employment over the period determined under
paragraph 10 less, subject to sub-paragraphs (5) to (7), any expenses wholly and exclusively
paid in that period for the purposes of that employment.

(5) Subject to paragraph (6), no deduction is to be made under paragraph (3)(a) or (4) in
respect of—

    (a) any capital expenditure,

    (b) the depreciation of any capital asset,

    (c) any sum employed or intended to be employed in the setting up or expansion of the
employment,

    (d) any loss incurred before the beginning of the period determined under paragraph 10
(calculation of earnings of self-employed earners),

    (e) the repayment of capital on any loan taken out for the purposes of the employment,

    (f) any expenses incurred in providing business entertainment,

    (g) where the individual provides accommodation to another person in the dwelling the
individual occupies as their home, any expenses paid by the individual in providing the
accommodation to that person.

(6) A deduction is made under sub-paragraph (3)(a) or (4) in respect of the repayment of
capital on any loan used for—

    (a) the replacement in the course of business of equipment or machinery, and

    (b) the repair of an existing business asset except to the extent that any sum is payable
under an insurance policy for its repair.

(7) A deduction is not made in respect of any expenses under sub-paragraph (3)(a) or (4)
where the Scottish Ministers are not satisfied that the expenses have been incurred or, having
regard to the nature of the expense and its amount, that it has been reasonably incurred.

(8) For the avoidance of doubt—

    (a) a deduction is not made under sub-paragraph (3)(a) or (4) in respect of any sum
unless it has been expended for the purposes of the business,

    (b) a deduction is made under sub-paragraph (3)(a) or (4) in respect of—

        (i) the excess of any VAT paid over VAT received in the period determined under
paragraph 10 (calculation of earnings of self-employed earners),

        (ii) any income expended in the repair of an existing asset except to the extent that
any sum is payable under an insurance policy for its repair,

        (iii) any payment of interest on a loan taken out for the purposes of the employ-
ment.

(9) Where an individual is engaged in employment as a child minder the net profit of the employment is one-third of the earnings of that employment, less—

  (a) an amount in respect of—
    (i) income tax, and
    (ii) social security contributions payable under the 1992 Act, calculated in accordance with paragraph 13 (deduction of tax and contributions for self-employed earners), and
  (b) one half of any premiums paid in respect of a retirement annuity or personal pension scheme.

(10) Notwithstanding paragraph 10 (calculation of earnings for self-employed earners) and sub-paragraphs (1) to (5) of this paragraph, the Scottish Ministers may assess any item of an individual's earnings or expenditure over a period other than that determined under paragraph 10 as may, in the particular case, enable the weekly amount of that item of earnings or expenditure to be determined more accurately.

Deduction of tax and contributions for self-employed earners

13.—(1) The amount to be deducted in respect of income tax under paragraph 12(1)(b)(i), (3)(b)(i) or (9)(a)(i) (calculation of net profit for self-employed earners) is calculated on the basis of the amount of chargeable income and as if that income were assessable to income tax at the basic rate, or in the case of a Scottish taxpayer, the Scottish basic rate, of tax less only the personal reliefs to which the individual is entitled under Chapters 2, 3 and 3A of Part 3 of the Income Tax Act 2007 and as are appropriate to their circumstances; but, if the period determined under paragraph 10 (calculation of earnings of self-employed earners) is less than a year, the earnings to which the basic rate, or the Scottish basic rate, of tax is to be applied and the amount of the personal reliefs deductible under this sub-paragraph is calculated on a pro rata basis.

1.079

(2) The amount to be deducted in respect of social security contributions under paragraph 12(1)(b)(i), (3)(b)(ii) or (9)(a)(ii) is the total of—

  (a) the amount of Class 2 contributions payable under section 11(2) or, as the case may be, 11(8) of the 1992 Act at the rate applicable at the date on which a decision relating to the individual's entitlement to Carer Support Payment is made by the Scottish Ministers under these Regulations or, as the case may be, on appeal by the First-tier Tribunal for Scotland, except where the individual's chargeable income is equal to or less than the amount specified in section 11(4)(a) of that Act (lower profits threshold) for the tax year in which that date falls; but if the assessment period is less than a year, the amount specified for that year is reduced pro rata, and
  (b) the amount of Class 4 contributions (if any) which would be payable under section 15 of the 1992 Act (Class 4 contributions recoverable under the Income Tax Acts) at the percentage rate applicable at the date on which a decision relating to the individual's entitlement to Carer Support Payment is made by the Scottish Ministers under these Regulations or, as the case may be, on appeal by the First-tier Tribunal for Scotland, on so much of the chargeable income as exceeds the lower limit but does not exceed the upper limit of profits and gains applicable for the tax year in which that date falls; but if the assessment period is less than a year, those limits are reduced pro rata.

(3) In this paragraph, "chargeable income" means—

  (a) in the case of employment as a child minder, one-third of the earnings of that employment, or
  (b) in all other cases, the earnings derived from the employment less any expenses deducted under paragraph 12(3)(a) or (4).

Sums to be disregarded in the calculation of earnings and profits

14. For the purposes of paragraphs 9(2) (calculation of net earnings of employed earners) and 12(2) (calculation of net profit of self-employed earners), the sums to be disregarded in the calculation of earnings and profits are—

  (a) any payment made to the individual by a person who normally resides with the individual, which is a contribution towards that person's living and accommodation costs, except where that person is residing with the individual in circumstances to which sub-paragraph (b) or (c) refers,
  (b) where the individual occupies a dwelling as their home and the dwelling is also occupied by another person and there is a contractual liability to make payments to the individual in respect of the occupation of the dwelling by that person or a member of their family—

    (i)   where the aggregate of any payments made in respect of any one week in respect of that dwelling by that person or a member of their family, or by that person and a member of their family, is less than £20, the whole of that amount, or

    (ii)   where the aggregate of those payments is £20 or more per week, £20,

(c)   where the individual occupies a dwelling as their home and they provide in that dwelling board and lodging accommodation, an amount, in respect of each person for whom that accommodation is provided for the whole or any part of a week, equal to—

    (i)   where the aggregate of those payments made in respect of any one week does not exceed £20, 100% of those payments, or

    (ii)   where the aggregate of those payments exceeds £20, £20 and 50% of the excess over £20,

(d)   except in the case of an individual who is absent from Great Britain and not disqualified for receiving any benefit, pension, allowance or supplement, by virtue of the Social Security Benefit (Persons Abroad) Regulations 1975—

    (i)   any earnings derived from employment which are payable in a country outside the United Kingdom for such period during which there is a prohibition against the transfer to the United Kingdom of those earnings,

    (ii)   where a payment of earnings is made in a currency other than sterling, any banking charge or commission payable in converting that payment into sterling,

(e)   any earnings which are due to be paid before the start of the award of Carer Support Payment and which would otherwise fall to be taken into account in the same award week as a payment of the same kind and from the same source,

(f)   any payment made by a local authority to the individual with whom a person is accommodated by virtue of arrangements made under section 22C (ways in which looked after children are to be accommodated and maintained) of the Children Act 1989 (provision of accommodation and maintenance for a child whom they are looking after), section 81 (ways in which looked after children are to be accommodated and maintained) of the Social Services and Well-being (Wales) Act 2014, or section 26 (manner of provision of accommodation to child looked after by local authority) of the Children (Scotland) Act 1995 or by a voluntary organisation under section 59(1)(a) (provision of accommodation by voluntary organisations) of the Children Act 1989.

(g)   any payment made by a health authority, an integrated care board, the National Health Service Commissioning Board, a local authority or a voluntary organisation to the individual in respect of a person who is not normally a member of the individual's household but is temporarily in their care,

(h)   any payment paid at intervals of at least one year and derived from employments as—

    (i)   a part-time fire fighter employed by a fire and rescue authority under the Fire and Rescue Services Act 2004 or by the Scottish Fire and Rescue Service established under section 1A of the Fire (Scotland) Act 2005,

    (ii)   an auxiliary coastguard in respect of coast rescue activities,

    (iii)   a person engaged part-time in the manning or launching of a lifeboat,

    (iv)   a member of any territorial reserve force prescribed in Part I of schedule 1 of the Employment and Support Allowance Regulations 2013,

(i)   any amount by way of refund of income tax deducted from profits or emoluments chargeable to income tax under schedule D or E of the Income and Corporation Taxes Act 1988,

(j)   in the case of employment as an employed earner, any advance of earnings or any loan made by the individual's employer,

(k)   any earnings, other than items to which sub-paragraph (l) applies, paid or due to be paid from the individual's employment as an employed earner which ended before the day in respect of which the individual first satisfied the eligibility criteria for Carer Support Payment set out in Part 3 of these Regulations,

(l)   this sub-paragraph applies to—

    (i)   any payment by way of occupational or personal pension, and

    (ii)   except in a case where the individual's employment terminated by reason of retirement at a time when they had attained pensionable age (within the meaning given by the rules in paragraph 1 of schedule 4 of the Pensions Act 1995)—

      (aa)   any payment or remuneration of the nature described in paragraph 8(1)(e) or (j), and

      (bb)   any award or sum of the nature described in paragraph 8(1)(g) or (h) (including any payment made following the settlement of a complaint to an employment tribunal or of court proceedings).

Care charges to be deducted in the calculation of earnings

15.—(1) This paragraph applies where an individual is—   **1.080**

  (a) entitled to Carer Support Payment in accordance with these Regulations, and

  (b) incurring relevant care charges.

(2) In this paragraph—

"close relative" means a parent, son, daughter, brother, sister or partner,

"relevant care charges" means the charges paid by the individual for care which is provided by a person, who is not a close relative of either the cared for person or the individual, for—

  (a) the cared for person, or

  (b) any child under the age of 16 on the date on which the award week begins in respect of whom the individual or their partner is entitled to Child Benefit under section 141 of the 1992 Act because the individual is unable to care for any of those persons because they are carrying out duties in connection with their employment,

"cared for person" means the cared for person in respect of whom entitlement to Carer Support Payment arises.

PART II

UPDATING MATERIAL

VOLUME I
NON MEANS TESTED BENEFITS

Commentary by

Ian Hooker

John Mesher

Edward Mitchell

Christopher Ward

Nick Wikeley

p.112, *amendment to the Social Security Contributions and Benefits Act 1992 s.70 (Invalid Care Allowance)*

With effect from November 19, 2023, art.2 of the Carer's Assistance (Carer Support Payment) (Scotland) Regulations 2023 (Consequential Modifications) Order 2023 (SI 2023/1214) amended s.70 as follows: **2.001**

(1) Delete subsection (7) and substitute: —
"(7) No person shall be entitled for the same day to—
   (a) more than one allowance under this section; or
   (b) both an allowance under this section and carer support payment.
(7ZA) Where, apart from this subsection, two or more persons would have a relevant entitlement for the same day in respect of the same severely disabled person, one of them only shall have that entitlement and that shall be such one of them—
   (a) as they may jointly elect in the prescribed manner; or
   (b) as may, in default of such an election, be determined by the Secretary of State in the Secretary of State's discretion.
(7ZB) Subsection (7ZC) applies where a person (A)—
   (a) (disregarding the effect of regulation 5(3) of the Carer's Assistance (Carer Support Payment) (Scotland) Regulations 2023) has, or would have, an entitlement to carer support payment; or
   (b) has, or would have, an entitlement to carer's allowance in respect of which the Scottish Ministers have the power to make decisions, for a day in respect of a severely disabled person.
(7ZC) Another person (B) shall not have a relevant entitlement for the same day in respect of the same severely disabled person unless—
   (a) A and B jointly elect in the prescribed manner that B shall have the relevant entitlement (and that A shall not have an entitlement mentioned in subsection (7ZB)) for that day in respect of that severely disabled person; or
   (b) in default of such an election, the Secretary of State is satisfied, following consultation with the Scottish Ministers, that—
     (i) the Scottish Ministers have decided, or will decide, that A shall not have an entitlement mentioned in subsection (7ZB); and
     (ii) B shall have the relevant entitlement, for that day in respect of that severely disabled person."
(2) In subsection (7A) delete "subsection (7)" and substitute "subsections (7ZA) and (7ZC)"
(3) In subsection (7A)(a) after "carer's allowance" insert "in respect of which the Secretary of State has the power to make decisions"
(4) After subsection (7A) insert—
"(7B) In subsections (7) and (7ZB), "carer support payment" means carer's assistance given in accordance with the Carer's Assistance (Carer Support Payment) (Scotland) Regulations 2023."

p.114, *annotation to the Social Security Contributions and Benefits Act 1992 s.70 (Invalid Care Allowance)*

2.002   Note that there is nothing in s.70 that requires a claimant, when they make a claim, to have the consent of the disabled person for whom they are caring. This may be important because the fact that someone is in receipt of CA may affect the entitlement to other benefits of the person who is cared for. It is possibly for this reason that the CA claim form makes provision for a signature of that person. See *SSWP v GK (ESA)* [2023] UKUT 273 (AAC).

The new Scottish benefit that will be an equivalent of Carer's Allowance has been introduced from November 19, 2023. It will be known as Carer Support Payment and will be paid to those who care for a severely disabled person where the claimant is normally resident in Scotland and on similar terms to those that would qualify for Carer's Allowance in England and Wales. Various amendments to this section and to the Invalid Care Allowance Regulations have been necessary to accommodate claimants who might move between Scotland and another part of the United Kingdom and *vice versa*.

p.230, *annotation to the Social Security Contributions and Benefits Act 1992 s.113 (General provisions as to disqualification and suspension)—Reciprocal agreements—amendment*

2.003   A Convention on Social Security Coordination between Iceland, Liechtenstein Norway and the UK was signed on June 30, 2023 and implemented by SI 2023/1060. It is not apparent that the Convention is fully in force at the time of writing: *https://www.gov.uk/government/collections/bilateral-and-multilateral-treaties-published-in-the-treaty-series-2018.*

p.245, *amendment to the Social Security Contributions and Benefits Act 1992 s.150 (Interpretation of Part X)*

2.004   With effect from November 16, 2023, art.4(2)(a) of the Carer's Assistance (Carer Support Payment) (Scotland) Regulations 2023 (Consequential Modifications) Order 2023 (SI 2023/1214) amended s.150 by inserting after subsection (1)(e) the words "(ea) carer support payment;".

p.246, *amendment to the Social Security Contributions and Benefits Act 1992 s.150 (Interpretation of Part X)*

2.005   With effect from November 16, 2023, art.4(2)(b) of the Carer's Assistance (Carer Support Payment) (Scotland) Regulations 2023 (Consequential Modifications) Order 2023 (SI 2023/1214) amended s.150 by inserting after the definition of "attendance allowance" in subsection (2) the words ""carer support payment" means carer's assistance given in accordance with the Carer's Assistance (Carer's Support Payment) (Scotland) Regulations 2023;".

p.336, *annotation to the new style Jobseekers Act 1995 s.2 (The contribution-based conditions)*

2.006   The Government's response to the SSAC's paper on *The future of working age contributory benefits for those not in paid work,* published on September 12, 2023, rejected the making of any changes to the contribution requirements, at least until after the complete migration of legacy benefit cases to universal credit.

p.339, *annotation to the new style Jobseekers Act 1995 s.4 (Amount payable by way of jobseeker's allowance)*

The Government's response to the SSAC's paper on *The future of working*   2.007
age contributory benefits for those not in paid work, published on September 12, 2023, rejected any review of the means-testing of the amount of new style JSA against pension income, saying that it "is unreasonable to pay full New Style JSA or ESA to people who had retired from their regular occupation with a significant occupational pension before reaching state pension age." Many in such circumstances are still in the labour market and £50 per week is scarcely significant, except perhaps by comparison with the measly level of new style JSA.

p.419, *annotation to the new style Jobseekers Act 1995 s.35 (Interpretation – "occupational pension scheme")*

Chief Constable of Derbyshire Constabulary v Clark [2023] EAT 135   2.008
contains a lengthy discussion of the legal background in answering the question whether a police disablement gratuity under reg.12 of the Police (Injury Benefit) Regulations 2006 (SI 2006/932) fell within the definition of "occupational pension scheme" in s.1 of the Pension Schemes Act 1993, as amended. See the entry in this Supplement for p.439 of Vol.II for further details.

p.523, *annotation to the Welfare Reform Act 2012 s.77 (Personal independence payment)*

Note that a Social Security Commissioner in Northern Ireland has held   2.009
that the UK is the competent country for the payment of PIP as a sickness benefit for the purposes of Regulation (EC) 883/2004 when the claimant was resident in the UK. This was so, notwithstanding that the claimant was already in receipt of a disability payment from the Irish Republic awarded when the claimant had been resident there (C9/23-24-NI Unreported).

p.563, *correction of General Note to the Pensions Act 2014 s.30 (Bereavement support payment)*

In the first paragraph of this note the third sentence should read as follows: 2.010
With effect from August 30, 2018, the Bereavement Benefits (Remedial) Order 2023 (SI 2023/134) has extended entitlement to a claimant who was living as a cohabiting partner with the deceased at the time of death and the claimant is, at that time, either pregnant or entitled to child benefit in the circumstances provided for in s.80(4) of the Pensions Act 2014. (i.e., the same circumstances as apply in the case of a surviving spouse or civil partner). (The Order goes on to provide that regulations might be made to provide for other circumstances in which the claimant might be entitled to child benefit. At the time of writing no such regulations have been made and it is difficult to envisage the circumstances in which it might be thought appropriate to extend entitlement to a cohabiting couple while

not at the same time applying that to a surviving spouse or civil partner. For this reason, it seems likely that this power has been included to mirror the power that exists in the 2014 Act that might be used to extend the circumstances of entitlement).

p.575, *annotation to the Pensions Act 2014 s.31 (Bereavement support payment: contribution condition and amendments)*

2.011   The decision in *R. (on the application of Jwanczuk) v SSWP* [2022] EWHC 2298, has been upheld in the Court of Appeal—see *R. (on the application of Jwanczuk) v SSWP* [2023] EWCA Civ 1156.

p.579, *annotation to Part 2 of Schedule 1 to the Pensions Act 2014 (Amount for pre-commencement qualifying years – how to calculate the amount for pre-commencement qualifying years)*

2.012   *FE* was followed by Upper Tribunal Judge Church in *DB v Secretary of State for Work & Pensions* [2023] UKUT 144 (AAC). Judge Church also rejected the argument that the failure to take into account the claimant's Australian residence was contrary to Article 14 of the European Convention on Human Rights (rights under the Convention to be enjoyed without discrimination on any ground) taken with Article 8 (right to respect for private and family life, home and correspondence). The claimant argued that residents of New Zealand and Canada were able to rely on their residence in those countries for the purposes of Step 2 in the calculation of the amount of state pension referable to pre-commencement qualifying years and that his inability to rely on his Australian residence was discriminatory contrary to Article 14. Judge Church rejected the submission that the claimant's situation fell within the ambit of Article 8, for Article 14 purposes, because he was unable to spend a reasonable amount of time with his family on account of pension-related financial limitations. This "purely financial consideration" had "too tenuous a link with his private and family life to bring his situation within Article 8". But, if the judge was wrong regarding 'ambit' the claimant failed to satisfy the other three elements necessary for a successful Article 14 claim identified by Lady Black in *R. (on the application of Stott) v Secretary of State for Justice* [2020] A.C. 51. Firstly, Judge Church doubted whether the different of treatment was based on country of residence, as the claimant argued, rather than the absence of an applicable reciprocal agreement between the UK and Australia. Secondly, the claimant was not in a relevantly similar position to his chosen comparators (that argument was precluded by the European Court of Human Rights' decision in *Carson v the United Kingdom* [2010] ECHR 338). Finally, the UK, in not affording the same advantages to Australian residents as those enjoyed by Canadians and New Zealanders, could not be characterised as an act that was manifestly without reasonable foundation.

p.604, *amendments to the Social Security (Credits) Regulations 1975 (SI 1975/556) reg.7A (Credits for carer's allowance)*

2.013   With effect from November 19, 2023, art.3 of the Carer's Assistance (Carer Support Payment) (Scotland) Regulations 2023 (Consequential Amendments) Order 2023 (SI 2023/1218) amended reg.7A as follows:

(a) in the heading, after "carer's allowance" insert "or carer support payment";

(b) in paragraph (1)—

    (i) after "carer's allowance", in both places it occurs, insert "or carer support payment";

    (ii) after "would have been so payable but for" insert "regulation 16 of the Carer's Assistance (Carer Support Payment) (Scotland) Regulations 2023 or";

(c) after paragraph (2) insert—

"(3) In this regulation "carer support payment" means carer's assistance given in accordance with the Carer's Assistance (Carer Support Payment) (Scotland) Regulations 2023."

p.652, *amendments to the Social Security (Contributions Credits for Parents and Carers) Regulations 2010 (SI 2010/19) reg.7 (Additional period in respect of entitlement to carer's allowance and relevant benefits)*

With effect from November 19, 2023, art.20(2) of the Carer's Assistance (Carer Support Payment) (Scotland) Regulations 2023 (Consequential Amendments) Order 2023 (SI 2023/1218) amended reg.7 as follows:
    2.014

(a) in the heading, after "carer's allowance" insert "or carer support payment";

(b) at the end of paragraph (1)(a), insert "or carer support payment under the Carer's Assistance (Carer Support Payment) (Scotland) Regulations 2023";

(c) at the end of paragraph (1)(b), insert "or carer support payment by virtue of those Regulations";

(d) at the end of paragraph (2), insert "or a payment under the Carer's Assistance (Carer Support Payment) (Scotland) Regulations 2023".

p.653, *amendment to the Social Security (Contributions Credits for Parents and Carers) Regulations 2010 (SI 2010/19) reg.10 (Applications: carers for 20 or more hours per week)*

With effect from November 19, 2023, art.20(3) of the Carer's Assistance (Carer Support Payment) (Scotland) Regulations 2023 (Consequential Amendments) Order 2023 (SI 2023/1218) amended reg.10 by inserting "or carer support payment" after "carer's allowance".
    2.015

p.750, *General Note to the Social Security Benefit (Persons Abroad) Regulations 1975 (SI 1975/563) reg.5*

It is now reg.3 of the Social Security Benefits Up-rating Regulations 2023 (SI 2023/340) which provides for the regulation to apply.
    2.016

p.777, *amendment to the Social Security (Attendance Allowance) Regulations 1991 (SI 1991/2740) reg.2C (Refugees and certain persons with leave to enter or remain in the United Kingdom)*

With effect from May 15, 2023, reg.4 of the Social Security (Habitual Residence and Past Presence) (Amendment) Regulations (SI 2023/532)
    2.017

amended reg.2C (1) by omitting the word "or" at the end of sub-para.(e) and inserting after sub-para.(f) the following:

"or

(g) leave to enter or remain in the United Kingdom granted under or outside the immigration rules, a right of abode in the United Kingdom within the meaning given in section 2 of the Immigration Act 1971 or does not require leave to enter or remain in the United Kingdom in accordance with section 3ZA of that Act, where the person—
   (i) was residing in Sudan before 15th April 2023; and
   (ii) left Sudan in connection with the violence which rapidly escalated on 15th April 2023 in Khartoum and across Sudan".

Note: this regulation applies only to England and Wales. Identical provision is made for Scotland with effect from May 17, 2023, by reg.2 of the Social Security (Residence Requirements) (Sudan) (Scotland) Regulations (SSI 2023/149).

With effect from October 27, 2023, reg.10 of the Social Security (Habitual Residence and Past Presence, and Capital Disregards) Regulations 2023 (SI 2023/1144) further amended reg.2C (1) as follows:

At the end of sub-para.(f) omit the word "or" and after sub-para.(g) insert—

", or

(h) leave to enter or remain in the United Kingdom granted under or outside the immigration rules, a right of abode in the United Kingdom within the meaning given in section 2 of the Immigration Act 1971 or does not require leave to enter or remain in the United Kingdom in accordance with section 3ZA of that Act, where the person—
   (i) was residing in Israel, the West Bank, the Gaza Strip, East Jerusalem, the Golan Heights or Lebanon immediately before 7th October 2023; and
   (ii) left Israel, the West Bank, the Gaza Strip, East Jerusalem, the Golan Heights or Lebanon in connection with the Hamas terrorist attack in Israel on 7th October 2023 or the violence which rapidly escalated in the region following the attack."

Note: This amendment applies only to England and Wales. Identical provision is made for Scotland with effect from October 26, 2023, by the Social Security (Residence and Presence Requirements) (Israel, West Bank, the Gaza Strip, East Jerusalem, the Golan Heights and Lebanon) (Scotland) Regulations 2023 (SSI 2023/309).

p.790, *amendment to the Social Security (Disability Living Allowance) Regulations 1991 (SI 1991/2890) reg.1 (Interpretation)*

2.018   With effect from July 7, 2023, reg.2 of the Scotland Act 2016 (Social Security) (Disability Living Allowance) (Amendment) Regulations 2023 (SI 2023/664) amended reg.1 as follows:

(1) by inserting after the definition of the "the NHS (Wales Act of 2006" the following:

""the Claims and Payments Regulations" means the Social Security (Claims and Payments) Regulations 1987;"

(2) and by inserting after the definition of the "mobility component" the following:

""the residence change date", in relation to a person, means the date on which the person becomes permanently resident in Scotland (whether or not the Secretary of State is notified of the move and whether or not any such notification takes place before or after the person moves to Scotland);

"the run-on period" has the meaning given in paragraph (6);"

(3) and by inserting after para.(5) the following:

"(6) "The run-on period", in relation to a person, is the period—

(a) beginning with the residence change date, and

(b) ending at the end of the day preceding the pay day which falls immediately after the end of the relevant period.

(7) For the purposes of paragraph (6)—

(a) "pay day" means the day on which a payment of disability living allowance is made in accordance with regulation 25 (1) of the Claims and Payments Regulations;

(b) "the relevant period" means the period of 13 weeks beginning with the residence change date.".

And the same regulation inserted after regulation 1 the following:

"Regulations 2 and 2ZA: the status condition and the award condition

1ZA.—(1) For the purposes of regulations 2 and 2ZA, a person satisfies the status condition if—

(a) they were, on the day on which they reached the age of 16, terminally ill and either—

(i) they are terminally ill, or

(ii) following a change in their prognosis, they are a person to whom the Secretary of State is required by regulation 3 (5) of the PIP Transitional Regulations to send a PIP notification but to whom such a notification has not yet been sent,

(b) they are an exempt person,

(c) they have ceased to be an exempt person and are a person—

(i) to whom the Secretary of State is required by regulation 3 (3) or (5) of the PIP Transitional Regulations to send a PIP notification, but

(ii) to whom such a notification has not yet been sent,

(d) no disability living allowance is payable to them only by virtue of regulation 8, 9 or 12A,

(e) they are a notified person but not a transfer claimant, or

(f) they are a transfer claimant and no assessment determination has been made on their claim for personal independence payment.

(2) For the purposes of regulations 2 and 2ZA, a person satisfies the award condition if they have an award of disability living allowance for the under 16 age group (whether the award is as originally made, as revised in accordance with section 9 of the 1998 Act or follows a supersession in accordance with section 10 of the 1998 Act).

(3) In this regulation—

(a) "PIP notification" means a notification under regulation 3(1) of the PIP Transitional Regulations;

(b) "the PIP Transitional Regulations" means the Personal Independence Payment (Transitional Provisions) Regulations 2013;

(c) "assessment determination", "exempt person", "notified person" and "transfer claimant" have the meanings given in regulation 2(1) of the PIP Transitional Regulations."

p.791, *amendment to the Social Security (Disability Living Allowance) Regulations 1991 (SI 1991/2890) reg.2 (Conditions as to residence and presence in Great Britain)*

2.019   With effect from July 7, 2023, reg.2(4) of the Scotland Act 2016 (Social Security) (Disability Living Allowance) (Amendment) Regulations 2023 (SI 2023/664) amended reg.2 as follows:

(1) in paragraph (1)—

    (i) in the words before sub-paragraph (a), for "regulations 2A" substitute "regulations 2ZA, 2ZB, 2A";

    (ii) in sub-paragraph (a)(ii), for "Great Britain" substitute "the relevant place";

(2) after paragraph (1) insert—

"(1ZZA) For the purposes of this regulation, the relevant place is—

    (a) if the person is either under the age of 16 or satisfies both the status condition and the award condition, England and Wales;

    (b) otherwise, Great Britain.";

(3) in paragraph (2), in the words before sub-paragraph (a)—

    (i) for "Great Britain", in the second place it occurs, substitute "the relevant area";

    (ii) after "his absence" insert "from Great Britain";

(4) after paragraph (2) insert—

"(2A) Where a person ("P") is required for the purposes of paragraph (1)(a)(ii) to be present in England and Wales, even though P is absent from England and Wales on any day, P is to be treated as though P were present in England and Wales on that day if—

    (a) P's absence on that day is by reason only of the fact that P is temporarily absent from England and Wales; and

    (b) P is present in Scotland.";

(5) in paragraph (3B), in the words before sub-paragraph (a), for "Great Britain", in the second place it occurs, substitute "the relevant area";

(6) after paragraph (3B) insert—

"(3BA) In paragraphs (2) and (3B), "the relevant area" means—

    (a) for the purposes of paragraph (1)(a)(ii), the relevant place;

    (b) for the purposes of paragraph (1)(a)(iii), Great Britain.";

(7) in paragraph (3C), for "if" substitute "only if".

And after regulation 2 insert—

"Persons who are entitled to disability living allowance: effect of move to Scotland

2ZA.—(1) This regulation applies where a relevant DLA entitled person becomes permanently resident in Scotland on or after 7th July 2023.

(2) In this regulation "relevant DLA entitled person" means a person who, at the end of the day preceding the residence change date—

    (a) is entitled to disability living allowance,

(b) is, or in accordance with regulation 2(2), (2A) or (3B) is treated for the purposes of regulation 2(1)(a)(ii) as, present in England and Wales, and

(c) is under the age of 16 or satisfies both the status condition and the award condition.

(3) The relevant DLA entitled person is to be treated as satisfying the condition in regulation 2(1)(a)(ii) for the duration of the run-on period.

(4) If—

(a) the relevant DLA entitled person has an award of any component of disability living allowance which is for a fixed term period, and

(b) the fixed term period is due to expire before the end of the run-on period,

the fixed term period is extended so that it expires at the end of the run-on period.

Persons with an ongoing claim for disability living allowance: effect of move to Scotland

2ZB.—(1) This regulation applies where a new DLA claimant has an ongoing claim for disability living allowance on the residence change date.

(2) For the purposes of this regulation—

(a) "new DLA claimant" means a person who—

(i) does not have an award of disability living allowance,

(ii) makes a claim for disability living allowance and is under the age of 16 on the date on which they make that claim ("the claim date"),

(iii) is, or in accordance with regulation 2(2), (2A) or (3B) is treated for the purposes of regulation 2(1)(a)(ii) as, present in England and Wales on the claim date,

(iv) becomes permanently resident in Scotland after the claim date and on or after 7th July 2023, and

(v) is, or in accordance with regulation 2(2), (2A) or (3B) is treated for the purposes of regulation 2(1)(a)(ii) as, present in England and Wales at the end of the day preceding the residence change date;

(b) a new DLA claimant has an ongoing claim for disability living allowance on the residence change date if their claim for disability living allowance has not—

(i) been decided by the Secretary of State under section 8 of the 1998 Act before that date,

(ii) been withdrawn in accordance with regulation 5(2) of the Claims and Payments Regulations before that date, or

(iii) otherwise ceased, before that date, to be under consideration before being decided by the Secretary of State under section 8 of the 1998 Act.

(3) The Secretary of State must make a decision under section 8 of the 1998 Act on the new DLA claimant's claim for disability living allowance, unless the new DLA claimant withdraws the claim in accordance with regulation 5(2) of the Claims and Payments Regulations.

(4) For the purposes of the Secretary of State making such a decision, regulation 2 applies as if the amendments made to that regulation by the Scotland Act 2016 (Social Security) (Disability Living Allowance) (Amendment) Regulations 2023 had not been made.

(5) If the Secretary of State determines that the new DLA claimant is entitled to disability living allowance—
  (a) the new DLA claimant is to be treated as satisfying the condition in regulation 2(1)(a)(ii) until the end of the transfer day, and
  (b) if—
      (i) the new DLA claimant has an award of any component of disability living allowance which is for a fixed term period, and
      (ii) the fixed term period is due to expire before the end of the transfer day,
the fixed term period is extended so that it expires at the end of the transfer day.
(6) In this regulation—
  (a) "the transfer day", in relation to a person, means—
      (i) the final day of the run-on period, or
      (ii) if earlier, the day preceding the day on which the person's entitlement to Child Disability Payment begins in accordance with regulation 24 of the Disability Assistance for Children and Young People (Scotland) Regulations 2021;
  (b) any reference to the date on which a person makes a claim for disability living allowance (however expressed) is to be construed in accordance with regulation 6 of the Claims and Payments Regulations."

p.796, *amendment to the Social Security (Disability Living Allowance) Regulations 1991 (SI 1991/2890) reg.2C (Refugees and certain persons with leave to enter or remain in the United Kingdom)*

2.020 With effect from May 15, 2023, reg.4 of the Social Security (Habitual Residence and Past Presence) (Amendment) Regulations (SI 2023/532) amended reg.2C (1) by omitting the word "or" at the end of sub-para.(e) and inserting after sub-para.(f) the following:

"or
  (g) leave to enter or remain in the United Kingdom granted under or outside the immigration rules, a right of abode in the United Kingdom within the meaning given in section 2 of the Immigration Act 1971 or does not require leave to enter or remain in the United Kingdom in accordance with section 3ZA of that Act, where the person—
      (i) was residing in Sudan before 15th April 2023; and
      (ii) left Sudan in connection with the violence which rapidly escalated on 15th April 2023 in Khartoum and across Sudan".
Note: this regulation applies only to England and Wales. Identical provision is made for Scotland with effect from May 17, 2023, by reg.2 of the Social Security (Residence Requirements) (Sudan) (Scotland) Regulations (SSI 2023/149).

With effect from October 27, 2023, reg.10 of the Social Security (Habitual Residence and Past Presence, and Capital Disregards) Regulations 2023 (SI 2023/1144) further amended reg.2C(1) as follows:
At the end of sub-para.(f) omit the word "or" and after sub-para.(g) insert-

", or

(h) leave to enter or remain in the United Kingdom granted under or outside the immigration rules, a right of abode in the United Kingdom within the meaning given in section 2 of the Immigration Act 1971 or does not require leave to enter or remain in the United Kingdom in accordance with section 3ZA of that Act, where the person—

    (i) was residing in Israel, the West Bank, the Gaza Strip, East Jerusalem, the Golan Heights or Lebanon immediately before 7th October 2023; and

    (ii) left Israel, the West Bank, the Gaza Strip, East Jerusalem, the Golan Heights or Lebanon in connection with the Hamas terrorist attack in Israel on 7th October 2023 or the violence which rapidly escalated in the region following the attack."

Note: This amendment applies only to England and Wales. Identical provision is made for Scotland with effect from October 26, 2023, by the Social Security (Residence and Presence Requirements) (Israel, West Bank, the Gaza Strip, East Jerusalem, the Golan Heights and Lebanon) (Scotland) Regulations 2023 (SSI. 2023/309).

p.862, *amendment to the Social Security (Invalid Care Allowance) Regulations 1976 (SI 1976/409) reg.7 (Manner of electing the person entitled to [a carer's allowance] in respect of a severely disabled person where, but for [section 70(7) of the Contributions and Benefits Act], more than one person would be entitled to [a carer's allowance] in respect of that severely disabled person)*

With effect from November 19, 2023, reg.2 of the Carer's Assistance (Carer Support Payment) (Consequential and Miscellaneous Amendments and Transitional Provision) (Scotland) Regulations 2023 (SSI 2023/258) amended reg.7 of these regulations as follows:

    2.021

(1) For the heading substitute "manner of electing the person entitled to carer's allowance in respect of a severely disabled person where more than one person would be entitled".
(Note that this amendment has been replaced by a further amendment and with effect from the same date by the regulations below).

(2) In paragraph (1) for "section 37(7) of the Act" 22 substitute "section 70(7ZA) of the Contributions and Benefits Act"
(Note that this amendment is inaccurate and has been replaced with a further amendment from the same date by the regulations below).

(3) After paragraph (1) insert—
"(1A) For the purposes of section 70(7ZC) of the Contributions and Benefits Act which provides that where, apart from that section, one person (A) would have an entitlement mentioned in subsection (7ZB) and another person (B) would have an entitlement to carer's allowance for the same day in respect of the same severely disabled person, A and B may jointly elect in the prescribed manner which of them shall have such entitlement, an election shall be made by giving the Scottish Ministers a notice in writing signed by both A and B specifying that B shall have entitlement to carer's allowance and A shall not have an entitlement mentioned in subsection (7ZB).

(1B) For the purposes of section 70(7ZE) of the Contributions and Benefits Act which provides that where, apart from that section, one person (A) has, or would have an entitlement to universal credit carer element and another person (B) would have an entitlement to carer's allowance for the same day in respect of the same severely disabled person, A and B may jointly elect in the prescribed manner which of them shall have such entitlement, an election shall be made by giving the Scottish Ministers a notice in writing signed by both A and B specifying that B shall have an entitlement to carer's allowance and A shall not have entitlement to universal credit carer element."

(4) In paragraph (2) for "paragraph (1) substitute "paragraphs (1), (1A) or (1B)" and after the words "carer's allowance" insert ", carer support payment".
(Note that this amendment is further amended with effect from the same date by the regulations below).

(5) After paragraph (3) insert—
"(4) In paragraph (2), "carer support payment" means a payment made under the Carer's Assistance (Carer Support Payment) (Scotland) Regulations 2023."
(Note that this amendment is further amended with effect from the same date by the regulations below).

With effect from November 19, 2023, art.2 of the Carer's Assistance (Carer Support Payment) (Scotland) Regulations 2023 (Consequential Amendments) Order 2023 (SI 2023/1218) amended this regulation as follows:

(1) For the heading substitute "manner of electing the person entitled to a carer's allowance in respect of a severely disabled person for the purposes of section 70 of the Contributions and Benefits Act".
(2) In paragraph (1) for "section 70(7)" substitute "section 70(7ZA)"
(3) After paragraph (1) insert—
"(1C) For the purposes of section 70(7ZB) and (7ZC) of the Contributions and Benefits Act, which provides that where, apart from those subsections, one person (A) would have an entitlement mentioned in subsection (7ZB) and another person (B) would have a relevant entitlement for the same day in respect of the same severely disabled person, persons A and B may jointly elect in the prescribed manner that B shall have the relevant entitlement and that A shall not have an entitlement mentioned in subsection (7ZB), an election shall be made by giving the Secretary of State a notice in writing signed by both A and B specifying that B shall have the relevant entitlement and A shall not have an entitlement mentioned in subsection (7ZB)."
(4) In paragraph (2) for "paragraph (1)" substitute "paragraph (1) or (1C)" and after the words "carer's allowance" insert ", carer's support payment".
(5) After paragraph (3) insert—
"(5) In paragraph (2), "carer support payment" means carer's assistance given in accordance with the Carer's Assistance (Carer Support Payment) (Scotland) Regulations 2023.".

(Note that this amendment follows paragraph (3) yet is numbered paragraph (5). Paragraph (4) was introduced in the regulations above, but it and the new paragraph (5) are in nearly identical terms).

p.863, *annotation to the Social Security (Invalid Care Allowance) Regulations (SI 1976/409) reg.8 (Circumstances in which a person is or is not to be regarded as gainfully employed)*

Note too, that where a person's earnings fluctuate more than once, or where a person regularly has periods in which they do not work, earnings may be averaged by the application of regulation 8(3) of the Computation of Earnings Regulations (see Part III of this book) and for an example of the operation of that regulation see the decision of Judge Wright in *KR v SSWP (CA)* [2023] UKUT 202 (AAC). 2.022

p.865, *amendment to Social Security (Invalid Care Allowance) Regulations 1976 (SI 1976/409 reg.9 (Conditions relating to residence and presence in Great Britain)*

With effect from April 8, 2013, art.2(2) and Sch. para.2(2)(b) of the Armed Forces and Reserved Forces Compensation Scheme (Consequential Provisions: Subordinate Legislation) Order 2013 (SI 2013/591) amended this regulation by inserting after head (iii) of para.(2)(b) the following: 2.023

"(iiia) armed forces independence payment under the Armed Forces and Reserve Forces (Compensation Scheme) Order 2011; or"

With effect from November 20, 2023, reg.2 of the Disability Assistance (Miscellaneous Amendment) (Scotland) Regulations 2023 (SSI 2023/346) amended this regulation as follows:

(a) at the end of head (iiia), omit "or",
(b) at the end of head (iv), insert—
"(v) the care component of child disability payment at the middle or highest rate in accordance with regulation 11 of the Disability Assistance for Children and Young People (Scotland) Regulations 2021, or
(vi) the daily living component of adult disability payment at the standard or enhanced rate in accordance with regulation 5 of the Disability Assistance for Working Age People (Scotland) Regulations 2022".

p.868, *amendment to the Social Security (Invalid Care Allowance) Regulations 1976 (SI 1976/409) reg.9C (Refugees and certain persons with leave to enter or remain in the United Kingdom)*

With effect from May 15, 2023 reg.4 of the Social Security (Habitual Residence and Past Presence) (Amendment) Regulations (SI 2023/532) amended reg.9C (1) by omitting the word "or" at the end of sub-para.(e) and inserting after sub-para.(f) the following: 2.024

"or
(g) leave to enter or remain in the United Kingdom granted under or outside the immigration rules, a right of abode in the United

Kingdom within the meaning given in section 2 of the Immigration Act 1971 or does not require leave to enter or remain in the United Kingdom in accordance with section 3ZA of that Act, where the person—

    (i) was residing in Sudan before 15th April 2023; and

   (ii) left Sudan in connection with the violence which rapidly escalated on 15th April 2023 in Khartoum and across Sudan".

Note: this regulation applies only to England and Wales. Identical provision is made for Scotland with effect from May 17, 2023, by reg.2 of the Social Security (Residence Requirements) (Sudan) (Scotland) Regulations (SSI 2023/149).

With effect from October 27, 2023, reg.10 of the Social Security (Habitual Residence and Past Presence, and Capital Disregards) Regulations 2023 (SI 2023/1144) further amends reg.9C(1) as follows:

At the end of sub-para.(f) omit the word "or" and after sub-para.(g) insert—

", or

(h) leave to enter or remain in the United Kingdom granted under or outside the immigration rules, a right of abode in the United Kingdom within the meaning given in section 2 of the Immigration Act 1971 or does not require leave to enter or remain in the United Kingdom in accordance with section 3ZA of that Act, where the person—

    (i) was residing in Israel, the West Bank, the Gaza Strip, East Jerusalem, the Golan Heights or Lebanon immediately before 7th October 2023; and

   (ii) left Israel, the West Bank, the Gaza Strip, East Jerusalem, the Golan Heights or Lebanon in connection with the Hamas terrorist attack in Israel on 7th October 2023 or the violence which rapidly escalated in the region following the attack.".

Note: This amendment applies only to England and Wales. Identical provision is made for Scotland with effect from October 26, 2023, by the Social Security (Residence and Presence Requirements) (Israel, West Bank, the Gaza Strip, East Jerusalem, the Golan Heights and Lebanon) (Scotland) Regulations 2023 (SSI 2023/309).

p.909, *amendment to the Social Security (Personal Independence Payment) Regulations 2013 (SI 2013/377) reg.23A (Refugees and certain persons with leave to enter or remain in the United Kingdom)*

2.025   With effect from May 15, 2023 reg.5 of the Social Security (Habitual Residence and Past Presence) (Amendment) Regulations (SI 2023/532) amended reg.23A (1) by omitting the word "or" at the end of sub-para.(e) and inserting after sub-para.(f) the following:

"or

(g) leave to enter or remain in the United Kingdom granted under or outside the immigration rules, a right of abode in the United Kingdom within the meaning given in section 2 of the Immigration Act 1971 or does not require leave to enter or remain in the United Kingdom in accordance with section 3ZA of that Act, where the person—

    (i) was residing in Sudan before 15th April 2023; and
    (ii) left Sudan in connection with the violence which rapidly esca-
       lated on 15th April 2023 in Khartoum and across Sudan".
Note: this regulation applies only to England and Wales. Identical provision is made for Scotland with effect from May 17, 2023, by reg.3
of the Social Security (Residence Requirements) (Sudan) (Scotland)
Regulations (SSI 2023/149).

With effect from October 27, 2023, reg.10 of the Social Security (Habitual
Residence and Past Presence, and Capital Disregards) Regulations 2023
(SI 2023/1144) further amends reg.9C(1) as follows:
At the end of sub-para.(f) omit the word "or" and after sub-para.(g)
insert—

", or
(h) leave to enter or remain in the United Kingdom granted under
    or outside the immigration rules, a right of abode in the United
    Kingdom within the meaning given in section 2 of the Immigration
    Act 1971 or does not require leave to enter or remain in the United
    Kingdom in accordance with section 3ZA of that Act, where the
    person—
      (i) was residing in Israel, the West Bank, the Gaza Strip, East
        Jerusalem, the Golan Heights or Lebanon immediately before
        7th October 2023; and
      (ii) left Israel, the West Bank, the Gaza Strip, East Jerusalem, the
        Golan Heights or Lebanon in connection with the Hamas ter-
        rorist attack in Israel on 7th October 2023 or the violence which
        rapidly escalated in the region following the attack.".
Note: This amendment applies only to England and Wales. Identical
provision is made for Scotland with effect from October 26, 2023, by
the Social Security (Residence and Presence Requirements) (Israel, West
Bank, the Gaza Strip, East Jerusalem, the Golan Heights and Lebanon)
(Scotland) Regulations 2023 (SSI 2023/309).

p.1018, *amendment to the Social Security (Deferral of Retirement Pensions)
Regulations 2005 (SI 2005/453) reg.3 (Amount of retirement pension not
included in the calculation of the lump sum)*

With effect from November 19, 2023, art.15 of the Carer's Assistance
(Carer Support Payment) (Scotland) Regulations 2023 (Consequential
Amendments) Order 2023 (SI 2023/1218) amended reg.3(1)(a) by inserting after sub-paragraph (iv) the words "(v) carer support payment under
the Carer's Assistance (Carer's Support Payment) (Scotland) Regulations
2023;".   2.026

p.1059, *amendment to the Social Security (Widow's Benefit and Retirement
Pensions) Regulations 1979 (SI 1979/642) reg.4 (Days to be treated as days
of increment)*

With effect from November 19, 2023, art.4(2) of the Carer's Assistance
(Carer Support Payment) (Scotland) Regulations 2023 (Consequential
Amendments) Order 2023 (SI 2023/1218) amended reg.4(1)(b) by   2.027

inserting after sub-paragraph (iv) the words "(v) carer support payment under the Carer's Assistance (Carer's Support Payment) (Scotland) Regulations 2023; and".

p.1070, *amendment to the Social Security (Widow's Benefit and Retirement Pensions) Regulations 1979 (SI 1979/642) reg.10 (Conditions for entitlement to Category D retirement pension)*

2.028
With effect from December 31, 2023, reg.2 of the Social Security (Widow's Benefit and Retirement Pensions) (Amendment) Regulations 2023 (SI 2023/1237) amended reg.10 by numbering the existing provision as paragraph (1), and inserting the following thereafter—

"(2) Paragraph (1)(b) does not apply where, on the day or date determined in accordance with that paragraph, the person is ordinarily resident in an EEA state or Switzerland and one of the following provisions applies to that person—

(a) the Convention on Social Security between the Government of the United Kingdom of Great Britain and Northern Ireland and the Government of Ireland, signed on 1st February 2019;

(b) the Agreement between the United Kingdom of Great Britain and Northern Ireland and the Swiss Confederation on Citizens' Rights following the Withdrawal of the United Kingdom from the European Union and the Free Movement of Persons Agreement, signed on 25th February 2019;

(c) the Agreement on the Withdrawal of the United Kingdom of Great Britain and Northern Ireland from the European Union and the European Atomic Energy Community, signed on 24th January 2020;

(d) the Agreement on arrangements between Iceland, the Principality of Liechtenstein, the Kingdom of Norway and the United Kingdom of Great Britain and Northern Ireland following the withdrawal of the United Kingdom from the European Union, the EEA Agreement and other agreements applicable between the United Kingdom and the EEA EFTA States by virtue of the United Kingdom's membership of the European Union, signed on 28th January 2020;

(e) the Protocol on Social Security Coordination to the Trade and Cooperation Agreement between the United Kingdom of Great Britain and Northern Ireland, of the one part, and the European Union and the European Atomic Energy Community, of the other part, signed on 30th December 2020;

(f) the Convention on Social Security Coordination between the United Kingdom of Great Britain and Northern Ireland and the Swiss Confederation, signed on 9th September 2021;

(g) the Convention on Social Security Coordination between Iceland, the Principality of Liechtenstein, the Kingdom of Norway and the United Kingdom of Great Britain and Northern Ireland, signed on 30th June 2023".

p.1070, *annotation to the Social Security (Widow's Benefit and Retirement Pensions) Regulations 1979 (SI 1979/642) reg.10 (Conditions for entitlement to Category D retirement pension)*

Regulation 10(2) enables a person resident in a European Economic Area (EEA) state or Switzerland to continue to claim a Category D retirement pension provided that the claimant is covered by one of the Conventions or Agreements specified in the regulation. This provision is necessary in anticipation of the Retained EU Law (Revocation and Reform) Act 2023 which will disapply the effect of the European Court of Justice's judgment in *Stewart v Secretary of State for Work & Pensions* (Case C-503/09). *Stewart* effectively modifies the Great Britain residency conditions in reg.10(1) so that residents in an EEA state or Switzerland may nevertheless claim a Category D pension. Regulation 10(2) maintains the *Stewart* position, following implementation of the 2023 Act, in respect of persons falling within reg.10(2). 2.029

p.1076, *amendment to the Social Security (Widow's Benefit and Retirement Pensions) Regulations 1979 (SI 1979/642) reg.17 (Provisions relating to age addition for persons not in receipt of a retirement pension)*

With effect from November 19, 2023, art.4(3) of the Carer's Assistance (Carer Support Payment) (Scotland) Regulations 2023 (Consequential Amendments) Order 2023 (SI 2023/1218) amended reg.17(1) by inserting after sub-para.(g) the words "(ga) the Carer's Assistance (Carer's Support Payment) (Scotland) Regulations 2023". 2.030

p.1104, *amendment to the State Pension Regulations 2015 (SI 2015/173) reg.11 (Days which are not included in determining the period of deferral)*

With effect from November 19, 2023, art.27(2) of the Carer's Assistance (Carer Support Payment) (Scotland) Regulations 2023 (Consequential Amendments) Order 2023 (SI 2023/1218) amended reg.11(2) by inserting after sub-paragraph (vi) the words "(v) carer support payment under the Carer's Assistance (Carer's Support Payment) (Scotland) Regulations 2023 ("carer support payment")". 2.031

p.1115, *amendment to the State Pension Regulations 2015 (SI 2015/173) reg.28 (Credits for spouses and civil partners of members of Her Majesty's forces)*

With effect from November 19, 2023, art.27(3) of the Carer's Assistance (Carer Support Payment) (Scotland) Regulations 2023 (Consequential Amendments) Order 2023 (SI 2023/1218) amended reg.28(4)(a)(i) by inserting after "carer's allowance" the words "or carer support payment". 2.032

p.1116, *amendment to the State Pension Regulations 2015 (SI 2015/173) reg.29 (Credits under the 1975 Regulations)*

With effect from November 19, 2023, art.27(4) of the Carer's Assistance (Carer Support Payment) (Scotland) Regulations 2023 (Consequential Amendments) Order 2023 (SI 2023/1218) amended reg.29(2)(b) by inserting after "carer's allowance" the words "or carer support payment". 2.033

p.1118, *amendment to the State Pension Regulations 2015 (SI 2015/173) reg.33 (Credits for spouses and civil partners of members of Her Majesty's forces)*

2.034 With effect from November 19, 2023, art.27(5) of the Carer's Assistance (Carer Support Payment) (Scotland) Regulations 2023 (Consequential Amendments) Order 2023 (SI 2023/1218) amended reg.33(4)(a)(ii) by inserting after "carer's allowance" the words "or carer support payment".

p.1122, *amendment to the State Pension Regulations 2015 (SI 2015/173) reg.38 (Credits for an additional period in respect of entitlement to carer's allowance and relevant benefits)*

2.035 With effect from November 19, 2023, art.27(6) of the Carer's Assistance (Carer Support Payment) (Scotland) Regulations 2023 (Consequential Amendments) Order 2023 (SI 2023/1218) amended the heading of reg.38 by inserting after "carer's allowance" the words "or carer support payment".

p.1122, *amendment to the State Pension Regulations 2015 (SI 2015/173) reg.38 (Credits for an additional period in respect of entitlement to carer's allowance and relevant benefits)*

2.036 With effect from November 19, 2023, art.27(6) of the Carer's Assistance (Carer Support Payment) (Scotland) Regulations 2023 (Consequential Amendments) Order 2023 (SI 2023/1218) amended reg.38(1)(a) by inserting after "the 1992 Act" the words "or carer support payment under the Carer's Assistance (Carer Support Payment) (Scotland) Regulations 2023".

p.1122, *amendment to the State Pension Regulations 2015 (SI 2015/173) reg.38 (Credits for an additional period in respect of entitlement to carer's allowance and relevant benefits)*

2.037 With effect from November 19, 2023, art.27(6) of the Carer's Assistance (Carer Support Payment) (Scotland) Regulations 2023 (Consequential Amendments) Order 2023 (SI 2023/1218) amended reg.38(1)(b) by inserting after "that subsection" the words "or carer support payment by virtue of those Regulations".

p.1122, *amendment to the State Pension Regulations 2015 (SI 2015/173) reg.38 (Credits for an additional period in respect of entitlement to carer's allowance and relevant benefits)*

2.038 With effect from November 19, 2023, art.27(6) of the Carer's Assistance (Carer Support Payment) (Scotland) Regulations 2023 (Consequential Amendments) Order 2023 (SI 2023/1218) amended reg.38(2) by inserting after "the 1992 Act" the words "or carer support payment under the Carer's Assistance (Carer Support Payment) (Scotland) Regulations 2023".

p.1137, *amendment to the Jobseeker's Allowance Regulations 2013 (SI 2013/378) reg.2(2) (General interpretation)*

2.039 With effect from November 19, 2023, art.24(2) of the Carer's Assistance (Carer Support Payment) (Scotland) Regulations 2023 (Consequential

Amendments) Order 2023 (SI 2023/1218) amended reg.2(2) by inserting the following after the definition of "benefit week":

""carer support payment" means carer's assistance given in accordance with the Carer's Assistance (Carer Support Payment) (Scotland) Regulations 2023;"

p.1153, *annotation to the Jobseeker's Allowance Regulations 2013 (SI 2013/378) reg.9 (Expected hours)*

See the entry in this Supplement for p.472 of Vol.II, on reg.88 of the Universal Credit Regulations, for the administrative changes made with effect from October 25, 2023, to the identification of expected hours for universal credit purposes. But note that the press release announcing those changes was expressly in terms of that benefit, so that it is not clear whether there might be any change of approach in relation to new style JSA.

2.040

p.1201, *amendment to the Jobseeker's Allowance Regulations 2013 (SI 2013/378) reg.36(1) (Waiting days)*

With effect from November 19, 2023, art.24(3) of the Carer's Assistance (Carer Support Payment) (Scotland) Regulations 2023 (Consequential Amendments) Order 2023 (SI 2023/1218) amended reg.36(1) by substituting ", carer's allowance or carer support payment" for "carer's allowance". Carer support payment is newly defined in reg.2(2) by reference to the Scottish legislation (see the entry for p.1137 and Part I of this Supplement). Where the General Note to reg.36 mentions carer's allowance it should be taken as including carer support payment.

2.041

pp.1205–1206, *amendments to the Jobseeker's Allowance Regulations 2013 (SI 2013/378) reg.39 (Linking periods)*

With effect from November 19, 2023, art.24(4) of the Carer's Assistance (Carer Support Payment) (Scotland) Regulations 2023 (Consequential Amendments) Order 2023 (SI 2023/1218) amended reg.39(2)(a) and (4) by inserting "or carer support payment" after "Benefits Act" and "carer's allowance" respectively. Carer support payment is newly defined in reg.2(2) by reference to the Scottish legislation (see the entry for p.1137 and Part I of this Supplement). Where the General Note to reg.39 mentions carer's allowance it should be taken as including carer support payment.

2.042

p.1212, *amendment to the Jobseeker's Allowance Regulations 2013 (SI 2013/378) reg.42(3)(c)(iii) (Remunerative work)*

With effect from November 19, 2023, art.24(5) of the Carer's Assistance (Carer Support Payment) (Scotland) Regulations 2023 (Consequential Amendments) Order 2023 (SI 2023/1218) amended reg.42(3)(c)(iii) by inserting "or carer support payment" after "Benefits Act". Carer support payment is newly defined in reg.2(2) by reference to the Scottish legislation (see the entry for p.1137 and Part I of this Supplement).

2.043

p.1252, *amendment to the Jobseeker's Allowance Regulations 2013 (SI 2013/378) reg.60(2)(c)(i) (Earnings of self-employed earners)*

2.044   With effect from November 6, 2023, reg.107 of and para.1 of Sch. to the Health and Care Act 2022 (Further Consequential Amendments) (No.2) Regulations 2023 (SI 2023/1071) amended reg.60(2)(c)(i) by substituting "NHS England" for "the National Health Service Commissioning Board".

p.1280, *amendment to the Employment and Support Allowance Regulations 2013 (SI 2013/379) reg.2 (Interpretation)*

2.045   With effect from November 19, 2023, art.25(2) of the Carer's Assistance (Carer Support Payment) (Scotland) Regulations 2023 (Consequential Amendments) Order 2023 (SI 2023/1218) amended reg.2 by inserting after the definition of "carer's allowance" the following new definition:

""carer support payment" means carer's assistance given in accordance with the Carer's Assistance (Carer Support Payment) (Scotland) Regulations 2023;".

p.1292, *amendment to the Employment and Support Allowance Regulations 2013 (SI 2013/379) reg.9 (Relaxation of the first contribution condition)*

2.046   With effect from November 19, 2023, art.25(3) of the Carer's Assistance (Carer Support Payment) (Scotland) Regulations 2023 (Consequential Amendments) Order 2023 (SI 2023/1218) amended reg.9 by inserting "or carer support payment" after "carer's allowance".

p.1315, *amendment to the Employment and Support Allowance Regulations 2013 (SI 2013/379) reg.37(7) (A claimant who works to be treated as not entitled to an employment and support allowance)*

2.047   With effect from November 6, 2023, reg.107 of, and the Sch. to, the Health and Care Act 2022 (Further Consequential Amendments) (No. 2) Regulations 2023 (SI 2023/1071) substituted "NHS England" for "National Health Service Commissioning Board" in sub-paragraph (7)(b)(i).

p.1326, *amendments to the Employment and Support Allowance Regulations 2013 (SI 2013/379) reg.47 (Claimants subject to no work-related requirements)*

2.048   With effect from November 19, 2023, art.25(4)(a) and (b) of the Carer's Assistance (Carer Support Payment) (Scotland) Regulations 2023 (Consequential Amendments) Order 2023 (SI 2023/1218) amended reg.47 by inserting "or have entitlement to carer support payment" after "carer's allowance" in para.(1)(a) and by substituting for para.(2)(a) and (b) the following:

"(a) satisfies the conditions for entitlement to a carer's allowance, or would do so but for the fact that—
   (i) their earnings have exceeded the limit prescribed for the purposes of that allowance; or

(ii) they are—
    (aa) resident, or treated as resident, in Scotland; or
    (bb) resident outside of Great Britain and have a genuine and sufficient link to Scotland; or
(b) is entitled to carer support payment."

p.1327, *amendment to the Employment and Support Allowance Regulations 2013 (SI 2013/379) reg.47(5) (Claimants subject to no work-related requirements)*

With effect from November 19, 2023, art.25(4)(c) of the Carer's Assistance (Carer Support Payment) (Scotland) Regulations 2023 (Consequential Amendments) Order 2023 (SI 2023/1218) amended reg.47(5) by inserting after the definition of "severely disabled" the following new definition:

2.049

""sufficient" has the meaning given in paragraph 3 of Schedule 1 to the Carer's Assistance (Carer Support Payment) (Scotland) Regulations 2023;".

p.1359, *amendment to the Employment and Support Allowance Regulations 2013 (SI 2013/379) reg.85 (Waiting days)*

With effect from November 19, 2023, art.25(5) of the Carer's Assistance (Carer Support Payment) (Scotland) Regulations 2023 (Consequential Amendments) Order 2023 (SI 2023/1218) amended reg.85(2)(a) by inserting "carer support payment" after "carer's allowance".

2.050

p.1375, *amendment to the Employment and Support Allowance Regulations 2013 (SI 2013/379) reg.100 (Modification in the calculation of income)*

With effect from November 19, 2023, art.25(6) of the Carer's Assistance (Carer Support Payment) (Scotland) Regulations 2023 (Consequential Amendments) Order 2023 (SI 2023/1218) amended reg.100(b) by inserting "carer support payment" after "carer's allowance".

2.051

PART III

UPDATING MATERIAL

VOLUME II
UNIVERSAL CREDIT, STATE PENSION CREDIT AND THE SOCIAL FUND

Commentary by

John Mesher

Tom Royston

Nick Wikeley

p.14, *amendment to the State Pension Credit Act 2002 s.2 (Guarantee credit)*

With effect from November 16, 2023, reg.5(2) of the Carer's Assistance (Carer Support Payment) (Scotland) Regulations 2023 (Consequential Modifications) Order 2023 (SI 2023/1214) amended s.2 by inserting "or carer support payment" after "Contributions and Benefits Act" in subs.(8)(a) and inserting "or payment" after "an allowance" in subs.(8)(b).

3.001

p.38, *amendment to the State Pension Credit Act 2002 s.17 (Other interpretation provisions)*

With effect from November 16, 2023, reg.5(3) of the Carer's Assistance (Carer Support Payment) (Scotland) Regulations 2023 (Consequential Modifications) Order 2023 (SI 2023/1214) amended s.17 by inserting after the definition of "capital" the following new definition:

3.002

""carer support payment" means carer's assistance given in accordance with the Carer's Assistance (Carer Support Payment) (Scotland) Regulations 2023;".

p.55, *Welfare Reform Act 2012, GENERAL NOTE–'Assessment periods'*

The main text refers to the Secretary of State having sought permission to appeal against the Court of Appeal's decision in *Bui v Secretary of State for Work and Pensions* [2023] EWCA Civ 566, in which it declared unlawful the blanket refusal of UC advances to claimants without a national insurance number. The Supreme Court refused permission on October 18, 2023.

3.003

p.59, *Welfare Reform Act 2012, GENERAL NOTE–'The benefit cap'*

The main text observed that the benefit cap rates were in April 2023 up-rated to take account of annual inflation, for the first time since the rates were inserted into s.96 of the Act in 2016. The main text also observed that it was not known whether this was a one-off or whether there would be regular up-rating. The absence of any mention of benefit cap up-rating in the Autumn Statement 2023 implies that the rates will be frozen for 2024–25 at least.

3.004

p.100, *annotation to the Welfare Reform Act 2012 s.19(2)b) (Claimants subject to no work-related requirements)*

Note that although s.19(2)(b) of the WRA 2012 (no work-related requirements can be imposed on anyone with "regular and substantial caring responsibilities for a severely disabled person") has not been directly amended, recipients of Scottish carer support payment have with effect from November 19, 2023, been put on a par with recipients of UK carer's allowance by amendments to the meaning of that phrase in reg.30 of the Universal Credit Regulations (see the entry for p.276 setting out the effect of art.23(4) of the Carer's Assistance (Carer Support Payment) (Scotland) Regulations 2023 (Consequential Amendments) Order 2023 (SI 2023/1218)).

3.005

p.102, *annotation to the Welfare Reform Act 2012 s.20 (Claimants subject to work-focused interview requirement only)*

3.006   It was announced in a press release of July 24, 2023 that (as presaged in general terms in the Spring Budget 2023) from that date responsible carers of a child aged one would be required to meet a work coach, presumably for a work-focused interview with a purpose identified in reg.93 of the Universal Credit Regulations, every three months, instead of every six months. See the note to s.21 for the position of responsible carers of a child aged two.

pp.103–104, *annotation to the Welfare Reform Act 2012 s.21 (Claimants subject to work preparation requirement)*

3.007   It was announced in a press release of July 24, 2023 that (as presaged in general terms in the Spring Budget 2023) from that date responsible carers of a child aged two would be required to meet a work coach, presumably for a work-focused interview with a purpose identified in reg.93 of the Universal Credit Regulations, every month, instead of every three months. Under s.21 there is a discretion to impose a work preparation requirement under s.16. In such cases, the current guidance document deposited in the House of Commons Library suggests that the "default maximum expected hours" for action under such a requirement, to be specified under s.16(2), would be 16. That would, just as in cases where reg.88 applies and as recognised in the guidance, be subject to the constraints of the claimant's individual circumstances, including health conditions and caring responsibilities, and external realities, such as the actual availability and affordability of childcare. See the notes to s.22 and regs 88 and 97 for the position of responsible carers of children aged three and above.

pp.104–105, *annotation to the Welfare Reform Act 2012 s.22 (Claimants subject to all work-related requirements)*

3.008   Since April 2017 healthy responsible carers of children aged three and above have in principle been subject to the Secretary of State's duty under s.22(2) to impose work search and work availability requirements (though note the potential exemptions under regs 89, 90 (conditionality earnings threshold) and 91 (some foster parents and friend or family carers) of the Universal Credit Regulations). That is subject to the rule in reg.97(2) that those requirements must be limited to the claimant's expected number of hours a week under reg.88. With effect from October 25, 2023, the administrative guidance on the maximum hours to be considered under reg.88 introduced a significant increase, according to the press release of that date to give such claimants more support to get back to work. However, the legal structure for identifying the proper level of expected hours under reg.88 has not changed. See the entry for p.472 for the details.

p.191, *annotation to Social Security (Additional Payments) Act 2023 s.1 (Means-teste additional payments: main payments*

3.009   The second qualifying day was September 17, 2023: see the Social Security Additional Payments (Second Qualifying Day) Regulations 2023 (SI 2023/1017).

p.206, *amendment to the Universal Credit Regulations 2013 (SI 2013/376) reg.2 (Interpretation)*

With effect from November 19, 2023, art.23 of the Carer's Assistance (Carer Support Payment) (Scotland) Regulations 2023 (Consequential Amendments) Order 2023 (SI 2023/1218) inserts the following after the definition of "carer element":

3.010

""carer support payment" means carer's assistance given in accordance with the Carer's Assistance (Carer Support Payment) (Scotland) Regulations 2023;".

p.224, *amendment to the Universal Credit Regulations 2013 (SI 2013/376) reg.9 (Persons treated as not being in Great Britain)*

With effect from May 15, 2023, reg.3 of the Social Security (Habitual Residence and Past Presence) (Amendment) Regulations 2023 (SI 2023/532) inserts the following after reg.9(4)(zc):

3.011

"(zd) a person who was residing in Sudan before 15th April 2023, left Sudan in connection with the violence which rapidly escalated on 15th April 2023 in Khartoum and across Sudan and—
  (i) has been granted leave in accordance with immigration rules made under section 3(2) of the Immigration Act 1971;
 (ii) has a right of abode in the United Kingdom within the meaning given in section 2 of that Act; or
(iii) does not require leave to enter or remain in the United Kingdom in accordance with section 3ZA of that Act;".

With effect from October 27, 2023, reg.2 of the Social Security (Habitual Residence and Past Presence, and Capital Disregards) (Amendment) Regulations 2023 (SI 2023/1144) inserts the following after reg.9(4)(zd):

"(ze) a person who was residing in Israel, the West Bank, the Gaza Strip, East Jerusalem, the Golan Heights or Lebanon immediately before 7th October 2023, who left Israel, the West Bank, the Gaza Strip, East Jerusalem, the Golan Heights or Lebanon in connection with the Hamas terrorist attack in Israel on 7th October 2023 or the violence which rapidly escalated in the region following the attack and—
  (i) has been granted leave in accordance with immigration rules made under section 3(2) of the Immigration Act 1971;
 (ii) has a right of abode in the United Kingdom within the meaning given in section 2 of that Act; or
(iii) does not require leave to enter or remain in the United Kingdom in accordance with section 3ZA of that Act;".

p.227, *annotation to the Universal Credit Regulations 2013 (SI 2013/376) reg.9 (Persons treated as not being in Great Britain) GENERAL NOTE*

The main text refers to the case of *Secretary of State for Work and Pensions v AT* [2022] UKUT 330 (AAC). In *Secretary of State for Work and Pensions v AT* [2023] EWCA Civ 1307 (November 8, 2023) the Court of Appeal unanimously dismissed the Secretary of State's appeal. On February 7, 2024 the Supreme Court refused the Secretary of State's further

3.012

application for permission to appeal, so the decision of the Upper Tribunal is now final.

p.265, *annotation to the Universal Credit Regulations 2013 (SI 2013/376) reg.24A (Availability of the child element where maximum exceeded)*

3.013   The main text refers to the fact that SI 2018/1129 did not address the situation of households whose first or second child is the result of non-consensual conception or multiple birth. In *AT v Secretary of State for Work and Pensions* [2023] UKUT 148 (AAC), the Upper Tribunal rejected a claim that this situation breached the Convention rights of a woman who had conceived two children non-consensually, followed by a third consensually. It commented (at para.30) that [a] 'judicial review challenge, alleging irrationality in the terms of the ordering provision, might well have a more promising prospect of success', but went on to state (at para.31) 'these are not judicial review proceedings and the Upper Tribunal's jurisdiction is in any event limited in that regard'.

p.273, *amendment to the Universal Credit Regulations 2013 (SI 2013/376) reg.28 (Period for which the LCWRA element is not to be included)*

3.014   With effect from June 29, 2023, reg.4 of the Social Security and Universal Credit (Miscellaneous Amendments) Regulations 2023 (SI 2023/543) inserts the following after reg.28(5):

"(6) Paragraph (1) does not apply where a claimant has limited capability for work and it is subsequently determined that they have limited capability for work and work-related activity.".

p.275, *amendment to the Universal Credit Regulations 2013 (SI 2013/376) reg.29 (Award to include the carer element)*

3.015   With effect from November 19, 2023, art.23 of the Carer's Assistance (Carer Support Payment) (Scotland) Regulations 2023 (Consequential Amendments) Order 2023 (SI 2023/1218) makes amendments such that reg.29 now appears as follows below. This version also corrects an error in the main text (the omission of Amendment 1):

Award to include the carer element

29.—(1) An award of universal credit is to include an amount ("the carer element") specified in the table in regulation 36 where a claimant has regular and substantial caring responsibilities for a severely disabled person, but subject to [3 paragraphs (2) to (6)] [1 and section [3 70] of the Contributions and Benefits Act (entitlement by different persons to the carer element and to carer's allowance [3 or carer support payment] in respect of the same severely disabled person].

(2) In the case of joint claimants, an award is to include the carer element for both joint claimants if they both qualify for it, but only if they are not caring for the same severely disabled person.

(3) Where two or more persons have regular and substantial caring responsibilities for the same severely disabled person, an award of universal credit may only include the carer element in respect of one them and that

is the one they jointly elect or, in default of election, the one the Secretary of State determines.

[[2] (4) Where an amount would, apart from this paragraph, be included in an award in relation to a claimant by virtue of paragraphs (1) to (3), and the claimant has limited capability for work and work-related activity (and, in the case of joint claimants, the LCWRA element has not been included in respect of the other claimant), only the LCWRA element may be included in respect of the claimant.]

[[3] (5) Paragraph (6) applies where—

(a) a person (A)—
    (i) has, or would have but for regulation 5(3) of the Carer's Assistance (Carer Support Payment) (Scotland) Regulations 2023, an entitlement to carer support payment; or
    (ii) has, or would have but for section 70 of the Contributions and Benefits Act, an entitlement to carer's allowance in respect of which the Scottish Ministers have the power to make decisions; and
(b) another person (B) has, or would have but for this regulation, an entitlement to the carer element of universal credit for the same day in respect of the same severely disabled person; and
(c) section 70 of the Contributions and Benefits Act does not apply to the decision in respect of B's entitlement to universal credit.

(6) The universal credit award of B shall not include a carer element unless—

(a) A and B jointly elect that B shall have entitlement to the carer element and that A shall not have an entitlement mentioned in paragraph (5)(a) for that day in respect of that severely disabled person; or
(b) in default of such an election, the Secretary of State is satisfied, following consultation with the Scottish Ministers, that—
    (i) Scottish Ministers have decided, or will decide, that A shall not have an entitlement mentioned in paragraph (5)(a); and
    (ii) B shall have a carer element included in their award of universal credit, for that day in respect of that severely disabled person.]

AMENDMENTS

1. Universal Credit and Miscellaneous Amendments Regulations 2015 (SI 2015/1754) reg.13 (November 4, 2015).

2. Employment and Support Allowance and Universal Credit (Miscellaneous Amendments and Transitional and Savings Provisions) Regulations 2017 (SI 2017/204) reg.4(1) and (6) (April 3, 2017).

3. Carer's Assistance (Carer Support Payment) (Scotland) Regulations 2023 (Consequential Amendments) Order 2023 (SI 2023/1218) art.23 (November 19, 2023).

p.276, *amendment to the Universal Credit Regulations 2013 (SI 2013/376) reg.30 (Meaning of "regular and substantial caring responsibilities for a severely disabled person")*

With effect from November 19, 2023, art.23 of the Carer's Assistance (Carer Support Payment) (Scotland) Regulations 2023 (Consequential

3.016

Amendments) Order 2023 (SI 2023/1218) makes the following amendments:

- for paragraph (1) substitute—

  "(1) For the purposes of Part 1 of the Act and these Regulations, a person has regular and substantial caring responsibilities for a severely disabled person if—
  - (a) they satisfy the conditions for entitlement to a carer's allowance or would do so but for the fact that—
    - (i) their earnings have exceeded the limit prescribed for the purposes of that allowance; or (ii) they are—
      - (aa) resident, or treated as resident, in Scotland; or
      - (bb) resident outside of Great Britain and have a genuine and sufficient link to Scotland; or
  - (b) they are entitled to carer support payment.";

- in paragraph (2), for "paragraph (1)" substitute "paragraph (1)(a)";

- after paragraph (3) insert—

  "(4) For the purposes of paragraph (1), "sufficient" has the meaning given in paragraph 3 of Schedule 1 to the Carer's Assistance (Carer Support Payment) (Scotland) Regulations 2023.".

p.280, *amendment to the Universal Credit Regulations 2013 (SI 2013/376) reg. 34 (Amount of childcare costs element)*

3.017   With effect from June 28, 2023, reg. 2 of the Universal Credit (Childcare) (Amendment) Regulations 2023 (SI 2023/593) amends reg. 34 by substituting the following for paragraph 3:

"(3) "Other relevant support" means payments out of funds provided by the Secretary of State or by Scottish or Welsh Ministers in connection with the claimant's participation in work-related activity or training but does not include payments made by the Secretary of State where—
  (a) the claimant—
    (i) has taken up, or is due to take up, paid work; or
    (ii) has increased, or is due to increase, their hours of paid work;
  (b) the claimant is required to pay the charges for relevant childcare before they receive a payment of universal credit that reflects the increase in the claimant's earned income as a result of sub-paragraph (a); and
  (c) if the payment is not taken into account in determining the charges paid by the claimant for childcare the claimant will be less likely to continue in paid work or maintain the increase in hours of paid work.".

p.284, *amendment to the Universal Credit Regulations 2013 (SI 2013/376) reg. 36 (Table showing amounts of elements)*

3.018   With effect from June 28, 2023, reg. 2 of the Universal Credit (Childcare) (Amendment) Regulations 2023 (SI 2023/593) amends reg. 36 by:

- in the row under "Childcare costs element" showing the maximum amount for one child, for "£646.35" substituting "£950.92";

- in the row under "Childcare costs element" showing the maximum amount for two or more children, for "£1,108.04" substituting "£1,630.15".

p.285, *annotation to the Universal Credit Regulations 2013 (SI 2013/376) reg.36 (Table showing amounts of elements)*

The main text discusses the variable approach which has been adopted to annual uprating in recent years. For 2024–25 the Secretary of State intends to up-rate all elements by the September 2023 CPI inflation rate of 6.7%: HM Treasury, *Autumn Statement 2023* (CP 977, 22 November 2023), 3.   3.019

p.300, *annotation to the Universal Credit Regulations 2013 (SI 2013/376) reg.46 (What is included in capital? – claimant holding as trustee)*

Gill v Thind [2023] EWCA Civ 1276 confirms that in declaration cases the burden of proving an intention to create a trust is the balance of probabilities, not some higher standard (Arnold LJ at para.58, with some more general helpful discussion at paras 55–59).   3.020

p.350, *annotation to the Universal Credit Regulations 2013 (SI 2013/376) reg.54 (Calculation of earned income—general principles)*

The decision in *JN v SSWP (UC)* [2023] UKUT 49 (AAC) has been reported as [2023] AACR 7.   3.021

pp.367–369, *annotation to the Universal Credit Regulations 2013 (SI 2013/376) reg.55 (Employed earnings)*

The Court of Appeal in *Commissioners for HMRC v E.ON UK plc* [2023] EWCA Civ 1383 has overturned the decision of the Tax and Chancery Chamber of the Upper Tribunal ([2022] UKUT 196 (TCC)) noted in the main volume and decided that the First-tier Tribunal had not erred in finding the "facilitation payment" in issue to be taxable as earnings from employment. The judgment of Nugee LJ provides a remarkably accessible description of the general principles to be applied. He concludes that the UTTCC created a false dichotomy between the payment being in return for employees' consent to adverse prospective changes in the final salary pension scheme and it being an inducement to provide future services on changed terms and that it was such an inducement (so taxable), the relevant change being that to the pension scheme. His view was that the previous case law, analysed in detail by Falk LJ, did not stand in the way of that straightforward conclusion.   3.022

The decision in *SK and DK v SSWP (UC)* [2023] UKUT 21 (AAC) has been reported as [2023] AACR 5.

p.392, *annotation to the Universal Credit Regulations 2013 (SI 2013/376) reg.60(3) and (4) (Notional earned income – services provided at less than going rate)*

The decision referred to in the main volume as *CIS/11482/1966* was reported as *R(IS) 2/98* and is relied on in ADM H3255.   3.023

pp.396–398, *annotation to the Universal Credit Regulations 2013 (SI 2013/376) reg.61 (Information for calculating earned income—real time information etc.)*

3.024   The decision in *JN v SSWP (UC)* [2023] UKUT 49 (AAC) has been reported as [2023] AACR 7.

The decision in *SK and DK v SSWP (UC)* [2023] UKUT 21 (AAC) has been reported as [2023] AACR 5.

p.408, *annotation to the Universal Credit Regulations 2013 (SI 2013/376) reg.62 (Minimum income floor)*

3.025   As and when the administrative changes announced on October 24, 2023 to the calculation of expected hours under reg.88 for responsible carers of children aged three to 12 begin to work through into an increased number of hours (see the entry for p.472 for discussion of the relationship of those changes with the terms of reg.88, which have not been amended), there will be an effect on the calculation of the level of earnings to constitute the minimum income floor under reg.62(2) and (3) for those in gainful self-employment. Those provisions adopt the levels of the individual or couple threshold (known as the conditionality earnings threshold) in reg.90. That effect was announced as a specific measure in para.5.34 of the *Autumn Statement 2023* (CP977, November 22, 2023), according to the Correction Note issued on December 1, 2023 to operate from January 2024, but appears to be an inevitable knock-on effect of the October 2023 administrative changes.

p.420, *amendment to the Universal Credit Regulations 2013 (SI 2013/376) reg.66(1)(b)) (What is included in unearned income?)*

3.026   With effect from November 19, 2023, art.23(5) of the Carer's Assistance (Carer Support Payment) (Scotland) Regulations 2023 (Consequential Amendments) Order 2023 (SI 2023/1218) amended reg.66(1)(b) by inserting the following after head (iii):

"(iiia) carer support payment but only up to a maximum of the amount a claimant would receive if they had an entitlement to carer's allowance,"

Carer support payment (CSP) is newly defined in reg.2 by reference to the Scottish legislation (see the entry for p.206 and Part I of this Supplement). Its roll-out started in selected areas in November 2023. Note that in so far as the amount of the CSP exceeds what the claimant would have been entitled to in carer's allowance under British legislation the excess does not count as unearned income under reg.66(1)(b) (nor as an analogous benefit under reg.66(1)(c). That is in accordance with the Fiscal Framework Agreement governing the provision of devolved benefits in Scotland (see para.6.9 of the Explanatory Memorandum to SI 2023/1218). Initially, CSP is to be paid at the same rate as carer's allowance.

p.439, *annotation to the Universal Credit Regulations 2013 (SI 2013/376) reg.67 (Meaning of retirement pension income)*

3.027   *Chief Constable of Derbyshire Constabulary v Clark* [2023] EAT 135 contains a lengthy discussion of the legal background in answering the question whether a police disablement gratuity under reg.12 of the Police Injury Benefit Regulations 2006 falls within the definition of "occupational pension scheme" in s.1 of the Pension Schemes Act 1993, as amended. The gratuity was payable to officers injured in the execution of their duty who had ceased to be a member of a police force and who became totally and permanently disabled as a result of the injury, within 12 months of the injury. The two claimants were refused gratuities because more than 12 months had elapsed between the injury and the disablement. They wished to challenge that ground of refusal in an employment tribunal (ET) as demonstrating disability discrimination. The ET would only have jurisdiction if the gratuity formed part of an occupational pension scheme. The scheme of injury benefits was separated from the arrangements for police pensions. The President of the EAT, Eady J, held that the gratuity did not fall within the Pension Schemes Act definition because, although it was a condition of payment that the officer had ceased to be a member of a police force, entitlement could only be established at the point where the officer was deemed to be totally and permanently disabled. The regulation did not require any causative link between the ceasing of employment and the injury or disablement. Thus, the benefit was not provided on retirement or termination of service.

pp.440–442, *annotation to the Universal Credit Regulations 2013 (SI 2013/376) reg.68 (Person treated as having student income)*

See the following entry for discussion of *IB v Gravesham BC and SSWP (HB)* [2023] UKUT 193 (AAC); [2024] P.T.S.R. 130 on what are reasonable steps to acquire a student or postgraduate loan for the purposes of reg.68(5) and the deeming of having such a loan.   3.028

SSWP v AD (UC) [2023] UKUT 272 (AAC) confirms that under regs 68(5) and 69(1) it is irrelevant to the amount of a student loan (i.e. a loan towards maintenance under the relevant student support regulations) that is to be taken into account that the claimant had to use £9,250 of the loan to pay fees (not having qualified for a fees loan because of earlier periods of study). The definition in reg.68(7) is based on objective criteria relating to the source of the funds and their characterisation under the student support regulations, rather than how the particular student intends to use or actually uses the funds. The First-tier Tribunal went wrong in applying the exclusion in reg.70(a) of payments intended to meet tuition fees or examination fees, because reg.70 applies only to grants, not loans.

p.442, *annotation to the Universal Credit Regulations 2013 (SI 2013/376) reg.69 (Calculation of student income—student loans and postgraduate loans)*

See, in relation to the housing benefit equivalent of the rule in regs.68(5) and 69(1) treating students as having the maximum student or postgraduate loan in respect of an academic year that they could acquire by taking reasonable steps to do so, the decision of Judge Poynter in *IB v Gravesham BC and SSWP (HB)* [2023] UKUT 193 (AAC); [2024] P.T.S.R. 130 declining to follow *CH/4429/2006*. There, Commissioner Powell had held that "reasonable" qualified only the mechanical steps that had to be taken to acquire a loan and was not concerned with matters such as the motives or religious beliefs of the claimant. The facts of *IB* were on all   3.029

fours with those of *CH/4429/2006*, in that the claimant was a devout and observant Muslim, who did not take out student loans otherwise available to him because that would have involved the paying of interest, which he conscientiously believed was forbidden by his religion. Nonetheless, the local authority treated him as possessing income from the loans, so that he failed the housing benefit means test. That decision was upheld by the First-tier Tribunal, considering itself bound by *CH/4429/2006*. The Upper Tribunal substituted the decision that on the particular facts the claimant's entitlement to housing benefit was to be recalculated on the basis that he did not possess any income from the loans that he had not applied for.

The judge's view was that the reasoning in *CH/4429/2006* proceeded on a false basis and contained additional errors of logic. The Commissioner had stated in para.4 that the practical effect of the provision was that a student who was "entitled to a student loan", the use of which words was said to be deliberate, was to suffer a diminution in the amount of housing benefit. That was the apparent basis for the conclusion about the meaning of reasonable steps in para.11 of his decision. The judge points out that those words do not appear anywhere in the applicable Regulations, and that the test actually set out is in terms of what could be acquired by taking reasonable steps and does not assume the making of an application. A straightforward analysis of the steps that would be necessary to acquire a student loan would include scrutinising the terms on which the loan was offered, deciding whether to accept those terms and, if so, completing and submitting the application form and finally signing an agreement accepting the paying of interest. The judge concludes that the steps to be considered under the regulation therefore cannot be restricted to the "mechanical", the particular question of whether to accept the terms being one that would involve issues of judgment for anyone (e.g. about whether to accept the future burden of debt and interest payments). Moreover, while the Commissioner had noted that it was difficult to see how the necessary steps to acquire a loan could in themselves be said to be unreasonable except in the most exceptional cases, Judge Poynter suggests that, if personal circumstances were to be ignored, it would be inconceivable that the mechanics of applying for a student loan could ever require students to take steps that were unreasonable. In order for the words "reasonable steps" to be given some practical application, as must be assumed to have been intended, the interpretation adopted in *CH/4429/2006* could not be correct. For those and other subsidiary reasons, the judge declined to follow that decision.

Judge Poynter formulated the correct test to be applied, without the *CH/4429/2006* limitation and in line with the established approach in other areas of social security law, as follows:

"139. I therefore conclude that "reasonable steps" means steps that are reasonable in all the circumstances including all the personal characteristics of the individual who was eligible to have applied for the student loan. That includes strong conscientious religious or other objections to the payment of interest.

140. I would, however, add that all the circumstances includes the interests of the wider public as represented by the Secretary of State and that assessing reasonableness will need to give those interests weight (see

paragraphs 190–191 below). Without being prescriptive, I suggest that an omission to acquire a loan that is based on purely financial considerations is unlikely to outweigh those interests."

He rejected the Secretary of State's submission that that approach would involve direct discrimination against claimants who did not share IB's particular religious views. That was because (para.142):

"[t]he line drawn by my interpretation is not between Muslims and non-Muslims nor even between people who have conscientious objections to taking out a student loan and those who don't. Rather it is between, on the one hand, any student whose personal circumstances as a whole are such that—for whatever reason—he cannot take reasonable steps to acquire a student loan and, on the other, all students who are not so circumstanced. Those two groups are not in analogous situations. The latter could reasonably acquire the loan that [the regulation] takes into account as their income. The former cannot."

The judge also rejected the submission that his interpretation would make the housing benefit scheme unworkable and invite numerous, possibly opportunistic, claims, pointing out the limited scope for students to qualify for housing benefit (as for other means-tested benefits, including universal credit), the fact that to benefit from the rule the claimant would have to turn down the advantages of actually receiving the loan on offer and the difficulties that claimants might have in showing a genuine conscientious religious or other objection to the payment of interest. The latter point might easily be tested by seeing if the particular claimant had any interest-bearing bank or building society accounts, a credit card or a non-Sharia mortgage. Finally, there was the limiting factor of the need to take into account when judging reasonableness the interests of the wider public, in the form of the government policy that the costs of education are usually to be funded from the education budget rather than the social security benefit.

However, in substituting his own decision in *IB* Judge Poynter had no doubt that the claimant's personal circumstances, in particular his sincere and strongly held religious conviction that it would be a major sin to pay interest, outweighed any loss to public funds or dent in the government's general policy.

The result is that at the moment there are two conflicting decisions of equal authority. A First-Tier Tribunal may therefore choose to follow the decision whose reasoning it finds more convincing. In doing so it can give weight to the fact that *IB* contains a detailed review of the reasoning in *CH/4429/2006*.

pp.451–452, *amendments to the Universal Credit Regulations 2013 (SI 2013/376) reg.76 (Special schemes for compensation etc.)*

With effect from July 9, 2023, reg.8 of the Social Security (Income and Capital Disregards) (Amendment) Regulations 2023 (SI 2023/640) amended reg.76 so as to read as follows (the marking of pre-existing amendments as shown in the 2023/24 main volume has been omitted, so that the square brackets below mark only the July 2023 amendments, and see the rest of this entry for subsequent amendments):

3.030

"Special schemes for compensation etc.

76.—(1) This regulation applies where a person receives a payment from a scheme established or approved by the Secretary of State or from a trust established with funds provided by the Secretary of State for the purpose of—

(a) providing compensation or support in respect of any of the following—

  (i) a person having been diagnosed with variant Creutzfeldt-Jacob disease or infected from contaminated blood products,

  (ii) the bombings in London on 7th July 2005,

  (iii) persons who have been interned or suffered forced labour, injury, property loss or loss of a child during the Second World War;

  (iv) the terrorist attacks in London on 22nd March 2017 or 3rd June 2017,

  (v) the bombing in Manchester on 22nd May 2017,

  (vi) [...];

  (vii) historic institutional child abuse in the United Kingdom;

(b) supporting persons with a disability to live independently in their accommodation.

(1A) This regulation also applies where a person receives a payment from—

(a) the National Emergencies Trust, registered charity number 1182809;

(b) the Child Migrants Trust, registered charity number 1171479, under the scheme for former British child migrants; or

(c) [...]

(d) the scheme established by the Windrush Compensation Scheme (Expenditure) Act 2020.

[(e) the Post Office or the Secretary of State for the purpose of providing compensation or support which is—

  (i) in connection with the failings of the Horizon system; or

  (ii) otherwise payable following the judgment in *Bates and Others v Post Office Ltd* ((No. 3) "Common Issues").]

[(1B) This regulation also applies where a person receives a payment made for the purpose of providing compensation or support in respect of the fire on 14th June 2017 at Grenfell Tower.

(1C) This regulation also applies where a person—

(a) receives a vaccine damage payment or is a person for whose benefit a vaccine damage payment is made;

(b) is the partner of a person referred to in sub-paragraph (a) and receives a payment by or on behalf of that person which is derived from a vaccine damage payment;

(c) was the partner of a person referred to in sub-paragraph (a) immediately before the latter's death and receives a payment from their estate which is derived from a vaccine damage payment;

(d) in a case where a vaccine damage payment is made to the personal representative of a person who was severely disabled as a result of vaccination ("P"), was P's partner immediately before P's death and receives a payment from P's estate which is derived from a vaccine damage payment.]

(2) Any such payment, if it is capital, is to be disregarded in the calculation of the person's capital and, if it is income, is to be disregarded in the calculation of the person's income.

(3) In relation to a claim for universal credit made by the partner, parent, son or daughter of a diagnosed or infected person referred to in paragraph (1)(a)(i) a payment received from the scheme or trust, or from the diagnosed or infected person or from their estate is to be disregarded if it would be disregarded in relation to an award of state pension credit by virtue of paragraph 13 or 15 of Schedule 5 to the State Pension Credit Regulations 2002.

[(4) In this regulation—
"the Horizon system" means any version of the computer system used by the Post Office known as Horizon, Horizon Legacy, Horizon Online or HNG-X;
"the Post Office" means Post Office Limited (registered number 02154540);
"vaccine damage payment" means a payment made under the Vaccine Damage Payments Act 1979.]"

The Explanatory Memorandum to SI 2023/640 provides a detailed description of the changes made by the amendments. In brief, the category of Grenfell Tower payments is widened by taking it out of para.(1), restricted to payments from schemes established or approved by the Secretary of State or from trusts established with funds from the Secretary of State, and para. (1A)(c), restricted to payments from the Royal Borough of Kensington and Chelsea or registered charities, and putting it in a stand-alone category in para.(1B), where the source of the payment of compensation or support is irrelevant. Other sources of compensation have more recently come to light, including in particular settlements of civil litigation, which will now be covered by the disregard in para.(2).

One-off payments under the Vaccine Damage Payments Act 1979, which now covers Covid-19 vaccinations, are already partially dealt with by reg.75 (compensation for personal injury), but only where the payment is awarded to the person who has suffered the personal injury in the form of severe disability. That case is now expressly covered by para.(1C)(a), but the rest of para.(1C) extends the disregard to payments received by the partner of the severely disabled person, either during that person's life or after their death.

The new para.(1)(e) provides disregards for any payments from the Post Office or the Secretary of State in connection with the failings of the Horizon computer accounting system (defined in para.(4)) or the decision in the named test case on the Post Office's liability to a group of postmasters. The neutral citation number of the decision, as set out in a footnote to the regulation, is [2019] EWHC 606 (QB). Paragraph 7.3 of the Explanatory Memorandum describes the compensation schemes currently in being.

With effect from August 30, 2023, reg.3 of the Social Security (Infected Blood Capital Disregard) (Amendment) Regulations 2023 (SI 2023/894) substituted the following for reg.76(3):

"(3) In relation to a claim for universal credit made by a person other than the diagnosed or infected person referred to in paragraph (1)(a) (i), a payment received from the scheme or trust, or which derives from a payment received from the scheme or trust, is to be disregarded if it would be disregarded in relation to an award of state pension credit by virtue of paragraph 13 or 15 of Schedule 5 to the State Pension Credit Regulations 2002."

See the entry for p.897 for the amendment to para.15 of Sch.V to the State Pension Credit Regulations from the same date, adding a new sub-para.(5A) disregarding payments, deriving from payments from a scheme as a result of the recommendation for interim payments of £100,000 made by the Infected Blood Inquiry on July 29, 2022, from the estate of the person to a son, daughter, step-son or step-daughter. See the minutes of the July 19, 2023 meeting of the Social Security Advisory Committee for further details and in particular Annex B, setting out the significant changes in the drafting of the amending regulations as compared with the draft form presented to the SSAC. Payments to a former partner out of the estate are covered by para.13 of Sch.V

With effect from October 27, 2023, reg.9 of the Social Security (Habitual Residence and Past Presence, and Capital Disregards) (Amendment) Regulations 2023 (SI 2023/1144) amended reg.76(1A) by omitting "or" at the end of sub-para.(d) (although that word appears not to have been part of the text as at October 27, 2023), substituting "; or" for the full stop at the end of sub-para.(e) and inserting the following after sub-para.(e):

"(f) the Victims of Overseas Terrorism Compensation Scheme established by the Ministry of Justice in 2012 under section 47 of the Crime and Security Act 2010."

That scheme is administered by the Criminal Injuries Compensation Authority. It enables compensation to be paid to persons injured and to partners or close family members of persons killed, where the injury or death is directly attributable to a designated incident. Payments for personal injury would be disregarded as capital under reg.75 (indefinitely only if held on trust, otherwise for 52 weeks), but will now if necessary be disregarded indefinitely under para.(1A)(f), along with payments to family members (not previously covered). The amending regulations were made under urgency procedures following the UK's designation of some aspects of the violence in Israel from October 7, 2023 as incidents of terrorism, but many other incidents have been designated (as listed on the scheme's website).

p.468, *amendment to the Universal Credit Regulations 2013 (SI 2013/376) reg. 83 (Exceptions—entitlement or receipt of certain benefits)*

3.031 With effect from November 19, 2023, art.23 of the Carer's Assistance (Carer Support Payment) (Scotland) Regulations 2023 (Consequential Amendments) Order 2023 (SI 2023/1218) makes the following amendment to reg.83(1): after sub-para.(i) insert "(ia) a claimant, or a qualifying young person for whom a claimant is responsible, is entitled to carer support payment;".

p.472, *annotation to the Universal Credit Regulations 2013 (SI 2013/376) reg.88 (Expected hours)*

3.032 It was announced in a press release of October 25, 2023 that (as presaged in general terms in the Spring Budget 2023) from that date healthy carers of children aged three to 12, but not those who were self-employed, would be "supported to increase their chances of getting a job or up their work hours", i.e. "will agree with their Work Coach to spend more time in work or applying for jobs, up to a maximum of 30 hours a week. Commitments will be tailored to parents' personal circumstances, including the availability of childcare." Previously, the "default maximum expected hours" were 16 per week for carers of three and four-year-olds and 25 for five to 12-year-olds. There has been no change in the underlying legislation, so the mechanism for giving effect to the change is the identification of the expected hours in reg.88, which sets the limit to required hours of work search (including paid or voluntary work and work preparation: reg.95(1)(a)(i) and (2)) and work availability under reg.97(2), and in particular the circumstances in which a number of hours less than 35 must identified (para.(2)(a) to (c)). Heads (a) and (aa) depend on the number of hours compatible with the relevant caring responsibilities and head (b) (where the child is of compulsory school age, but under 13) depends on the number of hours compatible with the child's normal school hours. On the face of it, at least for existing claimants coming within para.(2), the conclusion on what is so compatible could not be altered merely by an administrative alteration in the "default maximum expected hours" (there has been no alteration for para.(2)(a), where the default number of 35 under para.(1) applies subject to the conditions of para.(2)(a)). However, one unexpressed argument must be, because of the specific mention of this factor in the press release, that the increases in the amounts that universal credit claimants can claim for childcare from June 28, 2023 and the improvements in the meeting of upfront costs has made it possible for more hours than previously to be compatible with caring responsibilities or normal school hours. It might additionally be argued that previously more hours of work search, preparation and work had actually been compatible, but that work coaches had been constrained by the lower administratively set default maximum expected hours (even though those default hours could not be legally binding), so that there is scope for an increase.

Everything will (or ought to) depend on the particular circumstances of individual cases, including the actual availability of childcare in the locality concerned and the claimant's personal circumstances, including of course the effects of any physical or mental impairment of the claimant (para.(2)(c)). Although the press release says that claimants "will agree" to spend more time in work search etc., any approach that the expected hours for the affected groups should automatically be increased unless the claimant shows some special reason why not would be improper. The test in law remains that of compatibility in individual circumstances, without any initial presumptions about what the expected hours should be.

The press release says nothing about how often affected claimants will be expected to meet their work coach, but since the frequency for claimants subject to the work preparation requirement has been increased to once a month (see the entry for pp.103–104), the expectation for the present group of claimants would presumably be no less.

Expected hours under reg.88 are also relevant to the operation of the minimum income floor under reg.62 for those in gainful self-employment. See the entry for p.408.

p.473, *amendment to the Universal Credit Regulations 2013 (SI 2013/376) reg.89(1)(b)) (Claimants subject to no work-related requirements)*

3.033   With effect from November 19, 2023, art.23(7) of the Carer's Assistance (Carer Support Payment) (Scotland) Regulations 2023 (Consequential Amendments) Order 2023 (SI 2023/1218) amended reg.89(1)(b) by inserting ", or have entitlement to carer support payment" after "carer's allowance". Carer support allowance (CSP) is newly defined in reg.2 (see the entry for p.206 and Part I of this Supplement) by reference to the Scottish legislation. Note that although s.19(2)(b) of the WRA 2012 (no work-related requirements can be imposed on anyone with "regular and substantial caring responsibilities for a severely disabled person") has not been directly amended, recipients of CSP have been put on a par with recipients of UK carer's allowance by amendments to the meaning of that phrase in reg.30 (see the entry for p.276).

pp.487–488, *annotation to the Universal Credit Regulations 2013 (SI 2013/376) reg.97(2) (Work search requirement and work availability requirement–limitations)*

3.034   See the entry for p.472 for the administrative changes relevant to the identification under reg.88 of the expected hours for carers of children.

p.561, *amendment to the Universal Credit Regulations 2013 (SI 2013/376) Sch.4 (No deduction for housing cost contributions in respect of certain non-dependants)*

3.035   With effect from November 19, 2023, art.23 of the Carer's Assistance (Carer Support Payment) (Scotland) Regulations 2023 (Consequential Amendments) Order 2023 (SI 2023/1218) makes the following amendment to Sch.4:

after paragraph 16(2)(g), insert "(ga) a person in receipt of carer support payment;".

p.561, *annotation to the Universal Credit Regulations 2013 (SI 2013/376) Sch.4 (No deduction for housing cost contributions in respect of certain non-dependants), GENERAL NOTE*

3.036   In *SM v Secretary of State for Work and Pensions (UHC)* [2023] UKUT 176 (AAC) the Upper Tribunal decided that in the context of the Sch.4 para.12(3) "overnight care condition", "regular" care means care that is provided "sufficiently often". The FTT had not correctly understood the meaning of "regular" and the findings of fact it made were therefore insufficient (paras 28–30). In principle even relatively infrequent and unpredictable overnight care could qualify a claimant for an extra room, albeit that frequency would be a relevant factor in deciding whether care was regular. However, that conclusion did not assist SM: it is implicit in the para.12(3) "overnight care condition" that care must be required, and the FTT had been entitled to find that the care being given was not required (para.31).

p.599, *annotation to the Universal Credit Regulations 2013 (SI 2013/376) Sch.10 para.4(1)(c) (Capital to be disregarded—premises intended to be occupied where the claimant is carrying out essential repairs or alterations)*

3.037   In *SH v London Borough of Southwark (HB)* [2023] UKUT 198 (AAC), Judge Hemingway held in para.23, in the context of reg.7(4) of the Housing Benefit Regulations and whether housing benefit could be paid for two properties, that the evaluation of whether repairs were essential had to take account of the claimant's individual characteristics, including impairment or vulnerability in consequence of ill-health, as had also been decided by Commissioner Williams in *CH/393/2002*. That tends to support the answer no to the question posed in the existing annotation about whether the works have to be essential for occupation by anyone. Under the supplementary benefit single payments scheme, "essential" was said to mean something like "necessary" in the sense in which luxuries are differentiated from the necessaries of life, importing a test of substantial need (*R(SB) 10/81*), but the ordinary word in para.4(1)(c) should be applied rather than some attempted further explanation.

p.656, *annotation to the Loans for Mortgage Interest Regulations 2017 (SI 2017/725) reg.13 (Standard rate to be applied under regs 11 and 12)*

From December 11, 2023, the standard rate will be 3.16% per annum. Announcements of variations in the standard rate now appear to be published at the following web address: *https://www.gov.uk/support-for-mortgage-interest/what-youll-get.*   **3.038**

p.659, *ERRATUM in annotation to the Loans for Mortgage Interest Regulations 2017 (SI 2017/725) reg.15 (Interest)*

From July 1 to December 31, 2023, the rate charged was 3.28% per annum. From January 1 to June 30, 2023, it was 3.03%. From June 1 to December 31, 2022, it was 1.4%. Announcements of variations in the rate now appear to be made at the following web address: **3.039**

https://www.gov.uk/support-for-mortgage-interest/what-youll-get.

pp.722–723, *amendment to the Universal Credit (Transitional Provisions) Regulations 2014 (SI 2014/1230) reg.9(1) (Treatment of ongoing entitlement to certain benefits: benefit cap)*

With effect from June 29, 2023, reg.6(2) of the Social Security and Universal Credit (Miscellaneous Amendments) Regulations 2023 (SI 2023/543) substituted "the Claims and Payments Regulations" for "the Universal Credit Regulations".   **3.040**

p.740, *amendment to the Universal Credit (Transitional Provisions) Regulations 2014 (SI 2014/1230) reg.21(4)(b) (Other claimants with limited capability for work: credit only cases)*

With effect from June 29, 2023, reg.6(3) of the Social Security and Universal Credit (Miscellaneous Amendments) Regulations 2023 (SI 2023/543) substituted "regulation 27(1)" for "regulation 27(1)(b)".   **3.041**

p.777, *amendment to the Universal Credit (Transitional Provisions) Regulations 2014 (SI 2014/1230) reg.53(10) (The transitional element—total legacy amount)*

With effect from June 29, 2023, reg.6(4) of the Social Security and Universal Credit (Miscellaneous Amendments) Regulations 2023 (SI 2023/543) substituted "for housing benefit in respect of specified or temporary accommodation" for "in respect of housing benefit" in para.(10).   **3.042**

pp.788 and 791, *amendments to the Universal Credit (Transitional Provisions) Regulations 2014 (SI 2014/1230) Sch.1 (Modification of tax credits legislation—finalisation of tax credits)*

3.043   With effect from June 29, 2023, reg.6(5) of the Social Security and Universal Credit (Miscellaneous Amendments) Regulations 2023 (SI 2023/543) omitted paragraphs 2(b), 25(a), 26(b) and 27(b) in Sch.1. This represents HMRC's response to the drafting ambiguity identified by the Upper Tribunal in *HMRC v AS (TC)* [2023] UKUT 67 (AAC).

p.792, *amendment to the Universal Credit (Transitional Provisions) Regulations 2014 (SI 2014/1230) Sch.2 para.5 (Claimants previously entitled to a severe disability premium)*

3.044   With effect from June 29, 2023, reg.6(6)(a) of the Social Security and Universal Credit (Miscellaneous Amendments) Regulations 2023 (SI 2023/543) substituted "if the higher SDP rate is payable on the first day of the award and no person becomes a carer for either of them in the first assessment period" for "if the higher SDP rate was payable" in para.5(b)(i) of Sch.2.

p.792, *amendment to the Universal Credit (Transitional Provisions) Regulations 2014 (SI 2014/1230) Sch.2 para.8 (Claimants previously entitled to a severe disability premium)*

3.045   With effect from June 29, 2023, reg.6(6)(b) of the Social Security and Universal Credit (Miscellaneous Amendments) Regulations 2023 (SI 2023/543) renumbered para.8 as para.8(1) and at the end inserted the following new sub-paragraph:

"(2) In paragraph 5(b)(i), the reference to a person being a carer for another person is to the person being entitled to, and in receipt of, a carer's allowance or having an award of universal credit which includes the carer element in respect of caring for that other person.";

With effect from November 19, 2023, art.26 of the Carer's Assistance (Carer Support Payment) (Scotland) Regulations 2023 (Consequential Amendments) Order 2023 (SI 2023/1218) amended para.8 by inserting "or carer support payment" after "a carer's allowance" in sub-para.(2) and inserting after that same sub-paragraph the following:

"(3) In paragraph (2) "carer support payment" means carer's assistance given in accordance with the Carer's Assistance (Carer Support Payment) (Scotland) Regulations 2023."

p.792, *amendment to the Universal Credit (Transitional Provisions) Regulations 2014 (SI 2014/1230) Sch.2 para.9 (Claimants previously entitled to a severe disability premium)*

3.046   With effect from June 29, 2023, reg.6(6)(c) of the Social Security and Universal Credit (Miscellaneous Amendments) Regulations 2023 (SI 2023/543) inserted the following new sub-paragraph after para.8:

"**9.** For the purposes of paragraph 3(b) and 5(b)(i), paragraph 6(6) of Schedule 4 to the Employment and Support Allowance Regulations 2008 or, as the case may be, the corresponding provision in relation to income support or income-based jobseeker's allowance, is to be disregarded.".

p.803, *amendment to the State Pension Credit Regulations 2002 (SI 2002/1792) reg.1 (Citation, commencement and interpretation)*

With effect from November 19, 2023, art.14(2) of the Carer's Assistance (Carer Support Payment) (Scotland) Regulations 2023 (Consequential Amendments) Order 2023 (SI 2023/1218) inserted after the definition of "care home service" the following new definition:

3.047

""carer support payment" means carer's assistance given in accordance with the Carer's Assistance (Carer Support Payment) (Scotland) Regulations 2023;".

p.805, *amendment to the State Pension Credit Regulations 2002 (SI 2002/1792) reg.1 (Citation, commencement and interpretation)*

With effect from July 9, 2023, reg.4(2)(a) of the Social Security (Income and Capital Disregards) (Amendment) Regulations 2023 (SI 2023/640) substituted for the definition of "Grenfell Tower payment" the following new definition:

3.048

""Grenfell Tower payment" means a payment made for the purpose of providing compensation or support in respect of the fire on 14th June 2017 at Grenfell Tower;".

pp.805 and 807, *amendments to the State Pension Credit Regulations 2002 (SI 2002/1792) reg.1 (Citation, commencement and interpretation)*

With effect from July 9, 2023, reg.4(2)(b) of the Social Security (Income and Capital Disregards) (Amendment) Regulations 2023 (SI 2023/640) inserted at the appropriate places the following new definitions:

3.049

""the Horizon system" means any version of the computer system used by the Post Office known as Horizon, Horizon Legacy, Horizon Online or HNG-X;";"
""the Post Office" means Post Office Limited (registered number 02154540);";"
""Post Office compensation payment" means a payment made by the Post Office or the Secretary of State for the purpose of providing compensation or support which is—
(a) in connection with the failings of the Horizon system; or
(b) otherwise payable following the judgment in *Bates and Others v Post Office Ltd* ((No. 3) "Common Issues");";"
""vaccine damage payment" means a payment made under the Vaccine Damage Payments Act 1979;".

With effect from October 27, 2023, reg.5(2)(b) of the Social Security (Habitual Residence and Past Presence, and Capital Disregards) (Amendment) Regulations 2023 (SI 2023/1144) inserted after the definition of "vaccine damage payment" the following new definition:

"the Victims of Overseas Terrorism Compensation Scheme" means the scheme of that name established by the Ministry of Justice in 2012 under section 47 of the Crime and Security Act 2010;".

p.807, *amendment to the State Pension Credit Regulations 2002 (SI 2002/1792) reg.1 (Citation, commencement and interpretation)*

3.050   With effect from July 9, 2023, reg.4(2)(c) of the Social Security (Income and Capital Disregards) (Amendment) Regulations 2023 (SI 2023/640) substituted ", a Windrush payment, a Post Office compensation payment or a vaccine damage payment" for "or a Windrush payment" in the definition of "qualifying person".

    With effect from October 27, 2023, the definition of "qualifying person" was further amended by reg.5(2)(a) of the Social Security (Habitual Residence and Past Presence, and Capital Disregards) (Amendment) Regulations 2023 (SI 2023/1144) which inserted ", the Victims of Overseas Terrorism Compensation Scheme" after "the National Emergencies Trust".

p.813, *amendment to the State Pension Credit Regulations 2002 (SI 2002/1792) reg.2(4) (Persons not in Great Britain)*

3.051   With effect from May 15, 2023, reg.2(1) and 2(2)(c) of the Social Security (Habitual Residence and Past Presence) (Amendment) Regulations 2023 (SI 2023/532) inserted the following new sub-paragraph after sub-para.(4) (zzc):

"(zzd) a person who was residing in Sudan before 15th April 2023, left Sudan in connection with the violence which rapidly escalated on 15th April 2023 in Khartoum and across Sudan and—
(i) has been granted leave in accordance with immigration rules made under section 3(2) of the Immigration Act 1971;
(ii) has a right of abode in the United Kingdom within the meaning given in section 2 of that Act; or
(iii) does not require leave to enter or remain in the United Kingdom in accordance with section 3ZA of that Act;".

p.825, *amendment to the State Pension Credit Regulations 2002 (SI 2002/1792) reg.6 (Amount of the guarantee credit)*

3.052   With effect from November 19, 2023, art.14(3) of the Carer's Assistance (Carer Support Payment) (Scotland) Regulations 2023 (Consequential Amendments) Order 2023 (SI 2023/1218) amended reg.6(5)(b) by inserting after "receipt of an allowance under section 70 of the 1992 Act" the phrase "or carer support payment".

p.841, *amendment to the State Pension Credit Regulations 2002 (SI 2002/1792) reg.15 (Income for the purposes of the Act)*

3.053   With effect from November 19, 2023, art.14(4) of the Carer's Assistance (Carer Support Payment) (Scotland) Regulations 2023 (Consequential Amendments) Order 2023 (SI 2023/1218) amended reg.15 by inserting after sub-para.(4)(f) the following:

"(g) regulation 16(2) of the Carer's Assistance (Carer Support Payment) (Scotland) Regulations 2023."

p.853, *amendment to the State Pension Credit Regulations 2002 (SI 2002/1792) reg.17B (Earnings of self-employed earners)*

With effect from November 6, 2023, reg.107 of, and the Sch. to, the Health and Care Act 2022 (Further Consequential Amendments) (No.2) Regulations 2023 (SI 2023/1071) substituted "NHS England" for "National Health Service Commissioning Board" in substituted sub-para. (2)(d)(ivb).   3.054

p.855, *amendment to the State Pension Credit Regulations 2002 (SI 2002/1792) reg.18 (Notional income)*

With effect from November 19, 2023, art.14(5) of the Carer's Assistance (Carer Support Payment) (Scotland) Regulations 2023 (Consequential Amendments) Order 2023 (SI 2023/1218) amended reg.18(1CA) by inserting after "the Social Security (Overlapping Benefits) Regulations 1979" the phrase "or regulation 16(2) of the Carer's Assistance (Carer Support Payment) (Scotland) Regulations 2023".   3.055

pp.866–867, *amendments to the State Pension Credit Regulations 2002 (SI 2002/1792) Sch.I para.1 (Additional amounts)*

With effect from November 19, 2023, art.14(6)(a) of the Carer's Assistance (Carer Support Payment) (Scotland) Regulations 2023 (Consequential Amendments) Order 2023 (SI 2023/1218) amended para.1 in the following ways: 3.056

  (i) in sub-paragraph (1)(a)(iii), after "(carer's allowance)" insert "or carer support payment";
 (ii) in the words after sub-paragraph (1)(b)—
    (aa) after "and either a person is entitled to, and in receipt of, an allowance under section 70 of the 1992 Act" insert "or carer support payment";
    (bb) after "in respect of caring for one only of the partners or, as the case may be, no person is entitled to, and in receipt of, such an allowance under section 70" insert "or carer support payment";
(iii) in sub-paragraph (1)(c)(iv), after "no person is entitled to and in receipt of an allowance under section 70 of the 1992 Act" insert "or carer support payment";
(iv) in sub-paragraph (2)(c), after "as not being in receipt of an allowance under section 70 of the 1992 Act" insert "or carer support payment";.

p.868, *amendments to the State Pension Credit Regulations 2002 (SI 2002/1792) Sch.I para.4 (Additional amounts)*

With effect from November 19, 2023, art.14(6)(b) of the Carer's Assistance (Carer Support Payment) (Scotland) Regulations 2023   3.057

(Consequential Amendments) Order 2023 (SI 2023/1218) amended para.4 in the following ways:

(i) in sub-paragraph (2), after "allowance under section 70 of the 1992 Act (carer's allowance)" insert "or carer support payment";

(ii) in sub-paragraph (3), after "allowance", in both places it occurs, insert "or payment";

(iii) in sub-paragraph (4)—

(aa) after "the allowance", in both places it occurs, insert "or payment";

(bb) after "that allowance" insert "or payment";

p.868, *amendment to the State Pension Credit Regulations 2002 (SI 2002/1792) Sch.I para.5 (Additional amounts)*

3.058   With effect from November 19, 2023, art.14(6)(c) of the Carer's Assistance (Carer Support Payment) (Scotland) Regulations 2023 (Consequential Amendments) Order 2023 (SI 2023/1218) amended para.5 by inserting "or carer support payment" after "allowance under section 70 of the 1992 Act".

p.879, *amendment to the State Pension Credit Regulations 2002 (SI 2002/1792) Sch.II para.14(8) (Housing costs: Persons residing with the claimant)*

3.059   With effect from July 9, 2023, reg.4(3) of the Social Security (Income and Capital Disregards) (Amendment) Regulations 2023 (SI 2023/640) inserted after sub-para.(bc) the following new sub-paragraph:

"(bd) any Post Office compensation payment;".

With effect from October 27, 2023, reg.5(3)(a) of the Social Security (Habitual Residence and Past Presence, and Capital Disregards) (Amendment) Regulations 2023 (SI 2023/1144) inserted ", the Victims of Overseas Terrorism Compensation Scheme" after "the National Emergencies Trust" in sub-para.(8)(b).

p.888, *amendment to the State Pension Credit Regulations 2002 (SI 2002/1792) Sch.III para.1 (Special groups)*

3.060   With effect from November 19, 2023, art.14(7) of the Carer's Assistance (Carer Support Payment) (Scotland) Regulations 2023 (Consequential Amendments) Order 2023 (SI 2023/1218) amended para.1(10)(d) by inserting "or carer support payment" after "allowance under section 70 of the 1992 Act".

p.892, *amendment to the State Pension Credit Regulations 2002 (SI 2002/1792) Sch.IV (Amounts to be disregarded in the calculation of income other than earnings)*

3.061   With effect from November 19, 2023, art.14(8) of the Carer's Assistance (Carer Support Payment) (Scotland) Regulations 2023 (Consequential Amendments) Order 2023 (SI 2023/1218) amended Sch.IV by inserting after para.18 the following new disregard:

"**19.** Any amount of carer support payment that is in excess of the amount the claimant would receive if they had an entitlement to carer's allowance under section 70 of the 1992 Act.".

pp.896–897, *amendments to the State Pension Credit Regulations 2002 (SI 2002/1792) Sch.V para.15 (Income from capital: capital disregarded for purpose of calculating income)*

With effect from July 9, 2023, reg.4(4) of the Social Security (Income and Capital Disregards) (Amendment) Regulations 2023 (SI 2023/640) inserted ", Post Office compensation payment or vaccine damage payment" after "Windrush payment" in sub-para.(1A) and substituted ", a Windrush payment, a Post Office compensation payment or a vaccine damage payment" for "or a Windrush payment" in each of sub-paras (2) to (6).

3.062

With effect from October 27, 2023, reg.5(3)(b) of the Social Security (Habitual Residence and Past Presence, and Capital Disregards) (Amendment) Regulations 2023 (SI 2023/1144) inserted ", the Victims of Overseas Terrorism Compensation Scheme" after "the National Emergencies Trust" in para.15(1) and (7).

p.897, *amendment to the State Pension Credit Regulations 2002 (SI 2002/1792) Sch.V para.15 (Income from capital: capital disregarded for purpose of calculating income)*

With effect from August 30, 2023, reg.2(1)(c) and (2) of the Social Security (Infected Blood Capital Disregard) (Amendment) Regulations 2023 (SI 2023/894) inserted after para.(5) the following new paragraph:

3.063

"(5A) Any payment out of the estate of a person, which derives from a payment to meet the recommendation of the Infected Blood Inquiry in its interim report published on 29th July 2022 made under or by the Scottish Infected Blood Support Scheme or an approved blood scheme to the estate of the person, where the payment is made to the person's son, daughter, step-son or step-daughter."

p.928, *amendment to the Social Fund Winter Fuel Payment Regulations 2000 (SI 2000/729) reg.2 (Social fund winter fuel payments)*

With effect from September 18, 2023, reg.2 of the Social Fund Winter Fuel Payment (Temporary Increase) Regulations 2023 (SI 2023/549) modifies reg.2 for the winter that follows the qualifying week beginning on September 18, 2023 so that it is applied as if:

3.064

- the references to £100 (in both places) were to £250;

- in paragraphs (1)(i), (2)(a) and (3), the reference to £200 were to £500;

- in paragraph (2)(b), the reference to £200 were to £350;

- in paragraph (2)(b), the reference to £150 were to £300; and

- the references to £300 (in both places) were to £600.

113

p.946, *amendment to the Social Fund Maternity and Funeral Expenses (General) Regulations 2005 (SI 2005/3061) reg.5 (Entitlement to Sure Start Maternity Grant)*

3.065   With effect from June 8, 2023, reg.3 of the Social Fund Maternity and Funeral Expenses (General) and Social Security (Claims and Payments) (Amendment) Regulations 2023 (SI 2023/545), makes the following amendments:

- omit paragraph (4);

- in paragraph (5), for "fourth" substitute "third";

- in paragraph (6), for "fifth" substitute "fourth".

p.952, *amendment to the Social Fund Maternity and Funeral Expenses (General) Regulations 2005 (SI 2005/3061) reg.5A (Entitlement to Sure Start Maternity Grant where another member of the claimant's family is under the age of 16)*

3.066   With effect from June 8, 2023, reg.3 of the Social Fund Maternity and Funeral Expenses (General) and Social Security (Claims and Payments) (Amendment) Regulations 2023 (SI 2023/545), inserts the following at the end of reg.5A:

"(8) A Sure Start Maternity Grant shall be awarded if—
    (a) at the date of claim, any existing member of the family is under the age of 16;
    (b) the claimant is a person to whom paragraph (9) or (10) applies;
    (c) no Sure Start Maternity Grant has been awarded to the claimant—
        (i) where the claimant is a person to whom paragraph (9) applies, on or after 15th August 2021;
        (ii) where the claimant is a person to whom paragraph (10) applies, on or after 24th February 2022; and
    (d) the other conditions for entitlement to the grant are satisfied.
(9) This paragraph applies where the claimant is—
    (a) a person who is granted leave in accordance with the immigration rules made under section 3(2) of the Immigration Act 1971 ("the 1971 Act") by virtue of—
        (i) Appendix Afghan Relocations and Assistance Policy of those rules; or
        (ii) the previous scheme for locally-employed staff in Afghanistan (sometimes referred to as the ex-gratia scheme); or
    (b) a person in Great Britain not coming within sub-paragraph (a) who left Afghanistan in connection with the collapse of the Afghan government that took place on 15th August 2021.
(10) This paragraph applies where the claimant is a person who was residing in Ukraine immediately before 1st January 2022, who left Ukraine in connection with the Russian invasion which took place on 24th February 2022 and who—
    (a) has a right of abode in the United Kingdom within the meaning given in section 2 of the 1971 Act;

(b) has been granted leave in accordance with immigration rules made under section 3(2) of the 1971 Act;

(c) has been granted, or is deemed to have been granted, leave outside those rules; or

(d) does not require leave to enter or remain in the United Kingdom in accordance with section 3ZA of the 1971 Act.".

p.973, *amendment to the Social Fund Maternity and Funeral Expenses (General) Regulations 2005 (SI 2005/3061) reg.10 (Deductions from an award of a funeral payment)*

With effect from November 19, 2023, art.16 of the Carer's Assistance   **3.067**
(Carer Support Payment) (Scotland) Regulations 2023 (Consequential Amendments) Order 2023 (SI 2023/1218) makes the following amendment to regulation 10(1A): after sub-paragraph (c) insert— "(ca)carer support payment under the Carer's Assistance (Carer Support Payment) (Scotland) Regulations 2023;".

PART IV

UPDATING MATERIAL

VOLUME III
ADMINISTRATION, ADJUDICATION AND
THE EUROPEAN DIMENSION

Commentary by

Will Rolt

Christopher Ward

p.21, *annotation to the Social Security Administration Act 1992 s.1 (Entitlement to benefit dependent on claim)*

The Court of Appeal's decision in *SSWP v Bui and Onekoya* [2023] EWCA Civ 566 is reported as [2023] AACR 9.

4.001

p.69, *annotation to the Social Security Administration Act 1992 s.71 (Overpayments—general)—Failure to disclose*

In *KI v HMRC (TC)* [2023] UKUT 212 (AAC) the lack of a legal duty to share information between the DWP and HMRC meant that there was no "official error" when information was not shared.

4.002

p.158, *annotation to the Social Security Administration Act 1992 s.187 (Certain benefit to be inalienable)*

In *McKenzie v Edinburgh City Council* [2023] SLT (Sh Ct) 127; [2023] 7 WLUK 332, the Sherriff Court held that benefits, even once paid into a claimant's bank account, remained protected under s.187 (and under the Social Security (Scotland) Act 2018, s.83 which has a similar effect). Confusion had resulted because a successful appeal against an earlier decision to contrary effect in another case (*North Lanarkshire Council v Crossan*) had not previously been published.

4.003

p.163, *amendment to the Social Security Administration Act 1992 s.191 (Interpretation—general)—correction*

With effect from April 8, 2002, limbs (b) and (c) of the definition of "income-related benefit" were repealed subject to savings by the Tax Credits Act 2002 Sch.6.

4.004

p.309, *amendment to the Social Security Act 1998 s.79 (Regulations and Orders)*

With effect from February 2, 2013, s.104(2) of the Welfare Reform Act 2012 inserted new paragraphs after subs.(6):

"(6A) The provision referred to in subsection (6) includes, in a case where regulations under this Act require or authorise the use of electronic communications, provision referred to in section 8(4) and (5) and 9(5) of the Electronic Communications Act 2000.

(6B) For the purposes of subsection (6A), references in section 8(4) and (5) and 9(5) of the Electronic Communications Act 2000 to an order under section 8 of that Act are to be read as references to regulations under this Act; and references to anything authorised by such an order are to be read as references to anything required or authorised by such regulations."

4.005

p.313, *amendment to the Social Security Act 1998 Sch.2 (Decisions against which no appeal lies)*

With effect from November 16, 2023, art.6 of the Carer's Assistance (Carer Support Payment) (Scotland) Regulations 2023 (Consequential

4.006

Modifications) Order 2023 (SI 2023/1214) amended Sch.2 to the Social Security Act 1998 by inserting "carer support payment and the carer element of universal credit" after "carer's allowance" in the heading to para.3 and by substituting for para.3 the following:

> "3. A decision as to whether a person has entitlement under section 70 (7ZA), (7ZC) or (7ZE) of the Contributions and Benefits Act."

pp.366–367, *amendments to the Welfare Reform Act 2012 s.132 (Unlawful disclosure of information supplied under section 131)*

4.007   With effect from February 7, 2023, reg.2 of, and Schedule to, the Judicial Review and Courts Act (Magistrates' Court Sentencing Powers) Regulations 2023 (SI 2023/149) amended subsection (3)(b) by deleting "twelve months" and inserting "the general limit in a magistrates' court".

As amended by the above provision with effect from February 7, 2023, and, with effect from April 28, 2022, by reg.5 of, and the Schedule to, the Criminal Justice Act 2003 (Commencement No.33) and Sentencing Act 2020 (Commencement No.2) Regulations 2022 (SI 2022/500) subs.(9) now reads:

> "In relation to an offence under this section committed in England and Wales before 2 May 2022 the reference in subsection (3)(b) to the general limit in a magistrates' court must be taken to be a reference to six months."

p.395, *annotation to the Social Security (Claims and Payments) Regulations 1987 (SI 1987/1968) reg.3 (Claims not required for entitlement to benefit in certain cases)*

4.008   *GM v SSWP (RP)* [2022] UKUT 85 (AAC) is now reported as [2023] AACR 2.

p.396, *amendment to the Social Security (Claims and Payments) Regulations 1987 (SI 1987/1968) reg.3A (Notification that claim not required for entitlement to a Category A or B retirement pension)*

4.009   With effect from November 19, 2023, reg.6 of the Carer's Assistance (Carer Support Payment) (Scotland) Regulations 2023 (Consequential Amendments) Order 2023 (SI 2023/1218) inserted into the definition of "non-exempt benefit" in para.(6) after "(a) carer's allowance;" the following:

> "(ab) carer support payment under the Carer's Assistance (Carer Support Payment) (Scotland) Regulations 2023;".

p.464, *amendment to the Social Security (Claims and Payments) Regulations 1987 (SI 1987/1968) reg.19 (Time for claiming benefit)*

4.010   With effect from June 8, 2023, reg.2 of the Social Fund Maternity and Funeral Expenses (General) and Social Security (Claims and Payments) (Amendment) Regulations 2023 (SI 2023/545) inserted the following after para.(7):

"(7A) Where—
    (a) a claim for a social fund payment in respect of maternity expenses (a "relevant social fund payment") is made by a person to whom paragraph (7B) or (7C) applies; and
    (b) both of the conditions in paragraph (7D) are met,
sub-paragraphs (a) to (f) of the entry in column (2) of Schedule 4 relating to the relevant social fund payment each have effect as if at the end there were added "or, if later, 8th December 2023".

(7B) This paragraph applies to a person who—
    (a) is granted leave in accordance with the immigration rules made under section 3(2) of the Immigration Act 1971 ("the 1971 Act") where such leave is granted by virtue of—
        (i) Appendix Afghan Relocations and Assistance Policy of those rules; or
        (ii) the previous scheme for locally-employed staff in Afghanistan (sometimes referred to as the ex-gratia scheme); or
    (b) does not come within sub-paragraph (a) and who left Afghanistan in connection with the collapse of the Afghan government that took place on 15th August 2021.

(7C) This paragraph applies to a person who was residing in Ukraine immediately before 1st January 2022, who left Ukraine in connection with the Russian invasion which took place on 24th February 2022 and who—
    (a) has a right of abode in the United Kingdom within the meaning given in section 2 of the 1971 Act;
    (b) has been granted leave in accordance with immigration rules made under section 3(2) of the 1971 Act;
    (c) has been granted, or is deemed to have been granted, leave outside those rules; or
    (d) does not require leave to enter or remain in the United Kingdom in accordance with section 3ZA of the 1971 Act.

(7D) The conditions for the purposes of paragraph (7A)(b) are that—
    (a) at the date of the claim for a relevant social fund payment, there is an existing member of the family (within the meaning given in regulation 5A of the Social Fund Maternity and Funeral Expenses (General) Regulations 2005); and
    (b) that existing member of the family is under the age of 16 on that date."

p.466, *annotation to the Social Security (Claims and Payments) Regulations 1987 (SI 1987/1968) reg. 19 (Time for claiming benefit)*

Note that reg.19(2) is to be read as if "three months" read "12 months" in the case of claims by those who, as a result of the Bereavement Benefits (Remedial) Order 2023 (SI 2023/134) have become eligible for widowed parent's allowance for any part of the period from August 30, 2018 to February 9, 2023: Remedial Order, art.3(2).

4.011

p.571, *amendment to the Universal Credit, Personal Independence Payment, Jobseeker's Allowance and Employment and Support Allowance (Claims and Payments) Regulations 2013 reg. 26 (Time within which a claim for universal credit is to be made)*

4.012   With effect from June 29, 2023, reg.5 of the Social Security and Universal Credit (Miscellaneous Amendments) Regulations 2023 (SI 2023/543) substituted for the words ", subject to a maximum extension of one month, to the date on" the wording "up to and including the day that would be the last day of the first assessment period for an award beginning on the first day in respect of".

p.626, *annotation to the Social Security and Child Support (Decision and Appeals) Regulations 1999 (SI 1999/991) reg.1 (Citation, commencement, application and interpretation)*

4.013   *KI v HMRC* [2023] UKUT 212 (AAC) "Official error"—failure of the automatic information sharing system between the DWP and HMRC to notify HMRC of an award of DLA did not amount to "official error". *AG v HMRC* [2013] UKUT 530 (AAC); *AM v HMRC (TC)* [2015] UKUT 345 (AAC); *JP v HMRC (TC)* [2013] UKUT 519 (AAC) not wrongly decided. *R. (on the application of Sier) v HBRB Cambridge CC* [2001] EWCA Civ 1523 distinguished.

p.640, *amendment to the Social Security and Child Support (Decision and Appeals) Regulations 1999 (SI 1999/991) reg.3 (Revision of decisions)*

4.014   With effect from December 14, 2022, reg.8 of the Social Security (Class 2 National Insurance Contributions Increase of Threshold) Regulations 2022 (SI 2022/1329) inserted a new paragraph after paragraph 8K:

"(8L) A decision made under section 8 or 10(34) in relation to maternity allowance may be revised at any time where, by virtue of regulation 7(1) of the Social Security (Crediting and Treatment of Contributions, and National Insurance Numbers) Regulations 2001 (treatment for the purpose of any contributory benefit of contributions paid under certain provisions relating to the payment and collection of contributions), a contribution is treated as paid on a date which falls on or before the date on which the decision was made."

p.821, *amendment to the Social Security (Information-sharing) Regulations 2012 (SI 2012/1483) reg.12 (Using purposes)*

4.015   With effect from April 1, 2023, the First-tier Tribunal for Scotland (Transfer of Functions of Valuation Appeals Committees) Regulations 2023 (SSI 2023/45) substituted for the previous reg.14(3)(d)(iii) the following:

"(iii) The First-tier Tribunal for Scotland or the Upper Tribunal for Scotland, established by section 1 of the Tribunals (Scotland) Act 2014;".

p.943, *annotation to the Social Security (Payments on Account of Benefit) Regulations 2013 (SI 2013/383) reg.5 (Payments on account of benefit where there is no award of benefit*

4.016   The Court of Appeal's decision in *SSWP v Bui and Onekoya* [2023] EWCA Civ 566 is reported as [2023] AACR 9.

p.967, *amendment to the Social Security (Recovery of Benefits) Regulations 1997 (SI 1997/2205) reg.2 (Exempted trusts and payments)*

With effect from July 9, 2023, reg.9 of the Social Security (Income and Capital Disregards) (Amendment) Regulations 2023 (SI 2023/640) inserted new sub-paragraphs after sub-para. (r):

4.017

"(s) any payment made for the purpose of providing compensation or support in respect of the fire on 14th June 2017 at Grenfell Tower;
(t) any payment made by the Post Office or the Secretary of State for the purpose of providing compensation or support which is—
 (i) in connection with the failings of the Horizon system; or
 (ii) otherwise payable following the judgment in Bates and Others v Post Office Ltd ((No. 3) "Common Issues")."

The same amending regulation inserted after paragraph (2):

"(3) In this regulation—
"the Horizon system" means any version of the computer system used by the Post Office known as Horizon, Horizon Legacy, Horizon Online or HNG-X;
"the Post Office" means Post Office Limited (registered number 02154540).".

p.981, *amendment to the Social Security (Recovery of Benefits) (Lump Sum Payments) Regulations 2008 (SI 2008/1596) reg.7 (Exempted trusts and payments)*

With effect from July 9, 2023, reg.10 of the Social Security (Income and Capital Disregards) (Amendment) Regulations 2023 (SI 2023/640) inserted new sub-paragraphs after sub-para.(o):

4.018

"(p) any payment made for the purpose of providing compensation or support in respect of the fire on 14th June 2017 at Grenfell Tower;
(q) any payment made by the Post Office or the Secretary of State for the purpose of providing compensation or support which is—
 (i) in connection with the failings of the Horizon system; or
 (ii) otherwise payable following the judgment in Bates and Others v Post Office Ltd ((No. 3) "Common Issues")."

The same amending regulation inserted after para.(2):

"(3) In this regulation—
"the Horizon system" means any version of the computer system used by the Post Office known as Horizon, Horizon Legacy, Horizon Online or HNG-X;
"the Post Office" means Post Office Limited (registered number 02154540).".

p.999, *amendment to the Social Security (Work-focused Interviews for Lone Parents) and Miscellaneous Amendments Regulations 2000 (SI 2000/1926) reg.2ZB (General requirement for lone parents entitled to income support to take part in an interview)*

With effect from November 19, 2023, reg.11 of the Carer's Assistance (Carer Support Payment) (Scotland) Regulations 2023 (SI 2023/1218)

4.019

inserted in para.(5)(a) after "or carer's allowance" the phrase ", or carer support payment under the Carer's Assistance (Carer Support Payment) (Scotland) Regulations 2023,".

p.1099, *annotation to the Tribunal Courts and Enforcement Act 2007 s.2 – the Upper Tribunal (Precedent)*

4.020   However, also note *His Majesty's Revenue and Customs v Secretary of State for Work and Pensions and GS (TC)* [2023] UKUT 9 (AAC) confirms that where there are two previous inconsistent decisions from Upper Tribunal Judges of co-ordinate jurisdiction, as a matter of precedent the second of those decisions should be followed in the absence of cogent reasons to the contrary. See *Re Lune Metal Products Ltd* [2006] EWCA Civ 1720 per Neuberger LJ at [9]. See too Lord Neuberger in *Willers v Joyce (Re Gubay (deceased) No.2)* [2016] UKSC 44 at [9], Lewison J in *Re Cromptons Leisure Machines Ltd* [2006] EWHC 3583 (Ch); [2007] B.C.C. 214 and HHJ Purle QC in *Re BXL Services* [2012] EWHC 1877 (Ch).

p.1129, *annotation to the Tribunals, Courts and Enforcement Act 2007 s.11 – Right to appeal to the Upper Tribunal (Procedural and other irregularities)*

4.021   In *Aspect Windows (Western) Limited v Adam Retter (as representative of the Estate of Mrs C McCorie* [2023] EAT 95, following the promulgation of the decision of the Employment Tribunal arising from a full merits hearing, one of the lay members of the tribunal posted on her LinkedIn page a link to a report about the decision in the Mail Online. Followers of hers then responded on LinkedIn and she responded to them. The unsuccessful respondent in the employment tribunal appealed on the basis that the LinkedIn posts gave rise to apparent bias against it. Having regard to the particular content of the posts, and applying the guidance in *Magill v Porter* [2001] UKHL 67 and other pertinent authorities, the Employment Appeal Tribunal concluded that, whatever else they might make of the wisdom or appropriateness of posting the link in the first place, the fair-minded and informed observer, having considered the contents of the post, would not in all the circumstances consider that the tribunal member was biased.

p.1139, *annotation to the Tribunals, Courts and Enforcement Act 2007 s.11A— Finality of decisions by Upper Tribunal about permission to appeal*

4.022   The effect of the Tribunals, Courts and Enforcement Act 2007 s.11A is to limit the supervisory jurisdiction of the High Court over a UT decision to refuse permission to appeal from a decision of the First Tier Tribunal by setting out, in s.11A(4), exceptions on which the UT decision could be reviewed. The decision in *R. (on the application of LA (Albania)) v Upper Tribunal (Immigration & Asylum Chamber)* [2023] EWCA Civ 1337 states that a mere assertion that one of the s.11A(4) exceptions applied was not sufficient to establish jurisdiction. A genuinely disputable question had to be shown for an applicant's judicial review claim to fall within s.11A(4). The Upper Tribunal had not acted in a procedurally defective way as to amount to a fundamental breach of the principles of natural justice. The Upper Tribunal had refused permission on the papers and addressed all the applicant's grounds of appeal against the First-tier Tribunal's decision, giving reasons why they were unarguable.

p.1282, *annotation to the Tribunal Procedure (First-tier Tribunal) (SEC) Rules 2008 (SI 2008/2685) r.25(2) (Medical and physical examination in appeals under s.12 of the Social Security Act 1998)*

Chaperones

The General Medical Council has stringent conditions on the conduct of intimate examinations. This is set out in The GMC Guidance (Intimate Examinations and Chaperones). In particular, a doctor conducting an intimate examination (which can include physical touching) must offer a chaperone to the appellant. The Guidance states that, "Intimate examinations can be embarrassing or distressing for patients and whenever you examine a patient you should be sensitive to what they may think of as intimate. This is likely to include examinations of breasts, genitalia and rectum, but could also include any examination where it is necessary to touch or even be close to the patient."

In the First-tier Tribunal where a chaperone has not been present a family member, judge or clerk are considered not to be appropriate chaperones. If a trained medical chaperone is not present, then it would be unwise for the medical member to conduct an examination. If a complaint is made where no medical chaperone was present, the GMC would have to investigate the complaint. In the event that there is no medical chaperone booked and it is deemed necessary to conduct an examination, the First-tier Tribunal is likely to consider it necessary to adjourn the hearing.

p.1294, *annotation to the Tribunal Procedure (First-tier Tribunal) (SEC) Rules 2008 (SI 2008/2685) r.27 (Taking evidence from overseas)*

SSHD v Agbabiaka (evidence from abroad, Nare guidance) [2021] UKUT 00286 (IAC) sets out guidance about when evidence can be taken from a person who is not in the United Kingdom, stating:

"1. There is an understanding among Nation States that one State should not seek to exercise the powers of its courts within the territory of another, without having the permission of that other State to do so. Any breach of that understanding by a court or tribunal in the United Kingdom risks damaging this country's relationship with other States with which it has diplomatic relations and is, thus, contrary to the public interest. The potential damage includes harm to the interests of justice.
2. The position of the Secretary of State for Foreign, Commonwealth and Development Affairs is that it is accordingly necessary for there to be permission from such a foreign State (whether on an individual or general basis) before oral evidence can be taken from that State by a court or tribunal in the United Kingdom. Such permission is not considered necessary in the case of written evidence or oral submissions.
3. Henceforth, it will be for the party to proceedings before the First-tier Tribunal who is seeking to have oral evidence given from abroad to make the necessary enquiries with the Taking of Evidence Unit (ToE) of the Foreign, Commonwealth and Development Office (FCDO), in order to ascertain whether the government of the foreign State has any objection to the giving of evidence to the Tribunal from its territory.

4.023

4.024

4. The First-tier Tribunal will need to be informed at an early stage of the wish to give evidence from abroad. The party concerned will need to give the Tribunal an indication of the nature of the proposed evidence (which need not, at this stage, be in the form of a witness statement).

5. The Tribunal's duty to seek to give effect to the overriding objective may require it, in particular, to consider alternatives to the giving of oral evidence where (for example) there are delays in the FCDO obtaining an answer from the foreign State. Each case will need to be considered on its merits.

6. The experience gained by the First-tier Tribunal in hearing oral evidence given in the United Kingdom by remote means during the Covid-19 pandemic is such that there should no longer be a general requirement for such evidence to be given from another court or tribunal hearing centre.

7. The guidance given by the Upper Tribunal in *Nare (evidence by electronic means) Zimbabwe* [2011] UKUT 00443 (IAC) is amended to the above extent."

From 7 April, 2022, His Majesty's Courts and Tribunals Service have assumed responsibility for contacting the ToE Unit on behalf of any party who has notified the tribunal that they propose to rely upon oral evidence from a person overseas.

If it becomes apparent at a hearing that a party or witness is joining from overseas and that the ToE Unit has not confirmed whether the state has given permission, the tribunal will consider the overriding objective (rule 2), and either a) adjourn the appeal with appropriate directions for making enquiries of the ToE Unit; or might b) decide the appeal.

It is suggested that although a party who is overseas may not give oral evidence in such circumstances, it would be permissible for them to make brief submissions about whether the tribunal should adjourn and the directions that might be made. Relevant factors may include the relevance and significance of the oral evidence, whether the party has failed to respond to directions asking them to inform the tribunal whether they wish to give oral evidence from overseas, and delay.

A further complication has arisen because it appears that, where a country has given permission to take evidence via video or telephone, this may be limited to nationals and residents of that country only. This means that those people just visiting (temporary visitors) may not be permitted to give evidence in any event. Clarification is being sought from FCDO but in the meantime it should be assumed that temporary any permission given does not extend to temporary visitors.

Permission is not required where persons wish to give oral evidence by video or telephone from England, Scotland, Wales, Northern Ireland, the Isle of Man, the Channel Islands, or from British Overseas Territories. Nor is there any requirement to seek permission from the tribunal in relation to documentary evidence or the production of a written witness statement or written evidence from abroad. This means, subject to the Tribunal Procedural Rules, that a party may rely upon written submissions, or written evidence that has been supplied by an individual who is situated within the territory of another state without needing to establish to the satisfaction of the tribunal that there is no legal or diplomatic barrier to their doing so.

p.1300, *annotation to the Tribunal Procedure (First-tier Tribunal) (SEC) Rules 2008 (SI 2008/2685) r.29 (Notice of hearings)*

See also *GK v SSWP* [2016] UKUT 465 (AAC) a tribunal's case man-   **4.025**
agement decision to hear an appeal at an earlier time on the scheduled day
must be guided by the overriding objective.

p.1310, *annotation to the Tribunal Procedure (First-tier Tribunal) (SEC) Rules 2008, (SI 2008/2685) r.33(1) (Notice of decisions)*

The decision in *Patel v SSHD* [2015] EWCA Civ 1175 was applied in   **4.026**
KK v SSWP (PIP) [2023] UKUT 151 (AAC). In this case the First-tier
Tribunal had announced one decision at the end of the substantive hearing
and then changed its mind after further discussion with the Appellant and
announced a different decision. The Upper Tribunal found that the First-
tier Tribunal had erred in law by changing its decision after it had been
promulgated orally at the end of the hearing.

p.1331, *annotation to the Tribunal Procedure (First-tier Tribunal) (SEC) Rules 2008 (SI 2008/2685) r.37(2) (Setting aside a decision which disposes of proceedings)*

The principle of taking a robust approach to set aside decisions is illus-   **4.027**
trated in *Herman v Information Commissioner and the Chief Constable of Kent
Police* [2023] UKUT 240 (AAC). The Upper Tribunal was dealing with an
appeal concerning Rule 41 of The Tribunal Procedure (First-tier Tribunal)
(General Regulatory Chamber) Rules 2009, which is in the same terms as
Rule 37. On 11.10.2017 the First-tier Tribunal had proceeded to determine
and refuse the Appellant's Freedom of Information Act 2000 application in
their absence and on the mistaken understanding that the Appellant had
refused to attend the hearing. Over four years later, on 20.02.2022, the
Appellant made an application to appeal the decision. On 31.08.2022 the
First-tier Tribunal extended time to admit the application but refused to
set aside the Tribunal's decision of 17.10.2017. The Upper Tribunal found
that the overall error of the First-tier Tribunal was in failing to weigh in its
consideration the central importance of an Appellant being able to attend
the oral hearing of their appeal. That was plainly a significant factor in
determining where the 'interests of justice' lay. The error of law the First-
tier Tribunal made in its refusal to set aside decision was to concentrate
solely on the underlying merits of the appeal and in not having any, or any
sufficient, regard to the Appellant's absence from the hearing and why that
was so. The Upper Tribunal noted that there had not been any application before the First-tier Tribunal that the merits of the appeal were so
poor that the appeal should have been struck out. Therefore, the First-tier
Tribunal was required to hold and oral hearing and the Appellant had been
entitled to attend. The Upper Tribunal referred to para.9 of *MK v SSWP
(ESA)* [2018] UKUT 33 (AAC), which references the relevant cases that
establish a concomitant between proceeding in an Appellant's absence and
being prepared to set aside. Dealing with the issue of delay it is noted that
the First-tier Tribunal's decision to admit the application of 20 February,
2022 was not challenged and had not been set aside and so remained in
place. That decision of the First-tier Tribunal was therefore binding in the

First-tier Tribunal proceedings and so binds the Upper Tribunal equally in remaking the First-tier Tribunal decision whether to set aside the 17 October, 2017 First-tier Tribunal's decision (see *R. (on the application of Majera) v SSHD* [2021] UKSC 46 [2022] A.C. 461).

p.1439, *annotation to the Human Rights Act 1988, s.2 (Interpretation of Convention rights)*

4.028   The Court's Rules have been further amended, up to and including October 30, 2023. They may be found at *https://www.echr.coe.int/documents/d/echr/Rules_Court_ENG* (*i.e.* the same address as previously). The main change is the introduction of a new procedure to deal with highly sensitive documents.

pp.1508–1509, *annotation to the Human Rights Act 1998, Sch.1—National authorities on art.14 read with art.1 of Protocol 1 in relation to specific benefits— (c) Bereavement*

4.029   The Court of Appeal has given MK permission to appeal against the Upper Tribunal's decision in *HM and MK v SSWP* [2023] UKUT 15 (AAC); a hearing is scheduled for March 2024.

The Court of Appeal has dismissed the Secretary of State's appeal against the decision in *Jwanczuk*: see [2023] EWCA Civ 1156.

p.1534, *United Kingdom withdrawal from the European Union—"Important note"*

4.030   For the Retained EU Law (Revocation and Reform) Act 2023, see the "New Legislation" part of this Supplement and the General Note to European Union (Withdrawal) Act 2018, s.4.

p.1540, *annotation to the European Union (Withdrawal) Act 2018 s.4 (Saving for rights etc. under section 2(1) of the ECA)*

4.031   While this correctly states the law as at the date (December 11, 2023) as at which the law in this volume is stated, note that s.4 is repealed from the end of 2023 by the Retained EU Law (Revocation and Reform) Act 2023 (as to which, see the "New Legislation" part of this Supplement).

p.1544, *annotation to the European Union (Withdrawal) Act 2018 s.5 (Exceptions to savings and incorporation)*

4.032   The Secretary of State's appeal in *Secretary of State for Work and Pensions v AT (UC)* has been dismissed by the Court of Appeal: [2023] EWCA Civ 1307.

The Supreme Court has since refused the Secretary of State's application for permission to appeal.

p.1550, *amendment to the European Union (Withdrawal) Act 2018 s.7 (Status of retained EU law)*

4.033   With effect from June 29, 2023, Retained EU Law (Revocation and Reform) Act 2023 s.10(2)(a) substituted for the existing s.7(5)(d) the following:

"(d) paragraph 16 of Schedule 8 (information about Scottish instruments which amend or revoke subordinate legislation under section 2(2) of the European Communities Act 1972),".

p.1552, *annotation to the European Union (Withdrawal) Act 2018 s.7A (General implementation of remainder of withdrawal agreement)*

For the "conduit pipe" effect of s.7A, see further now *SSWP v AT* [2023] EWCA Civ 1307 at [60]–[62].   4.034

p.1553, *annotation to the European Union (Withdrawal) Act 2018 s.7B (General implementation of EEA ETA and Swiss agreements)*

A Convention on Social Security Coordination between Iceland, Liechtenstein Norway and the UK was signed on 30 June, 2023 and implemented by SI 2023/1060. It is not apparent that the Convention is fully in force at the time of writing: 4.035

https://www.gov.uk/government/collections/bilateral-and-multilateral-treaties-published-in-the-treaty-series-2018.

p.1596, *Extracts from the Agreement on the withdrawal of the United Kingdom—Art.4 (Methods and principles relating to the effect, the implementation and the application of the Agreement)—General Note*

The Court of Appeal took a generally similar approach in dismissing the Secretary of State's appeal: [2023] EWCA Civ 1307 at [86]–[91].   4.036
The Supreme Court has since refused the Secretary of State's application for permission to appeal.

p.1598, *Extracts from the Agreement on the withdrawal of the United Kingdom—Part Two—Citizens' Rights—General Note*

From October 1, 2023 the Practice Directions which supplement the Civil Procedure Rules 1998 include a Practice Direction requiring notice to be given to the Independent Monitoring Authority of cases raising issues under this Part of the Withdrawal Agreement (or under the equivalent provision of the EEA EFTA Separation Agreement). Its text is as follows: 4.037

PRACTICE DIRECTION – CLAIMS RELATING TO EU AND EEA EFTA CITIZENS' RIGHTS UNDER PART 2 OF THE WITHDRAWAL AGREEMENT AND PART 2 OF THE EEA EFTA SEPARATION AGREEMENT

Introduction

1.1 The international treaties governing the United Kingdom's withdrawal from the European Union (the Withdrawal Agreement and the EEA EFTA Separation Agreement), provide for certain rights including—
(a) residency rights,
(b) the right to work and be self-employed,
(c) recognition of certain professional qualifications,
(d) the right to co-ordination of social security, and
(e) rights of non-discrimination on the grounds of nationality and equal treatment.

Scope and Interpretation

1.2 This Practice Direction applies to any proceedings in which a citizens' rights issue arises.

1.3 A 'citizens' rights issue' is an issue relating to rights arising under— (a) Part 2 of the Withdrawal Agreement; or (b) Part 2 of the EEA EFTA Separation Agreement.

Notice of proceedings

2.1 When a party serves a statement of case which raises a citizens' rights issue, that party must send a copy of the statement of case to the IMA at the same time.

2.2 Notice under paragraph 2.1 should be sent either – (a) by email; or (b) in hard copy to—The Independent Monitoring Authority for the Citizens' Rights Agreements 3rd Floor, Civic Centre Oystermouth Road Swansea SA1 3SN.

2.3 In the event of non-compliance with paragraphs 2.1 and 2.2—(a) the court will consider whether any order should be made or any step taken; but (b) any such order or step must not involve any sanction (including any stay, dismissal or striking out) or costs penalty or other costs order against the relevant or other party.

While the Civil Procedure Rules (and so Practice Directions associated with them) do not apply to the tribunals and there is no equivalent Practice Direction for tribunals at the time of writing, it would be open to a tribunal to serve the IMA so as to provide it with an opportunity to apply to be joined if it so wished.

p.1602, *Extracts from the Agreement on the withdrawal of the United Kingdom— Art. 13 (Residence rights)*

4.038   A similar argument on behalf of the Secretary of State was rejected by the Court of Appeal: see *SSWP v AT* [2023] EWCA Civ 1307 at [93]–[95].

The Supreme Court has since refused the Secretary of State's application for permission to appeal.

p.1626, *Extracts from the Agreement on the withdrawal of the United Kingdom— Art. 159 (Monitoring of the implementation and application of Part Two)*

4.039   For discussion of the Practice Direction which applies to cases in the courts raising issues relating to rights under Part Two, see the annotation to the General Note to Part Two (above).

p.1629, *Updating commentary on Art. 21 TFEU*

4.040   A similar argument on behalf of the Secretary of State was rejected by the Court of Appeal: see *SSWP v AT* [2023] EWCA Civ 1307 at [93]–[95].

The Supreme Court has since refused the Secretary of State's application for permission to appeal.

p.1631, *Updating commentary on the Charter of Fundamental Rights of the European Union Art. 1*

The Secretary of State's appeal was dismissed: see *SSWP v AT* [2023]   **4.041**
EWCA Civ 1307. The Court of Appeal reviewed the scope of the concept of "dignity" at [32]–[36] and at [104]–[113] rejected an argument by SSWP that Art.1 had no greater effect than does Art.4 (or Art.3 of the ECHR). SSWP's criticisms of the First-tier Tribunal's findings of fact and resulting conclusion, and the Upper Tribunal's endorsement of them, were dismissed at [170]–[176]. Green LJ does add "an important caveat or word of caution" at [177]–[179] that exploring the concept of "dignity" in any greater details, or its interaction with other rights conferred by the Charter or ECHR, will have to await other cases.
The Supreme Court has since refused the Secretary of State's application for permission to appeal.

p.1637, *Updating commentary on Directive 2004/38—Art. 24—Equal treatment*

The Secretary of State's appeal in *Secretary of State for Work and Pensions*   **4.042**
v AT (UC) has been dismissed: [2023] EWCA Civ 1307.
The Supreme Court has since refused the Secretary of State's application for permission to appeal.

p.1640, *Updating commentary on Regulation (EC) No. 883/2004 Art. 11 (Determination of the legislation applicable)—General rules*

In *SP v Department for Communities (PIP)* [2023] NiCom23, the claimant   **4.043**
was able to rely on art.11(3)(e) to claim personal independence payment from the UK, her state of residence, despite being in receipt of an invalidity pension from the Republic of Ireland, exported in reliance on art.7. The invalidity pension did not bring her within any of limbs (a) to (d) of art.11(3). Further, following *Konevod v SSWP* [2020] EWCA Civ 809 and *Harrington* * *v SSWP* [2023] EWCA Civ 433, art.11(3) was not displaced by the rules of Title III.
*The claimant's name is wrongly spelled as Herrington in the main volume. *Harrington* is now reported as [2023] AACR 8.

PART V

UPDATING MATERIAL

VOLUME IV
HMRC-ADMINISTERED SOCIAL SECURITY
BENEFITS AND SCOTLAND

Commentary by

Ian Hooker

Edward Mitchell

Nick Wikeley

p.51, *amendment to the Social Security Contributions and Benefits Act 1992 s.157(1) (Rates of payment)*

With effect from April 6, 2023, art.9 of the Social Security Benefits Up-rating Order 2023 (SI 2023/316) increased the weekly rate of SSP to £109.40.

5.001

p.156, *annotation to the Tax Credits Act 2002 s.2 (Function of Commissioners)*

In *GL v HMRC* [2023] UKUT 100 (AAC); [2023] 1 W.L.R. 4481 Deputy Upper Tribunal Judge Buley KC doubted the correctness of HMRC's argument that, in principle, they had discretion, in an exceptional case, to continue to pay tax credits to a person who, falling outside reg.4 of the Tax Credits (Residence) Regulations 2003, was not in the United Kingdom (s.3(3) of the Tax Credits Act 2002 provides that a claim for a tax credit may be made by a person "in the United Kingdom"). The judge suspected that HMRC may have mistakenly assumed that a recognised extra-statutory discretion, applicable in connection with HMRC's tax collection functions, was also applicable in connection with their tax credits functions. HMRC's case seemed to have overlooked the "fundamental problem" that their statutory powers to pay tax credits do not permit payment of a tax credit to a person who fails to satisfy the statutory conditions, and that s.2's authority to make payment of tax credits is to be read as an authority to make payment in accordance with, rather than outwith, the statutory scheme.

5.002

p.231, *annotation to the Tax Credits Act s.38 (Appeals)*

In *HMRC v Arrbab* [2024] EWCA Civ 16, the Court of Appeal held that the Upper Tribunal's decision *AB v HMRC* (TC) [2021] UKUT 328 (AAC) was wrongly decided. The wording of s.38(1A) was clear and did not admit of any other construction than that a right of appeal is excluded where a late request for a review under s.21A is made and HMRC refuse under s.21B to extend time. The Upper Tribunal mistakenly adopted the approach taken in *R. (CJ) v Secretary of State for Work and Pensions* [2017] UKUT 324 (AAC); [2018] AACR 5 without appreciating that CJ turned on the interpretation of social security appeal legislation that is not reflected in the appeal provisions of the Tax Credits Act 2002. However, the Court of Appeal went on to consider whether the secondary legislation that inserted s.38(1A), so as to purportedly restrict rights of appeal to the First-tier Tribunal, and hence s.38(1A) itself, was *ultra vires*. That secondary legislation – the Tax Credits, Child Benefit and Guardian's Allowance Reviews and Appeals Order 2014, SI 2014/886 – was made under enabling powers provided for by s.124 of the Finance Act 2008. Such powers, being powers that authorise secondary legislation to amend an Act of Parliament, are known as Henry VIII powers and, in the case of doubt as to their extent, must be interpreted restrictively (*R. (Public Law Project) v Secretary of State for Justice* [2016] UKSC 39; [2016] A.C. 1531). This includes a presumption that Henry VIII powers are assumed not to extend to authorising provision that restricts rights of appeal (*R. v Emmett* [1998] A.C. 773). The Court of Appeal held that "there is nothing in s.124 FA 2008 that makes clear that it authorises a provision which has the effect of making the

5.003

decision maker the effective gatekeeper of appeals to the FTT in the event of a late challenge, subject only to the possibility of judicial review". Section 38(1A) of the Tax Credits Act 2002 was struck out and, accordingly, to be treated as of no effect.

p.313, *amendment to the Income Tax (Earnings and Pensions) Act 2003 s.658 (Amount charged to tax)*

5.004   With effect from November 19, 2023, reg.2(2) of the Income Tax (Tax Treatment of Carer Support Payment and Exemption of Social Security Benefits) Regulations 2023 (SI 2023/1148) amended s.658(4) by inserting after "carer's allowance supplement" the words "carer support payment".

p.314, *amendment to the Income Tax (Earnings and Pensions) Act 2003 s.660 (Taxable benefits: United Kingdom benefits—Table A)*

5.005   With effect from November 19, 2023, reg.2(3) of the Income Tax (Tax Treatment of Carer Support Payment and Exemption of Social Security Benefits) Regulations 2023 (SI 2023/1148) amended Table A in s.660(1) by inserting the following entry after that for "carer's allowance supplement":

"

Carer support payment	CA(CSP)(S)R 2023	Regulation 3

"

p.316, *amendment to the Income Tax (Earnings and Pensions) Act 2003 s.661 (Taxable social security income)*

5.006   With effect from November 19, 2023, reg.2(4) of the Income Tax (Tax Treatment of Carer Support Payment and Exemption of Social Security Benefits) Regulations 2023 (SI 2023/1148) amended the list of benefits in s.661(1) by inserting after the entry for "carer's allowance supplement" the entry "carer support payment".

p.551, *annotation to the Welfare Reform Act (Commencement No.23 and Transitional and Transitory Provisions) Order 2015 (SI 2015/634) art.7 (Transitional provision: claims for…a tax credit)*

5.007   The provisions originally enacted in art.7 have been re-enacted in the main Universal Credit Transitional Regulations: see reg.6A of the Universal Credit (Transitional Provisions) Regulations 2014 (SI 2014/1230) below in this volume and the annotation thereto.

p.697, *amendment to the Tax Credits (Definition and Calculation of Income) Regulations 2002 (SI 2002/2006) reg.10(2) (Investment income)—Table 4 (Payments in the calculation of investment income) at item 9*

5.008   With effect from October 27, 2023, reg.3(2) of the Child Benefit and Tax Credits (Miscellaneous Amendments) Regulations 2023 (SI 2023/1139) amended Table 4 item 9 by inserting after "ITTOIA)" in column 1 "or under the Victims of Overseas Terrorism Compensation Scheme 2012 or any corresponding scheme established under section 47 of the Crime and Security Act 2010" and for the entry in column 2 inserting the following:

"The amount to which no liability to income tax arises under section 732 of ITTOIA."

p.716, *amendments to the Tax Credits (Definition and Calculation of Income) Regulations 2002 (SI 2002/2006) reg.19 (General disregards in the calculation of income)*

With effect from October 27, 2023, reg.3(3) of the Child Benefit and Tax Credits (Miscellaneous Amendments) Regulations 2023 (SI 2023/1139) amended Table 6 (Sums to be disregarded in the calculation of income) by inserting after item 43 the following disregard: 5.009

"**44.** An award of compensation made under the Victims of Overseas Terrorism Compensation Scheme 2012 or any corresponding scheme established under section 47 of the Crime and Security Act 2010.".

With effect from November 6, 2023, reg.6 of the Health and Care Act 2022 (Further Consequential Amendments) (No.2) Regulations 2023 (SI 2023/1071) substituted "NHS England" for "the National Health Service Commissioning Board" in Table 8 (Sums partly disregarded in the calculation of income), item 3, column 1, in para.(db).

p.721, *annotation to the Tax Credits (Definition and Calculation of Income) Regulations 2002 (SI 2002/2006) reg.19 (General disregards in the calculation of income)*

Table 6 now includes an entry (para.44) disregarding awards of compensation under the Victims of Overseas Terrorism Compensation Scheme 2012 or a corresponding scheme under s.47 of the Crime and Security Act 2010. 5.010

p.797, *annotation to the Tax Credits (Claims and Notifications) Regulations 2002 (SI 2002/2014) reg.20 (Increases of maximum rate of entitlement to a tax credit as a result of changes of circumstances to be dependent on notification)*

In *KI v HMRC* (TC) [2023] UKUT 212 (AAC) Upper Tribunal Judge Hemingway rejected the argument that the requirement in reg.20(1) to give notification in accordance with Part III of the Regulations was restricted to the reporting of changes of circumstances in the tax year in which they occur. A failure duly to notify a change of circumstances, that would increase the maximum rate of a tax credit, prevents such an increase regardless of the tax year in which the change of circumstances occurred. 5.011

p.857, *annotation to the Tax Credits (Residence) Regulations 2003 (SI 2003/654) reg.4 (Persons temporarily absent from the United Kingdom)*

In *GL v HMRC* [2023] UKUT 100 (AAC); [2023] 1 W.L.R. 4481 Deputy Tribunal Judge Buley KC held that it was irrelevant, for the purposes of reg.4, that a person's return to the UK had been prevented by Coronavirus-related foreign travel restrictions. The residency rules for 5.012

certain social security benefits were relaxed to take account of Coronavirus-related travel restrictions but no similar amendment was made to reg.4. Accordingly, a person whose absence from the UK exceeded 8 weeks due to pandemic-related restrictions on returning to the UK could not, on the application of reg.4, be considered temporarily absent from the UK. However, HMRC accepted before the Upper Tribunal that child tax credit was a "family benefit" within EU Regulation 833/2004, so that, for the purposes of Art.11 of that Regulation, the claimant remained subject to the legislation of the UK while absent in Spain. HMRC further conceded that Regulation 883/2004 required "the UK to treat a claimant's presence in another member state as though it were presence in the UK which prevents [application of] the domestic temporary absence conditions". Judge Buley accepted HMRC's concessions but emphasised that he was doing so without hearing argument.

Judge Buley in *GL* also expressed doubt as to the correctness of HMRC's argument that, in principle, they had discretion, in an exceptional case, to continue to pay tax credit to a person who, falling outside reg.4, was not in the United Kingdom (s.3(3) of the Tax Credits Act 2002 provides that a claim for a tax credit may be made by a person "in the United Kingdom"). The judge suspected that HMRC may have mistakenly assumed that a recognised extra-statutory discretion, applicable in connection with HMRC's tax collection functions, was also applicable in connection with HMRC's tax credits functions. HMRC's case seemed to have overlooked the "fundamental problem" that their statutory powers to pay tax credits do not permit payment of a tax credit to a person who fails to satisfy the statutory conditions.

p.860, *annotation to the Tax Credits (Official Error) Regulations 2003 (SI 2003/692) reg.2 (Interpretation)*

5.013   In *KI v HMRC* (TC) [2023] UKUT 212 (AAC) Upper Tribunal Judge Hemingway rejected the argument that 'a failure of an automatic information sharing system between the DWP and HMRC' amounted to an official error for the purposes of the 2003 Regulations. The claimant sought to rely on failure of the data feed between HMRC and the DWP to argue that his notification to the DWP of a change of circumstances relevant to tax credit entitlement sufficed as notification to HMRC. The claimant's argument was contrary to existing Upper Tribunal authority (*AG v HMRC* [2013] UKUT 530 (AAC)) and, in the absence of a specific legal duty requiring information sharing between the DWP and HMRC, could not succeed.

pp.909–912, *amendments to the Child Benefit (General) Regulations 2006 (SI 2006/223) reg.23(6) (Circumstances in which person treated as not being in Great Britain)*

5.014   With effect from May 15, 2023, reg.2(2) of the Child Benefit (General) (Amendment) Regulations 2023 (SI 2023/533) amended reg.23(6) by substituting for "January 2022" in sub-para.(s) the following:

"January 2022;
(t) left Sudan in connection with the violence which rapidly escalated on 15th April 2023 in Khartoum and across Sudan, providing that person was residing in Sudan immediately before 15th April 2023.".

With effect from October 27, 2023, reg.2 of the Child Benefit and Tax Credits (Miscellaneous Amendments) Regulations 2023 (SI 2023/1139) further amended reg.23 as follows:

(1) in para.(2) delete the words "Paragraphs (1) and (5)" and substitute "Paragraph (1) does"
(2) in para.(3) omit the words "and paragraph (5) shall not apply".
(3) omit paragraphs (5) to (7).

pp.915–918, *amendment to the Child Benefit (General) Regulations 2006 (SI 2006/223) reg. 27(5) (Circumstances in which person treated as not being in Northern Ireland)*

With effect from May 15, 2023, reg.2(3) of the Child Benefit (General) (Amendment) Regulations 2023 (SI 2023/533) amended reg.27(5) by substituting for "January 2022" in sub-para.(s) the following: 5.015

"January 2022;
(t) left Sudan in connection with the violence which rapidly escalated on 15th April 2023 in Khartoum and across Sudan, providing that person was residing in Sudan immediately before 15th April 2023.".

With effect from October 27, 2023, reg.2 of the Child Benefit and Tax Credits (Miscellaneous Amendments) Regulations 2023 (SI 2023/1139) further amended reg. 27 by omitting "and paragraph (4) shall not apply" in para.(2) and by omitting paragraphs (4) to (6).

p.1015, *amendment to the Statutory Maternity Pay (General) Regulations 1986 (SI 1986/1960) reg.6 (Prescribed rate of statutory maternity pay)*

With effect from April 2, 2023, art.10 of the Social Security Benefits   5.016
Up-rating Order 2023 (SI 2023/316) increased the weekly rate of SMP to £172.48.

p.1065, *amendment to the Statutory Paternity Pay and Statutory Adoption Pay (Weekly Rates) Regulations 2002 (SI 2002/2818) reg.2(a) (Weekly rate of payment of statutory paternity pay)*

With effect from April 2, 2023, art.11(1)(a) of the Social Security   5.017
Benefits Up-rating Order 2023 (SI 2023/316) increased the weekly rate of SPP to £172.48.

p.1066, *amendment to the Statutory Paternity Pay and Statutory Adoption Pay (Weekly Rates) Regulations 2002 (SI 2002/2818) reg.3(a) (Weekly rate of payment of statutory adoption pay)*

With effect from April 2, 2023, art. 11(1)(b) of the Social Security   5.018
Benefits Up-rating Order 2023 (SI 2023/316) increased the weekly rate of SAP to £172.48.

p.1206, *amendment to the Statutory Shared Parental Pay (General) Regulations 2014 (SI 2014/3051) reg.40(1)(a) (Weekly rate of payment of statutory shared parental pay)*

5.019   With effect from April 2, 2023, art.11(2) of the Social Security Benefits Up-rating Order 2023 (SI 2023/316) increased the weekly rate of statutory shared parental pay to £172.48.

p.1254, *amendment to the Statutory Parental Bereavement Pay (General) Regulations 2020 (SI 2020/233) reg.20(1)(a) (Weekly rate of payment)*

5.020   With effect from April 2, 2023, art.11(3) of the Social Security Benefits Up-rating Order 2023 (SI 2023/316) increased the weekly rate of statutory parental bereavement pay to £172.48.

p.1377, *amendments to the Childcare Payments Regulations 2015 (SI 2015/522) reg.14 (Variation of relevant maximum: delay in payment of allowances)*

5.021   With effect from November 16, 2023, reg.12(2) of the Carer's Assistance (Carer Support Payment) (Scotland) Regulations 2023 (Consequential Modifications) Order 2023 (SI 2023/1214) amended reg.14 by (a) omitting the "or" at the end of sub-para.(1)(a)(i), (b) inserting after sub-para.(1)(a)(i) new sub-paragraph "(ia) carer support payment under the Carer's Assistance (Carer Support Payment) (Scotland) Regulations 2023; or"; and (c) inserting "carer support payment" after "carer's allowance," in para.(4).

pp.1379–1380, *amendments to the Childcare Payments Regulations 2015 (SI 2015/522) reg.17 (Compensatory payments)*

5.022   With effect from November 16, 2023, reg.12(3) of the Carer's Assistance (Carer Support Payment) (Scotland) Regulations 2023 (Consequential Modifications) Order 2023 (SI 2023/1214) amended reg.17 by (a) omitting the "or" at the end of sub-para.(2)(b)(i), (b) inserting after sub-para.(2)(b)(i) new sub-paragraph "(ia) carer support payment under the Carer's Assistance (Carer Support Payment) (Scotland) Regulations 2023; or"; and (c) inserting "carer support payment" after "carer's allowance," in para.(8).

p.1390 and pp.1390–1418, *correction to the Childcare (Free of Charge for Working Parents) (England) Regulations 2022 (SI 2022/1134)*

5.023   The correct SI number for the Childcare (Free of Charge for Working Parents) (England) Regulations 2022 is SI 2022/1134 (and not SI 2016/1257). Accordingly on pp.1390-1418 the left-hand page running headers should read "The Childcare Regulations 2022", while the right-hand page running headers should read "(SI 2022/1134)".

pp.1394–1395, *amendments to the Childcare (Free of Charge for Working Parents) (England) Regulations 2022 (SI 2022/1134) reg.4 (Definitions)*

5.024   With effect from March 30, 2023, reg.11(a)-(d) of the Childcare and Inspection of Education, Children's Services and Skills (Fees) (Amendments) Regulations 2023 (SI 2023/276) amended reg.4 as follows:

(a) for the definition of "childminder" substitute—

""childminder" means an early years childminder within the meaning given in section 96(4) of the Childcare Act 2006 but as if the definition in that subsection was not subject to subsection (5) of that section;";

(b) after the definition of "inspection report" insert—

""limited capability for work" means limited capability for work under—

(a) regulation 39 of the Universal Credit Regulations 2013, or

(b) regulation 40 of the Universal Credit Regulations (Northern Ireland) 2016;

"limited capability for work and work-related activity" means limited capability for work and work-related activity under—

(a) regulation 40 of the Universal Credit Regulations 2013, or

(b) regulation 41 of the Universal Credit Regulations (Northern Ireland) 2016;";

(c) omit the definition of "Social Security Act";

(d) before the definition of "tax year" insert—

""specified benefit" has the meaning given in regulation 11A;".

p.1397, *amendment to the Childcare (Free of Charge for Working Parents) (England) Regulations 2022 (SI 2022/1134) reg.10 (Meaning of "partner")*

With effect from March 30, 2023, reg.12 of the Childcare and Inspection of Education, Children's Services and Skills (Fees) (Amendments) Regulations 2023 (SI 2023/276) amended reg.10 by inserting after paragraph (2) the following:

5.025

"(3) A person is not a member of the same household as, or living together with, another person if—

(a) the person is absent, and

(b) the absence exceeds, or is expected to exceed, 6 months.".

p.1398, *amendment to the Childcare (Free of Charge for Working Parents) (England) Regulations 2022 (SI 2022/1134) by insertion of new reg.11A (Meaning of "specified benefit")*

With effect from March 30, 2023, reg.13 of the Childcare and Inspection of Education, Children's Services and Skills (Fees) (Amendments) Regulations 2023 (SI 2023/276) inserted a new reg.11A after reg.11:

5.026

"Meaning of "specified benefit"

11A.—(1) A "specified benefit" is any of the following—

(a) carer's allowance under—

(i) section 70 of the Social Security Contributions and Benefits Act 1992, or

(ii) section 70 of the Social Security Contributions and Benefits (Northern Ireland) Act 1992;

(b) carer's assistance given in accordance with regulations made under section 28 of the Social Security (Scotland) Act 2018 except a young carer grant given under the Carer's Assistance (Young Carer Grants) (Scotland) Regulations 2019;

    (c) the carer element under—
        (i) regulation 29 of the Universal Credit Regulations 2013, or
        (ii) regulation 30 of the Universal Credit Regulations (Northern Ireland) 2016;
    (d) credits for incapacity for work or limited capability for work under—
        (i) regulation 8B of the Social Security (Credits) Regulations 1975, or
        (ii) regulation 8B of the Social Security (Credits) Regulations (Northern Ireland) 1975;
    (e) employment and support allowance under—
        (i) section 1 of the Welfare Reform Act 2007, or
        (ii) section 1 of the Welfare Reform Act (Northern Ireland) 2007;
    (f) long-term incapacity benefit under—
        (i) regulation 11(4) or 17(1) of the Social Security (Incapacity Benefit) (Transitional) Regulations 1995, or
        (ii) regulation 11(4) or 17(1) of the Social Security (Incapacity Benefit) (Transitional) Regulations (Northern Ireland) 1995;
    (g) long-term or short-term incapacity benefit under—
        (i) section 30A, 40 or 41 of the Social Security Contributions and Benefits Act 1992, or
        (ii) section 30A, 40 or 41 of the Social Security Contributions and Benefits (Northern Ireland) Act 1992;
    (h) severe disablement allowance under—
        (i) section 68 of the Social Security Contributions and Benefits Act 1992, or
        (ii) section 68 of the Social Security Contributions and Benefits (Northern Ireland) Act 1992.".

p.1399, *amendments to the Childcare (Free of Charge for Working Parents) (England) Regulations 2022 (SI 2022/1134) reg.14 (Conditions relating to parent)*

5.027   With effect from March 30, 2023, reg.14 of the Childcare and Inspection of Education, Children's Services and Skills (Fees) (Amendments) Regulations 2023 (SI 2023/276) amended reg.14 by substituting "mentioned in regulation 15(3)," for "(see regulation 10)" in para.(4)(a) and by omitting para.(5).

p.1399, *amendments to the Childcare (Free of Charge for Working Parents) (England) Regulations 2022 (SI 2022/1134) reg.15 (Conditions relating to partner of parent)*

5.028   With effect from March 30, 2023, reg.15 of the Childcare and Inspection of Education, Children's Services and Skills (Fees) (Amendments) Regulations 2023 (SI 2023/276) amended reg.15 by substituting "(2) If a parent of a young child has a partner, the partner must be a person mentioned in paragraph (3) or (4)." for para.(2) and then inserting the following new paragraphs:

"(3) A person who—
    (a) meets the qualifying paid work requirement in regulation 16 or 17,
    (b) does not for the relevant tax year—
        (i) expect their adjusted net income to exceed £100,000,

    (ii) make a claim under section 809B of the Income Tax Act 2007 (claim for remittance basis to apply), or

    (iii) expect section 809E of Income Tax Act 2007 to apply (application of remittance basis without claim: other cases), and

(c) if a foster parent of the young child, has confirmation from the responsible local authority that it is satisfied that engaging in any paid work other than as a foster parent is consistent with the child's care plan.

(4) A person who is the partner of a parent mentioned in regulation 14(3) and who—

(a) has limited capability for work;

(b) has limited capability for work and work-related activity;

(c) is entitled to a specified benefit; or

(d) is a resident of an EEA State or Switzerland who is, under the law of the EEA State or Switzerland, entitled to a benefit of a kind that is substantially similar to a specified benefit.".

p.1401, *amendments to the Childcare (Free of Charge for Working Parents) (England) Regulations 2022 (SI 2022/1134) reg.16 (Qualifying paid work requirement: employee)*

With effect from March 30, 2023, reg.16 of the Childcare and Inspection of Education, Children's Services and Skills (Fees) (Amendments) Regulations 2023 (SI 2023/276) amended reg.16 by substituting for sub-para.(3)(a) the following: **5.029**

"(a) any period the person is—

  (i) a foster parent, or

  (ii) on specified leave other than adoption leave of the kind mentioned in sub-paragraph (b);".

The same amending regulation made the following further amendments in para.(4) of reg.16:

  (i) in the definition of "adoption leave", in para.(b), for "the Social Security Act" substitute "the Social Security Contributions and Benefits Act";

  (ii) after the definition of "national insurance number" insert—
""the Social Security Contributions and Benefits Act" means either of the following—
    (a) the Social Security Contributions and Benefits Act 1992;
    (b) the Social Security Contributions and Benefits (Northern Ireland) Act 1992";

  (iii) in the definition of "specified leave", in para.(a) for (i) to (v) substitute—
    "(i) ordinary or additional maternity leave;
    (ii) ordinary or additional adoption leave;
    (iii) shared parental leave;
    (iv) parental leave;
    (v) paternity leave;
    (vi) parental bereavement leave;";

  (iv) in paragraph (b), for "the Social Security Act" substitute "the Social Security Contributions and Benefits Act".

p.1403, *amendments to the Childcare (Free of Charge for Working Parents) (England) Regulations 2022 (SI 2022/1134) reg.18(3) (Minimum income requirement)*

5.030   With effect from March 30, 2023, reg.17 of the Childcare and Inspection of Education, Children's Services and Skills (Fees) (Amendments) Regulations 2023 (SI 2023/276) amended reg.18(3) in the definition of "relevant period" by substituting in sub-para.(a), for the words from "beginning with" to the end, the following:

"beginning with—
  (i) the day on which the declaration relating to the employee is made, or
  (ii) if regulation 7(1)(d) applies, the day on which the person expects to be a person mentioned in any of regulation 7(1)(a) to (c);";

The same amending regulation substituted "of three months beginning with the day on which the declaration relating to the employee is made" for "mentioned in paragraph (a)" in para.(b).

p.1414, *amendment to the Childcare (Free of Charge for Working Parents) (England) Regulations 2022 (SI 2022/1134) reg.45(3) (Duty to make arrangements with childcare provider chosen by parent)*

5.031   With effect from March 30, 2023, reg.18 of the Childcare and Inspection of Education, Children's Services and Skills (Fees) (Amendments) Regulations 2023 (SI 2023/276) amended reg.45(3)(c) by substituting "an early years childminder agency" for "a childcare agency".

p.1415, *amendment to the Childcare (Free of Charge for Working Parents) (England) Regulations 2022 (SI 2022/1134) reg.47 (Requirements permissible in arrangements)*

5.032   With effect from March 30, 2023, reg.19 of the Childcare and Inspection of Education, Children's Services and Skills (Fees) (Amendments) Regulations 2023 (SI 2023/276) amended reg.47(1)(f) by substituting "an early years childminder agency" for "a childcare agency".

pp.1477–1479, *amendments to the Social Security (Scotland) Act 2018 s.81 (Carer's Allowance Supplement)*

5.033   With effect from November 19, 2023, para.9(2)-(5) of Sch.1 to the Carer's Assistance (Carer Support Payment) (Scotland) Regulations 2023 (SSI 2023/302) made the following four amendments to s.81:

(1) In subs.(2), for para.(a) substitute—
  "(a) in receipt of—
    (i) a carer's allowance under section 70 of the Social Security Contributions and Benefits Act 1992, or
    (ii) carer support payment under the Carer's Assistance (Carer Support Payment) (Scotland) Regulations 2023 (S.S.I. 2023/302), and".
(2) In subs.(9), for para.(a) substitute—
  "(a) in receipt of—
    (i) a carer's allowance under section 70 of the Social Security Contributions and Benefits Act 1992, or

    (ii)   carer support payment under the Carer's Assistance (Carer Support Payment) (Scotland) Regulations 2023 (S.S.I. 2023/302),".

(3) In subs.(11), for para.(a) substitute—

"(a) in receipt of—

    (i)   a carer's allowance under section 70 of the Social Security Contributions and Benefits Act 1992, or

    (ii)   carer support payment under the Carer's Assistance (Carer Support Payment) (Scotland) Regulations 2023 (S.S.I. 2023/302),".

(4) In subs.(13), for para.(a) substitute—

"(a) in receipt of—

    (i)   a carer's allowance under section 70 of the Social Security Contributions and Benefits Act 1992, or

    (ii)   carer support payment under the Carer's Assistance (Carer Support Payment) (Scotland) Regulations 2023 (S.S.I. 2023/302),".

p.1516, *amendment to the Early Years Assistance (Best Start Grants) (Scotland) Regulations 2018 (SSI 2018/370) Sch.2 para.4 (Residence requirement—pregnancy and baby grant)*

With effect from May 17, 2023, at 5:54pm reg.4(2) of the Social Security (Residence Requirements) (Sudan) (Scotland) Regulations 2023 (SSI 2023/149) amended para.4 by inserting after sub-para.(2)(ac) the following new sub-paragraph:

5.034

"(ad) a person who was residing in Sudan before 15 April 2023, left Sudan in connection with the violence which rapidly escalated on 15 April 2023 in Khartoum and across Sudan and—
(i) has been granted leave in accordance with immigration rules made under section 3(2) of the Immigration Act 1971,
(ii) has a right of abode in the United Kingdom within the meaning given in section 2 of that Act, or
(iii) does not require leave to enter or remain in the United Kingdom in accordance with section 3ZA of that Act".

With effect from October 26, 2023, at 5:38pm reg.4(2) of the Social Security (Residence and Presence Requirements) (Israel, the West Bank, the Gaza Strip, East Jerusalem, the Golan Heights and Lebanon) (Scotland) Regulations 2023 (SSI 2023/309) further amended para.4 by inserting after sub-para.(2)(ad) the following new sub-paragraph:

"(ae) a person in Great Britain who was residing in Israel, the West Bank, the Gaza Strip, East Jerusalem, the Golan Heights or Lebanon immediately before 7 October 2023, left Israel, the West Bank, the Gaza Strip, East Jerusalem, the Golan Heights or Lebanon in connection with the Hamas terrorist attack in Israel on 7 October 2023 or the violence which rapidly escalated in the region following the attack and—
(i) has been granted leave in accordance with immigration rules made under section 3(2) of the Immigration Act 1971,
(ii) has a right of abode in the United Kingdom within the meaning given in section 2 of that Act, or

> (iii) does not require leave to enter or remain in the United Kingdom in accordance with section 3ZA of that Act,".

p.1521, *amendment to the Early Years Assistance (Best Start Grants) (Scotland) Regulations 2018 (SSI 2018/370) Sch.3 para.3 (Residence requirement—early learning grant)*

5.035 With effect from on May 17, 2023 at 5:54pm reg.4(3) of the Social Security (Residence Requirements) (Sudan) (Scotland) Regulations 2023 (SSI 2023/149) amended para.3 by inserting after sub-para.(2)(ac) the following new sub-paragraph:

> "(ad) a person who was residing in Sudan before 15 April 2023, left Sudan in connection with the violence which rapidly escalated on 15 April 2023 in Khartoum and across Sudan and—
> (i) has been granted leave in accordance with immigration rules made under section 3(2) of the Immigration Act 1971,
> (ii) has a right of abode in the United Kingdom within the meaning given in section 2 of that Act, or
> (iii) does not require leave to enter or remain in the United Kingdom in accordance with section 3ZA of that Act".

With effect from 26, 2023 at 5:38pm reg.4(3) of the Social Security (Residence and Presence Requirements) (Israel, the West Bank, the Gaza Strip, East Jerusalem, the Golan Heights and Lebanon) (Scotland) Regulations 2023 (SSI 2023/309) further amended para.3 by inserting after sub-para.(2)(ad) the following new sub-paragraph:

> "(ae) a person in Great Britain who was residing in Israel, the West Bank, the Gaza Strip, East Jerusalem, the Golan Heights or Lebanon immediately before 7 October 2023, left Israel, the West Bank, the Gaza Strip, East Jerusalem, the Golan Heights or Lebanon in connection with the Hamas terrorist attack in Israel on 7 October 2023 or the violence which rapidly escalated the region following the attack and—
> (i) has been granted leave in accordance with immigration rules made under section 3(2) of the Immigration Act 1971,
> (ii) has a right of abode in the United Kingdom within the meaning given in section 2 of that Act, or
> (iii) does not require leave to enter or remain in the United Kingdom in accordance with section 3ZA of that Act,".

p.1523, *amendment to the Early Years Assistance (Best Start Grants) (Scotland) Regulations 2018 (SSI 2018/370) Sch.4 para.4 (Residence requirement – school-age grant)*

5.036 With effect from May 17, 2023 at 5:54pm reg.4(4) of the Social Security (Residence Requirements) (Sudan) (Scotland) Regulations 2023 (SSI 2023/149) amended para.4 by inserting after sub-para.(2)(ac) the following new sub-paragraph:

> "(ad) a person who was residing in Sudan before 15 April 2023, left Sudan in connection with the violence which rapidly escalated on 15 April 2023 in Khartoum and across Sudan and—
> (i) has been granted leave in accordance with immigration rules made under section 3(2) of the Immigration Act 1971,

    (ii) has a right of abode in the United Kingdom within the meaning given in section 2 of that Act, or

   (iii) does not require leave to enter or remain in the United Kingdom in accordance with section 3ZA of that Act".

With effect from October 26, 2023 at 5:38pm reg.4(4) of the Social Security (Residence and Presence Requirements) (Israel, the West Bank, the Gaza Strip, East Jerusalem, the Golan Heights and Lebanon) (Scotland) Regulations 2023 (SSI 2023/309) further amended para.4 by inserting after sub-para.(2)(ad) the following new sub-paragraph:

"(ae) a person in Great Britain who was residing in Israel, the West Bank, the Gaza Strip, East Jerusalem, the Golan Heights or Lebanon immediately before 7 October 2023, left Israel, the West Bank, the Gaza Strip, East Jerusalem, the Golan Heights or Lebanon in connection with the Hamas terrorist attack in Israel on 7 October 2023 or the violence which rapidly escalated in the region following the attack and—

    (i) has been granted leave in accordance with immigration rules made under section 3(2) of the Immigration Act 1971,

    (ii) has a right of abode in the United Kingdom within the meaning given in section 2 of that Act, or

   (iii) does not require leave to enter or remain in the United Kingdom in accordance with section 3ZA of that Act,".

p.1537, *amendment to the Carer's Assistance (Young Carer Grants) (Scotland) Regulations 2019 (SSI 2019/324) reg.6 (Conditions relating to the person or persons being care for)*

With effect from November 19, 2023, reg.7 of the Carer's Assistance (Carer Support Payment) (Consequential and Miscellaneous Amendments and Transitional Provision) (Scotland) Regulations 2023 (SSI 2023/258) amended reg.6(3)(a) by substituting "Carer Support Payment payable under the Carer's Assistance (Carer Support Payment) (Scotland) Regulations 2023" for "carer's assistance, payable under section 28 of the Social Security (Scotland) Act 2018".

        5.037

p.1538, *amendment to the Carer's Assistance (Young Carer Grants) (Scotland) Regulations 2019 (SSI 2019/324) reg.7 (Further eligibility conditions)*

With effect from November 19, 2023, para.11(2) of Sch.1 to the Carer's Assistance (Carer Support Payment) (Scotland) Regulations 2023 (SSI 2023/302) inserted "at any point in the qualifying period or" after "young carer grant if," in reg.7(1) and omitted "in respect of any of the persons being cared for".

        5.038

p.1539, *amendment to the Carer's Assistance (Young Carer Grants) (Scotland) Regulations 2019 (SSI 2019/324) reg.8 (Conditions relating to residence)*

With effect from May 17, 2023 at 5:54pm reg.6(2) of the Social Security (Residence Requirements) (Sudan) (Scotland) Regulations 2023 (SSI 2023/149) amended reg.8 by inserting after sub-para.(2)(ab) the following new sub-paragraph:

        5.039

"(ac) a person who was residing in Sudan before 15 April 2023, left Sudan in connection with the violence which rapidly escalated on 15 April 2023 in Khartoum and across Sudan and—
   (i) has been granted leave in accordance with immigration rules made under section 3(2) of the Immigration Act 1971,
   (ii) has a right of abode in the United Kingdom within the meaning given in section 2 of that Act, or
   (iii) does not require leave to enter or remain in the United Kingdom in accordance with section 3ZA of that Act".

With effect from October 26, 2023 at 5:38pm reg.6(2) of the Social Security (Residence and Presence Requirements) (Israel, the West Bank, the Gaza Strip, East Jerusalem, the Golan Heights and Lebanon) (Scotland) Regulations 2023 (SSI 2023/309) further amended reg.8 by inserting after sub-para.(2)(ac) the following new sub-paragraph:

"(ad) a person in Great Britain who was residing in Israel, the West Bank, the Gaza Strip, East Jerusalem, the Golan Heights or Lebanon immediately before 7 October 2023, left Israel, the West Bank, the Gaza Strip, East Jerusalem, the Golan Heights or Lebanon in connection with the Hamas terrorist attack in Israel on 7 October 2023 or the violence which rapidly escalated in the region following the attack and—
   (iv) has been granted leave in accordance with immigration rules made under section 3(2) of the Immigration Act 1971,
   (v) has a right of abode in the United Kingdom within the meaning given in section 2 of that Act, or
   (vi) does not require leave to enter or remain in the United Kingdom in accordance with section 3ZA of that Act,".

p.1584, *amendment to the Carer's Allowance Supplement and Young Carer Grants (Residence Requirements and Procedural Provisions) (EU Exit) (Scotland) Regulations 2020 (SSI 2020/475) reg.7 (Determination of entitlement to a carer's allowance supplement without application for individuals resident outside Scotland)*

5.040 With effect from November 19, 2023, para.10(2) of Sch.1 to the Carer's Assistance (Carer Support Payment) (Scotland) Regulations 2023 (SSI 2023/302) substituted for sub-para.7(b)(i) the following:

"(i) the Scottish Ministers establish that the individual has received an award of—
   (aa) carer's allowance under section 70 of the Social Security Contributions and Benefits Act 1992,
   (bb) carer support payment under the Carer's Assistance (Carer Support Payment) (Scotland) Regulations 2023 (S.S.I. 2023/302),".

p.1593, *amendment to the Disability Assistance for Children and Young People (Scotland) Regulations 2021 (SSI 2021/174) reg.2 (Interpretation—general)*

5.041 With effect from November 20, 2023, reg.3(2) of the Disability Assistance (Miscellaneous Amendment) (Scotland) Regulations 2023 (SSI 2023/346) amended reg.2 by inserting the following new definition after the definition of "the 2018 Act":

""the ADP Regulations" means the Disability Assistance for Working Age People (Scotland) Regulations 2022,".

p.1595, *amendments to the Disability Assistance for Children and Young People (Scotland) Regulations 2021 (SSI 2021/174) reg.4 (Age criteria)*

With effect from November 20, 2023, reg.3(3) of the Disability Assistance (Miscellaneous Amendment) (Scotland) Regulations 2023 (SSI 2023/346) amended reg.4 by inserting ", (1C)" after "(1B)" and substituting a new para.(1B) as follows:

5.042

"(1B) Child Disability Payment may continue to be paid in respect of an individual who is over the age of 17 years—
(a) where they are an individual to whom regulation 15 (entitlement under special rules for terminal illness) applies,
(b) until the age of 19 years where the individual is a transferring individual in terms of Part 3 of the schedule, and reaches the age of 18 on or before 31 December 2023, except where paragraph (1C) applies,
(c) until the age of 19 years where they are an individual mentioned in regulation 35 (individuals in respect of whom Disability Living Allowance is paid in another part of the United Kingdom immediately before moving to Scotland) who reaches the age of 18 on or before 31 December 2023, except where paragraph (1C) applies,
(d) where the individual does not fall within sub-paragraph (a), (b) or (c) and—
  (i) they are awaiting a determination of their entitlement to Adult Disability Payment, or
  (ii) a determination has been made that the individual is entitled to Adult Disability Payment but payment has not begun,
until the age of 19 years, or the individual becomes entitled to Adult Disability Payment in accordance with regulation 58(2)(a) of the ADP Regulations, whichever is earlier.
(1C) Where an individual falls within paragraph (1B)(b) or (c) and—
(a) a determination of their entitlement to Adult Disability Payment is made within the period of 4 weeks before the date on which the individual reaches the age of 19, and
(b) that determination is that the individual is entitled to Adult Disability Payment,
Child Disability Payment may continue to be paid in respect of the individual after they reach the age of 19 until the day before the day on which the individual becomes entitled to Adult Disability Payment in accordance with regulation 58(2)(a) of the ADP Regulations."

p.1598, *amendment to the Disability Assistance for Children and Young People (Scotland) Regulations 2021 (SSI 2021/174) reg.5(10A) (Residence and presence conditions)*

With effect from May 17, 2023 at 5:54pm reg.7(2) of the Social Security (Residence Requirements) (Sudan) (Scotland) Regulations 2023 (SSI

5.043

2023/149) amended reg.5(10A) by omitting "or" at the end of sub-para.(e) and by inserting after sub-para.(f) the following new sub-paragraph:

", or

(g) has leave to enter or remain in the United Kingdom granted under or outside the immigration rules, has a right of abode in the United Kingdom within the meaning given in section 2 of the Immigration Act 1971 or does not require leave to enter or remain in the United Kingdom in accordance with section 3ZA of that Act, where the individual—
  (i) was residing in Sudan before 15 April 2023, and
  (ii) left Sudan in connection with the violence which rapidly escalated on 15 April 2023 in Khartoum and across Sudan".

With effect from October 26, 2023 at 5:38pm reg.7(2) of the Social Security (Residence and Presence Requirements) (Israel, the West Bank, the Gaza Strip, East Jerusalem, the Golan Heights and Lebanon) (Scotland) Regulations 2023 (SSI 2023/309) further amended reg.5(10A) by omitting "or" at the end of sub-para.(f) and by inserting after sub-para.(g) the following new sub-paragraph:

", or

(h) has leave to enter or remain in the United Kingdom granted under or outside the immigration rules, has a right of abode in the United Kingdom within the meaning given in section 2 of the Immigration Act 1971 or does not require leave to enter or remain in the United Kingdom in accordance with section 3ZA of that Act, where the individual—
  (i) was residing in Israel, the West Bank, the Gaza Strip, East Jerusalem, the Golan Heights or Lebanon immediately before 7 October 2023, and
  (ii) left Israel, the West Bank, the Gaza Strip, East Jerusalem, the Golan Heights or Lebanon in connection with the Hamas terrorist attack in Israel on 7 October 2023 or the violence which rapidly escalated in the region following the attack".

p.1601, *amendment to the Disability Assistance for Children and Young People (Scotland) Regulations 2021 (SSI 2021/174)—insertion of new reg.9A (No entitlement to care component where UK is not competent state)*

5.044 With effect from November 20, 2023, reg.3(4) of the Disability Assistance (Miscellaneous Amendment) (Scotland) Regulations 2023 (SSI 2023/346) inserted after reg. 9 (Persons residing outside the United Kingdom to whom a relevant EU Regulation applies) the following new regulation:

"No entitlement to care component where UK is not competent state
9A. An individual to whom a relevant EU Regulation applies is not entitled to the care component for a period unless during that period the United Kingdom is competent for payment of sickness benefits in cash to the individual for the purposes of the relevant EU Regulation in question.".

p.1619, *amendments to the Disability Assistance for Children and Young People (Scotland) Regulations 2021 (SSI 2021/174) reg.29 (When a decrease in level or cessation of entitlement takes effect)*

With effect from November 20, 2023, reg.3(5) of the Disability Assistance (Miscellaneous Amendment) (Scotland) Regulations 2023 (SSI 2023/346) amended reg.29 by inserting after sub-para. (a) the following new sub-paragraph:

5.045

"(aa) in the case of a determination without application under regulation 31(b), on the date of the individual's death,",

and by inserting after sub-para.(b)(i) the following new sub-paragraph:

"(ia) where the Scottish Ministers make a determination that the individual is entitled to Adult Disability Payment, on the day that the entitlement to Adult Disability Payment begins in terms of regulation 58 of the ADP Regulations,".

p.1623, *amendment to the Disability Assistance for Children and Young People (Scotland) Regulations 2021 (SSI 2021/174) reg.34 (Determination to effect a deduction decision)*

With effect from November 20, 2023, reg.3(6) of the Disability Assistance (Miscellaneous Amendment) (Scotland) Regulations 2023 (SSI 2023/346) amended reg.34(3)(b) by inserting "Payment" after "Child Disability".

5.046

p.1630, *amendment to the Disability Assistance for Children and Young People (Scotland) Regulations 2021 (SSI 2021/174) Sch. Pt 3 para.8 (Notice of intention to transfer to Child Disability Payment)*

With effect from November 20, 2023, reg.3(7) of the Disability Assistance (Miscellaneous Amendment) (Scotland) Regulations 2023 (SSI 2023/346) amended para.8 of Part 3 by substituting a new sub-para. (3) as follows:

5.047

"(3) Where a notice under sub-paragraph (1) is given—
(a) to a transferring individual who, before a determination is made under paragraph 9(1), ceases to be ordinarily resident in Scotland, or
(b) in error where the individual is neither—
    (i) ordinarily resident in Scotland, nor
    (ii) an individual who is habitually resident in an EEA state, Gibraltar or Switzerland and has a genuine and sufficient link to Scotland,
the duty on the Scottish Ministers in paragraph 9(1) does not apply."

p.1633, *amendment to the Disability Assistance for Children and Young People (Scotland) Regulations 2021 (SSI 2021/174) Sch. Pt3 para.14 (Appointees)*

With effect from November 20, 2023, reg.3(8) of the Disability Assistance (Miscellaneous Amendment) (Scotland) Regulations 2023 (SSI 2023/346) amended para.14 of Part 3 by inserting the following new sub-paragraph after sub-para (2):

5.048

"(3) The duty in sub-paragraph (2) does not apply where the Scottish Ministers have already appointed the person mentioned in sub-paragraph (1) to act on behalf of that transferring individual under section 85A or 85B of the 2018 Act."

p.1651, *amendment to the Disability Assistance for Working Age People (Scotland) Regulations 2022 (SSI 2022/54) reg.15(7) (Residence and presence conditions)*

5.049   With effect from May 17, 2023 at 5:54pm reg.8(2) of the Social Security (Residence Requirements) (Sudan) (Scotland) Regulations 2023 (SSI 2023/149) amended reg.15(7) by omitting "or" at the end of sub-para.(c) and by inserting after sub-para.(d) the following new sub-paragraph:

", or
(e) has leave to enter or remain in the United Kingdom granted under or outside the immigration rules, has a right of abode in the United Kingdom within the meaning given in section 2 of the Immigration Act 1971 or does not require leave to enter or remain in the United Kingdom in accordance with section 3ZA of that Act, where the individual—
(i) was residing in Sudan before 15 April 2023, and
(ii) left Sudan in connection with the violence which rapidly escalated on 15 April 2023 in Khartoum and across Sudan".

With effect from October 26, 2023 at 5:38pm reg.8(2) of the Social Security (Residence and Presence Requirements) (Israel, the West Bank, the Gaza Strip, East Jerusalem, the Golan Heights and Lebanon) (Scotland) Regulations 2023 (SSI 2023/309) further amended reg.15(7) by omitting "or" at the end of sub-para.(d) and by inserting after sub-para.(e) the following new sub-paragraph:

", or
(f) has leave to enter or remain in the United Kingdom granted under or outside the immigration rules, has a right of abode in the United Kingdom within the meaning given in section 2 of the Immigration Act 1971 or does not require leave to enter or remain in the United Kingdom in accordance with section 3ZA of that Act, where the individual—
(i) was residing in Israel, the West Bank, the Gaza Strip, East Jerusalem, the Golan Heights or Lebanon immediately before 7 October 2023, and
(ii) left Israel, the West Bank, the Gaza Strip, East Jerusalem, the Golan Heights or Lebanon in connection with the Hamas terrorist attack in Israel on 7 October 2023 or the violence which rapidly escalated in the region following the attack".

p.1654, *amendment to the Disability Assistance for Children and Young People (Scotland) Regulations 2021 (SSI 2021/174)—insertion of new reg.20A (No entitlement to daily living component where UK is not competent state)*

5.050   With effect from November 20, 2023, reg.4(2) of the Disability Assistance (Miscellaneous Amendment) (Scotland) Regulations 2023 (SSI 2023/346) inserted after reg.20 (Persons residing outside the United Kingdom to whom a relevant EU Regulation applies) the following new regulation:

"No entitlement to daily living component where UK is not competent state

20A. An individual to whom a relevant EU Regulation applies is not entitled to the daily living component for a period unless during that period the United Kingdom is competent for payment of sickness benefits in cash to the individual for the purposes of the relevant EU Regulation in question."

p.1672, *amendment to the Disability Assistance for Children and Young People (Scotland) Regulations 2021 (SSI 2021/174) reg.46 (When a decrease in level or cessation of entitlement takes effect)*

With effect from November 20, 2023, reg.4(3) of the Disability Assistance (Miscellaneous Amendment) (Scotland) Regulations 2023 (SSI 2023/346) amended reg.46 by inserting after sub-para.(1)(a) the following new sub-paragraph:

5.051

"(aa) in the case of a determination without application under regulation 48(b), on the date of the individual's death,".

p.1679, *amendment to the Disability Assistance for Children and Young People (Scotland) Regulations 2021 (SSI 2021/174) reg.58 (Applications by individuals entitled to Child Disability Payment)*

With effect from November 20, 2023, reg.4(4) of the Disability Assistance (Miscellaneous Amendment) (Scotland) Regulations 2023 (SSI 2023/346) amended reg.46 by substituting for para.(1) the following:

5.052

"(1) This regulation applies where an individual who is entitled to Child Disability Payment submits the required data in terms of regulation 35(4) on a day on which the individual is still entitled to Child Disability Payment and makes an application for Adult Disability Payment—
(a) on a day on which the individual is still entitled to Child Disability Payment,
(b) on a day on which the individual is no longer entitled to Child Disability Payment, where that day falls within the period of 8 weeks starting on the day on which the individual submitted the required data, or
(c) on a day on which the individual is no longer entitled to Child Disability Payment, where that day is after the expiry of the 8 week period mentioned in sub-paragraph (b) and the Scottish Ministers are satisfied that there is good reason why the application was not made sooner.";

and substituting for para.(2) the following:

"(2) Where, on the basis of that application, the Scottish Ministers make a determination of the individual's entitlement to Adult Disability Payment ("Adult Disability Payment determination"), and on the date of that determination—
(a) the individual is still entitled to Child Disability Payment, the date on which their entitlement to Adult Disability Payment begins is to be—
    (i) the day after the first day on which the individual is to be paid Child Disability Payment after the date of the Adult Disability

Payment determination in accordance with regulation 25(b)
(i) of the Disability Assistance for Children and Young People
(Scotland) Regulations 2021, or

(ii) 7 days after the first day on which the individual is to be paid
Child Disability Payment after the date of the Adult Disability
Payment determination in accordance with regulation 25(b)
(ii) of the Disability Assistance for Children and Young People
(Scotland) Regulations 2021,

(b) the individual is no longer entitled to Child Disability Payment, the
date on which their entitlement to Adult Disability Payment begins
is to be the date on which the Scottish Ministers make the Adult
Disability Payment determination.".

p.1691, *amendment to the Disability Assistance for Children and Young People
(Scotland) Regulations 2021 (SSI 2021/174) Sch.2 Pt 3 para.8 (Notice of
intention to transfer to Adult Disability Payment)*

5.053   With effect from November 20, 2023, reg.4(5) of the Disability Assistance
(Miscellaneous Amendment) (Scotland) Regulations 2023 (SSI 2023/346)
amended Sch.2 Pt 3 para.8 by substituting for sub-para (3) the following:

"(3) Where a notice under sub-paragraph (1) is given—

(a) to a transferring individual who, before a determination is made
under paragraph 9(1), ceases to be ordinarily resident in Scotland, or

(b) in error where the individual is neither—
(i) ordinarily resident in Scotland, nor
(ii) an individual who is habitually resident in an EEA state,
Gibraltar or Switzerland and has a genuine and sufficient link
to Scotland,

the duty on the Scottish Ministers in paragraph 9(1) does not apply."

p.1693, *amendment to the Disability Assistance for Children and Young People
(Scotland) Regulations 2021 (SSI 2021/174) Sch.2 Pt 3 para.12 (Change of
circumstances)*

5.054   With effect from November 20, 2023, reg.4(6) of the Disability Assistance
(Miscellaneous Amendment) (Scotland) Regulations 2023 (SSI 2023/346)
amended Sch.2 Pt 3 para.12 by substituting for sub-para (1) the following:

"(1) The Scottish Ministers must make a determination of an individual's
entitlement to Adult Disability Payment (the "review determination"),
without receiving an application, where—

(a) the individual, before a determination under paragraph 9(1) (the
"transfer determination") is made, reported a change of circumstances to the Secretary of State for Work and Pensions, which
had not been taken into account for the individual's entitlement to
Personal Independence Payment,

(b) the Scottish Ministers have made a transfer determination, and

(c) the individual has not requested a re-determination under section
41 of the 2018 Act, or appealed under section 46 of the 2018 Act, in
relation to the transfer determination."

p.1695, *amendment to the Disability Assistance for Children and Young People (Scotland) Regulations 2021 (SSI 2021/174) Sch.2 Pt 3 para.15 (Appointees)*

With effect from November 20, 2023, reg.4(7) of the Disability Assistance (Miscellaneous Amendment) (Scotland) Regulations 2023 (SSI 2023/346) amended Sch.2 Part 3 para.15 by inserting after sub-para (2) the following:

    "(3) The duty in sub-paragraph (2) does not apply where the Scottish Ministers have already appointed the person mentioned in sub-paragraph (1) to act on behalf of that transferring individual under section 85B of the 2018 Act."

5.055

p.1695, *correction to the Disability Assistance for Working Age People (Transitional Provisions and Miscellaneous Amendments) (Scotland) Regulations 2022 (SSI 2022/217)*

    The correct SSI number for the Disability Assistance for Working Age People (transitional Provisions and Miscellaneous Amendments) (Scotland) Regulations 2022 is SSI 2022/217 (and not SI 2022/517). The right-hand page running headers for pp.1697–1703 need to be corrected accordingly.

5.056

p.1698, *amendment to the Disability Assistance for Working Age People (Transitional Provisions and Miscellaneous Amendments) (Scotland) Regulations 2022 (SSI 2022/217) reg.3 (notice of intention to transfer to Adult Disability Payment)*

With effect from November 20, 2023, reg.5(2) of the Disability Assistance (Miscellaneous Amendment) (Scotland) Regulations 2023 (SSI 2023/346) amended reg.3(3) by substituting the following new paragraph:

5.057

    "(3) Where a notice under paragraph (1) is given—
    (a) to a transferring individual who, before a transfer determination is made ceases to be ordinarily resident in Scotland, or
    (b) in error where the individual is neither—
        (i) ordinarily resident in Scotland, nor
        (ii) an individual who is habitually resident in an EEA state, Gibraltar or Switzerland and has a genuine and sufficient link to Scotland,
the duty on the Scottish Ministers in regulation 4(1) does not apply."

p.1702, *amendment to the Disability Assistance for Working Age People (Transitional Provisions and Miscellaneous Amendments) (Scotland) Regulations 2022 (SSI 2022/217) reg.10 (Modification of the ADP Regulations: transferring individuals)*

With effect from November 20, 2023, reg.5(3) of the Disability Assistance (Miscellaneous Amendment) (Scotland) Regulations 2023 (SSI 2023/346) amended reg.10 by omitting paras, (f) and (g).

5.058

p.1703, *amendment to the Disability Assistance for Working Age People (Transitional Provisions and Miscellaneous Amendments) (Scotland) Regulations 2022 (SSI 2022/217) reg.11 (Appointees)*

5.059   With effect from November 20, 2023, reg.5(4) of the Disability Assistance (Miscellaneous Amendment) (Scotland) Regulations 2023 (SSI 2023/346) amended reg.11 by inserting after para.(2) the following new paragraph:

"(3) The duty in paragraph (2) does not apply where the Scottish Ministers have already appointed the person mentioned in paragraph (1) to act on behalf of that transferring individual under section 85B of the 2018 Act."

p.1704, *amendment to the Disability Assistance for Working Age People (Transitional Provisions and Miscellaneous Amendments) (Scotland) Regulations 2022 (SSI 2022/217) reg.14 (Change of circumstances)*

5.060   With effect from November 20, 2023, reg.5(5) of the Disability Assistance (Miscellaneous Amendment) (Scotland) Regulations 2023 (SSI 2023/346) substituted a new reg.14 as follows:

"Change of circumstances
14. Where the Scottish Ministers are making a review determination of an individual's entitlement to Adult Disability Payment, where the individual, before a transfer determination is made, reported a change of circumstances to the Secretary of State for Work and Pensions which had not been taken into account for the individual's entitlement to Disability Living Allowance, the change of circumstances—
(a) is not to be regarded as relating to the individual's entitlement to Disability Living Allowance, and
(b) is to be taken into consideration by the Scottish Minister in making the review determination."

p.1704, *amendment to the Disability Assistance for Working Age People (Transitional Provisions and Miscellaneous Amendments) (Scotland) Regulations 2022 (SSI 2022/217) reg.15 (When an increase in level of entitlement takes effect)*

5.061   With effect from November 20, 2023, reg.5(6) of the Disability Assistance (Miscellaneous Amendment) (Scotland) Regulations 2023 (SSI 2023/346) inserted after para.(2) the following new paragraph:

"(3) Where paragraph (1) applies, regulation 45 of the ADP Regulations does not apply.".

p.1704, *amendment to the Disability Assistance for Working Age People (Transitional Provisions and Miscellaneous Amendments) (Scotland) Regulations 2022 (SSI 2022/217) reg.16 (When a decrease in level or cessation of entitlement takes effect)*

5.062   With effect from November 20, 2023, reg.5(7) of the Disability Assistance (Miscellaneous Amendment) (Scotland) Regulations 2023 (SSI 2023/346) substituted a new regulation 16 as follows:

"**When a decrease in level or cessation of entitlement takes effect**
16.—(1) Where an individual's entitlement to Adult Disability Payment
is determined in the review determination to be at a lower rate than, or
the same rate as awarded by, the transfer determination, entitlement
under the review determination will take effect on the day that the
Scottish Ministers make the review determination.

(2) Where paragraph (1) applies, regulation 46 of the ADP Regulations
does not apply."

PART VI

CUMULATIVE UPDATING MATERIAL

VOLUME V
INCOME SUPPORT AND THE LEGACY BENEFITS

Commentary by

John Mesher

Tom Royston

Nick Wikeley

Replace Vol.II pp.1027–1145 with the following:

PART I

SOCIAL SECURITY STATUTES

p.15, *amendment to the Social Security Contributions and Benefits Act 1992 s.126(7) (Trade disputes)*

With effect from April 10, 2023, art.23 of the Social Security Benefits Up-rating Order 2023 (SI 2023/316) substituted "£47.00" for "£42.50" (as had been in effect from April 11, 2022) in subs.(7).

6.001

p.18, *annotation to the Social Security Contributions and Benefits Act 1992 s.126(5)(b) (Trade disputes—relevant sum)*

Note that the amount of the "relevant sum" for the purposes of s.126(5) (b) is specified in subs.(7), not (6). With effect from April 10, 2023 the sum was increased to £47 (see the entry for p.15).

6.002

pp.19–20, *annotation to the Social Security Contributions and Benefits Act 1992 s.134(1) (Exclusions from benefit)*

In the Institute for Government and the Social Security Advisory Committee's 2021 joint report *Jobs and benefits: The Covid-19 challenge* it was noted that if the capital limit had risen in line with prices since 2006 it would be close to £23,500 (or £25,000: different figures are given) and recommended that the limit should be increased to £25,000 and subsequently automatically indexed to maintain its real value (pp.22 and 31). That recommendation was summarily rejected in the Government's response of March 22, 2022.

6.003

p.33, *annotation to the old style Jobseekers Act 1995 GENERAL NOTE*

The two remaining prohibitions on claiming universal credit have now been removed. The former exception for "frontier workers" was removed with effect from March 30, 2022 by the Welfare Reform Act 2012 (Commencement No.34 and Commencement No.9, 21, 23, 31 and 32 and Transitional Provisions (Amendment)) Order 2022 (SI 2022/302) and the discretion given to the Secretary of State under reg.4 of the Transitional Provisions Regulations 2014 (SI 2014/1230) to determine (for the safeguarding of efficient administration or ensuring the efficient testing of administrative systems) that no claims for universal credit were to be accepted in an area or category of case was removed with effect from July 25, 2022 by reg.2 of the Universal Credit (Transitional Provisions) Amendment Regulations 2022 (SI 2022/752). There is thus now no exception, however remote, to the proposition that any new claim for JSA can only be for new style JSA.

6.004

p.72, *annotation to the Jobseekers Act 1995 s.13(1) (Income and capital: income-based jobseeker's allowance)*

6.005 In the Institute for Government and the Social Security Advisory Committee's 2021 joint report *Jobs and benefits: The Covid-19 challenge* it was noted that if the capital limit had risen in line with prices since 2006 it would be close to £23,500 (or £25,000: different figures are given) and recommended that the limit should be increased to £25,000 and subsequently automatically indexed to maintain its real value (pp.22 and 31). That recommendation was summarily rejected in the Government's response of March 22, 2022.

p.81, *annotation to the old style Jobseekers Act 1995 s.15(2) (Effect on other claimants—trade disputes)*

6.006 With effect from April 10, 2023 the "prescribed sum" for the purposes of s.15(2)(d) was increased to £47 (see the entry for p.1086).

p.124, *correction to the old style Jobseekers Act 1995 s.20E (Contracting out)*

6.007 The text in s.20E(1)–(3) should be replaced with the following:

"(1) The following functions of the Secretary of State may be exercised by, or by employees of, such person (if any) as the Secretary of State may authorise for the purpose, namely—
 (a) [2...]
 (b) [2...]
 (c) [2...]
 (d) [3...]
 (e) [3...]
 (f) [3...]
(2) The following functions of officers of the Secretary of State may be exercised by, or by employees of, such person (if any) as the Secretary of State may authorise for the purpose, namely—
 (a) specifying places and times, and being contacted, under section 8;
 (b) entering into or varying any jobseeker's agreement under section 9 or 10 and referring any proposed agreement or variation to the Secretary of State under section 9 or 10;
 (c) giving notifications under section 16[2...];
 (d) [2...].
(3) Regulations may provide for any of the following functions of the Secretary of State to be exercisable by, or by employees of, such person (if any) as the Secretary of State may authorise for the purpose—
 (a) any function under regulations under section 8,[2...] 17A[2...][3...], except the making of an excluded decision (see subsection (4));
 (b) the function under section 9(1) of the 1998 Act (revision of decisions) so far as relating to decisions (other than excluded decisions) that relate to any matter arising under any such regulations;
 (c) the function under section 10(1) of the 1998 Act (superseding of decisions) so far as relating to decisions (other than excluded decisions) of the Secretary of State that relate to any matter arising under any such regulations;

(d) any function under Chapter 2 of Part 1 of the 1998 Act (social security decisions), except section 25(2) and (3) (decisions involving issues arising on appeal in other cases), which relates to the exercise of any of the functions within paragraphs (a) to (c)."

p.133, *annotation to the old style Jobseekers Act 1995 s.35 (Interpretation— definition of "employment officer")*

Note in relation to the schemes whose providers have been designated as employment officers that the Work Programme has ceased to operate and that reg.8(3) of the SAPOE Regulations has been revoked with effect from March 22, 2022 (see the entry for p.1187).

6.008

PART II

INCOME SUPPORT REGULATIONS

p.229, *amendments to the Income Support (General) Regulations 1987 (SI 1987/1967) reg.2 (Interpretation)*

With effect from July 26, 2021, Sch.1 para.2 of the Social Security (Scotland) Act 2018 (Disability Assistance for Children and Young People) (Consequential Modifications) Order 2021 (SI 2021/786) inserts the following definitions:

6.009

"child disability payment" has the meaning given in regulation 2 of the DACYP Regulations;
"DACYP Regulations" means the Disability Assistance for Children and Young People (Scotland) Regulations 2021;

With effect from January 1, 2022, reg.2(2) of the Social Security (Income and Capital Disregards) (Amendment) Regulations 2021 (SI 2021/1405) inserts the following definitions:

"child abuse payment" means a payment from a scheme established or approved by the Secretary of State for the purpose of providing compensation in respect of historic institutional child abuse in the United Kingdom;"
"Windrush payment" means a payment made under the Windrush Compensation Scheme (Expenditure) Act 2020;"

With effect from January 1, 2022, reg.2(2) of the Social Security (Income and Capital Disregards) (Amendment) Regulations 2021 (SI 2021/1405) inserts ", a child abuse payment or a Windrush payment" into the definition of "qualifying person", after "Grenfell Tower payment".
With effect from March 21, 2022, art.2(2) of the Social Security (Disability Assistance for Working Age People) (Consequential Amendments) Order 2022 (SI 2022/177) inserts the following definition:

"adult disability payment" has the meaning given in regulation 2 of the Disability Assistance for Working Age People (Scotland) Regulations 2022;

With effect from July 9, 2023, reg.2 of the Social Security (Income and Capital Disregards) (Amendment) Regulations 2023 (SI 2023/640) amends reg.2 as follows:

- for the definition of "Grenfell Tower payment" substitute—
  ""Grenfell Tower payment" means a payment made for the purpose of providing compensation or support in respect of the fire on 14th June 2017 at Grenfell Tower;";
- insert the following definitions:
  - "the Horizon system" means any version of the computer system used by the Post Office known as Horizon, Horizon Legacy, Horizon Online or HNG-X;
  - "the Post Office" means Post Office Limited (registered number 02154540);
  - "Post Office compensation payment" means a payment made by the Post Office or the Secretary of State for the purpose of providing compensation or support which is—
    (a) in connection with the failings of the Horizon system; or
    (b) otherwise payable following the judgment in Bates and Others v Post Office Ltd ((No. 3) "Common Issues")(10);
  - "vaccine damage payment" means a payment made under the Vaccine Damage Payments Act 1979(11);";
- in the definition of "qualifying person", for "or a Windrush payment" substitute ", a Windrush payment, a Post Office compensation payment or a vaccine damage payment".

With effect from October 27, 2023, reg.3 of the Social Security (Habitual Residence and Past Presence, and Capital Disregards) (Amendment) Regulations 2023 (SI 2023/1144) amends reg.2 as follows:

- in the definition of "qualifying person", after "the National Emergencies Trust" insert ", the Victims of Overseas Terrorism Compensation Scheme";
- insert the following definition:

"the Victims of Overseas Terrorism Compensation Scheme" means the scheme of that name established by the Ministry of Justice in 2012 under section 47 of the Crime and Security Act 2010;

With effect from November 19, 2023, art.5 of the Carer's Assistance (Carer Support Payment) (Scotland) Regulations 2023 (Consequential Amendments) Order 2023 (SI 2023/1218) amends reg.2 as follows:

after the definition of "care home" insert—

""carer support payment" means carer's assistance given in accordance with the Carer's Assistance (Carer Support Payment) (Scotland) Regulations 2023;".

p.275, *amendments to the Income Support (General) Regulations 1987 (SI 1987/1967) reg.4 (Temporary absence from Great Britain)*

6.010   With effect from July 26, 2021, Sch.1 para.3 of the Social Security (Scotland) Act 2018 (Disability Assistance for Children and Young People)

(Consequential Modifications) Order 2021 (SI 2021/786) makes the following amendment:

> In reg.4(2)(c)(v)(aa) after "allowance", insert ", the care component of child disability payment at the highest rate in accordance with the DACYP Regulations (see regulation 11(5) of those Regulations)".

With effect from March 21, 2022, art.2(3) of the Social Security (Disability Assistance for Working Age People) (Consequential Amendments) Order 2022 (SI 2022/177) makes the following amendment:

> In reg.4(2)(c)(v)(aa) (temporary absence from Great Britain):
> (a) for "or" after "armed forces independence payment" substitute ",";
> (b) after "personal independence payment" insert "or the enhanced rate of the daily living component of adult disability payment".

p.314, *annotation to the Income Support (General) Regulations 1987 (SI 1987/1967) reg.17 (Applicable amounts)*

The Social Security (Coronavirus) (Further Measures) Regulations 2020 (SI 2020/371), followed by the Universal Credit (Extension of Coronavirus Measures) Regulations 2021 (SI 2021/313), had the effect that for the 18 months to October 2021, the standard allowances of UC were uplifted by £20 per week. Similar measures were employed for working tax credit: the Coronavirus Act 2020 s.77, followed by the Coronavirus Act 2020 Functions of Her Majesty's Revenue and Customs (Covid-19 support scheme: working households receiving tax credits) Direction (7 April 2021).   6.011

Recipients of IS, ESA and JSA did not receive an uplift. In *R. (T) v Secretary of State for Work and Pensions,* the legality of this differential treatment was challenged (unsuccessfully) as being unlawfully discriminatory contrary to the ECHR.

In [2022] EWHC 351 (Admin) (18 February 2022) the High Court: (i) rejected the claim that there was unlawful discrimination against people with the status of being a legacy benefit claimant, on the basis that being a legacy benefit claimant was not a status within the scope of ECHR art.14 (paras 22–24); and (ii) rejected the claim that there was unlawful discrimination against disabled people, on the basis that the discrimination was justified (paras 30–38). Permission to appeal to the Court of Appeal was refused on point (i) but given on point (ii). In [2023] EWCA Civ 24 (17 January 2023), the Court of Appeal confirmed that the disability discrimination was justified. The Secretary of State's focus was on prioritising people likely to be facing a recent reduction in income, and on adopting an approach she considered technically practicable (paras 53–54). In that context, the High Court did not err by deciding that the limitation of uplift to UC and WTC was a proportionate means of achieving a legitimate aim.

pp.329–331, *amendment to the Income Support (General) Regulations 1987 (SI 1987/1967) reg.21AA (Special cases: supplemental—persons from abroad)*

The text in the main volume at para.2.167 should be replaced with the following: 6.012

"[¹ Special cases: supplemental—persons from abroad

21AA.—(1) "Person from abroad" means, subject to the following provisions of this regulation, a claimant who is not habitually resident in the United Kingdom, the Channel Islands, the Isle of Man or the Republic of Ireland.

(2) No claimant shall be treated as habitually resident in the United Kingdom, the Channel Islands, the Isle of Man or the Republic of Ireland unless he has a right to reside in (as the case may be) the United Kingdom, the Channel Islands, the Isle of Man or the Republic of Ireland other than a right to reside which falls within paragraph (3) [¹² or (3A)].

(3) A right to reside falls within this paragraph if it is one which exists by virtue of, or in accordance with, one or more of the following—

(a) regulation 13 of the [¹² Immigration (European Economic Area) Regulations 2016];

(b) regulation 14 of those Regulations, but only in a case where the right exists under that regulation because the claimant is—

(i) a jobseeker for the purpose of the definition of "qualified person" in regulation 6(1) of those Regulations, or

(ii) a family member (within the meaning of regulation 7 of those Regulations) of such a jobseeker; [¹⁴ or]

[⁷[¹²(bb) regulation 16 of those Regulations, but only in a case where the right exists under that regulation because the claimant satisfies the criteria in paragraph (5) of that regulation;]]

[¹⁴ (c)–(e) . . .]

[¹² (3A) A right to reside falls within this paragraph if it exists by virtue of a claimant having been granted limited leave to enter, or remain in, the United Kingdom under the Immigration Act 1971 by virtue of—

(a) Appendix EU to the immigration rules made under section 3(2) of that Act; [¹⁵ . . .]

(b) being a person with a Zambrano right to reside as defined in Annex 1 of Appendix EU to the immigration rules made under section 3(2) of that Act.][¹⁵; or

(c) having arrived in the United Kingdom with an entry clearance that was granted under Appendix EU (Family Permit) to the immigration rules made under section 3(2) of that Act.]

[¹³ (3B) Paragraph (3A)(a) does not apply to a person who—

(a) has a right to reside granted by virtue of being a family member of a relevant person of Northern Ireland; and

(b) would have a right to reside under the [¹² Immigration (European Economic Area) Regulations 2016] if the relevant person of Northern Ireland were an EEA national, provided that the right to reside does not fall within paragraph (3).]

(4) A claimant is not a person from abroad if he is—

[¹⁷(zza) a person granted leave in accordance with the immigration rules made under section 3(2) of the Immigration Act 1971, where such leave is granted by virtue of—

(i) the Afghan Relocations and Assistance Policy; or

(ii) the previous scheme for locally-employed staff in Afghanistan (sometimes referred to as the ex-gratia scheme);

(zzb) a person in Great Britain not coming within sub-paragraph (zza) or [¹⁸ (h)] who left Afghanistan in connection with the collapse of the Afghan government that took place on 15th August 2021;]

[[18](zzc) a person in Great Britain who was residing in Ukraine immediately before 1st January 2022, left Ukraine in connection with the Russian invasion which took place on 24th February 2022 and—
    (i) has been granted leave in accordance with immigration rules made under section 3(2) of the Immigration Act 1971; [[19] . . .]
    (ii) has a right of abode in the United Kingdom within the meaning given in section 2 of that Act;] [[19] or
    (iii) does not require leave to enter or remain in the United Kingdom in accordance with section 3ZA of that Act;]
[[20](zzd) a person who was residing in Sudan before 15th April 2023, left Sudan in connection with the violence which rapidly escalated on 15th April 2023 in Khartoum and across Sudan and—
    (i) has been granted leave in accordance with immigration rules made under section 3(2) of the Immigration Act 1971;
    (ii) has a right of abode in the United Kingdom within the meaning given in section 2 of that Act; or
    (iii) does not require leave to enter or remain in the United Kingdom in accordance with section 3ZA of that Act;]
[[21](zze) a person who was residing in Israel, the West Bank, the Gaza Strip, East Jerusalem, the Golan Heights or Lebanon immediately before 7th October 2023, who left Israel, the West Bank, the Gaza Strip, East Jerusalem, the Golan Heights or Lebanon in connection with the Hamas terrorist attack in Israel on 7th October 2023 or the violence which rapidly escalated in the region following the attack and—
    (i) has been granted leave in accordance with immigration rules made under section 3(2) of the Immigration Act 1971;
    (ii) has a right of abode in the United Kingdom within the meaning given in section 2 of that Act; or
    (iii) does not require leave to enter or remain in the United Kingdom in accordance with section 3ZA of that Act;]
[[10](za) a qualified person for the purposes of [[16] regulation 6 of the Immigration (European Economic Area) Regulations 2016] as a worker or a self-employed person;
  (zb) a family member of a person referred to in sub-paragraph (za) [[13] . . .];
  (zc) a person who has a right to reside permanently in the United Kingdom by virtue of regulation 15(1)(c), (d) or (e) of those Regulations;]
[[13](zd) a family member of a relevant person of Northern Ireland, with a right to reside which falls within paragraph (3A)(a), provided that the relevant person of Northern Ireland falls within sub-paragraph (za), or would do so but for the fact that they are not an EEA national;]
[[14](ze) a frontier worker within the meaning of regulation 3 of the Citizens' Rights (Frontier Workers) (EU Exit) Regulations 2020;
  (zf) a family member, of a person referred to in sub-paragraph (ze), who has been granted limited leave to enter, or remain in, the United Kingdom by virtue of Appendix EU to the immigration rules made under section 3(2) of the Immigration Act 1971;]
  (g) a refugee within the definition in Article 1 of the Convention relating to the Status of Refugees done at Geneva on 28th July 1951, as extended by Article 1(2) of the Protocol relating to the Status of Refugees done at New York on 31st January 1967;

[³[⁹(h) a person who has been granted leave or who is deemed to have been granted leave outside the rules made under section 3(2) of the Immigration Act 1971 [¹⁸ . . .];

(hh) a person who has humanitarian protection granted under those rules;] [⁹ or]

(i) a person who is not a person subject to immigration control within the meaning of section 115(9) of the Immigration and Asylum Act and who is in the United Kingdom as a result of his deportation, expulsion or other removal by compulsion of law from another country to the United Kingdom; [⁵ . . .] [⁹ . . .]

[¹³ (5) In this regulation—

"EEA national" has the meaning given in regulation 2(1) of the Immigration (European Economic Area) Regulations 2016;

"family member" has the meaning given in regulation 7(1)(a), (b) or (c) of the Immigration (European Economic Area) Regulations 2016 except that regulation 7(4) of those Regulations does not apply for the purposes of paragraphs (3B) and (4)(zd);

"relevant person of Northern Ireland" has the meaning given in Annex 1 of Appendix EU to the immigration rules made under section 3(2) of the Immigration Act 1971.]

[¹⁴ (6) In this regulation references to the Immigration (European Economic Area) Regulations 2016 are to be read with Schedule 4 to the Immigration and Social Security Co-ordination (EU Withdrawal) Act 2020 (Consequential, Saving, Transitional and Transitory Provisions) Regulations 2020.]"

AMENDMENTS

1. Social Security (Persons from Abroad) Amendment Regulations 2006 (SI 1026/2006) reg.6(3) (April 30, 2006).

2. Social Security (Lebanon) Amendment Regulations 2006 (SI 2006/1981) reg.2 (July 25, 2006). The amendment ceased to have effect from January 31, 2007.

3. Social Security (Persons from Abroad) Amendment (No. 2) Regulations 2006 (SI 2006/2528) reg.2 (October 9, 2006).

4. Social Security (Bulgaria and Romania) Amendment Regulations 2006 (SI 2006/3341) reg.2 (January 1, 2007).

5. Social Security (Habitual Residence) (Amendment) Regulations 2009 (SI 2009/362) reg.2 (March 18, 2009).

6. Social Security (Miscellaneous Amendments) (No. 3) Regulations 2011 (SI 2011/2425) reg.7(1) and (3) (October 31, 2011).

7. Social Security (Habitual Residence) (Amendment) Regulations 2012 (SI 2012/2587) reg.2 (November 8, 2012).

8. Social Security (Croatia) Amendment Regulations 2013 (SI 2013/1474) reg.2 (July 1, 2013).

9. Social Security (Miscellaneous Amendments) (No. 3) Regulations 2013 (SI 2013/2536) reg.4(1) and (5) (October 29, 2013).

10. Social Security (Habitual Residence) (Amendment) Regulations 2014 (SI 2014/902) reg.2(1) (May 31, 2014).

11. Social Security (Updating of EU References) (Amendment) Regulations 2018 (SI 2018/1084) reg.4 and Sch. para.6 (November 15, 2018).

12. Social Security (Income-related Benefits) (Updating and Amendment) (EU Exit) Regulations 2019 (SI 2019/872) reg.2 (May 7, 2019).

13. Social Security (Income-Related Benefits) (Persons of Northern Ireland—Family Members) (Amendment) Regulations 2020 (SI 2020/683) reg.2 (August 24, 2020).

14. Immigration and Social Security Co-ordination (EU Withdrawal) Act 2020 (Consequential, Saving, Transitional and Transitory Provisions) (EU Exit) Regulations 2020 (SI 2020/1309) reg.53 (December 31, 2020 at 11.00pm).

15. Immigration (Citizens' Rights etc.) (EU Exit) Regulations 2020 (SI 2020/1372) reg.8 (December 31, 2020 at 11.00 pm).

16. Social Security (Income-related Benefits) (Updating and Amendment) (EU Exit) Regulations (SI 2019/872) reg.2 (May 7, 2019).

17. Social Security (Habitual Residence and Past Presence) (Amendment) Regulations 2021 (SI 2021/1034) reg.2 (September 15, 2021).

18. Social Security (Habitual Residence and Past Presence) (Amendment) Regulations 2022 (SI 2022/344) reg.2 (March 22, 2022).

19. Social Security (Habitual Residence and Past Presence) (Amendment) (No. 2) Regulations 2022 (SI 2022/990) reg.2 (October 18, 2022).

20. Social Security (Habitual Residence and Past Presence) (Amendment) Regulations 2023 (SI 2023/532), reg.2 (May 15, 2023).

21. Social Security (Habitual Residence and Past Presence, and Capital Disregards) (Amendment) Regulations 2023, reg.2 (SI 2023/1144) (October 27, 2023).

p.355, *annotation to the Income Support (General) Regulations 1987 (SI 1987/1967) reg.23 (Calculation of the income and capital of members of claimant's family and of a polygamous marriage)*

In line 4 of p.355, for "on the exclusion of", substitute "so as to exclude" and in line 5 for "s.11", substitute "ss.11 and 12". 6.013

p.385, *annotation to the Income Support (General) Regulations 1987 (SI 1987/1967) reg.35(1)(d) (Earnings of employed earners—holiday pay)*

Replace the second paragraph of 2.265 (starting "Holiday pay") with the following:

Holiday pay outside this sub-paragraph is to be treated as capital (reg.48(3)), with no disregard. It then appears that it cannot be taken into account as actual income, whether it would in the absence of reg.48(3) be regarded as earnings under the general meaning in reg.35(1) or as income other than earnings. In either case there is also a disregard (Sch.8, paras 1–2, and Sch.9, para.32). 6.014

p.396, *annotation to the Income Support (General) Regulations 1987 (SI 1987/1967) reg.37 (Earnings of self-employed earners*

The two Business Interruption Loan Schemes and the Bounce Back Loan Scheme ceased to operate on March 31, 2021, to be replaced by the Recovery Loan Scheme. 6.015

p.412, *annotation to the Income Support (General) Regulations 1987 (SI 1987/1967) reg.40(1) (Calculation of income other than earnings)*

Add to the non-exhaustive list of benefits disregarded as income under Sch.9, various Scottish benefits (paras 81–87 of Sch.9). 6.016

p.421, *amendment to the Income Support (General) Regulations 1987 (SI 1987/1967) reg.42(4ZB) (Notional income—exceptions)*

6.017 With effect from January 1, 2022, reg.2(3) of the Social Security (Income and Capital Disregards) (Amendment) Regulations 2021 (SI 2021/1405) amended para.(4ZB) by substituting the following for "a payment of income which is a Grenfell Tower payment":

"any of the following payments of income—

(a) a Grenfell Tower payment;
(b) a child abuse payment;
(c) a Windrush payment."

All of those payments are defined in reg.2(1). See the entry for p.684 for discussion of the nature of child abuse and Windrush payments.

With effect from July 9, 2023, reg.2(3) of the Social Security (Income and Capital Disregards) (Amendment) Regulations 2023 (SI 2023/640) amended reg.42(4ZA) by inserting the following after sub-para.(c):

"(d) a Post Office compensation payment."

Such payments are newly defined in reg.2(1), where there is now also an expanded definition of Grenfell Tower payments. See the entry for pp.451–452 of Vol.II in this Supplement for the background.

pp.431–433, *annotation to the Income Support (General) Regulations 1987 (SI 1987/1967) reg.42(4) and (4ZA) (Notional income—third parties)*

6.018 Note the extended exception to the operation of para.(4) (see the entry for p.421).

p.438, *annotation to the Income Support (General) Regulations 1987 (SI 1987/967) reg.45 (Capital limit)*

6.019 In the Institute for Government and the Social Security Advisory Committee's 2021 joint report *Jobs and benefits: The Covid-19 challenge* it was noted that if the capital limit of £16,000 had risen in line with prices since 2006 it would be close to £23,500 (or £25,000: different figures are given) and recommended that the limit should be increased to £25,000 and subsequently automatically indexed to maintain its real value (pp.22 and 31). That recommendation was summarily rejected in the Government's response of March 22, 2022.

p.439, *annotation to the Income Support (General) Regulations 1987 (SI 1987/1967) reg.46 (Calculation of capital)*

6.020 At some point, the valuation of digital assets, such as non-fungible tokens, cryptocurrency etc., may have to be addressed, including how they fit into the notions of capital and of personal possessions. There is extensive discussion of the existing legal framework in the Law Commission's *Digital Assets: Consultation Paper* (Law Com. No.256, July 28, 2022). Now see *Digital Assets: Final report* (Law Com. No.412, June 27, 2023).

pp.440–441, *annotation to the Income Support (General) Regulations 1987 (SI 1987/1967) reg.46 (Calculation of capital)*

The text in the paragraph starting "See also" on p.440 to the paragraph ending "had ceased." on p.441 should be deleted.

6.021

Insert the following text on p.441 between the paragraph starting "However" and the heading *"Beneficial ownership"*:

Interests under a will or intestacy when someone has died

The DMG (paras 29169–29175) contains guidance adopting in para.29174 the general principle that a beneficiary under a will or intestacy has no legal or equitable interest in any specific property while the estate remains unadministered. The personal representative in those circumstances has full ownership of the assets of the estate. That principle was applied by the Tribunal of Commissioners in *R(SB) 5/85*, relying on the foundational Privy Council decision in *Commissioner of Stamp Duties (Queensland) v Livingston* [1965] A.C. 694.

However, there are two important qualifications. The first is that, even where the *Livingston* principle applies, the beneficiary has a right to have the deceased's estate properly administered. That is a chose in action that has a market value. It can be transferred and can be borrowed against. Depending on the particular circumstances, the market value can be considerable and not far off the value that would be put on the asset(s) in question if owned outright. That point was made clearly by Commissioner Howell in para.28 of his decision in *R(IS) 1/01* and nothing to the contrary was said in the Court of Appeal in *Wilkinson v Chief Adjudication Officer*, reported as part of *R(IS) 1/01*, in upholding the Commissioner's decision. Nor is *R(SB) 5/85* to the contrary: the Commissioners there expressly noted that the claimant had a chose in action (para.7). It is submitted that that is the basis on which the later decision of Commissioner Howell in *CIS/1189/2003* is to be supported. The claimant there was the sole residuary beneficiary under her mother's will and the estate, whose main asset was a property that the claimant did not live in, remained unadministered for several years, so that the property had not actually vested in the claimant. In para.11, the Commissioner said that the claimant was beneficially entitled to the property from the date of her mother's death subject only to the formalities needed to perfect her title, so that for all practical purposes she had an entitlement equivalent to full beneficial ownership. That proposition can easily be misinterpreted, but in para.12, the Commissioner noted that as the claimant was the sole *residuary* beneficiary, it was para.28 of *R(IS) 1/01* that was applicable. So the valuation was of the claimant's chose in action, but in the circumstances the difference in value from that of full beneficial ownership was negligible.

The second qualification is that the position may be different where there has been a specific gift of some asset, as was the case in *R(IS) 1/01*, where the will of the claimant's mother gave the claimant and her brother equal shares in some income bonds and other money in a bank account and in a property. The matter was put very strongly by Commissioner Howell in para.27 of his decision, where he said that the *Livingston* principle had:

"never had any application to property specifically devised or bequeathed by a will. Such property becomes in equity the property of the legatee as soon as the testator dies, subject only to the right of the personal representative to resort to it for payment of debts if the remainder of the estate is insufficient for this purpose [citations omitted]."

No specific comment on that proposition was made in the judgments of the Court of Appeal in *Wilkinson*, but Mummery LJ did note generally that the evidence did not suggest that there was any question of the executors needing to have recourse to the property for payment of debts or that there was any other legal obstacle to the immediate completion of the administration of the estate and to an assent by the executors vesting the property in the names of the claimant and her brother as joint owners. That strongly suggests that what was being considered was a valuation of the claimant's chose in action, rather than of some equitable interest. It is submitted that that is the proper approach. The valuation would therefore be sensitive to the possibilities mentioned by Mummery LJ in the particular case, as well as to the value of the underlying asset. That approach would hold also for personal property or money, although there it should be noted that the process of the personal representative giving an assent, i.e. an indication that a certain asset is not required for administration purposes and may pass under the will or (possibly) an intestacy into the ownership of the beneficiary, does not need to be in writing and may be implied from conduct.

p.443, *annotation to the Income Support (General) Regulations 1987 (SI 1987/967) reg. 46 (Calculation of capital—claimant holding as trustee)*

6.022   In line 10 of the paragraph starting "One particular", insert the following between "return it" and the full stop:

"(a result most recently confirmed by the decision of the Privy Council in the *Prickly Bay* case)"

p.446, *annotation to the Income Support (General) Regulations 1987 (SI 1987/967) reg. 46 (Calculation of capital—claimant holding as trustee)*

6.023   Note, in relation to the discussion of cases in which the *Quistclose* principle has or has not been applied, that the Privy Council in *Prickly Bay Waterside Ltd v British American Insurance Co Ltd* [2022] UKPC 8; [2022] 1 W.L.R. 2087, while accepting the value of summaries of principles, in particular of those established by the judgment of Lord Millett in *Twinsectra Ltd v Yardley* [2002] 2 A.C. 164, warned against not going back to the "core analysis" in that judgment. It was emphasised again that it is not enough that money is provided for a particular purpose. The question is whether the parties intended that the money should be at the free disposition of the recipient. An intention that it should not be need not be mutual, in the sense of being shared or reciprocated, but could be imposed by one party and acquiesced in by the other. A *Quistclose* trust is a default trust, so can be excluded or moulded by the terms of the parties' express agreements. In the particular case, involving complex commercial transactions in which a sum was loaned to a bank that contracted to guarantee payment of the purchase price of a property on future completion, it was significant to the outcome that a *Quistclose* trust had not been established that there had been no requirement that the sum be segregated by the bank from its other funds. It is submitted that in other contexts, such as family or other relatively informal arrangements more likely to be encountered in the social security context, a lack of segregation, say into a separate account, would not carry nearly such weight.

p.451, *annotation to the Income Support (General) Regulations 1987 (SI 1987/1967) reg.46 (Calculation of capital—claimant holding as trustee)*

Note the decision of the Supreme Court, by a majority of three to two, in   6.024
Guest v Guest [2022] UKSC 27; [2022] 3 W.L.R. 911 on proprietary estoppel and the nature of the remedies available in equity. Lord Briggs, giving the majority judgment, conducted an exhaustive survey of the English and Australian case law, as well as academic debate, and rejected the theory that the aim of the remedy was to compensate the person given a promise or assurance about the acquisition of property for the detriment suffered in reliance on the promise or assurance, rather than primarily to hold the person who had given the promise or assurance to the promise or assurance, which would usually prevent the unconscionability inherent in the repudiation of the promise or assurance that had been detrimentally relied on (paras 71 and 61). However, the remedy was a flexible one dependent on the circumstances. Lord Briggs summarised the principles as follows:

"74. I consider that, in principle, the court's normal approach should be as follows. The first stage (which is not in issue in this case) is to determine whether the promisor's repudiation of his promise is, in the light of the promisee's detrimental reliance upon it, unconscionable at all. It usually will be, but there may be circumstances (such as the promisor falling on hard times and needing to sell the property to pay his creditors, or to pay for expensive medical treatment or social care for himself or his wife) when it may not be. Or the promisor may have announced or carried out only a partial repudiation of the promise, which may or may not have been unconscionable, depending on the circumstances.

75. The second (remedy) stage will normally start with the assumption (not presumption) that the simplest way to remedy the unconscionability constituted by the repudiation is to hold the promisor to the promise. The promisee cannot (and probably would not) complain, for example, that his detrimental reliance had cost him more than the value of the promise, were it to be fully performed. But the court may have to listen to many other reasons from the promisor (or his executors) why something less than full performance will negate the unconscionability and therefore satisfy the equity. They may be based on one or more of the real-life problems already outlined. The court may be invited by the promisor to consider one or more proxies for performance of the promise, such as the transfer of less property than promised or the provision of a monetary equivalent in place of it, or a combination of the two.

76. If the promisor asserts and proves, the burden being on him for this purpose, that specific enforcement of the full promise, or monetary equivalent, would be out of all proportion to the cost of the detriment to the promisee, then the court may be constrained to limit the extent of the remedy. This does not mean that the court will be seeking precisely to compensate for the detriment as its primary task, but simply to put right a

disproportionality which is so large as to stand in the way of a full specific enforcement doing justice between the parties. It will be a very rare case where the detriment is equivalent in value to the expectation, and there is nothing in principle unjust in a full enforcement of the promise being worth more than the cost of the detriment, any more than there is in giving specific performance of a contract for the sale of land merely because it is worth more than the price paid for it. An example of a remedy out of all proportion to the detriment would be the full enforcement of a promise by an elderly lady to leave her carer a particular piece of jewellery if she stayed on at very low wages, which turned out on valuation by her execu-tors to be a Faberge worth millions. Another would be a promise to leave a generous inheritance if the promisee cared for the promisor for the rest of her life, but where she unexpectedly died two months later."

Thus, in circumstances where proprietary estoppel might be in play (as would probably now be the case on similar facts to *R(SB) 23/85* and *R(SB) 7/87*), great care would be needed in establishing the primary facts and, outside the clearest cases, in a deeper investigation of the principles of law governing the nature of any remedy available. And would a repudia-tion of a promise when the promisor would otherwise be forced to rely on a means-tested benefit be unconscionable? However, even if it were to be concluded that the claimant did not hold the property in question on trust for someone else, the possibility of a claim in equity, e.g. for some monetary compensation, may well affect the valuation of the property.

p.457, *amendment to the Income Support (General) Regulations 1987 (SI 1987/1967) reg.48(10) (Income treated as capital—exceptions)*

6.025   With effect from January 1, 2022, reg.2(4) of the Social Security (Income and Capital Disregards) (Amendment) Regulations 2021 (SI 2021/1405) amended para.(10) by inserting the following after sub-para.(ab):

> "(ac) which is a child abuse payment;
> (ad) which is a Windrush payment; or"

Both of those payments are defined in reg.2(1). See the entry for p.684 for discussion of their nature. The "or" following sub-para.(ab), omitted in error in the main volume, has also been removed.

With effect from July 9, 2023, reg.2(4) of the Social Security (Income and Capital Disregards) (Amendment) Regulations 2023 (SI 2023/640) amended reg.48(10) by omitting "or" at the end of sub-para.(ad) and inserting the following:

> "(ae) which is a Post Office compensation payment."

Such payments are newly defined in reg.2(1), where there is now also an expanded definition of Grenfell Tower payments (see sub-para.(ab)). See the entry for pp.451–452 of Vol.II in this Supplement.

With effect from October 27, 2023, reg.3(3)(a) of the Social Security (Habitual Residence and Past Presence, and Capital Disregards) (Amendment) Regulations 2023 (SI 2023/1144) amended reg.48(10)(c) by inserting ", the Victims of Overseas Terrorism Compensation Scheme" after "the National Emergencies Trust". That scheme is newly defined in reg.2(1). See the entry for pp.684–685 for the background.

p.467, *amendment to the Income Support (General) Regulations 1987 (SI 1987/1967) reg.51(3A) and (3B) (Notional capital—exceptions)*

With effect from January 1, 2022, reg.2(5) of the Social Security (Income and Capital Disregards) (Amendment) Regulations 2021 (SI 2021/1405) amended para.(3B) by substituting the following for "a payment of capital which is a Grenfell Tower payment":   6.026

"any of the following payments of capital—
  (a) a Grenfell Tower payment;
  (b) a child abuse payment;
  (c) a Windrush payment."

All of those payments are defined in reg.2(1). See the entry for p.684 for discussion of the nature of child abuse and Windrush payments.

With effect from July 9, 2023, reg.2(5) of the Social Security (Income and Capital Disregards) (Amendment) Regulations 2023 (SI 2023/640) amended reg.51(3B) by inserting the following after sub-para.(c):

"(d) a Post Office compensation payment;
  (f) a vaccine damage payment."

Such payments are newly defined in reg.2(1), where there is now also an expanded definition of Grenfell Tower payments (see sub-para.(a)). See the entry for pp.451–452 of Vol.II in this Supplement.

With effect from October 27, 2023, reg.3(3)(b) of the Social Security (Habitual Residence and Past Presence, and Capital Disregards) (Amendment) Regulations 2023 (SI 2023/1144) amended reg.51(3A)(a) by inserting ", the Victims of Overseas Terrorism Compensation Scheme" after "the National Emergencies Trust". That scheme is newly defined in reg.2(1). See the entry for pp.684–685 for the background.

p.482, *annotation to the Income Support (General) Regulations 1987 (SI 1987/1967) reg.51(1) (Notional capital—deprivation)*

See the entry for pp.1029–30 for the acceptance of the position under reg.113(1) of the JSA Regulations 1996 in *DB v DfC (JSA)* [2021] NICom 43. There, it was found that the claimant had deprived herself of capital while in receipt of income-related ESA. It was inherently improbable that when doing so, more than a year before she claimed JSA, she had possible entitlement to JSA or income support in mind. The tribunal had failed to make necessary findings of fact in concluding that her purpose had been the securing of entitlement to JSA. The principle would apply even more so to reg.51(1), where the test of purpose is still restricted to income support (but contrast the position reg.115(1) of the ESA Regulations 2008).   6.027

The decision also illustrates that on a new claim neither the decision-maker nor a tribunal on appeal is bound by the findings of fact on capital that have underpinned a decision of non-entitlement on capital grounds. The basis of the ESA decision, that the claimant as at that date still had actual capital of more than £40,000, did not have to be adopted on the JSA claim.

pp.520–523, *annotations to the Income Support (General) Regulations 1987 (SI 1987/1967) reg.61 (Interpretation—students—meaning of "Full-time course")*

6.028   The principles derived from the case law, taking into account Court of Appeal decisions not all of which are discussed in the main volume, have recently very helpfully been summarised by Judge Rowley in para.19 of *BK v SSWP (UC)* [2022] UKUT 73 (AAC) (some references added by annotator):

"a. Whether or not a person is undertaking a full-time course is a question of fact for the tribunal having regard to the circumstances in each particular case (*R/SB 40/83* at [13]; *R(SB) 41/83* at [12]). Parameters have been set, as appear below:

b. The words 'full-time' relate to the course and not to the student. Specifically, they do not permit the matter to be determined by reference to the amount of time which the student happens to dedicate to their studies (*R/SB 40/83* at [14], [15]; *R(SB) 2/91* at [7]; *R(SB) 41/83* at [11]).

c. Evidence from the educational establishment as to whether or not the course is full-time is not necessarily conclusive, but it ought to be accepted as such unless it is inconclusive on its face, or is challenged by relevant evidence which at least raises the possibility that it ought to be rejected (*R/SB 40/83* at [18]), and any evidence adduced in rebuttal should be weighty in content (*R/SB 41/83* at [12]). See also *Flemming v Secretary of State for Work and Pensions* [2002] EWCA Civ 641; [2002] 1 W.L.R. 2322 [also reported as *R(G) 2/02*] at [21]–[22] and [38]; and *Deane v Secretary of State for Work and Pensions* [2010] EWCA Civ 699; [2011] 1 W.L.R. 743 [also reported at [2010] AACR 42] where the Court of Appeal repeated an earlier statement in *Flemming* that:

"38 . . . A tribunal of fact should, I think be very slow to accept that a person expects or intends to devote—or does, in fact, devote—significantly less time to the course than those who have conduct of the course expect of him, and very slow to hold that a person who is attending a course considered by the educational establishment to be a part-time course is to be treated as receiving full-time education because he devotes significantly more time than that which is expected of him . . . "

d. If the course is offered as a full-time course, the presumption is that the recipient is in full-time education. There may be exceptions to the rule, such where a student is granted exemptions from part of the course: *Deane* [51]."

In *BK* itself, the claimant was on a one-year MA course at Goldsmiths, University of London, described by that institution as full-time and involving more than 24 hours of study per week. Letters from the Department concerned confirmed six contact hours of teaching in two terms, with an expectation of at least six hours per week in independent study. A dissertation was to be written in the third term. The First-tier Tribunal rejected the claimant's argument that those letters, and the fact that he could arrange his time to be available for work, showed that the course was not full-time. Judge Rowley held that it did not err in law in doing so and that in saying that Goldsmiths' description was "determinative" of the nature of the course it had not strayed into regarding the description as conclusive, but had applied the test in para.19(c) above.

p.526, *annotation to the Income Support (General) Regulations 1987 (SI 1987/1967) reg.61 (Interpretation—"postgraduate loan")*

The value of a postgraduate loan under the English scheme described (there are different schemes for other UK countries) has been increased to £11,836 for courses starting on or after August 1, 2022 and to £12,167 for courses starting on or after August 1, 2023.

6.029

p.527, *annotation to the Income Support (General) Regulations 1987 (SI 1987/1967) reg.61 (Interpretation—student loan)*

See the entry for p.539 below.

6.030

p.539, *annotation to the Income Support (General) Regulations 1987 (SI 1987/1967) reg.66A (Treatment of student loans and postgraduate loans)*

See, in relation to the housing benefit equivalent of the rule in reg.66A(3)(b) and (4) treating students as possessing the maximum student or postgraduate loan in respect of an academic year that they could acquire by taking reasonable steps to do so, the decision of Judge Poynter in *IB v Gravesham BC and SSWP (HB)* [2023] UKUT 193 (AAC); [2024] P.T.S.R. 130 declining to follow *CH/4429/2006*. There, Commissioner Powell had held that "reasonable" qualified only the mechanical steps that had to be taken to acquire a loan and was not concerned with matters such as the motives or religious beliefs of the claimant. The facts of IB were on all fours with those of *CH/4429/2006*, in that the claimant was a devout and observant Muslim, who did not take out student loans otherwise available to him because that would have involved the paying of interest, which he conscientiously believed was forbidden by his religion. Nonetheless, the local authority treated him as possessing income from the loans, so that he failed the housing benefit means test. That decision was upheld by the First-tier Tribunal, considering itself bound by *CH/4429/2006*. The Upper Tribunal substituted the decision that on the particular facts the claimant's entitlement to housing benefit was to be recalculated on the basis that he did not possess any income from the loans that he had not applied for.

6.031

The judge's view was that the reasoning in *CH/4429/2006* proceeded on a false basis and contained additional errors of logic. The Commissioner had stated in para.4 that the practical effect of the provision was that a student who was "entitled to a student loan", the use of which words was said to be deliberate, was to suffer a diminution in the amount of housing benefit. That was the apparent basis for the conclusion about the meaning of reasonable steps in para.11 of his decision. The judge points out that those words do not appear anywhere in the applicable Regulations, and that the test actually set out is in terms of what could be acquired by taking reasonable steps and does not assume the making of an application. A straightforward analysis of the steps that would be necessary to acquire a student loan would include scrutinising the terms on which the loan was offered, deciding whether to accept those terms and, if so, completing and submitting the application form and finally signing an agreement accepting the paying of interest. The judge concludes that the steps to be considered under the regulation therefore cannot be restricted to the "mechanical", the particular question of whether to accept the terms being one that would involve issues of judgment for anyone (e.g.

about whether to accept the future burden of debt and interest payments). Moreover, while the Commissioner had noted that it was difficult to see how the necessary steps to acquire a loan could in themselves be said to be unreasonable except in the most exceptional cases, Judge Poynter suggests that, if personal circumstances were to be ignored, it would be inconceivable that the mechanics of applying for a student loan could ever require students to take steps that were unreasonable. In order for the words "reasonable steps" to be given some practical application, as must be assumed to have been intended, the interpretation adopted in *CH/4429/2006* could not be correct. For those and other subsidiary reasons, the judge declined to follow that decision.

Judge Poynter formulated the correct test to be applied, without the *CH/4429/2006* limitation and in line with the established approach in other areas of social security law, as follows:

> "139. I therefore conclude that "reasonable steps" means steps that are reasonable in all the circumstances including all the personal characteristics of the individual who was eligible to have applied for the student loan. That includes strong conscientious religious or other objections to the payment of interest.
> 140. I would, however, add that all the circumstances includes the interests of the wider public as represented by the Secretary of State and that assessing reasonableness will need to give those interests weight (see paragraphs 190–191 below). Without being prescriptive, I suggest that an omission to acquire a loan that is based on purely financial considerations is unlikely to outweigh those interests."

He rejected the Secretary of State's submission that that approach would involve direct discrimination against claimants who did not share his particular religious views. That was because (para.142):

> "[t]he line drawn by my interpretation is not between Muslims and non-Muslims nor even between people who have conscientious objections to taking out a student loan and those who don't. Rather it is between, on the one hand, any student whose personal circumstances as a whole are such that—for whatever reason—he cannot take reasonable steps to acquire a student loan and, on the other, all students who are not so circumstanced. Those two groups are not in analogous situations. The latter could reasonably acquire the loan that [the regulation] takes into account as their income. The former cannot."

The judge also rejected the submission that his interpretation would make the housing benefit scheme unworkable and invite numerous, possibly opportunistic, claims, pointing out the limited scope for students to qualify for housing benefit (as for other means-tested benefits, including income support), the fact that to benefit from the rule the claimant would have to turn down the advantages of actually receiving the loan on offer and the difficulties that claimants might have in showing a genuine conscientious religious or other objection to the payment of interest. The latter point might easily be tested by seeing if the particular claimant had any interest-bearing bank or building society accounts, a credit card or a non-Sharia mortgage. Finally, there was the limiting factor of the need to take into account when judging reasonableness the interests of the wider public, in the form of the government policy that the costs of education are usually to be funded from the education budget rather than the social security benefit.

However, in substituting his own decision in *IB* Judge Poynter had no doubt that the claimant's personal circumstances, in particular his sincere and strongly held religious conviction that it would be a major sin to pay interest, outweighed any loss to public funds or dent in the government's general policy.

The result is that at the moment there are two conflicting decisions of equal authority. A First-tier Tribunal may therefore choose to follow the decision whose reasoning it finds more convincing. In doing so it can give weight to the fact that *IB* contains a detailed review of the reasoning in *CH/4429/2006*.

p.550, *amendments to the Income Support (General) Regulations 1987 (SI 1987/1967) Sch.1B (Prescribed categories of persons)*

With effect from July 26, 2021, Sch.1 para.4 of the Social Security (Scotland) Act 2018 (Disability Assistance for Children and Young People) (Consequential Modifications) Order 2021 (SI 2021/786) makes the following amendments: **6.032**

- In para.4(a) of Sch.1B (persons caring for another person):
  - in para.(i), after "Contributions and Benefits Act" insert ", the care component of child disability payment at the highest or middle rate in accordance with the DACYP Regulations (see regulation 11(5) of those Regulations),";
  - in para.(iii), after "disability living allowance", insert ", child disability payment";
  - after para.(iiia), insert "(iiib) the person being cared for ("P") has claimed entitlement to the care component of child disability payment in accordance with regulation 24 (when an application is to be treated as made and beginning of entitlement to assistance) of the DACYP Regulations, an award at the highest or middle rate has been made in respect of P's claim, and where the period for which the award is payable has begun, P is in receipt of that payment;".

With effect from March 21, 2022, art.2(4)–(5) of the Social Security (Disability Assistance for Working Age People) (Consequential Amendments) Order 2022 (SI 2022/177) makes the following amendments:

- In para.4(a) (persons caring for another person) of Sch.1B (prescribed categories of person):
  - in sub-para.(i):
    - for "or" after "(see regulation 11(5) of those Regulations)," substitute ",";
    - after "2012 Act" insert "or the daily living component of adult disability payment at the standard or enhanced rate in accordance with regulation 5 of the Disability Assistance for Working Age People (Scotland) Regulations 2022";
  - in sub-para.(iii):
    - for "or" after "armed forces independence payment" substitute ",";
    - after "personal independence payment" insert "or adult disability payment";
  - after sub-para.(iv) insert "(v)the person being cared for has claimed entitlement to the daily living component of adult disability payment in accordance with regulation 35 (when an

application is to be treated as made and beginning of entitlement to assistance) of the Disability Assistance for Working Age People (Scotland) Regulations 2022, an award at the standard or enhanced rate has been made in respect of that claim and, where the period for which the award is payable has begun, that person is in receipt of the payment;".

- In para.7A (certain persons in receipt of the daily living component of personal independence payment) of Sch.1B:
  - in the heading, after "personal independence payment" insert "or adult disability payment";
  - after "at the enhanced rate" insert "or the daily living component of adult disability payment at the enhanced rate".

With effect from November 19, 2023, art.5 of the Carer's Assistance (Carer Support Payment) (Scotland) Regulations 2023 (Consequential Amendments) Order 2023 (SI 2023/1218) makes the following amendments to paragraph 4(b) of Schedule 1B:

- after "carer's allowance" insert "or carer support payment";
- for "that allowance" substitute "a carer's allowance".

pp.571–572, *amendments to the Income Support (General) Regulations 1987 (SI 1987/1967) Sch.2 (Applicable amounts)*

6.033   The text in the main volume at paras 2.606–2.626 should be replaced with the following:

Regulations 17 [³ (1)] and 18

"SCHEDULE 2

APPLICABLE AMOUNTS

[³⁵ PART I

PERSONAL ALLOWANCES

2.606   **1.**—The weekly amounts specified in column (2) below in respect of each person or couple specified in column (1) shall be the weekly amounts specified for the purposes of regulations 17(1) and 18(1) (applicable amounts and polygamous marriages).

Column (1) Person or Couple	Column (2) Amount
(1) Single claimant aged—	(1)
(a) except where head (b) or (c) of this sub-paragraph applies, less than 18;	(a) [⁸⁵ £67.20];
[²⁸(b) less than 18 who falls within any of the circumstances specified in paragraph 1A;]	(b) [⁸⁵ £67.20];
(c) less than 18 who satisfies the condition in [⁶⁵ paragraph 11(1)(a)]	(c) [⁸⁵ £67.20];
(d) not less than 18 but less than 25;	(d) [⁸⁵ £67.20];
(e) not less than 25.	(e) [⁸⁵ £84.80].

Column (1) Person or Couple	Column (2) Amount
(2) Lone parent aged—	(2)
(a) except where head (b) or (c) of this sub-paragraph applies, less than 18;	(a) [⁸⁵ £67.20];
[²⁸(b) less than 18 who falls within any of the circumstances specified in paragraph 1A;]	(b) [⁸⁵ £67.20];
(c) less than 18 who satisfies the condition in [⁶⁵ paragraph 11(1)(a)]	(c) [⁸⁵ £67.20];
(d) not less than 18.	(d) [⁸⁵ £84.80].
[²⁸(3) Couple—	(3)
(a) where both members are aged less than 18 and—	(a) [⁸⁵ £101.50];
(i) at least one of them is treated as responsible for a child; or	
(ii) had they not been members of a couple, each would have qualified for income support under regulation 4ZA [⁷¹ or income-related employment and support allowance]; or	
(iii) the claimant's partner satisfies the requirement of section 3(1)(f)(iii) of the Jobseekers Act 1995 (prescribed circumstances for persons aged 16 but less than 18); or	
(iv) there is in force in respect of the claimant's partner a direction under section 16 of the Jobseekers Act 1995 (persons under 18: severe hardship);	
(b) where both members are aged less than 18 and head (a) does not apply but one member of the couple falls within any of the circumstances specified in paragraph 1A;	(b) [⁸⁵ £67.20];
(c) where both members are aged less than 18 and heads (a) and (b) do not apply;	(c) [⁸⁵ £67.20];
(d) where both members are aged not less than 18;	(d) [⁸⁵ £133.30];
(e) where one member is aged not less than 18 and the other member is a person under 18 who—(2)	(e) [⁸⁵ £133.30];
(i) qualifies for income support under regulation 4ZA [⁷¹ or income-related employment and support allowance], or who would so qualify if he were not a member of a couple; or	
(ii) satisfies the requirements of section 3(1)(f)(iii) of the Jobseekers Act 1995 (prescribed circumstances for persons aged 16 but less than 18); or	
(iii) is the subject of a direction under section 16 of the Jobseekers Act 1995 (persons under 18: severe hardship);	
(f) where the claimant is aged not less than 18 but less than 25 and his partner is a person under 18 who—	(f) [⁸⁵ £67.20];
(i) would not qualify for income support under regulation 4ZA [⁷¹ or income-related employment and support allowance] if he were not a member of a couple; and	
(ii) does not satisfy the requirements of section 3(1)(f)(iii) of the Jobseekers Act 1995 (prescribed circumstances for persons aged 16 but less than 18); and	
(iii) is not the subject of a direction under section 16 of the Jobseekers Act 1995 (persons under 18: severe hardship);	
(g) where the claimant is aged not less than 25 and his (g) partner is a person under 18 who—	(g) [⁸⁵ £84.80].
(i) would not qualify for income support under regulation 4ZA [⁷¹ or income-related employment and support allowance] if he were not a member of a couple; and	

Column (1) Person or Couple	Column (2) Amount
(ii) does not satisfy the requirements of section 3(1)(f)(iii) of the Jobseekers Act 1995 (prescribed circumstances for persons aged 16 but less than 18); and (iii) is not the subject of a direction under section 16 of the Jobseekers Act 1995 (persons under 18: severe hardship).]]	

2.607

[²⁸ **1A.**—(1) The circumstances referred to in paragraph 1 are that—

(a) the person has no parents nor any person acting in the place of his parents;

(b) the person—

    (i) is not living with his parents nor any person acting in the place of his parents; and

    (ii) in England and Wales, was being looked after by a local authority pursuant to a relevant enactment who placed him with some person other than a close relative of his; or in Scotland, was in the care of a local authority under a relevant enactment and whilst in that care was not living with his parents or any close relative, or was in custody in any institution to which the Prison Act 1952 or the Prisons (Scotland) Act 1989 applied immediately before he attained the age of 16;

(c) the person is in accommodation which is other than his parental home, and which is other than the home of a person acting in the place of his parents, who entered that accommodation—

    (i) as part of a programme of rehabilitation or resettlement, that programme being under the supervision of the probation service or a local authority; or

    (ii) in order to avoid physical or sexual abuse; or

    (iii) because of a mental or physical handicap or illness and needs such accommodation because of his handicap or illness;

(d) the person is living away from his parents and any person who is acting in the place of his parents in a case where his parents are or, as the case may be, that person is, unable financially to support him and his parents are, or that person is—

    (i) chronically sick or mentally or physically disabled; or

    (ii) detained in custody pending trial or sentence upon conviction or under sentence imposed by a court; of

    (iii) prohibited from entering or re-entering Great Britain; or

(e) the person of necessity has to live away from his parents and any person acting in the place of his parents because—

    (i) he is estranged from his parents and that person; or

    (ii) he is in physical or moral danger; or

    (iii) there is a serious risk to his physical or mental health.

(2) In this paragraph—

(a) "chronically sick or mentally or physically disabled" has the same meaning it has in regulation 13(3)(b) (circumstances in which persons in relevant education are to be entitled to income support);

(b) in England and Wales, any reference to a person acting in place of a person's parents includes a reference to—

    (i) where the person is being looked after by a local authority or voluntary organisation who place him with a family, a relative of his, or some other suitable person, the person with whom the person is placed, whether or not any payment is made to him in connection with the placement; or

    (ii) in any other case, any person with parental responsibility for the child, and for this purpose "parental responsibility" has the meaning it has in the Children Act 1989 by virtue of section 3 of that Act;

(c) in Scotland, any reference to a person acting in place of a person's parents includes a reference to a local authority or voluntary organisation where the person is in their care under a relevant enactment, or to a person with whom the person is boarded out by a local authority or voluntary organisation whether or not any payment is made by them.]

2.608

[³⁵ **2.**—[⁵⁹ . . .]]

2.609

[¹⁷ **2A.**—[⁵⁵ . . .]]

PART II

Regulations 17[³ (1)](c) [³ and 18(1)](d)

FAMILY PREMIUM

3.—[⁵⁹ . . .] **2.610**

PART III

Regulations 17[³ (1)](d) [³ and 18(1)](e)

PREMIUMS

4.—Except as provided in paragraph 5, the weekly premiums specified in Part IV of this **2.611** Schedule shall, for the purposes of regulations 17[³(1)](d)[³ and 18(1)](e), be applicable to a claimant who satisfies the condition specified in [⁴² paragraphs 8A] [¹⁰ to 14ZA] in respect of that premium.

5.—Subject to paragraph 6, where a claimant satisfies the conditions in respect of more than one premium in this Part of this Schedule, only one premium shall be applicable to him and, if they are different amounts, the higher or highest amount shall apply.

[⁵⁸ **6.**—(1) Subject to sub-paragraph (2), the following premiums, namely—
  (a) a severe disability to which paragraph 13 applies;
  (b) an enhanced disability premium to which paragraph 13A applies;
  (c) [⁵⁹ . . .]; and
  (d) a carer premium to which paragraph 14ZA applies,

may be applicable in addition to any other premium that may apply under this Schedule.

(2) An enhanced disability premium in respect of a person shall not be applicable in addition to—
  (a) a pensioner premium under paragraph 9 or 9A; or
  (b) a higher pension premium under paragraph 10.]

7.—[¹⁰(1) Subject to sub-paragraph (2)] for the purposes of this Part of this Schedule, once a premium is applicable to a claimant under this Part, a person shall be treated as being in receipt of any benefit—
  (a) in the case of a benefit to which the Social Security (Overlapping Benefits) Regulations 1979 applies, for any period during which, apart from the provisions of those Regulations, he would be in receipt of that benefit; [⁸⁷ ...]
  (b) for any period spent by a claimant in undertaking a course of training or instruction provided or approved by the [¹² Secretary of State [⁶⁸ . . .]] under section 2 of the Employment and Training Act 1973 [¹¹, or by [⁶⁹ Skills Development Scotland,] Scottish Enterprise or Highlands and Islands Enterprise under section 2 of the Enterprise and New Towns (Scotland) Act 1990,] [⁷ or for any period during which he is in receipt of a training allowance]. [⁸⁷ ; and
  (c) in the case of carer support payment, for any period during which, apart from regulation 16 of the Carer's Assistance (Carer Support Payment) (Scotland) Regulations 2023, he would be in receipt of that benefit.]

[¹⁰(2) For the purposes of the carer premium under paragraph 14ZA, a person shall be treated as being in receipt of [⁴⁹ carer's allowance] by virtue of sub-paragraph (1)(a) [⁸⁷ or carer support payment by virtue of sub-paragraph (1)(c)] only if and for so long as the person in respect of whose care the allowance [⁸⁷ or payment] has been claimed remains in receipt of attendance allowance [¹⁵, [⁷⁵ . . .] the care component of disability living allowance at the highest or middle rate prescribed in accordance with section 37ZB(3) of the Social Security Act [SSCBA, s.72(3)]] [⁸², the care component of child disability payment at the highest or middle rate prescribed in accordance with the regulation 11(5) of the DACYP Regulations] [⁷⁵ or the daily living component of personal independence payment at the standard or enhanced rate in accordance with section 78(3) of the 2012 Act] [⁸³, the daily living component of adult disability payment at the standard or enhanced rate in accordance with regulation 5 of the Disability Assistance for Working Age People (Scotland) Regulations 2022] [⁷⁶ or armed forces independence payment].]

Lone Parent Premium

2.612   8.—[²⁹ . . .].

[⁴² Bereavement Premium

2.613   8A.—[⁶⁷ . . .]]

[Pensioner premium for persons under 75

2.614   [⁵⁴ **9.**—The condition is that the claimant has a partner aged [⁷⁰ not less than the qualifying age for state pension credit] but less than 75.]

Pensioner premium for persons 75 and over

2.615   [⁵⁴ **9A.**—The condition is that the claimant has a partner aged not less than 75 but less than 80.]]

Higher Pensioner Premium

2.616   **10.**—[⁵⁴ (1) [⁶⁵ Subject to sub-paragraph (6), the] condition is that—
(a)   the claimant's partner is aged not less than 80; or
(b)   the claimant's partner is aged less than 80 but [⁷⁰ not less than the qualifying age for state pension credit] and either—
     (i)   the additional condition specified in [⁵⁸ paragraph 12(1)(a), (c) or (d)] is satisfied; or
     (ii)   the claimant was entitled to, or was treated as being in receipt of, income support and—
          (aa)   the disability premium was or, as the case may be, would have been, applicable to him in respect of a benefit week within eight weeks of [⁷⁰ the day his partner attained the qualifying age for state pension credit]; and
          (bb)   he has, subject to sub-paragraph (3), remained continuously entitled to income support since his partner attained [⁷⁰ the qualifying age for state pension credit].]
(2) [. . .]
(3) For the purposes of this paragraph and paragraph 12—
(a)   once the higher pensioner premium is applicable to a claimant, if he then ceases, for a period of eight weeks or less, to be entitled to [⁴¹or treated as entitled to] income support, he shall, on becoming re-entitled to income support, thereafter be treated as having been continuously entitled thereto;
(b)   in so far as [⁵⁴ sub-paragraph (1)(b)(ii) is] concerned, if a claimant ceases to be entitled to [⁴¹or treated as entitled to] income support for a period not exceeding eight weeks which includes [⁷⁰ the day his partner attained the qualifying age for state pension credit], he shall, on becoming re-entitled to income support, thereafter be treated as having been continuously entitled thereto.
[³³ (4) In the case of a claimant who is a welfare to work beneficiary, references in sub-paragraphs (1)(b)(ii) [⁶⁵ . . .] and (3)(b) to a period of 8 weeks shall be treated as references to a period of [⁶⁴ 104 weeks].]
[⁴¹ (5) For the purposes of this paragraph, a claimant shall be treated as having been entitled to and in receipt of income support throughout any period which comprises only days on which he was participating in an employment zone programme and was not entitled to income support because, as a consequence of his participation in that programme, he was engaged in remunerative work or had income in excess of his applicable amount as prescribed in Part IV.]
[⁶⁵ (6) The condition is not satisfied if the claimant's partner to whom sub-paragraph (1) refers is a long-term patient.]

Disability Premium

2.617   **11.**—[⁶⁵ (1) Subject to sub-paragraph (2), the] condition is that—
(a)   where the claimant is a single claimant or a lone parent, [⁵⁴ . . .] the additional condition specified in paragraph 12 is satisfied; or
(b)   where the claimant has a partner, either—
     [⁵⁴ (i)   the claimant satisfies the additional condition specified in paragraph [⁵⁸ 12(1) (a), (b), (c) or (d)]; or]
     (ii)   his partner [⁷⁰ has not attained the qualifying age for state pension credit] and the additional condition specified in [⁵⁸ paragraph 12(1)(a), (c) or (d)] is satisfied by his partner.
[⁶⁵ (2) The condition is not satisfied if—
(a)   the claimant is a single claimant or a lone parent and (in either case) is a long-term patient;

(b) the claimant is a member of a couple or polygamous marriage and each member of the couple or polygamous marriage is a long-term patient; or

(c) the claimant is a member of a couple or a polygamous marriage and a member of that couple or polygamous marriage is—

(i) a long-term patient; and

(ii) the only member of the couple or polygamous marriage to whom sub-paragraph (1)(b) refers.]

Additional condition for the Higher Pensioner and Disability Premiums

12.—(1) Subject to sub-paragraph (2) and paragraph 7 the additional condition referred to in paragraphs 10 and 11 is that either—

   2.618

(a) the claimant or, as the case may be, his partner—

(i) is in receipt of one or more of the following benefits: attendance allowance, [[15] disability living allowance, [[76] armed forces independence payment,] [[75] personal independence payment,] [[83] adult disability payment,] [[50] the disability element or the severe disability element of working tax credit as specified in regulation 20(1)(b) and (f) of the Working Tax Credit (Entitlement and Maximum Rate) Regulations 2002]], mobility supplement, [[25] long-term incapacity benefit] under [[22] Part II of the Contributions and Benefits Act or severe disablement allowance under Part III of that Act] [[1]but, in the case of [[25] long-term incapacity benefit] or severe disablement allowance only where it is paid in respect of him]; or

(ii) is provided by the Secretary of State with an invalid carriage or other vehicle under section 5(2) of the National Health Service Act 1977 (other services) or, in Scotland, under section 46 of the National Health Service (Scotland) Act 1978 (provision of vehicles) or receives payments by way of grant from the Secretary of State under paragraph 2 of Schedule 2 to that 1977 Act (additional provisions as to vehicles) or, in Scotland, under that section 46; or

[[77] (iii) is certified as severely sight impaired or blind by a consultant ophthalmologist; or]

[[26] (b) the claimant—

(i) is entitled to statutory sick pay or [[27] is, or is treated as, incapable of work,] in accordance with the provisions of Part XIIA of the Contributions and Benefits Act and the regulations made thereunder (incapacity for work), and

(ii) has been so entitled or so incapable [[27], or has been treated as so incapable,] for a continuous period of not less than—

(aa) 196 days in the case of a claimant who is terminally ill within the meaning of section 30B(4) of the Contributions and Benefits Act; or

(bb) [[63] subject to [[65] paragraph 2A] of Schedule 7] 364 days in any other case; and for these purposes any two or more periods of entitlement or incapacity separated by a break of not more than 56 days shall be treated as one continuous period; or]

[[54] (c) the claimant's partner was in receipt of long-term incapacity benefit under Part II of the Contributions and Benefits Act when entitlement to that benefit ceased on account of the payment of a retirement pension under that Act [[81] or a state pension under Part 1 of the Pensions Act 2014] and—

(i) the claimant has since remained continuously entitled to income support;

(ii) the higher pensioner premium or disability premium has been applicable to the claimant; and

(iii) the partner is still alive;

(d) except where paragraph [[63] 2A [[65] . . .]] of Schedule 7 (patients) applies, the claimant or, as the case may be, his partner was in receipt of attendance allowance [[75], disability living allowance [[83], personal independence payment or adult disability payment]]—

(i) but payment of that benefit has been suspended under the [[60] Social Security (Attendance Allowance) Regulations 1991 [[75], the Social Security (Disability Living Allowance) Regulations 1991 or regulations made under section 86(1) (hospital in-patients) of the 2012 Act]] or otherwise abated as a consequence of the claimant or his partner becoming a patient within the meaning of regulation 21(3); and

(ii) a higher pensioner premium or disability premium has been applicable to the claimant.]

[[34](1A) In the case of a claimant who is a welfare to work beneficiary, the reference in sub-paragraph (1)(b) to a period of 56 days shall be treated as a reference to a period of [[64] 104 weeks].]

[[77] (2) For the purposes of sub-paragraph (1)(a)(iii), a person who has ceased to be certified as severely sight impaired or blind on regaining his eyesight shall nevertheless be treated as severely sight impaired or blind, as the case may be, and as satisfying the additional condition set out in that sub-paragraph for a period of 28 weeks following the date on which he ceased to be so certified.]

(3) [²⁶ . . .]

(4) For the purpose of [⁵⁸ sub-paragraph (1)(c) and (d)], once the higher pensioner premium is applicable to the claimant by virtue of his satisfying the condition specified in that provision, if he then ceases, for a period of eight weeks or less, to be entitled to income support, he shall on again becoming so entitled to income support, immediately thereafter be treated as satisfying the condition in [⁵⁸ sub-paragraph (1)(c) and (d)].

[⁴(5) For the purposes of sub-paragraph (1)(b), once the disability premium is applicable to a claimant by virtue of his satisfying the additional condition specified in that provision, he shall continue to be treated as satisfying that condition for any period spent by him in undertaking a course of training provided under section 2 of the Employment and Training Act 1973 [⁷ or for any period during which he is in receipt of a training allowance].]

[²⁵(6) For the purposes of [⁵⁸ sub-paragraph (1)(a)(i) and (c)], a reference to a person in receipt of long-term incapacity benefit includes a person in receipt of short-term incapacity benefit at a rate equal to the long-term rate by virtue of section 30B(4)(a) of the Contributions and Benefits Act (short-term incapacity benefit for a person who is terminally ill), or who would be or would have been in receipt of short-term incapacity benefit at such a rate but for the fact that the rate of short-term incapacity benefit already payable to him is or was equal to or greater than the long-term rate.]

[⁴⁰ [⁶¹ . . .]]

Severe Disability Premium

2.619

13.—(1) The condition is that the claimant is a severely disabled person.

(2) For the purposes of sub-paragraph (1), a claimant shall be treated as being a severely disabled person if, and only if—

(a) in the case of a single claimant[¹⁹, a lone parent or a claimant who is treated as having no partner in consequence of sub-paragraph (2A)]—

    (i) he is in receipt of attendance allowance [¹⁵ [⁷⁵ . . .] the care component of disability living allowance at the highest or middle rate prescribed in accordance with section 37ZB(3) of the Social Security Act [SSCBA, s.72(3)]] [⁷⁵ or the daily living component of personal independence payment at the standard or enhanced rate in accordance with section 78(3) of the 2012 Act] [⁸³ , the daily living component of adult disability payment at the standard or enhanced rate in accordance with regulation 5 of the Disability Assistance for Working Age People (Scotland) Regulations 2022] [⁷⁶ or armed forces independence payment], and

    (ii) subject to sub-paragraph (3), he has no non-dependants aged 18 or over [²³ normally residing with him or with whom he is normally residing,] and

    (iii) [⁴¹ no person is entitled to, and in receipt of, [⁴⁹ a carer's allowance] under section 70 of the Contributions and Benefits Act [⁸⁷ or carer support payment] [⁸⁰ or has an award of universal credit which includes the carer element] in respect of caring for him;]

(b) [⁴² in the case of a claimant who] has a partner—

    (i) he is in receipt of attendance allowance [¹⁵, [⁷⁵ . . .] the care component of disability living allowance at the highest or middle rate prescribed in accordance with section 37ZB(3) of the Social Security Act [SSCBA, s.72(3)]] [⁷⁵ or the daily living component of personal independence payment at the standard or enhanced rate in accordance with section 78(3) of the 2012 Act] [⁸³ , the daily living component of adult disability payment at the standard or enhanced rate in accordance with regulation 5 of the Disability Assistance for Working Age People (Scotland) Regulations 2022] [⁷⁶ or armed forces independence payment]; and

    (ii) his partner is also in receipt of such an allowance or, if he is a member of a polygamous marriage, all the partners of that marriage are in receipt thereof; and

    (iii) subject to sub-paragraph (3), he has no non-dependants aged 18 or over [²³ normally residing with him or with whom he is normally residing,]

and either [⁴¹ a person is entitled to, and in receipt of, [⁴⁹ a carer's allowance] [⁸⁷ or carer support payment] [⁸⁰ or has an award of universal credit which includes the carer element] in respect of caring for only one of the couple or, in the case of a polygamous marriage, for one or more but not all the partners of the marriage or, as the case may be, no person is entitled to, and in receipt of, such an allowance] [⁸⁷ or payment] [⁸⁰ or has such an award of universal credit] in respect of caring for either member of the couple or any partner of the polygamous marriage.

[^{19} (2A) Where a claimant has a partner who does not satisfy the condition in sub-paragraph (2)(b)(ii), and that partner is [^{77} severely sight impaired or blind or treated as severely sight impaired or blind] within the meaning of paragraph 12(1)(a)(iii) and (2), that partner shall be treated for the purposes of sub-paragraph (2) as if he were not a partner of the claimant.]

(3) For the purposes of sub-paragraph (2)(a)(ii) and (2)(b)(iii) no account shall be taken of—

(a) a person receiving attendance allowance [^{15}, [^{75} . . .] the care component of disability living allowance at the highest or middle rate prescribed in accordance with section 37ZB(3) of the Social Security Act [SSCBA, s.72(3)]] [^{75} or the daily living component of personal independence payment at the standard or enhanced rate in accordance with section 78(3) of the 2012 Act] [^{83} , the daily living component of adult disability payment at the standard or enhanced rate in accordance with regulation 5 of the Disability Assistance for Working Age People (Scotland) Regulations 2022] [^{76} or armed forces independence payment]; or

(b) [^{21} . . .]

(c) subject to sub-paragraph (4), a person who joins the claimant's household for the first time in order to care for the claimant or his partner and immediately before so joining the claimant or his partner was treated as a severely disabled person; [^{19} or (d) a person who is [^{77} severely sight impaired or blind or treated as severely sight impaired or blind] within the meaning of paragraph 12(1)(a)(iii) and (2).]

[^{1}(3A) For the purposes of sub-paragraph (2)(b) a person shall be treated [^{41} . . .]

(a) [^{41} as being in receipt of] attendance allowance [^{15}, or the care component of disability living allowance at the highest or middle rate prescribed in accordance with section 37ZB(3) of the Social Security Act [SSCBA, s.72(3)]] if he would, but for his being a patient for a period exceeding 28 days, be so in receipt;

(b) [^{41} as being entitled to and in receipt of [^{49} a carer's allowance] [^{87} or carer support payment] [^{80} or having an award of universal credit which includes the carer element] if he would, but for the person for whom he was caring being a patient in hospital for a period exceeding 28 days, be so entitled and in receipt [^{80} of carer's allowance [^{87} or carer support payment] or have such an award of universal credit].]]

[^{75} (c) as being in receipt of the daily living component of personal independence payment at the standard or enhanced rate in accordance with section 78(3) of the 2012 Act if he would, but for a suspension of benefit in accordance with regulations under section 86(1) (hospital in-patients) of the 2012 Act, be so in receipt [^{83} ;

(d) as being in receipt of the daily living component of adult disability payment at the standard or enhanced rate in accordance with regulation 5 of the [^{84} Disability Assistance for Working Age People (Scotland) Regulations 2022], if they would, but for regulation 28 (effect of admission to hospital on ongoing entitlement to Adult Disability Payment) of those Regulations, be so in receipt.]]

[^{22} (3ZA) For the purposes of sub-paragraph (2)(a)(iii) and (2)(b), no account shall be taken of an award of [^{49} a carer's allowance] [^{87}, carer support payment] [^{80} or universal credit which includes the carer element] to the extent that payment of such an award is back-dated for a period before [^{66} the date on which the award is first paid].]

(4) Sub-paragraph (3)(c) shall apply only for the first 12 weeks following the date on which the person to whom that provision applies first joins the claimant's household.

[^{45} (5) In sub-paragraph (2)(a)(iii) and (b), references to a person being in receipt of [^{49} a carer's allowance] [^{80} or as having an award of universal credit which includes the carer element] shall include references to a person who would have been in receipt of that allowance [^{80} or had such an award] but for the application of a restriction under section [^{72} 6B or] 7 of the Social Security Fraud Act 2001 (loss of benefit provisions).]

[^{80} (6) For the purposes of this paragraph, a person has an award of universal credit which includes the carer element if the person has an award of universal credit which includes an amount which is the carer element under regulation 29 of the Universal Credit Regulations 2013.]

[^{43} **Enhanced disability premium**

13A.—[^{75} ^{76} (1) Subject to sub-paragraph (2), the condition is that—

(a) the claimant; or

(b) the claimant's partner, if any, who has not attained the qualifying age for state pension credit, is a person to whom sub-paragraph (1ZA) applies.

(1ZA) This sub-paragraph applies to the person mentioned in sub-paragraph (1) where—

(a) armed forces independence payment is payable to that person;

2.620

    (b)   the care component of disability living allowance is, or would, but for a suspension of benefit in accordance with regulations under section 113(2) of the Contributions and Benefits Act or but for an abatement as a consequence of hospitalization, be payable to that person at the highest rate prescribed under section 72(3) of that Act; [82 . . .

   (ba)   the care component of child disability payment is payable to that person at the highest rate in accordance with the DACYP Regulations (see regulation 11(5) of those Regulations); [83 . . .]]

    (c)   the daily living component of personal independence payment is, or would, but for regulations made under section 86(1) (hospital in-patients) of the 2012 Act, be payable to that person at the enhanced rate in accordance with section 78(2) of that Act [83]; or

    (d)   the daily living component of adult disability payment is, or would, but for regulation 28 (effect of admission to hospital on ongoing entitlement to Adult Disability Payment) of the [84 Disability Assistance for Working Age People (Scotland) Regulations 2022], be payable to that person at the enhanced rate in accordance with regulation 5 of those Regulations.]]

[73 (1A) Where the condition in sub-paragraph (1) ceases to be satisfied because of the death of a child or young person, the condition is that the claimant [74 or partner] is entitled to child benefit in respect of that person under section 145A of the Contributions and Benefits Act (entitlement after death of child or qualifying young person).]

[65 (2) The condition is not satisfied if the person to whom sub-paragraph (1) refers is—

    (a)   [50 . . .]

    (b)   a single claimant or a lone parent and (in either case) is a long-term patient;

    (c)   a member of a couple or polygamous marriage and each member of the couple or polygamous marriage is a long-term patient; or

    (d)   a member of a couple or polygamous marriage who—

        (i)   is a long-term patient; and

       (ii)   is the only member of the couple or polygamous marriage to whom sub-paragraph (1) refers.]

Disabled Child Premium

2.621   **14.**—[59 . . . 65]

[10 **Carer premium**

2.622   **14ZA.**—(1) [13 Subject to sub-paragraphs (3) and (4),] the condition is that the claimant or his partner is, or both of them are, [41 entitled to [49 a carer's allowance] under section 70 of the Contributions and Benefits Act] [87 or carer support payment].

(2) [57 . . .]

[41 [48 (3) Where a carer premium is awarded but—

    (a)   the person in respect of whose care the [49 carer's allowance] [87 or carer support payment] has been awarded dies; or

    (b)   in any other case the person in respect of whom a carer premium has been awarded ceases to be entitled [57 . . .] to [49 a carer's allowance] [87 or carer support payment], the condition for the award of the premium shall be treated as satisfied for a period of eight weeks from the relevant date specified in sub-paragraph (3A) below.

(3A) The relevant date for the purposes of sub-paragraph (3) above shall be—

    (a)   [57 where sub-paragraph (3)(a) applies,] the Sunday following the death of the person in respect of whose care [49 a carer's allowance] [87 or carer support payment] has been awarded or the date of death if the death occurred on a Sunday;

    (b)   [57 . . .]

    (c)   in any other case, the date on which the person who has been entitled to [4946 a carer's allowance] [87 or carer support payment] ceases to be entitled to that allowance [87 or payment].]

(4) Where a person who has been entitled to [49 a carer's allowance] [87 or carer support payment] ceases to be entitled to that allowance [87 or payment] and makes a claim for income support, the condition for the award of the carer premium shall be treated as satisfied for a period of eight weeks from the date on which

[48 (a) the person in respect of whose care the [49 carer's allowance] [87 or carer support payment] has been awarded dies;

    (b)   [57 . . .]

[57 (c) in any other case, the person who has been entitled to a carer's allowance [87 or carer support payment] ceased to be entitled to that allowance [87 or payment].]]]]

[³ Persons in receipt of concessionary payments

14A.—For the purpose of determining whether a premium is applicable to a person [¹² under paragraphs 12 to 14ZA], any concessionary payment made to compensate that person for the non-payment of any benefit mentioned in those paragraphs shall be treated as if it were a payment of that benefit.]

2.623

[⁸ Person in receipt of benefit

14B.—For the purposes of this Part of this Schedule, a person shall be regarded as being in receipt of any benefit if, and only if, it is paid in respect of him and shall be so regarded only for any period in respect of which that benefit is paid.]

2.624

[³⁷ Part IV

Weekly Amounts of Premiums Specified in Part III

Column (1) *Premium*	Column (2) *Amount*
15.—(1) [²⁹ . . .] 　[⁴²(1A) [⁶⁷ . . .]] [⁵⁴(2) Pensioner premium for persons to whom paragraph 9 applies. (2A) Pensioner premium for persons to whom paragraph 9A applies. (3) Higher pensioner premium for persons to whom paragraph 10 applies.]	(1) [²⁹ . . .]. 　[⁴² (1A) [⁶⁷ . . .]] (2) [⁵⁴ . . .] (2A) [⁵⁴ . . .] (3) [⁵⁴ . . .]
(4) Disability Premium— 　(a)　where the claimant satisfies the condition in [⁶⁵ paragraph 11(1)(a)]; 　(b)　where the claimant satisfies the condition in [⁶⁵ paragraph 11(1)(b)].	(4) 　(a)　[⁸⁶ £39.85]. 　(b)　[⁸⁶ £56.80].
(5) Severe Disability Premium— 　(a)　where the claimant satisfies the condition in paragraph 13(2)(a); 　(b)　where the claimant satisfies the condition in paragraph 13(2)(b). 　　(i)　if there is someone in receipt of [⁴⁹ a carer's allowance] [⁸⁷ or carer support payment] or if he or any partner satisfies that condition only by virtue of paragraph 13(3A); 　　(ii)　if no-one is in receipt of such an allowance [⁸⁷ or payment].	(5) 　(a)　[⁸⁶ £76.40]; 　(b) 　　(i)　[⁸⁶ £76.40]; 　　(ii)　[⁸⁶ £152.80];
(6) [⁵⁹ . . .]	(6) [⁵⁹ . . .]
(7) Carer Premium—	(7) [⁸⁶ £42.75] in respect of each person who satisfied the condition specified in paragraph 14ZA.]
[⁴³ (8) Enhanced disability premium where the conditions in paragraph 13A are satisfied—	(8) 　　(a)　[⁵⁹ . . .] 　　(b)　[⁸⁶ £19.55] in respect of each person who is neither— 　　　(i)　a child or young person; nor 　　　(ii)　a member of a couple or a polygamous marriage, in respect of whom the conditions specified in paragraph 13A are satisfied:

2.625

2.625

Column (1) *Premium*	Column (2) *Amount*
	(c) [⁸⁶ £27.90] where the claimant is a member of a couple or a polygamous marriage and the conditions specified in paragraph 13A are satisfied in respect of a member of that couple or polygamous marriage.]

PART V

ROUNDING OF FRACTIONS

2.626 **16.** Where income support is awarded for a period which is not a complete benefit week and the applicable amount in respect of that period results in an amount which includes a fraction of a penny that fraction shall be treated as a penny."

AMENDMENTS

1. Income Support (General) Amendment Regulations 1988 (SI 1988/663) reg.29 (April 11, 1988).

2. Income Support (General) Amendment No. 3 Regulations 1988 (SI 1988/1228) reg.9 (September 12, 1988).

3. Income Support (General) Amendment No. 4 Regulations 1988 (SI 1988/1445) reg.19 (September 12, 1988).

4. Income Support (General) Amendment No. 5 Regulations 1988 (SI 1988/2022) reg.17(*b*) (December 12, 1988).

5. Income Support (General) Amendment No. 5 Regulations 1988 (SI 1988/2022) reg.17(*a*) (April 10, 1989).

6. Income Support (General) Amendment Regulations 1989 (SI 1989/534) reg.5 (October 9, 1989).

7. Income Support (General) Amendment No. 3 Regulations 1989 (SI 1989/1678) reg.6 (October 9, 1989).

8. Income Support (General) Amendment Regulations 1990 (SI 1990/547) reg.17 (April 9, 1990).

9. Income Support (General) Amendment No. 2 Regulations 1990 (SI 1990/1168) reg.2 (July 2, 1990).

10. Income Support (General) Amendment No. 3 Regulations 1990 (SI 1990/1776) reg.8 (October 1, 1990).

11. Enterprise (Scotland) Consequential Amendments Order 1991 (SI 1991/3870) art.9 (April, 1991).

12. Income Support (General) Amendment Regulations 1991 (SI 1991/236) reg.2 (April 8, 1991).

13. Income Support (General) Amendment No. 4 Regulations 1991 (SI 1991/236) reg.15 (August 5, 1991).

14. Income Support (General) Amendment No. 4 Regulations 1991 (SI 1991/1559) reg.15 (October 7, 1991).

15. Disability Living Allowance and Disability Working Allowance (Consequential Provisions) Regulations 1991 (SI 1991/2742) reg.11(4) (April 6, 1992).

16. Income Support (General) Amendment Regulations 1992 (SI 1992/468) reg.6 (April 6, 1992).

17. Social Security Benefits (Amendments Consequential Upon the Introduction of community Care) Regulations 1992 (SI 1992/3147) reg.2 (April 1, 1993).

18. Social Security Benefits (Miscellaneous Amendments) Regulations 1993 (SI 1993/518) reg.5 (April 1, 1993).

19. Income-related Benefits Schemes (Miscellaneous Amendments) (No. 2) Regulations 1993 (SI 1993/1150) reg.3 (May 25, 1993).

[20.]

21. Income-related Benefits Schemes (Miscellaneous Amendments) (No. 4) Regulations 1993 (SI 1993/2119) reg.18 (October 4, 1993).

22. Income-related Benefits Schemes (Miscellaneous Amendments) (No. 5) Regulations 1994 (SI 1994/2139) reg.30 (October 3, 1994).

23. Income-related Benefits Schemes (Miscellaneous Amendments) (No. 6) Regulations 1994 (SI 1994/3061) reg.2(3) (December 2, 1994).

24. Income-related Benefits Schemes (Miscellaneous Amendments) Regulations 1995 (SI 1995/516) reg.24 (April 10, 1995).

25. Disability Working Allowance and Income Support (General) Amendment Regulations 1995 (SI 1995/482) reg.16 (April 13, 1995).

26. Disability Working Allowance and Income Support (General) Amendment Regulations 1995 (SI 1995/482) reg.17 (April 13, 1995).

27. Income-related Benefits Schemes and Social Security (Claims and Payments) (Miscellaneous Amendments) Regulations 1995 (SI 1995/2303) reg.6(8) (October 2, 1995).

28. Income Support (General) (Jobseeker's Allowance Consequential Amendments) Regulations 1996 (SI 1996/206) reg.23 and Sch.2 (October 7, 1996).

29. Child Benefit, Child Support and Social Security (Miscellaneous Amendments) Regulations 1996 (SI 1996/1803) reg.39 (April 7, 1997).

30. Income-related Benefits and Jobseeker's Allowance (Personal Allowances for Children and Young Persons) (Amendment) Regulations 1996 (SI 1996/2545) reg.2 (April 7, 1997).

31. Income-related Benefits and Jobseeker's Allowance (Amendment) (No. 2) Regulations 1997 (SI 1997/2197) regs 7(5) and (6)(a) (October 6, 1997).

32. Social Security Amendment (Lone Parents) Regulations 1998 (SI 1998/766) reg.12 (April 6, 1998).

33. Social Security (Welfare to Work) Regulations 1998 (SI 1998/2231) reg.13(3) (a) (October 5, 1998).

34. Social Security (Welfare to Work) Regulations 1998 (SI 1998/2231) reg.13(3) (b) (October 5, 1998).

35. Social Security Benefits Up-rating Order 1999 (SI 1999/264) art.18(3) and Sch.4 (April 12, 1999).

36. Social Security Benefits Up-rating Order 1999 (SI 1999/264) art.18(4)(b) (April 12, 1999).

37. Social Security Benefits Up-rating Order 1999 (SI 1999/264) art.18(5) and Sch.5 (April 12, 1999).

38. Social Security Amendment (Personal Allowances for Children and Young Persons) Regulations 1999 (SI 1999/2555) reg.2(1)(b) and (2)(April 10, 2000).

39. Social Security and Child Support (Tax Credits) Consequential Amendments Regulations 1999 (SI 1999/2566) reg.2(2) and Sch.2 Pt II (October 5, 1999).

40. Social Security (Miscellaneous Amendments) (No. 2) Regulations 1999 (SI 1999/2556) reg.2(8) (October 4, 1999).

41. Social Security (Miscellaneous Amendments) Regulations 2000 (SI 2000/681) reg.4 (April 3, 2000).

42. Social Security Amendment (Bereavement Benefits) Regulations 2000 (SI 2000/2239) reg.2(3) (April 9, 2001).

43. Social Security Amendment (Enhanced Disability Premium) Regulations 2000 (SI 2629) reg.2(c) (April 9, 2001).

44. Social Security Amendment (Residential Care and Nursing Homes) Regulations 2001 (SI 2001/3767) reg.2 and Sch. Pt I para.14 (April 8, 2002).

45. Social Security (Loss of Benefit) (Consequential Amendments) Regulations 2002 (SI 2002/490) reg.2 (April 1, 2002).

46. Social Security Amendment (Residential Care and Nursing Homes) Regulations 2001 (SI 2001/3767) reg.2 and Sch. Pt I para.14 (as amended by Social Security Amendment (Residential Care and Nursing Homes) Regulations 2002 (SI 2002/398) reg.4(2)) (April 8, 2002).

47. Social Security Amendment (Personal Allowances for Children and Young Persons) Regulations 2002 (SI 2002/2019) reg.2 (October 14, 2002).

48. Social Security Amendment (Carer Premium) Regulations 2002 (SI 2002/2020) reg.2 (October 28, 2002).

49. Social Security Amendment (Carer's allowance) Regulations 2002 (SI 2002/2497) reg.3 and Sch.2 (April 1, 2003).

50. Social Security (Working Tax Credit and Child Tax Credit) (Consequential Amendments) Regulations 2003 (SI 2003/455) regs 1(5) and 2 and Sch.1 para.20(b) (April 7, 2003).

51. Social Security Benefits Up-Rating Order 2003 (SI 2003/526) art.17(3) and Sch.2 (April 7, 2003).

52. Social Security Benefits Up-Rating Order 2003 (SI 2003/526) art.17(5) and Sch.3 (April 7, 2003).

53. Social Security Benefits Up-Rating Order 2003 (SI 2003/526) art.17(4) (April 7, 2003).

54. State Pension Credit (Consequential, Transitional and Miscellaneous Provisions) Regulations 2002 (SI 2002/3019) reg.29(5) (October 6, 2003).

55. Social Security (Removal of Residential Allowance and Miscellaneous Amendments) Regulations 2003 (SI 2003/1121) reg.2 and Sch.1 para.6 (October 6, 2003).

56. Social Security (Hospital In-Patients and Miscellaneous Amendments) Regulations 2003 (SI 2003/1195) reg.3 (May 21, 2003).

57. Social Security (Miscellaneous Amendments) (No. 2) Regulations 2003 (SI 2003/2279) reg.2(3) (October 1, 2003).

58. Income Support (General) Amendment Regulations 2003 (SI 2003/2379) reg.2 (October 6, 2003).

59. Social Security (Working Tax Credit and Child Tax Credit) (Consequential Amendments) Regulations 2003 (SI 2003/455) reg.2 and Sch.1 para.20 (April 6, 2004, except in "transitional cases" and see further the note to reg.17 of the Income Support Regulations).

60. Social Security (Miscellaneous Amendments) (No. 2) Regulations 2004 (SI 2004/1141) reg.6 (May 12, 2004).

61. Social Security (Back to Work Bonus and Lone Parent Run-on) (Amendment and Revocation) Regulations 2003 (SI 2003/1589) reg.2(d) (October 25, 2004).

62. Civil Partnership (Pensions, Social Security and Child Support) (Consequential, etc. Provisions) Order 2005 (SI 2005/2877) art.2(3) and Sch.3 para.13(3) (December 5, 2005).

63. Social Security (Hospital In-Patients) Regulations 2005 (SI 2005/3360) reg.4 (April 10, 2006).

64. Social Security (Miscellaneous Amendments) (No. 4) Regulations 2006 (SI 2006/2378) reg.5(7) (October 2, 2006).

65. Social Security (Miscellaneous Amendments) Regulations 2007 (SI 2007/719) reg.2(7) (April 9, 2007). As it relates to paras 13A(2)(a) and 14, the amendment only affects "transitional cases". See further the note to reg.17 of the Income Support Regulations and the commentary below.

66. Social Security (Miscellaneous Amendments) Regulations 2007 (SI 2007/719) reg.2(7)(e) (April 2, 2007).

67. Social Security (Miscellaneous Amendments) (No. 5) Regulations 2007 (SI 2007/2618) reg.2 and Sch. (October 1, 2007).

68. Social Security (Miscellaneous Amendments) Regulations 2008 (SI 2008/698) reg.2(12) (April 14, 2008).

69. Social Security (Miscellaneous Amendments) Regulations 2009 (SI 2009/583) reg.2(1) and (3) (April 6, 2009).

70. Social Security (Equalisation of State Pension Age) Regulations 2009 (SI 2009/1488) reg.3 (April 6, 2010).

71. Social Security (Miscellaneous Amendments) (No. 2) Regulations 2010 (SI 2010/641) reg.2(1) and (9) (April 13, 2010).

72. Social Security (Loss of Benefit) Amendment Regulations 2010 (SI 2010/1160) reg.10(1) and (3) (April 1, 2010).

73. Social Security (Miscellaneous Amendments) Regulations 2011 (SI 2011/674) reg.3(5) (April 11, 2011).

74. Social Security (Miscellaneous Amendments) (No. 3) Regulations 2011 (SI 2011/2425) reg.7(1) and (7) (October 31, 2011).

75. Personal Independence Payment (Supplementary Provisions and Consequential Amendments) Regulations 2013 (SI 2013/388) reg.8 and Sch. para.11(1) and (5) (April 8, 2013).

76. Armed Forces and Reserve Forces Compensation Scheme (Consequential Provisions: Subordinate Legislation) Order 2013 (SI 2013/591) art.7 and Sch. para.4(1) and (5) (April 8, 2013).

77. Universal Credit and Miscellaneous Amendments (No. 2) Regulations 2014 (SI 2014/2888) reg.3(2)(a) (November 26, 2014).

78. Welfare Benefits Up-rating Order 2015 (SI 2015/30) art.6 and Sch.1 (April 6, 2015).

79. Social Security Benefits Up-rating Order 2015 (SI 2015/457) art.14(5) and Sch.3 (April 6, 2015).

80. Universal Credit and Miscellaneous Amendments Regulations 2015 (SI 2015/1754) reg.14 (October 28, 2015).

81. Pensions Act 2014 (Consequential, Supplementary and Incidental Amendments) Order 2015 (SI 2015/1985) art.8(1) and (3) (April 6, 2016).

82. Social Security (Scotland) Act 2018 (Disability Assistance for Children and Young People) (Consequential Modifications) Order 2021 (SI 2021/786) Sch.1 para.5 (July 26, 2021).

83. Social Security (Disability Assistance for Working Age People) (Consequential Amendments) Order 2022 (SI 2022/177) art.2(6) (March 21, 2022).

84. Social Security (Disability Assistance for Working Age People) (Consequential Amendments) (No. 2) Order 2022 (SI 2022/530) art.2(2) (June 6, 2022).

85. Social Security Benefits Up-rating Order 2023 (SI 2023/316) art.21(1) and (3) and Sch.2 (April 10, 2023).

86. Social Security Benefits Up-rating Order 2023 (SI 2023/316) art.21(1) and (5) and Sch.3 (April 10, 2023).

87. Carer's Assistance (Carer Support Payment) (Scotland) Regulations 2023 (Consequential Amendments) Order 2023 (SI 2023/1218) art.5 (November 19, 2023).

DEFINITIONS

"adult disability payment"—see reg.2(1).
"attendance allowance"—*ibid.*
"benefit week"—*ibid.*
"carer support payment""—see reg.2(1).
"child"—see SSCBA s.137(1).
"child disability payment"—see reg.2(1).
"claimant"—*ibid.*
"close relative"—*ibid.*
"couple"—*ibid.*
"the DACYP Regulations"—*ibid.*
"disability living allowance"—*ibid.*
"family"—see SSCBA s.137(1).
"invalid carriage or other vehicle"—see reg.2(1).
"lone parent"—*ibid.*

"mobility supplement"—*ibid.*
"non-dependent"—see reg.3.
"partner"—see reg.2(1).
"personal independence payment"—*ibid.*
"polygamous marriage"—*ibid.*
"preserved right"—see reg.2(1) and reg.19.
"single claimant"—see reg.2(1).
"Social Security Act"—*ibid.*
"welfare to work beneficiary"—*ibid.*
"young person"—*ibid.*, reg.14.
For the General Note to Sch.2, see Vol.V paras 2.627–2.650.

p.605, *amendments to the Income Support (General) Regulations 1987 (SI 1987/1967) Sch.3 para.18 (Housing costs—non-dependant deductions)*

6.034   With effect from April 10, 2023, art.21 of the Social Security Benefits Up-rating Order 2023 (SI 2023/316) makes the following amendments:

- in sub-para.(1)(a) for "£102.85" substitute "£115.75";
- in sub-para.(1)(b) for "£15.95" substitute "£18.10";
- in sub-para.(2)(a) for "£149.00" substitute "£162.00";
- in sub-para.(2)(b):
  (i) for "£35.65" substitute "£41.60";
  (ii) for "£149.00" substitute "£162.00"; and
  (iii) for "£217.00" substitute "£235.00";

- in sub-para.(2)(c):
  (i) for "£50.30" substitute "£57.10";
  (ii) for "£217.00" substitute "£235.00"; and
  (iii) for "£283.00" substitute "£308.00";

- in sub-para.(2)(d):
  (i) for "£82.30" substitute "£93.40";
  (ii) for "£283.00" substitute "£308.00"; and
  (iii) for "£377.00" substitute "£410.00"; and

- in sub-para.(2)(e):
  (i) for "£93.70" substitute "£105.35";
  (ii) for "£377.00" substitute "£410.00"; and
  (iii) for "£469.00" substitute "£511.00".

p.606, *amendments to the Income Support (General) Regulations 1987 (SI 1987/1967) Sch.3 para.18 (Housing costs—non-dependant deductions)*

6.035   With effect from July 26, 2021, para.6 of Sch.1 to the Social Security (Scotland) Act 2018 (Disability Assistance for Children and Young People) (Consequential Modifications) Order 2021 (SI 2021/786) inserts into sub-paragraph (6)(b), after paragraph (ii), "(iia) the care component of child disability payment;" and inserts into sub-paragraph (8)(a), after "disability living allowance", ", child disability payment".

With effect from January 1, 2022, reg.2(6) of the Social Security (Income and Capital Disregards) (Amendment) Regulations 2021 (SI 2021/1405) inserts into para.18(8)(b), after "Grenfell Tower payment", ", child abuse payment or Windrush payment".

With effect from March 21, 2022, art.2(7) of the Social Security (Disability Assistance for Working Age People) (Consequential Amendments) Order 2022 (SI 2022/177) makes the following amendments:

in para.18(6)(b)(iii) omit "or" at the end;
after para.18(6)(b)(iii) insert "(iiia) the daily living component of adult disability payment; or"; and
in para.18(8)(a), for "or personal independence payment" substitute ", personal independence payment, adult disability payment".

With effect from July 9, 2023, reg.2 of the Social Security (Income and Capital Disregards) (Amendment) Regulations 2023 (SI 2023/640) amends para.18 as follows:

- in paragraph 18(8)(b) (non-dependant deductions), for "or Windrush payment" insert ", Windrush payment or Post Office compensation payment".

p.631, *amendment to the Income Support (General) Regulations 1987 (SI 1987/1967) Sch.8, para.6A (Sums to be disregarded in the calculation of earnings)*

With effect from November 19, 2023, art.5(5) of the Carer's Assistance (Carer Support Payment) (Scotland) Regulations 2023 (Consequential Amendments) Order 2023 (SI 2023/1218) amended para.6A(1) by inserting "or carer support payment" after "carer's allowance" in the first place where that occurs. Carer support payment is newly defined in reg.2(1) by reference to the Scottish legislation (see the entry for p.229 and Pt I of this Supplement). **6.036**

p.642, *amendments to the Income Support (General) Regulations 1987 (SI 1987/1967) Sch.9 paras 6 and 9 (Sums to be disregarded in the calculation of income other than earnings—mobility component and AA, care component and daily living component)*

With effect from March 21, 2022, art.2(8)(a) of the Social Security (Disability Assistance for Working Age People) (Consequential Amendments) Order 2022 (SI 2022/177) amended para.6 to read as follows (square brackets indicate only the present amendment, those indicating previous amendments having been omitted): **6.037**

"**6.**—The mobility component of disability living allowance[,] the mobility component of personal independence payment [or the mobility component of adult disability payment]."

With effect from March 21, 2022, art.2(8)(b) of the same Order amended para.9 to read as follows (square brackets indicate only the present amendment, those indicating previous amendments having been omitted):

"**9.**—Any attendance allowance, the care component of disability living allowance[,] the daily living component of personal independence payment [or the daily living component of adult disability payment]."

"Adult disability payment" is defined in reg.2(1) by reference to reg.2 of the Disability Assistance for Working Age People (Scotland) Regulations 2022 (SSI 2022/54) (see Vol.IV of this series).

p.644, *amendment to the Income Support (General) Regulations 1987 (SI 1987/1967) Sch.9 para.21(2) (Sums to be disregarded in the calculation of income other than earnings—income in kind)*

6.038   With effect from January 1, 2022, reg.2(7)(a) of the Social Security (Income and Capital Disregards) (Amendment) Regulations 2021 (SI 2021/1405) amended sub-para.(2) by inserting ", a child abuse payment or a Windrush payment" after "Grenfell Tower payment". All of those payments are defined in reg.2(1). See the entry for p.684 for discussion of the nature of child abuse and Windrush payments.

p.646, *amendments to the Income Support (General) Regulations 1987 (SI 1987/1967) Sch.9 para.27 (Sums to be disregarded in the calculation of income other than earnings—payments for persons temporarily in care of claimant)*

6.039   With effect from July 1, 2022, reg.99 of and Sch. to the Health and Care Act 2022 (Consequential and Related Amendments and Transitional Provisions) Regulations 2022 (SI 2022/634) amended para.27(da) by substituting the following for the text after "(da)":

"an integrated care board established under Chapter A3 of Part 2 of the National Health Service Act 2006;"

With effect from November 6, 2023, reg.2 of the Health and Care Act 2022 (Further Consequential Amendments) (No.2) Regulations 2023 (SI 2023/1071) amended para.27(db) by substituting "NHS England" for "the National Health Service Commissioning Board".

p.648, *amendment to the Income Support (General) Regulations 1987 (SI 1987/1967) Sch.9 para.39(1A) (Sums to be disregarded in the calculation of income other than earnings)*

6.040   With effect from January 1, 2022, reg.2(7)(b) of the Social Security (Income and Capital Disregards) (Amendment) Regulations 2021 (SI 2021/1405) amended para.39 by substituting the following for sub-para.(1A):

"(1A) Any—
(a)   Grenfell Tower payment;
(b)   child abuse payment;
(c)   Windrush payment."

In addition, reg.2(7)(c) amended sub-paras (2) to (6) by inserting ", a child abuse payment or a Windrush payment" after "Grenfell Tower payment" in each place where those words occur. All of those payments are defined in reg.2(1).

See the entry for p.684 (Sch.10 (Capital to be disregarded) para.22) for some technical problems arising from the date of effect of these amendments. Because all the payments so far made from the approved historic institutional child abuse schemes and from the Windrush Compensation Scheme have been in the nature of capital, the question of disregarding income has not yet arisen.

With effect from July 9, 2023, reg.2(7) of the Social Security (Income and Capital Disregards) (Amendment) Regulations 2023 (SI 2023/640) amended para.39(1A) by adding the following after head (c):

"(d)   a Post Office compensation payment."

Such payments are newly defined in reg.2(1), where there is now also an expanded definition of Grenfell Tower payments (see head (a)). With effect from the same date, the words substituted in sub-paras (2) to (6) have been further amended by substituting ", a Windrush payment, a Post Office compensation payment or a vaccine damage payment" for "or a Windrush payment". "Vaccine damage payment" is also newly defined in reg.2(1). See the entry for pp.451–452 of Vol.II in this Supplement for the background.

p.651, *amendments to the Income Support (General) Regulations 1987 (SI 1987/1967) Sch.9 (Sums to be disregarded in the calculation of income other than earnings)*

With effect from July 26, 2021, art.11(2) of the Social Security (Scotland) Act 2018 (Disability Assistance, Young Carer Grants, Short-term Assistance and Winter Heating Assistance) (Consequential Provision and Modifications) Order 2021 (SI 2021/886) inserted the following after para.85:   **6.041**

"**86.** Any disability assistance given in accordance with regulations made section 31 of the Social Security (Scotland) Act 2018."

The relevant regulations under s.31 of the 2018 Act so far are the Disability Assistance for Children and Young People (Scotland) Regulations 2021 (SSI 2021/174), also in effect from July 26, 2021, providing for the benefit known as a child disability payment. The regulations also authorise the payment of short-term assistance, to be disregarded under para.85.

With effect from November 19, 2023, art.5(6) of the Carer's Assistance (Carer Support Payment) (Scotland) Regulations 2023 (Consequential Amendments) Order 2023 (SI 2023/1218) inserted the following after para.86:

"**87.** Any amount of carer support payment that is in excess of the amount the claimant would receive if they had an entitlement to carer's allowance under section 70 of the Contributions and Benefits Act."

Carer support payment (CSP) is newly defined in reg.2(1) by reference to the Scottish legislation (see the entry for p.229 and Pt I of this Supplement). Note that CSP in general counts as income and that the disregard is limited to any excess of the amount of the CSP over what the claimant would have been entitled to in carer's allowance under British legislation. That is in accordance with the Fiscal Framework Agreement governing the provision of devolved benefits in Scotland (see para.6.9 of the Explanatory Memorandum to SI 2023/1218). Initially, CSP is to be paid at the same rate as carer's allowance.

p.665, *annotations to the Income Support (General) Regulations 1987 (SI 1987/1967) Sch.9 paras 6 and 9 (Sums to be disregarded in the calculation of income other than earnings—mobility component and AA, care component and daily living component)*

Note the amendments to paras 6 and 9 on p.642 to take account of the introduction of Scottish adult disability payment (see Vol.IV of this series).   **6.042** *p.676, annotation to the Income Support (General) Regulations 1987 (SI 1987/1967) Sch.9, para.31A (Sums to be disregarded in the calculation of income other than earnings—local welfare provision)*

6.043 No doubt, payments from the Household Support Fund, in operation from October 2021 to March 2022, constituted "local welfare provision", as with the schemes mentioned in the main volume. See para.18A of Sch.10 for the capital disregard.

p.676, annotation to the Income Support (General) Regulations 1987 (SI 1987/1967) Sch.9 para.34 (Sums to be disregarded in the calculation of income other than earnings—payments by trade unions during trade disputes)

6.044 The relevant sum was increased to £47 with effect from April 10, 2023 (see the entries for pp.15 and 18).

p.677, annotation to the Income Support (General) Regulations 1987 (SI 1987/1967) Sch.9 para.39 (Sums to be disregarded in the calculation of income other than earnings—payments from certain funds)

6.045 See the entries for pp.648 and 684 for the extension in a new sub-para. (1A) of the funds covered to child abuse compensation payments from certain schemes and to payments under the Windrush Compensation Scheme.

p.681, amendment to the Income Support (General) Regulations 1987 (SI 1987/1967) Sch.10, para.7(1)(a) (Capital to be disregarded)

6.046 With effect from July 26, 2021, art.11(3) of the Social Security (Scotland) Act 2018 (Disability Assistance, Young Carer Grants, Short-term Assistance and Winter Heating Assistance) (Consequential Provision and Modifications) Order 2021 (SI 2021/886) substituted "84, 85 or 86" for "84 or 85". See the entry for p.651 for the new para.86 of Sch.9.

p.682, amendment to the Income Support (General) Regulations 1987 (SI 1987/1967) Sch.10 para.7A (Capital to be disregarded—widowed parent's allowance)

6.047 With effect from February 9, 2023, para.1(a) of the Schedule to the Bereavement Benefits (Remedial) Order 2023 (SI 2023/134) inserted the following after para.7 of Sch.10:

"7A. Any payment of a widowed parent's allowance made pursuant to section 39A of the Contributions and Benefits Act (widowed parent's allowance)—
(a) to the survivor of a cohabiting partnership (within the meaning in section 39A(7) of the Contributions and Benefits Act) who is entitled to a widowed parent's allowance for a period before the Bereavement Benefits (Remedial) Order 2023 comes into force, and
(b) in respect of any period of time during the period ending with the day before the survivor makes the claim for a widowed parent's allowance,

but only for a period of 52 weeks from the date of receipt of the payment."

The legislation on widowed parent's allowance (WPA), and bereavement support payment (BSP) that replaced it for deaths after April 5, 2017, was declared incompatible with the ECHR by discriminating against children whose parents were cohabiting but not married to each other or in a civil partnership (see *Re McLaughlin's Application for Judicial Review* [2018] UKSC 48; [2018] 1 W.L.R. 4250 and *R. (Jackson) v Secretary of State for Work and Pensions* [2020] EWHC 183 (Admin); [2020] 1 W.L.R. 1441 in Vol.I of this series). The Remedial Order allows retrospective claims to be made for those benefits from August 30, 2018 onwards and accordingly for arrears of benefit to be paid if the conditions of entitlement are met. The new para.7A, and the amended para.72 on BSP, deal with the consequences of such payments on income support entitlement, although with somewhat differing outcomes.

The Explanatory Memorandum misleadingly asserts in para.7.15 that the Remedial Order provides for payments of arrears under the Order to be treated as capital and disregarded for the purposes of income-related benefits, in line with assurances that had been given by the government to the Joint Committee on Human Rights and in its response to public consultation on a draft of the Order (see *Draft Bereavement Benefits (Remedial Order 2022: Second Report* (HC 834, HL Paper 108) (December 6, 2022), para.61). However, it is absolutely plain that the amendments made by the Order do nothing to deem any payment of arrears to be capital. The new provisions like para.7A merely provide for a disregard of the payment for 52 weeks in so far as it is properly to be regarded as capital. It has been firmly established at least since the decision in *R(SB) 4/89* (see para.2.245 of the 2021/22 main volume) that cumulative arrears of social security benefits that would have been income if paid on time retain their nature as income though paid as a lump sum. Then, as a result of regs 29 and 31 the periodical payments are to be treated for income support purposes as paid on the date on which they were due to be paid (i.e. in the past) for the payment period starting with that date. Thus, if a claimant receiving a sum of arrears of WPA had been in receipt of income support (or another "legacy" income-related benefit) for some part of the period to which the WPA is properly to be attributed as income (subject to the £10 per week disregard under Sch.9 para.16(h)) that would trigger the Secretary of State's power to revise the decision(s) awarding income support (Social Security and Child Support (Decisions and Appeals) Regulations 1999 (SI 1999/991) reg.3(7) and SSA 1998 s.9(3) in Vol.III of this series) and, if exercised, the creation of an overpayment that would be recoverable under the SSAA s.74, either by abatement of the amount payable by way of arrears of WPA or, if that was not exercised by recovery from the claimant.

That that is the legal position was effectively conceded by Viscount Younger, the Minister for Work and Pensions in the House of Lords, in a letter of February 2, 2023 to Baroness Sherlock (deposited in the Library of the House of Lords), in which he said this:

"It is right that usual rules apply in these cases, to ensure that we don't treat cohabitee claimants differently to those claimants who were in a legal union with the deceased. WPA is taken into account as income when assessing entitlement to other means-tested benefits. Where a claimant was in receipt of a legacy income-related benefit during the period of entitlement for WPA, we will offset any overpayment of the relevant benefit from the retrospective lump sum of WPA and pay a net WPA award. Where a claimant was in receipt of Universal Credit during the period of WPA entitlement, the claimant may incur an overpayment of Universal Credit as a consequence of receiving a retrospective WPA award. We will make this clear to claimants, so that they are able to make an informed choice about making a claim."

The Explanatory Memorandum appears not so far to have been corrected and DMG Memo 2/23 makes no mention of this issue.

There remains something for the new para.7A to bite on. Because of the £10 weekly disregard, even if the abatement process is applied over the entire period to which the arrears of WPA are attributed, there will be some amount of arrears payable, which according to accepted principle would metamorphose from income into capital at the end of the period to which it is properly attributable as income (see *R(IS) 3/93* and paras 2.208 and 2.209 of the 2020/21 main volume). Such capital is to be disregarded for 52 weeks, as would capital deriving from weeks in the past in which no income-related benefit was in payment. If the abatement process had been available but did not take place, it is arguable that the arrears of income would only metamorphose into capital after deduction of the liability to recovery of the overpayment (*R(SB) 2/83* and *R(SB) 35/83*).

Note that the outcome for BSP (see the amendment to para.72) is different because BSP is disregarded entirely as income for income support purposes (Sch.9 para.80).

pp.684–685, *amendments to the Income Support (General) Regulations 1987 (SI 1987/1967) Sch.10 para.22 (Capital to be disregarded)*

6.048   With effect from January 1, 2022, reg.2(8)(a) of the Social Security (Income and Capital Disregards) (Amendment) Regulations 2021 (SI 2021/1405) amended sub-para.(1A) by inserting ", child abuse payment, Windrush payment" after "Grenfell Tower payment" and amended sub-paras (2) to (6) by inserting ", a child abuse payment or a Windrush payment" after "Grenfell Tower payment" in each place where those words occur. All of those payments are defined in reg.2(1).

There are some technical problems with the addition only with effect from January 1, 2022 of the disregards of payments from approved schemes providing compensation in respect of historic institutional child abuse in the UK (para.(1)(a)(vii)) and from the Windrush Compensation Scheme. All the schemes so far in existence provide payments in the nature of capital.

The Explanatory Memorandum to the amending regulations reveals that four child abuse compensation schemes had been approved by the Secretary of State as at January 1, 2022: under the Historical Institutional Abuse (Northern Ireland) Act 2019; under the Redress for Survivors (Historical Child Abuse in Care) (Scotland) Act 2021; the London Borough of Lambeth Redress Scheme and the London Borough of Islington's proposed support payment scheme. All provide one-off capital payments. The Memorandum also reveals that payments under the Northern Ireland and Lambeth schemes could have been made prior to January 1, 2022. The application of the disregards provided under SI 2021/1405 to such pre-January 2022 payments has been authorised by a ministerial direction from the Secretary of State, acting under "common law powers" (see the letters of December 3, 2021 between the Permanent Secretary and the Secretary of State, published on the internet). The Windrush Compensation Scheme has also been making payments for some time. The correspondence above states that extra-statutory arrangements agreed with HM Treasury provided for the disregard in practice of such payments in means-tested benefits from the outset. It might be thought that the delay in putting that outcome on a proper statutory basis is symptomatic of the way in which the victims of that scandal have been treated.

Those arrangements raise questions as to what a tribunal on appeal should do if it has evidence of receipt prior to January 1, 2022 of a payment that would have been disregarded under the amendments if it had been received on or after that date. The legislation that a tribunal is bound to apply would not allow a disregard of such a payment unless it fell within an existing "personal injury" disregard in para.12 or 12A (possible for some historic institutional child abuse payments, though not for payments to next of kin or those who had merely been in "harm's way" or for Windrush Compensation Scheme payments). However, if an express submission from the DWP recorded the practical result of the application of the disregard either on the basis of a ministerial direction or an extra-statutory arrangement, it would appear that the issue of the treatment of the payment would not arise on the appeal (see SSA 1998 s.12(8)(a)) and it is submitted that it would then be irrational for the tribunal to exercise its discretion to consider the issue nonetheless. If evidence of a payment that had not been taken into account as capital emerged in the course of an appeal, but there was no express DWP submission to explain that outcome, it is submitted that a tribunal with knowledge of the matters mentioned above could still legitimately conclude that the issue did not arise on the appeal and decline to exercise its discretion under s.12(8)(a). Memo DMG 15/21 on the effect of the amendment to Sch.10 says nothing about these questions, although it does name the currently approved historic institutional child abuse schemes and give the date of approval (December 10, 2021).

With effect from July 9, 2023, reg.2(8) of the Social Security (Income and Capital Disregards) (Amendment) Regulations 2023 (SI 2023/640) amended para.22(1A) by adding the following after "Windrush payment":

", Post Office compensation payment or vaccine damage payment"

Such payments are newly defined in reg.2(1), where there is now also an expanded definition of Grenfell Tower payments. With effect from the same date, the words substituted in sub-paras (2) to (6) have been further amended by substituting ", a Windrush payment, a Post Office compensation payment or a vaccine damage payment" for "or a Windrush payment".

With effect from August 30, 2023, reg.2(1)(a) of the Social Security (Infected Blood Capital Disregard) (Amendment) Regulations 2023 (SI 2023/894) amended para.22 by inserting the following after sub-para.(5):

"(5A) Any payment out of the estate of a person, which derives from a payment to meet the recommendation of the Infected Blood Inquiry in its interim report published on 29th July 2022 made under or by the Scottish Infected Blood Support Scheme or an approved blood scheme to the estate of the person, where the payment is made to the person's son, daughter, step-son or step-daughter."

Sir Brian Langstaff's interim report recommended that an interim payment of £100,000 should be made to all those infected from contaminated blood and blood products and all bereaved partners already registered on one of the four UK infected blood support schemes and those who registered before the inception of any future scheme. The Government committed that where the infected person or their bereaved partner died after registering for such a scheme but before the interim payment could be made, it would be paid to their estate. The amendment is intended to secure that a payment derived from an interim infected blood compensation payment from the estate will be disregarded as capital for income support purposes if it is made to a deceased person's son, daughter, step-son or step-daughter.

With effect from October 27, 2023, reg.3(3)(c) of the Social Security (Habitual Residence and Past Presence, and Capital Disregards) (Amendment) Regulations 2023 (SI 2023/1144) amended para.22(1) and (7) by inserting ", the Victims of Overseas Terrorism Compensation Scheme" after "the National Emergencies Trust" in both places. That scheme is newly defined in reg.2(1). It was set up under s.47 of the Crime and Security Act 2010 and is administered by the Criminal Injuries Compensation Authority. It enables compensation to be paid to persons injured and to partners or close family members of persons killed, where the injury or death is directly attributable to a designated incident. Payments for personal injury would be disregarded as capital under paras 12 and 12A (indefinitely only if held on trust, otherwise for 52 weeks), but will now if necessary be disregarded indefinitely under para.22, along with payments to family members (not currently covered). The amending regulations were made under urgency procedures following the UK's designation of some aspects of the violence in Israel from October 7, 2023 as incidents of terrorism, but many other incidents have been designated (as listed on the scheme's website).

p.685, *amendment to the Income Support (General) Regulations 1987 (SI 1987/1967) Sch.10 para.29 (Capital to be disregarded—payments in kind)*

6.049   With effect from January 1, 2022, reg.2(8)(b) of the Social Security (Income and Capital Disregards) (Amendment) Regulations 2021 (SI 2021/1405) amended para.29 by inserting ", child abuse payment or Windrush payment" after "Grenfell Tower payment". All of those payments are defined in reg.2(1). See also the entry for p.684.

p.689, *amendment to the Income Support (General) Regulations 1987 (SI 1987/1967) Sch.10 para.72 (Capital to be disregarded—bereavement support payment)*

6.050   With effect from February 9, 2023, para.1(b) of the Schedule to the Bereavement Benefits (Remedial) Order 2023 (SI 2023/134) amended para.72 by making the existing text sub-para.(1) and inserting the following:

"(2) Where bereavement support payment under section 30 of the Pensions Act 2014 is paid to the survivor of a cohabiting partnership (within the meaning in section 30(6B) of the Pensions Act 2014) in respect of a death occurring before the day the Bereavement Benefits (Remedial) Order 2023 comes into force, any amount of that payment which is—

(a)   in respect of the rate set out in regulation 3(1) of the Bereavement Support Payment Regulations 2017, and

(b)   paid as a lump sum for more than one monthly recurrence of the day of the month on which their cohabiting partner died,

but only for a period of 52 weeks from the date of receipt of the payment."

See the entry for p.682 for the general background. The operation of this amendment is much more straightforward than that of the new para.7A on widowed parent's allowance. Although a payment of arrears of bereavement support payment (BSP) is in its nature a payment of income and attributable to the past period in respect of which it is due, the payment could not affect any entitlement to income support in that past period because it would be disregarded entirely as income (Sch.9 para.80). The amount of the arrears would thus immediately metamorphose into capital, which would then be disregarded under para.72(2) subject to the 52 week limit.

p.695, *annotation to the Income Support (General) Regulations 1987 (SI 1987/1967) Sch.10 (Capital to be disregarded)*

In the list of categories of disregards of capital, insert the following between the entry for para.7 and the entry for para.8:   6.051

"*Para.7A*   Arrears of widowed parent's allowance;"

p.697, *annotation to the Income Support (General) Regulations 1987 (SI 1987/1967) Sch.10 (Capital to be disregarded)*

With effect from June 28, 2022 "Cost of living payments" under the   6.052
Social Security (Additional Payments) Act 2022 (see Part I of Vol.II of this series), both those to recipients of specified means-tested benefits and "disability" payments, are not to be taken into account for any income support purposes by virtue of s.8(b) of the Act. The same effect was achieved with effect from March 23, 2023 in relation to payments under the Social Security (Additional Payments) Act 2023 (s.8(b) of that Act). See Pt I of Vol.II for the text of both Acts.

p.707, *annotation to the Income Support (General) Regulations 1987 (SI 1987/1967) Sch.10 (Capital to be disregarded–arrears of certain benefits)*

With effect from October 18, 2021, the Social Security Benefits   6.053
(Claims and Payments) (Amendment) Regulations 2021 (SI 2021/1065) have permitted the payment of arrears of many benefits to be made in instalments, where necessary to protect the interests of the beneficiary and the latter agrees. Once such payments become capital (see the main volume), presumably the 52-week limit on the para.7(1) disregard runs separately from the date of receipt of each instalment. The application of the conditions in para.7(2) for a longer disregard might be more problematic.

p.709, *annotation to the Income Support (General) Regulations 1987 (SI 1987/1967) Sch.10 para.7A (Capital to be disregarded—arrears of widowed parent's allowance)*

Insert the following before the note to para.8:

6.054   *"Paragraph 7A*
This new disregard as capital of arrears of widowed parent's allowance was introduced with effect from February 9, 2023. See the entry for p.682 for the text and discussion of its effect."

p.711, *annotation to the Income Support (General) Regulations 1987 (SI 1987/1967) Sch.10 para.12 (Capital to be disregarded—trusts derived from payments made in consequence of personal injury)*

6.055   Note that *R(IS) 15/96*, mentioned in para.2.819, holds that payments made under the Criminal Injuries Compensation Scheme are in consequence of personal injury.

p.714, *annotation to the Income Support (General) Regulations 1987 (SI 1987/1967) Sch.10 para.18A (Capital to be disregarded—local welfare provision)*

6.056   There has been no specific provision made under Sch.10 (or the equivalent old style ESA or JSA provisions) to disregard 2022 Energy Rebate Scheme payments as capital, as has been done for universal credit in the Universal Credit (Energy Rebate Scheme Disregard) Regulations 2022 (SI 2022/257) (see Pt II of Vol.II). That is because the payments to be administered by local authorities (the £150 council tax rebate for properties in bands A–D and under the discretionary scheme for the vulnerable) are considered already to be covered by para.18A.

p.717, *annotation to the Income Support (General) Regulations 1987 (SI 1987/1967) Sch.10, para.28 (Capital to be disregarded—premises intended to be occupied: essential repairs or alterations needed)*

6.057   In the second paragraph of this annotation in the main volume, the reference to the Housing Benefit Regulations should be to para.28 of Sch.6, not para.27 of Sch.5. Further, the works must be required to make the property fit for occupation by the claimant, not fit for human habitation as suggested in the first paragraph. There might sometimes be no difference in the practical effect, but sometimes there will be. In *SH v London Borough of Southwark (HB)* [2023] UKUT 198 (AAC), Judge Hemingway held in para.23, in the context of reg.7(4) of the Housing Benefit Regulations, that the evaluation of whether repairs were essential had to take account of the claimant's individual characteristics, including impairment or vulnerability in consequence of ill-health, as had also been decided by Commissioner Williams in *CH/393/2002*. "Essential" probably means something like "necessary" in the sense in which luxuries are differentiated from the necessaries of life, importing a test of substantial need (*R(SB) 10/81* on the supplementary benefit single payments scheme), but the ordinary word in para.28 should be applied rather than some attempted further explanation.

p.721, *annotation to the Income Support (General) Regulations 1987 (SI 1987/1967) Sch.10 para.72 (Capital to be disregarded—bereavement support payments)*

See the entry for p.689 for the text of the amendment with effect from February 9, 2023 extending this disregard to arrears of payments made under the Bereavement Benefits (Remedial) Order 2023 (SI 2023/134) and discussion of its effect.

6.058

p.722, *annotation to the Income Support (Liable Relatives) Regulations 1990 (SI 1990/1777) reg.2 (Prescribed amounts for the purposes of section 24A of the Act)*

With effect from November 19, 2023, art.7 of the Carer's Assistance (Carer Support Payment) (Scotland) Regulations 2023 (Consequential Amendments) Order 2023 (SI 2023/1218) amended reg.2(1)(e) by inserting "or carer support payment under the Carer's Assistance (Carer Support Payment) (Scotland) Regulations 2023," after "carer's allowance".

6.059

p.742, *amendment to the Fines (Deductions from Income Support) Regulations 1992 (SI 1992/2182) reg.4 (Deductions from offender's income support, universal credit, state pension credit or jobseeker's allowance)*

With effect from October 29, 2021, reg.2 of the Fines (Deductions from Income Support) (Miscellaneous Amendments) Regulations 2021 (SI 2021/1077) substitutes a new reg.4(1B):

6.060

"(1B) The amount that may be deducted under paragraph (1A) is 5 per cent. of the appropriate universal credit standard allowance for the offender for the assessment period in question, as specified under regulation 36 of the UC Regulations."

This amendment follows the decision of Kerr J in *R. (Blundell) v SSWP* [2021] EWHC 608 (Admin); [2021] P.T.S.R. 1342, where the Secretary of State's policy on deductions was found to be unlawfully fettering her discretion about the amount to deduct under reg.4(1B). The new regulation removes that discretion, by limiting deductions to the smallest amount which could previously have been deducted.

PART III

OLD STYLE JOBSEEKER'S ALLOWANCE REGULATIONS

p.787, *annotation to the Jobseeker's Allowance Regulations 1996 (SI 1996/207)*

Insert the following text at the end of the GENERAL NOTE as a new paragraph:

6.061

Note that after July 25, 2022, there are no longer any circumstances in which it is possible to make a new claim for old style JSA: see the entry for p.33.

p.787, *amendments to the Jobseeker's Allowance Regulations 1996 (SI 1996/207), reg.1 (Citation, commencement, interpretation and application)*

6.062   With effect from July 26, 2021, Sch.3 para.2 of the Social Security (Scotland) Act 2018 (Disability Assistance for Children and Young People) (Consequential Modifications) Order 2021 (SI 2021/786) inserts the following definitions:

"child disability payment" has the meaning given in regulation 2 of the DACYP Regulations;

"DACYP Regulations" means the Disability Assistance for Children and Young People (Scotland) Regulations 2021;

With effect from January 1, 2022, reg.3(2) of the Social Security (Income and Capital Disregards) (Amendment) Regulations 2021 (SI 2021/1405) inserts the following definitions:

"child abuse payment" means a payment from a scheme established or approved by the Secretary of State for the purpose of providing compensation in respect of historic institutional child abuse in the United Kingdom;"

"Windrush payment" means a payment made under the Windrush Compensation Scheme (Expenditure) Act 2020;"

With effect from January 1, 2022, reg.3(2) of the Social Security (Income and Capital Disregards) (Amendment) Regulations 2021 (SI 2021/1405) inserts ", a child abuse payment or a Windrush payment" into the definition of "qualifying person", after "Grenfell Tower payment".

In the definition of "qualifying person", after "Grenfell Tower payment" inserts ", a child abuse payment or a Windrush payment".

With effect from March 21, 2022, art.5 of the Social Security (Disability Assistance for Working Age People) (Consequential Amendments) Order 2022 (SI 2022/177) inserts the following definition:

"adult disability payment" has the meaning given in regulation 2 of the Disability Assistance for Working Age People (Scotland) Regulations 2022;

With effect from July 9, 2023, reg.3 of the Social Security (Income and Capital Disregards) (Amendment) Regulations 2023 (SI 2023/640) amends reg.1 as follows:

- for the definition of "Grenfell Tower payment" substitute—
  ""Grenfell Tower payment" means a payment made for the purpose of providing compensation or support in respect of the fire on 14th June 2017 at Grenfell Tower;";
- insert the following definitions:
  - "the Horizon system" means any version of the computer system used by the Post Office known as Horizon, Horizon Legacy, Horizon Online or HNG-X;
  - "the Post Office" means Post Office Limited (registered number 02154540);
  - "Post Office compensation payment" means a payment made by the Post Office or the Secretary of State for the purpose of providing compensation or support which is—

(a) in connection with the failings of the Horizon system; or
(b) otherwise payable following the judgment in Bates and Others v Post Office Ltd ((No. 3) "Common Issues") (10);

● "vaccine damage payment" means a payment made under the Vaccine Damage Payments Act 1979(11);";

● in the definition of "qualifying person", for "or a Windrush payment" substitute ", a Windrush payment, a Post Office compensation payment or a vaccine damage payment".

With effect from October 27, 2023, reg.4 of the Social Security (Habitual Residence and Past Presence, and Capital Disregards) (Amendment) Regulations 2023 (SI 2023/1144) amends reg.1 as follows:

● in the definition of "qualifying person", after "the National Emergencies Trust" insert ", the Victims of Overseas Terrorism Compensation Scheme";

● insert the following definition:

"the Victims of Overseas Terrorism Compensation Scheme" means the scheme of that name established by the Ministry of Justice in 2012 under section 47 of the Crime and Security Act 2010(20);

With effect from November 19, 2023, art.8 of the Carer's Assistance (Carer Support Payment) (Scotland) Regulations 2023 (Consequential Amendments) Order 2023 (SI 2023/1218) amends reg.1 as follows:

after the definition of "care home" insert—

""carer support payment" means carer's assistance given in accordance with the Carer's Assistance (Carer Support Payment) (Scotland) Regulations 2023;".

pp.851–852, *Jobseeker's Allowance Regulations 1996 (SI 1996/207) reg.16 (Further circumstances in which a person is to be treated as available: permitted period)*

Note that there has been no amendment to reg.16, equivalent to that made for universal credit and new style JSA purposes by SI 2022/108 (see the notes to reg.97(4) and (5) of the Universal Credit Regulations 2013 in Pt II of Vol.II of this series and to reg.14(3) of the JSA Regulations 2013 in Vol.I of this series), to reduce the maximum length of a "permitted period" from 13 weeks to four.

6.063

pp.872–873, *Jobseeker's Allowance Regulations 1996 (SI 1996/207) reg.20 (Further circumstances in which a person is to be treated as actively seeking employment: permitted period)*

Note that there has been no amendment to reg.20, equivalent to that made for universal credit and new style JSA purposes by SI 2022/108 (see the notes to reg.97(4) and (5) of the Universal Credit Regulations 2013 in Pt II of Vol.II of this series and to reg.14(3) of the JSA Regulations 2013 in Vol.I of this series), to reduce the maximum length of a "permitted period" from 13 weeks to four.

6.064

p.896, *amendments to the Jobseeker's Allowance Regulations 1996 (SI 1996/207) reg.46(1) (Waiting days)*

6.065   With effect from November 19, 2023, art.8(3) of the Carer's Assistance (Carer Support Payment) (Scotland) Regulations 2023 (Consequential Amendments) Order 2023 (SI 2023/1218) amended reg.46(1)(a) and (d) by substituting ", carer's allowance or carer support payment" for "carer's allowance" in both places. Carer support payment is newly defined in reg.1(3) by reference to the Scottish legislation (see the entry for p.789 and Part I of this Supplement).

pp.902–903, *amendments to the Jobseeker's Allowance Regulations 1996 (SI 1996/207) reg.48(2) and (3) (Linking periods)*

6.066   With effect from November 19, 2023, art.8(4) of the Carer's Assistance (Carer Support Payment) (Scotland) Regulations 2023 (Consequential Amendments) Order 2023 (SI 2023/1218) amended reg.48(2)(a) and (3) by inserting "or carer support payment" after "Benefits Act" in para.(2)(a) and after "carer's allowance" in para.(3). Carer support payment is newly defined in reg.1(3) by reference to the Scottish legislation (see the entry for p.789 and Part I of this Supplement).

pp.910–912, *amendments to the Jobseeker's Allowance Regulations 1996 (SI 1996/207) reg.51 (Remunerative work)*

6.067   The text in the main volume at para.3.166 should be replaced with the following:

"Remunerative work

51.—(1) For the purposes of the Act "remunerative work" means—
(a) in the case of [⁵ a claimant], work in which he is engaged or, where his hours of work fluctuate, is engaged on average, for not less than 16 hours per week; and
(b) in the case of any partner of the claimant, work in which he is engaged or, where his hours of work fluctuate, is engaged on average, for not less than 24 hours per week; [¹ and
(c) in the case of a non-dependant, or of a child or young person to whom paragraph 18 of Schedule 6 refers, work in which he is engaged or, where his hours of work fluctuate, is engaged on average, for not less than 16 hours per week,]
and for those purposes, [³ "work" is work] for which payment is made or which is done in expectation of payment.
    (2) For the purposes of paragraph (1), the number of hours in which [⁵ a claimant] or his partner is engaged in work shall be determined—
(a) where no recognisable cycle has been established in respect of a person's work, by reference to the number of hours or, where those hours are likely to fluctuate, the average of the hours, which he is expected to work in a week;
(b) where the number of hours for which he is engaged fluctuate, by reference to the average of hours worked over—

(i) if there is a recognisable cycle of work, and sub-paragraph (c) does not apply, the period of one complete cycle (including, where the cycle involves periods in which the person does not work, those periods but disregarding any other absences);

(ii) in any other case, the period of five weeks immediately before the date of claim or the date of [⁴ supersession], or such other length of time as may, in the particular case, enable the person's average hours of work to be determined more accurately;

(c) [⁷ . . .]

(3) In determining in accordance with this regulation the number of hours for which a person is engaged in remunerative work—

(a) that number shall include any time allowed to that person by his employer for a meal or for refreshments, but only where the person is, or expects to be, paid earnings in respect of that time;

(b) no account shall be taken of any hours in which the person is engaged in an employment or scheme to which any one of paragraphs (a) to (h) of regulation 53 (person treated as not engaged in remunerative work) applies;

(c) no account shall be taken of any hours in which the person is engaged otherwise than in an employment as an earner in caring for—

(i) a person who is in receipt of attendance allowance [¹ . . .] [⁹ , the care component of disability living allowance at the highest or middle rate [¹¹ the care component of child disability payment at the highest or middle rate in accordance with regulation 11(5) of the DACYP Regulations] [¹⁰ , armed forces independence payment] [¹² . . .] the daily living component of personal independence payment at the standard or enhanced rate] [¹² , or the daily living component of adult disability payment at the standard or enhanced rate]; or

(ii) a person who has claimed an attendance allowance [¹ . . .] [⁹, disability living allowance [¹¹ child disability payment] [¹⁰ , armed forces independence payment] [¹² . . .] personal independence payment] [¹² or adult disability payment], but only for the period beginning with the date of claim and ending on the date the claim is determined or, if earlier, on the expiration of the period of 26 weeks from the date of claim; or

(iii) another person [² and] is in receipt of [⁶ carer's allowance] under Section 70 of the [¹ Benefits Act [¹³ or carer support payment]; or

(iv) a person who has claimed either attendance allowance or disability living allowance and has an award of attendance allowance or the care component of disability living allowance at one of the two higher rates prescribed under section 72(4) of the Benefits Act for a period commencing after the date on which that claim was made] [⁹ ; or

[¹¹ (iva) a person who has claimed child disability payment and has an award of the care component of child disability payment at the highest or middle rate in accordance with regulation 11(5) of the DACYP Regulations for a period commencing after the date on which the claim was made;] or

209

(v) a person who has claimed personal independence payment and has an award of the daily living component at the standard or enhanced rate under section 78 of the 2012 Act for a period commencing after the date on which that claim was made] [10 ; or

[12 (va) a person who has claimed adult disability payment and has an award of the daily living component at the standard or enhanced rate under regulation 5 of the Disability Assistance for Working Age People (Scotland) Regulations 2022 for a period commencing after the date on which that claim was made;] or

(vi) a person who has claimed and has an award of armed forces independence payment for a period commencing after the date on which that claim was made.]

[8 . . .]"

AMENDMENTS

1. Jobseeker's Allowance (Amendment) Regulations 1996 (SI 1996/15160) reg.9 (October 7, 1996).

2. Jobseeker's Allowance (Amendment) Regulations 1996 (SI 1996/1516) reg.20 and Sch. (October 7, 1996).

3. Social Security (Miscellaneous Amendments) Regulations 1997 (SI 1997/454) reg.2(5) (April 7, 1997).

4. Social Security Act 1998 (Commencement No. 11, and Savings and Consequential Provisions) Order 1999 (SI 1999/2860 (C.75)) art.3(1) and (12) and Sch.12 para.5 (October 18, 1999)

5. Jobseeker's Allowance (Joint Claims) Regulations 2000 (SI 2000/1978) reg.2(5) and Sch.2 para.14 (March 19, 2001).

6. Social Security (Miscellaneous Amendments) Regulations 2003 (SI 2003/511) reg.3(4) and (5) (April 1, 2003).

7. Social Security (Miscellaneous Amendments) Regulations 2009 (SI 2009/583) reg.4(1) and (4) (April 6, 2009).

8. Social Security (Miscellaneous Amendments) (No. 3) Regulations 2011 (SI 2011/2425) reg.10(1) and (3) (October 31, 2011).

9. Personal Independence Payment (Supplementary Provisions and Consequential Amendments) Regulations 2013 (SI 2013/388) reg.8 and Sch. para.16(1) and (3) (April 8, 2013).

10. Armed Forces and Reserve Forces Compensation Scheme (Consequential Provisions: Subordinate Legislation) Order 2013 (SI 2013/591) art.7 and Sch. para.10(1) and (3) (April 8, 2013).

11. Social Security (Scotland) Act 2018 (Disability Assistance for Children and Young People) (Consequential Modifications) Order 2021 (SI 2021/786) Sch.3 para.3 (July 26, 2021).

12. Social Security (Disability Assistance for Working Age People) (Consequential Amendments) Order 2022 (SI 2022/177) art.5(3) (March 21, 2022).

13. Carer's Assistance (Carer Support Payment) (Scotland) Regulations 2023 (Consequential Amendments) Order 2023 (SI 2023/1218) art.8 (November 19, 2023).

DEFINITIONS

"the Act"—see reg.1(3).
"adult disability payment"—*ibid.*
"attendance allowance"—*ibid.*
"the Benefits Act"—see Jobseekers Act s.35(1).

"child"—*ibid.*
"child disability payment"—see reg.1(3).
"claimant"—see Jobseekers Act s.35(1).
"date of claim"—see reg.1(3).
"DACYP Regulations"—*ibid.*
"disability living allowance"—*ibid.*
"earnings"—*ibid.*
"employment"—see reg.3.
"partner"—see reg.1(3).
"payment"—*ibid.*
"personal independence payment"—*ibid.*
"week"—*ibid.*
"young person"—*ibid.*, reg.76.
For the General Note to reg.51, see Vol.V paras 3.167–3.169.

p.923, *amendment to the Jobseeker's Allowance Regulations 1996 (SI 1996/207) reg.55ZA(2)(a) (Extended period of sickness)*

With effect from July 1, 2022, reg.4(1) of the Social Security (Medical Evidence) and Statutory Sick Pay (Medical Evidence) (Amendment) (No. 2) Regulations 2022 (SI 2022/630) omitted the words "a doctor's" between "form of" and "statement".   6.068

p.970, *annotation to the Jobseeker's Allowance Regulations 1996 (SI 1996/207) reg.83 (Applicable amounts)*

On the lawfulness of not uplifting the amounts paid in IS, JSA and ESA by £20 per week (as was done with UC for 18 months during the coronavirus pandemic), see the annotation to the Income Support (General) Regulations 1987 (SI 1987/1967) reg.17 (Applicable amounts), above.   6.069

pp.974–977, *amendments to the Jobseeker's Allowance Regulations 1996 (SI 1996/207) reg.85A (Special cases: supplemental—persons from abroad)*

The text in the main volume at para.3.278 should be replaced with the following: 6.070

"**85A.**—(1) "Person from abroad" means, subject to the following provisions of this regulation, a claimant who is not habitually resident in the United Kingdom, the Channel Islands, the Isle of Man or the Republic of Ireland.
[¹⁰ (2) No claimant shall be treated as habitually resident in the United Kingdom, the Channel Islands, the Isle of Man or the Republic of Ireland unless—
(a) [¹² subject to the exceptions in paragraph (2A),] the claimant has been living in any of those places for the past three months; and
(b) the claimant has a right to reside in any of those places, other than a right to reside which falls within paragraph (3) [¹³ or (3A)].]
[¹² (2A) The exceptions are where the claimant has at any time during the period referred to in paragraph (2)(a)—
(a) paid either Class 1 or Class 2 contributions by virtue of regulation 114, 118, 146 or 147 of the Social Security (Contributions) Regulations 2001 or by virtue of an Order in Council having effect under section 179 of the Social Security Administration Act 1992; or

(b) been a Crown servant posted to perform overseas the duties of a Crown servant; or

(c) been a member of Her Majesty's forces posted to perform overseas the duties of a member of Her Majesty's forces.]

(3) A right to reside falls within this paragraph if it is one which exists by virtue of, or in accordance with, one or more of the following—

(a) regulation 13 of the [¹³ Immigration (European Economic Area) Regulations 2016]; [¹⁵ or]

[⁷[¹³(aa) regulation 16 of those Regulations, but only in a case where the right exists under that regulation because the claimant satisfies the criteria in paragraph (5) of that regulation;]]

(b) [¹⁵ . . .]

(c) [¹⁵ . . .]

[¹³ (3A) A right to reside falls within this paragraph if it exists by virtue of a claimant having been granted limited leave to enter, or remain in, the United Kingdom under the Immigration Act 1971 by virtue of—

(a) Appendix EU to the immigration rules made under section 3(2) of that Act; [¹⁶ . . .]

(b) being a person with a Zambrano right to reside as defined in Annex 1 of Appendix EU to the immigration rules made under section 3(2) of that Act.] [¹⁶; or

(c) having arrived in the United Kingdom with an entry clearance that was granted under Appendix EU (Family Permit) to the immigration rules made under section 3(2) of that Act.]

[¹⁴ (3B) Paragraph (3A)(a) does not apply to a person who—

(a) has a right to reside granted by virtue of being a family member of a relevant person of Northern Ireland; and

(b) would have a right to reside under the Immigration (European Economic Area) Regulations 2016 if the relevant person of Northern Ireland were an EEA national, provided that the right to reside does not fall within paragraph (3A).]

(4) A claimant is not a person from abroad if he is—

[¹⁶(zza) a person granted leave in accordance with the immigration rules made under section 3(2) of the Immigration Act 1971, where such leave is granted by virtue of—

(i) the Afghan Relocations and Assistance Policy; or

(ii) the previous scheme for locally-employed staff in Afghanistan (sometimes referred to as the ex-gratia scheme);

(zzb) a person in Great Britain not coming within sub-paragraph (zza) or [¹⁷ (h)] who left Afghanistan in connection with the collapse of the Afghan government that took place on 15th August 2021;]

[¹⁷(zzc) a person in Great Britain who was residing in Ukraine immediately before 1st January 2022, left Ukraine in connection with the Russian invasion which took place on 24th February 2022 and—

(i) has been granted leave in accordance with immigration rules made under section 3(2) of the Immigration Act 1971; [¹⁸ . . .]

(ii) has a right of abode in the United Kingdom within the meaning given in section 2 of that Act;] [¹⁸ or

(iii) does not require leave to enter or remain in the United Kingdom in accordance with section 3ZA of that Act;]

[¹⁹(zzd) a person who was residing in Sudan before 15th April 2023, left Sudan in connection with the violence which rapidly escalated on 15th April 2023 in Khartoum and across Sudan and—

    (i) has been granted leave in accordance with immigration rules made under section 3(2) of the Immigration Act 1971(10);

    (ii) has a right of abode in the United Kingdom within the meaning given in section 2 of that Act(11); or

    (iii) does not require leave to enter or remain in the United Kingdom in accordance with section 3ZA of that Act;]

[²⁰(zze) a person who was residing in Israel, the West Bank, the Gaza Strip, East Jerusalem, the Golan Heights or Lebanon immediately before 7th October 2023, who left Israel, the West Bank, the Gaza Strip, East Jerusalem, the Golan Heights or Lebanon in connection with the Hamas terrorist attack in Israel on 7th October 2023 or the violence which rapidly escalated in the region following the attack and—

    (i) has been granted leave in accordance with immigration rules made under section 3(2) of the Immigration Act 1971;

    (ii) has a right of abode in the United Kingdom within the meaning given in section 2 of that Act; or

    (iii) does not require leave to enter or remain in the United Kingdom in accordance with section 3ZA of that Act;]

[¹¹(za) a qualified person for the purposes of regulation 6 of the [¹³ Immigration (European Economic Area) Regulations 2016] as a worker or a self-employed person;

  (zb) a family member of a person referred to in sub-paragraph (za) [¹⁴ . . .];

  (zc) a person who has a right to reside permanently in the United Kingdom by virtue of regulation 15(1)(c), (d) or I of those Regulations;]

[¹⁴(zd) a family member of a relevant person of Northern Ireland, with a right to reside which falls within paragraph (3A)(a), provided that the relevant person of Northern Ireland falls within sub-paragraph (za), or would do so but for the fact that they are not an EEA national;]

[¹⁵(ze) a frontier worker within the meaning of regulation 3 of the Citizens' Rights (Frontier Workers) (EU Exit) Regulations 2020;

  (zf) a family member, of a person referred to in sub-paragraph (ze), who has been granted limited leave to enter, or remain in, the United Kingdom by virtue of Appendix EU to the immigration rules made under section 3(2) of the Immigration Act 1971;]

  (g) a refugee within the definition in Article 1 of the Convention relating to the Status of Refugees done at Geneva on 28th July 1951, as extended by Article 1(2) of the Protocol relating to the Status of Refugees done at New York on 31st January 1967;

[³[⁹(h) a person who has been granted leave or who is deemed to have been granted leave outside the rules made under section 3(2) of the Immigration Act 1971 [¹⁷ . . .]]

  (hh) a person who has humanitarian protection granted under those rules;] [⁹ or]

  (i) a person who is not a person subject to immigration control within the meaning of section 115(9) of the Immigration and Asylum Act and who is in the United Kingdom as a result of his deportation, expulsion or other removal by compulsion of law from another country to the United Kingdom; [⁵ . . .]

[⁹ . . .]

[¹⁴ (5) In this regulation—

"EEA national" has the meaning given in regulation 2(1) of the Immigration (European Economic Area) Regulations 2016;

"family member" has the meaning given in regulation 7(1)(a), (b) or (c) of the Immigration (European Economic Area) Regulations 2016 except that regulation 7(4) of those Regulations does not apply for the purposes of paragraphs (3B) and (4)(zd);

"relevant person of Northern Ireland" has the meaning given in Annex 1 of Appendix EU to the immigration rules made under section 3(2) of the Immigration Act 1971.]

[¹⁵ (6) In this regulation references to the Immigration (European Economic Area) Regulations 2016 are to be read with Schedule 4 to the Immigration and Social Security Co-ordination (EU Withdrawal) Act 2020 (Consequential, Saving, Transitional and Transitory Provisions) Regulations 2020.]"

AMENDMENTS

1. Social Security (Persons from Abroad) Amendment Regulations 2006 (SI 1026/2006) reg.7(3) (April 30, 2006).

2. Social Security (Lebanon) Amendment Regulations 2006 (SI 2006/1981) reg.3 (July 25, 2006). The amendment ceased to have effect from January 31, 2007.

3. Social Security (Persons from Abroad) Amendment (No. 2) Regulations 2006 (SI 2006/2528) reg.3 (October 9, 2006).

4. Social Security (Bulgaria and Romania) Amendment Regulations 2006 (SI 2006/3341) reg.3 (January 1, 2007).

5. Social Security (Habitual Residence) (Amendment) Regulations 2009 (SI 2009/362) reg.3 (March 18, 2009).

6. Social Security (Miscellaneous Amendments) (No. 3) Regulations 2011 (SI 2011/2425) reg.10(1) and (7) (October 31, 2011).

7. Social Security (Habitual Residence) (Amendment) Regulations 2012 (SI 2012/2587) reg.3 (November 8, 2012).

8. Social Security (Croatia) Amendment Regulations 2013 (SI 2013/1474) reg.3 (July 1, 2013).

9. Social Security (Miscellaneous Amendments) (No. 3) Regulations 2013 (SI 2013/2536) reg.6(1) and (8) (October 29,2013).

10. Jobseeker's Allowance (Habitual Residence) Amendment Regulations 2013 (SI 3196/2013) reg.2 (January 1, 2014).

11. Social Security (Habitual Residence) (Amendment) Regulations 2014 (SI 2014/902) reg.3 (May 31, 2014).

12. Jobseeker's Allowance (Habitual Residence) Amendment Regulations 2014 (SI 2014/2735) reg.3 (November 9, 2014).

13. Social Security (Income-related Benefits) (Updating and Amendment) (EU Exit) Regulations 2019 (SI 2019/872) reg.3 (May 7, 2019).

14. Social Security (Income-Related Benefits) (Persons of Northern Ireland— Family Members) (Amendment) Regulations 2020 (SI 2020/683) reg.3 (August 24, 2020).

15. Immigration and Social Security Co-ordination (EU Withdrawal) Act 2020 (Consequential, Saving, Transitional and Transitory Provisions) (EU Exit) Regulations 2020 (SI 2020/1309) reg.55 (December 31, 2020 at 11.00 pm).

16. Social Security (Habitual Residence and Past Presence) (Amendment) Regulations 2021 (SI 2021/1034), reg.2 (September 15, 2021).

17. Social Security (Habitual Residence and Past Presence) (Amendment) Regulations 2022 (SI 2022/344) reg.2 (March 22, 2022).

18. Social Security (Habitual Residence and Past Presence) (Amendment) (No. 2) Regulations 2022 (SI 2022/990) reg.2 (October 18, 2022).

19. Social Security (Habitual Residence and Past Presence) (Amendment) Regulations 2023 (SI 2023/532), reg.2 (May 15, 2023).

20. Social Security (Habitual Residence and Past Presence, and Capital Disregards) (Amendment) Regulations 2023, reg.2 (SI 2023/1144) (October 27, 2023).

p.1014, *amendment to the Jobseeker's Allowance Regulations 1996 (SI 1996/207) reg.105(10A) (Notional income—exceptions)*

With effect from January 1, 2022, reg.3(3) of the Social Security (Income and Capital Disregards) (Amendment) Regulations 2021 (SI 2021/1405) amended para.(10A) by inserting the following after sub-para.(ab): 6.071

"(ac) a child abuse payment;
(ad) a Windrush payment;"

Those payments are defined in reg.1(3). See the entry for p.684 for discussion of the nature of those payments.

With effect from July 9, 2023, reg.3(3) of the Social Security (Income and Capital Disregards) (Amendment) Regulations 2023 (SI 2023/640) amended reg.105(10A) by inserting the following after sub-para.(ad):

"(ae) a Post Office compensation payment;"

Such payments are newly defined in reg.1(3), where there is now also an expanded definition of Grenfell Tower payments (see sub-para.(ab)). See the entry for pp.451–452 of Vol.II in this Supplement.

p.1021, *annotation to the Jobseeker's Allowance Regulations 1996 (SI 1996/207) reg.107 (Capital limit)*

In the Institute for Government and the Social Security Advisory Committee's 2021 joint report *Jobs and benefits: The Covid-19 challenge* it was noted that if the capital limit of £16,000 had risen in line with prices since 2006 it would be close to £23,500 (or £25,000: different figures are given) and recommended that the limit should be increased to £25,000 and subsequently automatically indexed to maintain its real value (pp.22 and 31). That recommendation was summarily rejected in the Government's response of March 22, 2022. 6.072

p.1023, *amendment to the Jobseeker's Allowance Regulations 1996 (SI 1996/207) reg.110(10) (Income treated as capital—exceptions)*

With effect from January 1, 2022, reg.3(4) of the Social Security (Income and Capital Disregards) (Amendment) Regulations 2021 (SI 2021/1405) amended para.(10) by inserting the following after sub-para.(ab): 6.073

"(ac) which is a child abuse payment;
(ad) which is a Windrush payment; or"

Those payments are defined in reg.1(3). See the entry for p.684 for discussion of the nature of those payments. The "or" following sub-para.(ab), omitted in error in the main volume, has also been removed.

With effect from July 9, 2023, reg.3(4) of the Social Security (Income and Capital Disregards) (Amendment) Regulations 2023 (SI 2023/640) amended reg.110(10) by omitting "or" at the end of sub-para.(ad) and inserting the following:

"(ae) which is a Post Office compensation payment;"

Such payments are newly defined in reg.1(3), where there is now also an expanded definition of Grenfell Tower payments (see sub-para.(ab)). See the entry of pp.451–452 of Vol.II in this Supplement

With effect from October 27, 2023, reg.4(3)(a) of the Social Security (Habitual Residence and Past Presence, and Capital Disregards) (Amendment) Regulations 2023 (SI 2023/1144) amended reg.110(10)(c) by inserting ", the Victims of Overseas Terrorism Compensation Scheme" after "the National Emergencies Trust". That scheme is newly defined in reg.1(3). See the entry for pp.684–685 on income support for the background.

p.1027, *amendments to the Jobseeker's Allowance Regulations 1996 (SI 1996/207) reg.113(3A) and (3B) (Notional capital—exceptions)*

6.074

With effect from January 1, 2022, reg.3(5) of the Social Security (Income and Capital Disregards) (Amendment) Regulations 2021 (SI 2021/1405) amended para.(3B) by substituting the following for "a payment of capital which is a Grenfell Tower payment":

"any of the following payments of capital—

(a) a Grenfell Tower payment;
(b) a child abuse payment;
(c) a Windrush payment."

All of those payments are defined in reg.1(3). See the entry of p.684 for discussion of the nature of child abuse and Windrush payments.

With effect from July 9, 2023, reg.3(5) of the Social Security (Income and Capital Disregards) (Amendment) Regulations 2023 (SI 2023/640) amended reg.113(3B) by inserting the following after sub-para.(c):

"(d) a Post Office compensation payment;
(e) a vaccine damage payment."

Such payments are newly defined in reg.1(3), where there is now also an expanded definition of Grenfell Tower payments (see sub-para.(a)). See the entry for pp.451–452 of Vol.II in this Supplement.

With effect from October 27, 2023, reg.4(3)(b) of the Social Security (Habitual Residence and Past Presence, and Capital Disregards) (Amendment) Regulations 2023 (SI 2023/1144) amended reg.113(3A)(a) by inserting ", the Victims of Overseas Terrorism Compensation Scheme" after "the National Emergencies Trust". That scheme is newly defined in reg.1(3). See the entry for pp.684–685 on income support for the background.

pp.1029–1030, *annotation to the Jobseeker's Allowance Regulations 1996 (SI 1996/207) reg.113(1) (Notional capital—deprivation)*

DB v DfC (JSA) [2021] NICom 43 takes the same approach as set out in the main volume to the scope of the Northern Ireland equivalent (in identical terms) of reg.113(1). The claimant had been entitled to old style ESA. On November 25, 2016 the decision was given that she was not entitled from August 2015, apparently on the basis that, although she asserted that she had disposed of some £40,000 of capital that she said did not belong to her, it was her capital and she had not shown that she had disposed of it. She claimed old style JSA on September 14, 2017. On October 16, 2017 it was decided that she was not entitled, on the basis that her actual capital exceeded £16,000, despite her further assertions of having depleted bank accounts. A revision of that decision and submissions made on appeal were hopelessly confused as between actual and notional capital, but the decision of October 16, 2017 was never formally changed. The appeal tribunal found that the claimant had deprived herself of more than £40,000 in 2016 for the principal purpose of bringing her capital below the limits to obtain benefits including JSA, so that she was treated as having notional income over £16,000 after the application of the diminishing notional capital rule (reg.114). The Chief Commissioner held, as had been submitted by the DfC, that because reg.113(1) could only bite when the claimant's purpose was securing entitlement to or increasing the amount of old style JSA or income support, the appeal tribunal had failed to make the necessary findings of fact or show that it had applied the legally correct approach. It was inherently improbable that when depriving herself of capital while in receipt of ESA, more than a year before she claimed JSA, the claimant had possible entitlement to JSA in mind.

6.075

The decision also illustrates that on a new claim neither the decision-maker nor a tribunal on appeal is bound by the findings of fact on capital that have underpinned a decision of non-entitlement on capital grounds. The basis of the ESA decision, that the claimant as at that date still had actual capital of more than £40,000, did not have to be adopted on the JSA claim.

p.1054, *annotation to the Jobseeker's Allowance Regulations 1996 (SI 1996/207) reg.136(4) and (5) (Treatment of student loans and postgraduate loans)*

See the entry for p.539 on income support for details of the decision in *IB v Gravesham BC and SSWP (HB)* [2023] UKUT 193 (AAC); [2024] P.T.S.R. 130 on when a claimant cannot acquire a loan by taking reasonable steps to do so.

6.076

pp.1059–1060, *amendments to the Jobseeker's Allowance Regulations 1996 (SI 1996/207) reg.140 (Hardship payments)*

With effect from July 26, 2021, Sch.3 para.4 of the Social Security (Scotland) Act 2018 (Disability Assistance for Children and Young People) (Consequential Modifications) Order 2021 (SI 2021/786) makes the following amendments to reg.140(1)(h):

6.077

- in para.(i), after "Benefits Act", insert ", the care component of child disability payment at the highest or middle rate in accordance with regulation 11(5) of the DACYP Regulations";
- in para.(ii), after "disability living allowance", insert ", child disability payment";
- after para.(iii), insert "(iiia) has claimed child disability payment and has an award of the care component of child disability payment at the highest or middle rate in accordance with regulation 11(5) of the DACYP Regulations for a period commencing after the date on which the claim was made; or".

With effect from March 21, 2022, art.5 of the Social Security (Disability Assistance for Working Age People) (Consequential Amendments) Order 2022 (SI 2022/177) makes the following amendments to reg.140(1)(h):

- in para.(i):
  - after "DACYP Regulations" for "or" substitute ",";
  - after "the 2012 Act" insert ", the daily living component of adult disability payment at the standard or enhanced rate in accordance with regulation 5 of the Disability Assistance for Working Age People (Scotland) Regulations 2022";
- in para.(ii):
  - after "armed forces independence payment" for "or" substitute ",";
  - after "personal independence payment" insert "or adult disability payment";
- after para.(iv) insert "(iva) has claimed adult disability payment and has an award of the daily living component of adult disability payment at the standard or enhanced rate in accordance with regulation 5 of the Disability Assistance for Working Age People (Scotland) Regulations 2022 for a period commencing after the date on which that claim was made; or".

pp.1071–1072, *amendments to the Jobseeker's Allowance Regulations 1996 (SI 1996/207) reg.146A (Meaning of "couple in hardship")*

6.078   With effect from July 26, 2021, Sch.3 para.5 of the Social Security (Scotland) Act 2018 (Disability Assistance for Children and Young People) (Consequential Modifications) Order 2021 (SI 2021/786) makes the following amendments to reg.146A(1)(e):

- in para.(i), after "Benefits Act", insert ", the care component of child disability payment at the highest or middle rate in accordance with regulation 11(5) of the DACYP Regulations";
- in para.(ii), after "disability living allowance", insert ", child disability payment";
- after para.(iii), insert "(iiia) has claimed child disability payment and has an award of the care component of child disability payment at the highest or middle rate in accordance with regulation 11(5) of the DACYP Regulations for a period commencing after the date on which the claim was made; or".

With effect from March 21, 2022, art.5(5) of the Social Security (Disability Assistance for Working Age People) (Consequential Amendments) Order 2022 (SI 2022/177) makes the following amendments to reg.146A(1)(e):

- in para.(i):
  - after "armed forces independence payment", for "or" substitute ",";
  - after "the 2012 Act" insert ", or the daily living component of adult disability payment at the standard or enhanced rate in accordance with regulation 5 of the Disability Assistance for Working Age People (Scotland) Regulations 2022";
- in para.(ii):
  - after "armed forces independence payment", for "or" substitute ",";
  - after "personal independence payment" insert "or adult disability payment";
- after para.(iv) insert "(iva) has claimed adult disability payment and has an award of the daily living component at the standard or enhanced rate in accordance with regulation 5 of the Disability Assistance for Working Age People (Scotland) Regulations 2022 for a period commencing after the date on which that claim was made; or".

p.1080, *amendment to the Jobseeker's Allowance Regulations 1996 SI 1996/207), reg.150 (amount of a jobseeker's allowance payable)*

With effect from November 19, 2023, art.8 of the Carer's Assistance (Carer Support Payment) (Scotland) Regulations 2023 (Consequential Amendments) Order 2023 (SI 2023/1218) makes the following amendment to reg.150(2):

after "carer's allowance," insert "carer support payment,".

6.079

p.1081, *amendment to the Jobseeker's Allowance Regulations 1996 SI 1996/207), reg.153 (modification in the calculation of income),*

With effect from November 19, 2023, art.8 of the Carer's Assistance (Carer Support Payment) (Scotland) Regulations 2023 (Consequential Amendments) Order 2023 (SI 2023/1218) makes the following amendment to reg.153(c):

after "carer's allowance," insert "carer support payment,".

6.080

p.1086, *amendment to the Jobseeker's Allowance Regulations 1996 (SI 1996/207) reg.172 (Trade disputes: prescribed sum)*

With effect from April 10, 2023, art.28 of the Social Security Benefits Up-rating Order 2023 (SI 2023/316) substituted "£47.00" for "£42.50" (as had been in effect from April 11, 2022).

6.081

pp.1087–1088, *amendments to the Jobseeker's Allowance Regulations 1996 (SI 1996/207) Sch.A1 (Categories of members of a joint-claim couple who are not required to satisfy the conditions in section 1(2B)(b))*

With effect from July 26, 2021, Sch.3 para.6 of the Social Security (Scotland) Act 2018 (Disability Assistance for Children and Young People) (Consequential Modifications) Order 2021 (SI 2021/786) makes the following amendments to para.3(a) (member caring for another person):

6.082

- in para.(i), after "Benefits Act", insert ", the care component of child disability payment at the highest or middle rate in accordance with regulation 11(5) of the DACYP Regulations";
- in para.(iv), after "disability living allowance", insert ", child disability payment";
- after para.(v), insert "(va) the person being cared for ("P") has claimed entitlement to the care component of child disability payment in accordance with regulation 24 (when an application is to be treated as made and beginning of entitlement to assistance) of the DACYP Regulations, an award at the highest or middle rate has been made in respect of P's claim, and where the period for which the award is payable has begun, P is in receipt of that payment;"

With effect from March 21, 2022, art.5(6) of the Social Security (Disability Assistance for Working Age People) (Consequential Amendments) Order 2022 (SI 2022/177) makes the following amendments to para.3(a) (member caring for another person):

- in para.3(a)(i) (member caring for another person):
  - after "armed forces independence payment" for "or" substitute "";
  - after "the 2012 Act" insert "or the daily living component of adult disability payment at the standard or enhanced rate in accordance with regulation 5 of the Disability Assistance for Working Age People (Scotland) Regulations 2022";
- in para.3(a)(iv):
  - after "armed forces independence payment" for "or" substitute "";
  - after "personal independence payment" insert "or adult disability payment";
- in para.3(a)(vi) omit "or" at the end; and
- after para.3(a)(vi) insert "(via) the person being cared for has claimed entitlement to the daily living component of adult disability payment in accordance with regulation 35 (when an application is to be treated as made and beginning of entitlement to assistance) of the Disability Assistance for Working Age People (Scotland) Regulations 2022, an award of the standard or enhanced rate of the daily living component has been made in respect of that claim and, where the period for which the award is payable has begun, that person is in receipt of that payment; or"

With effect from November 19, 2023, art.8 of the Carer's Assistance (Carer Support Payment) (Scotland) Regulations 2023 (Consequential Amendments) Order 2023 (SI 2023/1218) makes the following amendment to para.3(b):

after "carer's allowance," insert "or carer support payment".

p.1091, *amendments to the Jobseeker's Allowance Regulations 1996 (SI 1996/207) Sch.1 (Applicable amounts)*

6.083   Substitute the following for paras 3.479–3.508

Regulations 83 and 84(1)

"SCHEDULE 1

Applicable Amounts

[⁹ Part I

Personal Allowances

1.—The weekly amounts specified in column (2) below in respect of each person or couple specified in column (1) shall be the weekly amounts specified for the purposes of regulations 83 [²⁸ 84(1), 86A and 86B] (applicable amounts and polygamous marriages).

3.479

Column (1) Person or Couple	Column (2) Amount
(1) Single claimant aged—	1.
(a) except where head (b) or (c) of this sub-paragraph applies, less than 18;	(a) [⁵⁵ £67.20];
(b) less than 18 who falls within paragraph (2) of regulation 57 and who—	(b) [⁵⁵ £67.20];
(i) is a person to whom regulation 59, 60 or 61 applies [¹ . . .]; or	
(ii) is the subject of a direction under section 16;	
(c) less than 18 who satisfies the condition in [³³ paragraph 13(1)(a)] of Part 3;	
(d) not less than 18 but less than 25;	
(e) not less than 25.	(c) [⁵⁵ £67.20];
	(d) [⁵⁵ £67.20];
	(e) [⁵⁵ £84.80];
(2) Lone parent aged—	2.
(a) except where head (b) or (c) of this sub-paragraph applies, less than 18;	(a) [⁵⁵ £67.20];
(b) less than 18 who falls within paragraph (2) of regulation 57 and who—	(b) [⁵⁵ £67.20];
(i) is a person to whom regulation 59, 60 or 61 applies [¹ . . .]; or	
(ii) is the subject of a direction under section 16;	(c) [⁵⁵ £67.20];
(c) less than 18 who satisfies the condition in [³³ paragraph 13(1)(a)] [² of Part 3];	
(d) not less than 18.	(d) [⁵⁵ £84.80].
(3) Couple—	3.
(a) where both members are aged less than 18 and—	(a) [⁵⁵ £101.50];
(i) at least one of them is treated as responsible for a child; or	
(ii) had they not been members of a couple, each would have been a person to whom regulation 59, 60 or 61 (circumstances in which a person aged 16 or 17 is eligible for a jobseeker's allowance) applied or	
(iii) had they not been members of a couple, the claimant would have been a person to whom regulation 59, 60 or 61 (circumstances in which a person aged 16 or 17 is eligible for a	

Column (1) *Person or Couple*	Column (2) *Amount*
jobseeker's allowance) applied and his partner satisfies the requirements for entitlement to income support [[36] or an income-related employment and support allowance] other than the requirement to make a claim for it; or	
[[1](iv) they are married [[31] or civil partners]and one member a of the couple is person to whom regulation 59, 60 or 61 applies and the other member is registered in accordance with regulation 62; or	
(iva) they are married [[31] or civil partners] and each member of the couple is a person to whom regulation 59, 60 or 61 applies; or]	
(v) there is a direction under section 16 (jobseeker's allowance in cases of severe hardship) in respect of each member; or	
(vi) there is a direction under section 16 in respect of one of them and the other is a person to whom regulation 59, 60 or 61 applies [[1] . . .], or	
(vii) there is a direction under section 16 in respect of one of them and the other satisfies requirements for entitlement to income support [[36] or an income-related employment and support allowance] other than the requirement to make a claim for it;	
(b) where both members are aged less than 18 and sub-paragraph (3)(a) does not apply but one member of the couple falls within paragraph (2) of regulation 57 and either— (i) is a person to whom regulation 59, 60 or 61 applies [[1] . . .]; or (ii) is the subject of a direction under section 16 of the Act;	(b) [[55] £67.20];
(c) where both members are aged less than 18 and neither head (a) nor (b) of sub-paragraph (3) applies but one member of the couple— (i) is a person to whom regulation 59, 60 or 61 applies [[1] . . .]; or (ii) is the subject of a direction under section 16;	(c) [[55] £67.20];
(d) where both members are aged less than 18 and none of heads (a), (b) or (c) of sub-paragraph (3) apply but one member of the couple is a person who satisfies the requirements of [[33] paragraph 13(1)(a)];	(d) [[55] £67.20];
[[35] (e) where— (i) both members are aged not less than 18; or (ii) one member is aged not less than 18 and the other member is a person who is— (aa) under 18, and (bb) treated as responsible for a child;]	(e) [[55] £133.30];
(f) where [[35] paragraph (e) does not apply and] one member is aged not less than 18 and the other member is a person under 18 who— (i) is a person to whom regulation 59, 60 or 61 applies [[1] . . .]; or (ii) is the subject of a direction under section 16; [[38] or	(f) [[55] £133.30];

Column (1) Person or Couple	Column (2) Amount

(iii) satisfies requirements for entitlement to income support or who would do so if he were not a member of a couple, other than the requirement to make a claim for it; or
    (iv) satisfies requirements for entitlement to an income-related employment and support allowance other than the requirement to make a claim for it;]
(g) where one member is aged not less than 18 but less than 25 and the other member is a person under 18—
    (i) to whom none of the regulations 59 to 61 applies; or
    (ii) who is not the subject of a direction under section 16; and
    (iii) does not satisfy requirements for entitlement to income support [³⁶ or an income-related employment and support allowance] disregarding the requirement to make a claim for it;
(h) where one member is aged not less than 25 and the other member is a person under 18—
    (i) to whom none of the regulations 59 to 61 applies; or
    (ii) is not the subject of a direction under section 16; and
    (iii) does not satisfy requirements for entitlement to income support [³⁶ or an income-related employment and support allowance] disregarding the requirement to make a claim for it.
	(g) [⁵⁵ £67.20];
	
	(h) [⁵⁵ £84.80].

2.—[³⁰ . . .]	
3.—[²⁹ . . .]	

PART II

FAMILY PREMIUM

4.—[³⁰ . . .]

3.480

PART III

PREMIUMS

5.—Except as provided in paragraph 6, the weekly premiums specified in Part IV of this Schedule shall for the purposes of regulations 83(e) and 84(1)(f), be applicable to a claimant who satisfies the condition specified in [⁴ ¹⁵ paragraphs 9A] to 17 in respect of that premium.

3.481

6.—Subject to paragraph 7, where a claimant satisfies the conditions in respect of more than one premium in this Part of this Schedule, only one premium shall be applicable to him and, if they are different amounts, the higher or highest amount shall apply.

[¹⁶ **7.**—(1) Subject to sub-paragraph (2), the following premiums, namely—

(a) a severe disability premium to which paragraph 15 applies;

(b) an enhanced disability premium to which paragraph 15A applies;

(c) [³⁰ . . .]; and

(d) a carer premium in which paragraph 17 applies,

may be applicable in addition to any other premium which may apply under this Part of this Schedule.

(2) An enhanced disability premium in respect of a person shall not be applicable in addition to—

(a) a pensioner premium under paragraph 10 or 11; or

(b) a higher pensioner premium under paragraph 12.]

8.—(1) Subject to sub-paragraph (2) for the purposes of this Part of this Schedule, once a premium is applicable to a claimant under this Part, a person shall be treated as being in receipt of any benefit—

(a) in the case of a benefit to which the Social Security (Overlapping Benefits) Regulations 1979 applies, for any period during which, apart from the provisions of those Regulations, he would be in receipt of that benefit; [58 ...]

[3(b) for any period spent by a claimant in undertaking a course of training or instruction provided or approved by the Secretary of State [35 ...] under section 2 of the Employment and Training Act 1973, or by [37 Skills Development Scotland,] Scottish Enterprise or Highlands and Islands Enterprise under section 2 of the Enterprise and New Towns (Scotland) Act 1990 or for any period during which he is in receipt of a training allowance [58 ... ; and

(c) in the case of carer support payment, for any period during which, apart from regulation 16 of the Carer's Assistance (Carer Support Payment) (Scotland) Regulations 2023, he would be in receipt of that benefit.]]

(2) For the purposes of the carer premium under paragraph 17, a person shall be treated as being in receipt of [24 carer's allowance] by virtue of sub-paragraph (1)(a) [58 or carer support payment by virtue of sub-paragraph (1)(c)] only if and for so long as the person in respect of whose care the allowance [48 or payment] has been claimed remains in receipt of attendance allowance, [46 the care component of disability living allowance at the highest or middle rate prescribed in accordance with section 72(3) of the Benefits Act [52, the care component of child disability payment at the highest or middle rate prescribed in accordance with regulation 11(5) of the DACYP Regulations] [47, armed forces independence payment] [53,] the daily living component of personal independence payment at the standard or enhanced rate prescribed in accordance with section 78(3) of the 2012 Act] [53, or the daily living component of adult disability payment at the standard or enhanced rate prescribed in accordance with regulation 5 of the Disability Assistance for Working Age People (Scotland) Regulations 2022].

Lone Parent Premium

3.482   **9.**—[4 . . .]

[15 Bereavement Premium

3.483   **9A.**—[34 . . .]]

Pensioner premium for persons [40 over the qualifying age for state pension credit]

3.484   **10.**—The condition is that the claimant—

(a) is a single claimant or lone parent who has attained [40 the qualifying age for state pension credit]; or

(b) has attained [40 the qualifying age for state pension credit] and has a partner; or

(c) has a partner and the partner has attained [40 the qualifying age for state pension credit] but not the age of 75.

Pensioner premium where claimant's partner has attained the age of 75

3.485   **11.**—The condition is that the claimant has a partner who has attained the age of 75 but not the age of 80.

Higher Pensioner Premium

3.486   **12.**—(1) [33 Subject to sub-paragraph (5), the] condition is that—

(a) the claimant is a single claimant or lone parent who has attained [40 the qualifying age for state pension credit] and either—

(i) satisfies one of the additional conditions specified in paragraph 14(1)(a), (c), [51 (ca), (cb),] (e), (f) [51, (fa)] or (h); or

(ii) was entitled to either income support or income-based jobseeker's allowance [12, or was treated as being entitled to either of those benefits and the disability premium was or, as the case may be, would have been,] applicable to him in respect of a benefit week within 8 weeks of [40 the date he attained the qualifying age for state pension credit] and he has, subject to sub-paragraph (2), remained continuously entitled to one of those benefits since attaining that age; or

   (b) the claimant has a partner and—
      (i) the partner has attained the age of 80; or
     (ii) the partner has attained [⁴⁰ the qualifying age for state pension credit] but not the age of 80, and the additional conditions specified in paragraph 14 are satisfied in respect of him; or
   (c) the claimant—
      (i) has attained [⁴⁰ the qualifying age for state pension credit];
    [³(ii) satisfies the requirements of either sub-head (i) or (ii) of paragraph 12(1)(a); and]
    (iii) has a partner.
   (2) For the purposes of this paragraph and paragraph 14—
   (a) once the higher pensioner premium is applicable to a claimant, if he then ceases, for a period of eight weeks or less, to be entitled to either income support or income-based jobseeker's allowance [¹² or ceases to be treated as entitled to either of those benefits], he shall, on becoming re-entitled to either of those benefits, thereafter be treated as having been continuously entitled thereto;
   (b) in so far as sub-paragraphs (1)(a)(ii) and (1)(c)(ii) are concerned, if a claimant ceases to be entitled to either income support or an income-based jobseeker's allowance [¹² or ceases to be treated as entitled to either of those benefits] for a period not exceeding eight weeks which includes [⁴⁰ the date he attained the qualifying age for state pension credit], he shall, on becoming re-entitled to either of those benefits, thereafter be treated as having been continuously entitled thereto.
   [⁸(3) In this paragraph where a claimant's partner is a welfare to work beneficiary, sub-paragraphs (1)(a)(ii) and (2)(b) shall apply to him as if for the words "8 weeks" there were substituted the words "[³² 104 weeks]".]
   [¹² (4) For the purposes of this paragraph, a claimant shall be treated as having been entitled to income support or to an income-based jobseeker's allowance throughout any period which comprises only days on which he was participating in an employment zone programme and was not entitled to—
   (a) income support because, as a consequence of his participation in that programme, he was engaged in remunerative work or had income in excess of the claimant's applicable amount as prescribed in Part IV of the Income Support Regulations; or
   (b) a jobseeker's allowance because, as a consequence of his participation in that programme, he was engaged in remunerative work or failed to satisfy the condition specified in section 2(1)(c) or in section 3(1)(a).]
   [³³ (5) The condition is not satisfied if—
   (a) the claimant is a single claimant or a lone parent and (in either case) is a long-term patient;
   (b) the claimant is a member of a couple or polygamous marriage and each member of the couple or polygamous marriage is a long-term patient; or
   (c) the claimant is a member of a couple or a polygamous marriage and a member of that couple or polygamous marriage is—
      (i) a long-term patient; and
     (ii) the only member of the couple or polygamous marriage to whom sub-paragraph (1)(b) or (c) refers.]

Disability Premium

13. [³³—(1) Subject to sub-paragraph (2), the] condition is that the claimant—   **3.487**
   (a) is a single claimant or lone parent who has not attained [⁴⁰ the qualifying age for state pension credit] and satisfies any one of the additional conditions specified in paragraph 14(1)(a), (c), [⁵¹ (ca), (cb),] (e), (f) [⁵¹, (fa)] or (h); or
   (b) has not attained [⁴⁰ the qualifying age for state pension credit], has a partner and the claimant satisfies any one of the additional conditions specified in paragraph 14(1)(a), (c), [⁵¹ (ca), (cb),] (e), (f) [⁵¹, (fa)] or (h); or
   (c) has a partner and the partner has not attained [⁴⁰ the qualifying age for state pension credit] and also satisfies any one of the additional conditions specified in paragraph 14.
   [³³ (2) The condition is not satisfied if—
   (a) the claimant is a single claimant or a lone parent and (in either case) is a long-term patient;
   (b) the claimant is a member of a couple or polygamous marriage and each member of the couple or polygamous marriage is a long-term patient; or

(c) the claimant is a member of a couple or polygamous marriage and a member of that couple or polygamous marriage—

    (i) is a long-term patient; and

    (ii) is the only member of the couple or polygamous marriage to whom the condition in sub-paragraph (1)(b) or (c) refers.]

Additional conditions for Higher Pensioner and Disability Premium

3.488   **14.**—(1) The additional conditions specified in this paragraph are that—

(a) the claimant or, as the case may be, his partner, is in receipt [25 the disability element or the severe disability element of working tax credit as specified in regulation 20(1) (b) and (f) of the Working Tax Credit (Entitlement and Maximum Rate) Regulations 2002] or mobility supplement;

(b) the claimant's partner is in receipt of severe disablement allowance;

(c) the claimant or, as the case may be, his partner, is in receipt of attendance allowance or disability living allowance or is a person whose disability living allowance is payable, in whole or in part, to another in accordance with regulation 44 of the Claims and Payments Regulations (payment of disability living allowance on behalf of third party);

[46 (ca) the claimant or, as the case may be, his partner, is in receipt of personal independence payment or is a person whose personal independence payment is payable, in whole or in part, to another in accordance with regulation 58(2) of the Universal Credit etc. Claims and Payments Regulations (payment to another person on the claimant's behalf);]

[53 (caa) the claimant or, as the case may be, the claimant's partner, is in receipt of adult disability payment or is a person whose adult disability payment is payable, in whole or in part, to another in accordance with regulation 33 of the Disability Assistance for Working Age People (Scotland) Regulations 2022 (making payments);]

[47 (cb) the claimant or, as the case may be, the claimant's partner, is in receipt of armed forces independence payment or is a person whose armed forces independence payment is payable, in whole or in part, to another in accordance with article 24D of the Armed Forces and Reserve Forces (Compensation Scheme) Order 2011;]

(d) the claimant's partner is in receipt of long-term incapacity benefit or is a person to whom section 30B(4) of the Benefits Act (long term rate of incapacity benefit payable to those who are terminally ill) applies;

(e) the claimant or, as the case may be, his partner, has an invalid carriage or other vehicle provided to him by the Secretary of State under section 5(2)(a) of and Schedule 2 to the National Health Service Act 1977 or under section 46 of the National Health Service (Scotland) Act 1978 or provided by the Department of Health and Social Services for Northern Ireland under article 30(1) of the Health and Personal Social Services (Northern Ireland) Order 1972, or receives payments by way of grant from the Secretary of State under paragraph 2 of Schedule 2 to the Act of 1977 (additional provisions as to vehicles) or, in Scotland, under section 46 of the Act of 1978;

(f) the claimant or, as the case may be, his partner, is a person who is entitled to the mobility component of disability living allowance but to whom the component is not payable in accordance with regulation 42 of the Claims and Payments Regulations (cases where disability living allowance not payable);

[46 (fa) the claimant or, as the case may be, his partner, is a person who is entitled to the mobility component of personal independence payment but to whom the component is not payable in accordance with regulation 61 of the Universal Credit etc. Claims and Payments Regulations (cases where mobility component of personal independence payment not payable);]

[53 (fb) the claimant or, as the case may be, the claimant's partner, is a person who is entitled to the mobility component of adult disability payment but to whom the component is not payable in accordance with regulation 34(6) of the Disability Assistance for Working Age People (Scotland) Regulations 2022 (amount and form of adult disability payment);]

(g) the claimant's partner was either—

    (i) in receipt of long term incapacity benefit under section 30A(5) of the Benefits Act immediately before attaining pensionable age and he is still alive;

    (ii) entitled to attendance allowance or disability living allowance but payment of that benefit was suspended in accordance with regulations under section 113(2) of the Benefits Act or otherwise abated as a consequence of [2 the partner] becoming a patient within the meaning of regulation 85(4) (special cases), [53 ; . . .]

(iii) entitled to personal independence payment but no amount is payable in accordance with regulations made under section 86(1) (hospital in-patients) of the 2012 Act] [⁵³ ; or

(iv) entitled to adult disability payment but no amount is payable in accordance with regulation 28 (effect of admission to hospital on ongoing entitlement to Adult Disability Payment) of the Disability Assistance for Working Age People (Scotland) Regulations 2022;]

and [⁵³ in any of the cases described in sub-paragraphs (i) to (iv),]the higher pensioner premium or disability premium had been applicable to the claimant or his partner;

[⁴⁸ (h) the claimant or, as the case may be, his partner, is certified as severely sight impaired or blind by a consultant ophthalmologist.]

[⁴⁸ (2) For the purposes of sub-paragraph (1)(h), a person who has ceased to be certified as severely sight impaired or blind on regaining his eyesight shall nevertheless be treated as severely sight impaired or blind, as the case may be, and as satisfying the additional condition set out in that sub-paragraph for a period of 28 weeks following the date on which he ceased to be so certified.]

Severe Disability Premium

15.—(1) In the case of a single claimant, a lone parent or a claimant who is treated as having **3.489** no partner in consequence of sub-paragraph (3), the condition is that—

(a) he is in receipt of attendance allowance [⁴⁶ , the care component of disability living allowance at the highest or middle rate prescribed in accordance with section 72(3) of the Benefits Act [⁴⁷ , armed forces independence payment] [⁵³ ,] the daily living component of personal independence payment at the standard or enhanced rate in accordance with section 78(3) of the 2012 Act] [⁵³ , or the daily living component of adult disability payment at the standard or enhanced rate in accordance with regulation 5 of the Disability Assistance for Working Age People (Scotland) Regulations 2022]; and

(b) subject to sub-paragraph (4), there are no non-dependants aged 18 or over normally residing with him or with whom he is normally residing; and

[¹¹(c) no person is entitled to, and in receipt of, [²⁴ a carer's allowance] under section 70 of the Benefits Act [⁵⁰ or has an award of universal credit which includes the carer element] in respect of caring for him;]

(2) Where the claimant has a partner, the condition is that—

(a) the claimant is in receipt of attendance allowance [⁴⁶ , the care component of disability living allowance at the highest or middle rate prescribed in accordance with section 72(3) of the Benefits Act [⁴⁷ , armed forces independence payment] [⁵³ ,] the daily living component of personal independence payment at the standard or enhanced rate in accordance with section 78(3) of the 2012 Act] [⁵³ , or the daily living component of adult disability payment at the standard or enhanced rate in accordance with regulation 5 of the Disability Assistance for Working Age People (Scotland) Regulations 2022]; and

(b) the partner is also in receipt of a qualifying benefit, or if he is a member of a polygamous marriage, all the partners of that marriage are in receipt of a qualifying benefit; and

(c) subject to sub-paragraph (4), there is no non-dependant aged 18 or over normally residing with him or with whom he is normally residing; and

(d) either—

(i) [¹¹ no person is entitled to, and in receipt of, [²⁴ a carer's allowance] under section 70 of the Benefits Act [⁵⁸ or carer support payment] [⁵⁰ or has an award of universal credit which includes the carer element] in respect of] caring for either member of the couple or all the members of the polygamous marriage; or

(ii) a person is engaged in caring for one member (but not both members) of the couple, or one or more but not all members of the polygamous marriage, and in consequence is [¹¹ entitled to] [²⁴ a carer's allowance] under section 70 of the Benefits Act [⁵⁸ or carer support payment] [⁵⁰ or has an award of universal credit which includes the carer element].

(3) Where the claimant has a partner who does not satisfy the condition in sub-paragraph (2)(b), and that partner is [⁴⁸ severely sight impaired or blind or treated as severely sight impaired or blind] within the meaning of paragraph 14(1)(h) and (2), that partner shall be treated for the purposes of sub-paragraph (2) as if he were not a partner of the claimant.

(4) The following persons shall not be regarded as a non-dependant for the purposes of sub-paragraphs (1)(b) and (2)(c)—

(a) a person in receipt of attendance allowance [⁴⁶ , the care component of disability living allowance at the highest or middle rate prescribed in accordance with section 72(3) of the Benefits Act [⁴⁷ , armed forces independence payment] [⁵³ ,] the daily living component of personal independence payment at the standard or enhanced rate in accordance with section 78(3) of the 2012 Act] [53 , or the daily living component of adult disability payment at the standard or enhanced rate in accordance with regulation 5 of the Disability Assistance for Working Age People (Scotland) Regulations 2022];

    (b) subject to sub-paragraph (6), a person who joins the claimant's household for the first time in order to care for the claimant or his partner and immediately before so joining the claimant or his partner satisfied the condition in sub-paragraph (1) or, as the case may be, (2);

    (c) a person who is [48 severely sight impaired or blind or treated as severely sight impaired or blind] within the meaning of paragraph 14(1)(h) and (2).

(5) For the purposes of sub-paragraph (2), a person shall be treated [11 . . .] (a) [11 as being in receipt of] attendance allowance, or the care component of disability living allowance at the highest or middle rate prescribed in accordance with section 72(3) of the Benefits Act if he would, but for his being a patient for a period exceeding 28 days, be so in receipt;

[46 (aa) as being in receipt of the daily living component of personal independence payment at the standard or enhanced rate in accordance with section 78 of the 2012 Act if he would, but for regulations made under section 86(1) (hospital in-patients) of the 2012 Act, be so in receipt;]

[53 (ab) as being in receipt of the daily living component of adult disability payment at the standard or enhanced rate in accordance with regulation 5 of the Disability Assistance for Working Age People (Scotland) Regulations 2022 if they would, but for regulation 28 (effect of admission to hospital on ongoing entitlement to Adult Disability Payment) of those Regulations be so in receipt;]

[11 (b) as being entitled to and in receipt of [24 a carer's allowance] [58 or carer support payment] [50 or having an award of universal credit which includes the carer element] if he would, but for the person for whom he was caring being a patient in hospital for a period exceeding 28 days, be so entitled and in receipt [50 of carer's allowance [58 or carer support payment] or have such an award of universal credit].]

(6) Sub-paragraph (4)(b) shall apply only for the first 12 weeks following the date on which the person to whom that provision applies first joins the claimant's household.

(7) For the purposes of sub-paragraph (1)(c) and (2)(d), no account shall be taken of an award of [24 carer's allowance] [58 carer support payment] [50 or universal credit which includes the carer element] to the extent that payment of such an award is backdated for a period before [34 the date on which the award is first paid].

(8) A person shall be treated as satisfying this condition if he would have satisfied the condition specified for a severe disability premium in income support in paragraph 13 of Schedule 2 to the Income Support Regulations by virtue only of regulations 4 to 6 of the Income Support (General) Amendment (No. 6) Regulations 1991 (savings provisions in relation to severe disability premium) and for the purposes of determining whether in the particular case regulation 4 of those Regulations had ceased to apply in accordance with regulation 5(2)(a) of those Regulations, a person who is entitled to an income-based jobseeker's allowance shall be treated as entitled to income support.

[20 (9) In sub-paragraphs (1)(c) and (2)(d), references to a person being in receipt of [24 a carer's allowance] [50 or as having an award of universal credit which includes the carer element] shall include references to a person who would have been in receipt of that allowance [50 or had such an award] but for the application of a restriction under section [39 6B or] 7 of the Social Security Fraud Act 2001 (loss of benefit provisions).]

[50 (10) For the purposes of this paragraph, a person has an award of universal credit which includes the carer element if the person has an award of universal credit which includes an amount which is the carer element under regulation 29 of the Universal Credit Regulations 2013.]

[16 **Enhanced disability premium**

3.490   **15A.**—[46 (1) Subject to sub-paragraph (2), the condition is that—

    (a) the claimant; or

    (b) the claimant's partner (if any), is a person who has not attained the qualifying age for state pension credit and is a person to whom sub-paragraph (1ZA) applies.

(1ZA) This sub-paragraph applies to the person mentioned in sub-paragraph (1) where—

    (a) the care component of disability living allowance is, or would, but for a suspension of benefit in accordance with regulations under section 113(2) of the Benefits Act or but for an abatement as a consequence of hospitalisation, be payable to that person at the highest rate prescribed under section 72(3) of the Benefits Act; or

[52 (aa) the care component of child disability payment is payable to that person at the highest rate in accordance with regulation 11(5) of the DACYP Regulations; or]

    (b) the daily living component of personal independence payment is, or would, but for a suspension of benefits in accordance with regulations under section 86(1) (hospital in-patients) of the 2012 Act, be payable to that person at the enhanced rate in accordance with section 78(2) of the 2012 Act] [47 ; or

[53 (ba) the daily living component of adult disability payment is, or would, but regulation 28 (effect of admission to hospital on ongoing entitlement to Adult Disability Payment) of the Disability Assistance for Working Age People (Scotland) Regulations 2022, be payable to that person at the enhanced rate in accordance with regulation 5 of those Regulations]

    (c) armed forces independence payment is payable to that person.]

[42 (1A) Where the condition in sub-paragraph (1) ceases to be satisfied because of the death of a child or young person, the condition is that the claimant is entitled to child benefit in respect of that person under section 145A of the Benefits Act (entitlement after death of child or qualifying young person).]

[33 (2) The condition is not satisfied where the person to whom sub-paragraph (1) refers is—

    (a) a child or young person—
        (i) whose capital if calculated in accordance with Part 8 of these Regulations in like manner as for the claimant, except as provided in regulation 106(1), would exceed £3,000; or
        (ii) who is a long-term patient;
    (b) a single claimant or a lone parent and (in either case) is a long-term patient;
    (c) a member of a couple or polygamous marriage and each member of the couple or polygamous marriage is a long-term patient; or
    (d) a member of a couple or polygamous marriage who is—
        (i) a long-term patient; and
        (ii) the only member of the couple or polygamous marriage to whom sub-paragraph (1) refers.]]

Disabled Child Premium

  16.—[30 . . . 33]   3.491

Carer Premium

  17.—(1) Subject to sub-paragraphs (3) and (4), the condition is that the claimant or his   3.492
partner is, or both of them are, [11 entitled to] [24 a carer's allowance] [58 or carer support payment] under section 70 of the Benefits Act.

  (2) [28 . . .]

[23 (3) Where a carer premium is awarded but—

    (a) the person in respect of whose care the [24 carer's allowance] [58 or carer support payment] has been awarded dies; or
    (b) in any other case the person in respect of whom a carer premium has been awarded ceases to be entitled [28 . . .] to [24 a carer's allowance] [58 or carer support payment], the condition for the award of the premium shall be treated as satisfied for a period of eight weeks from the relevant date specified in sub-paragraph (3A) below.

  (3A) The relevant date for the purposes of sub-paragraph (3) above shall be—

    (a) [28 where sub-paragraph (3)(a) applies,] the Sunday following the death of the person in respect of whose care [24 a carer's allowance] [58 or carer support payment] has been awarded or the date of death if the death occurred on a Sunday;
    (b) [28 . . .]
    (c) in any other case, the date of which the person who has been entitled to [24 a carer's allowance] [58 or carer support payment] ceases to be entitled to that allowance [58 or payment].]

  (4) Where a person who has been entitled to an invalid care allowance ceases to be entitled to that allowance and makes a claim for a jobseeker's allowance, the condition for the award of the carer premium shall be treated as satisfied for a period of eight weeks from the date on which

  [23 (a) the person in respect of whose care the [24 carer's allowance] [58 or carer support payment] has been awarded dies;
    (b) [28 . . .]
[28 (c) in any other case, the person who has been entitled to a carer's allowance [58 or carer support payment] ceased to be entitled to that allowance [58 or payment].]]

Persons in receipt of concessionary payments

3.493   **18.**—For the purpose of determining whether a premium is applicable to a person under paragraphs 14 to 17, any concessionary payment made to compensate that person for the non-payment of any benefit mentioned in those paragraphs shall be treated as if it were a payment of that benefit.

Person in receipt of benefit

3.494   **19.**—For the purposes of this Part of this Schedule, a person shall be regarded as being in receipt of any benefit if, and only if, it is paid in respect of him and shall be so regarded only for any period in respect of which that benefit is paid.

PART IV

WEEKLY AMOUNTS OF PREMIUMS SPECIFIED IN
PART III

Premium	*Amount*
20.—(1) [⁴ . . .]	(1) [⁴ . . .]
(1A) [³⁴ . . .];	(1A) [³⁴ . . .];
(2) Pensioner premium for persons [⁴⁰ who have attained the qualifying age for state pension credit]— (a) where the claimant satisfies the condition in paragraph 10(a); (b) where the claimant satisfies the condition in paragraph 10(b). (c) where the claimant satisfies the condition in paragraph 10(c).	(2) (a) [⁵⁶ £116.25]; (b) [⁵⁶ £173.55]; (c) [⁵⁶ £173.55];
(3) Pensioner premium for claimants whose partner has attained the age of 75 where the claimant satisfies the condition in paragraph 11;	(3) [⁵⁶ £173.55];
(4) Higher Pensioner Premium— (a) where the claimant satisfies the condition in paragraph 12(1)(a); (b) where the claimant satisfies the condition in paragraph 12(1)(b) or (c).	(4) (a) [⁵⁶ £116.25]; (b) [⁵⁶ £173.55];
(5) Disability Premium— (a) where the claimant satisfies the condition in [³³ paragraph 13(1)(a)]; (b) where the claimant satisfies the condition in [³³ paragraph 13(1)(b) or (c)].	(5) (a) [⁵⁶ £39.85]; (b) [⁵⁶ £56.80].
(6) Severe Disability Premium— (a) where the claimant satisfies the condition in paragraph 15(1); (b) where the claimant satisfies the condition in paragraph 15(2)— (i) if there is someone in receipt of [²⁴ a carer's allowance] [⁵⁸ or carer support payment] or [² if any partner of the claimant] satisfies that condition by virtue of paragraph 15(5); (ii) if no-one is in receipt of such an allowance [⁵⁸ or payment].	(6) (a) [⁵⁶ £76.40]; (b) (i) [⁵⁶ £76.40] (ii) [⁵⁶ £152.80]
(7) [³⁰ . . .]	(7) [³⁰ . . .]
(8) Carer Premium.	(8) [⁵⁶ £42.75] in respect of each person who satisfied the condition specified in paragraph 17.

Premium	Amount

[¹⁶ (9) Enhanced disability premium where the conditions in paragraph 15A are satisfied.]	[¹⁶ (9) (a) [³⁰ . . .]
	(b) [⁵⁶ £19.55] in respect of each person who is neither—
	   (i) a child or young person; nor
	   (ii) a member of a couple or a polygamous marriage, respect of whom the in conditions specified in paragraph 15A are satisfied;
	(c) [⁵⁶ £27.90] where the claimant is a member of a couple or a polygamous marriage and the conditions specified in paragraph 15A are satisfied in respect of a member of that couple or polygamous marriage.]

[¹⁴ PART IVA

PREMIUMS FOR JOINT-CLAIM COUPLES

20A.—Except as provided in paragraph 20B, the weekly premium specified in Part IVB of this Schedule shall, for the purposes of regulations 86A(c) and 86B(d), be applicable to a joint-claim couple where either or both members of a joint-claim couple satisfy the condition specified in paragraphs 20E to 20J in respect of that premium.

3.497

20B.—Subject to paragraph 20C, where a member of a joint-claim couple satisfies the conditions in respect of more than one premium in this Part of this Schedule, only one premium shall be applicable to the joint-claim couple in respect of that member and, if they are different amounts, the higher or highest amount shall apply.

[¹⁶ **20C.**—(1) Subject to sub-paragraph (2), the following premiums, namely—
(a) a severe disability premium to which paragraph 20I applies;
(b) an enhanced disability premium to which paragraph 20IA applies; and
(c) a carer premium to which paragraph 20J applies,
may be applicable in addition to any other premium which may apply under this Part of this Schedule.

(2) An enhanced disability premium in respect of a person shall not be applicable in addition to—
(a) a pensioner premium under paragraph 20E; or
(b) a higher pensioner premium under paragraph 20F.]

20D.—(1) Subject to sub-paragraph (2) for the purposes of this Part of this Schedule, once a premium is applicable to a joint-claim couple under this Part, a person shall be treated as being in receipt of any benefit—
(a) in the case of a benefit to which the Social Security (Overlapping Benefits) Regulations 1979 applies, for any period during which, apart from the provisions of those Regulations, he would be in receipt of that benefit; [⁵⁸ . . .]
(b) for any period spent by a person in undertaking a course of training or instruction provided or approved by the Secretary of State under section 2 of the Employment and Training Act 1973, or by [³⁷ Skills Development Scotland,] Scottish Enterprise or Highlands and Islands Enterprise under section 2 of the Enterprise and New Towns (Scotland) Act 1990, or for any period during which he is in receipt of a training allowance [⁵⁸ ; and
(c) in the case of carer support payment, for any period during which, apart from regulation 16 of the Carer's Assistance (Carer Support Payment) (Scotland) Regulations 2023, he would be in receipt of that benefit.]

(2) For the purposes of the carer premium under paragraph 20J, a person shall be treated as being in receipt of [²⁴ carer's allowance] by virtue of sub-paragraph (1)(a) [⁵⁸ or carer support payment by virtue of sub-paragraph (1)(c)] only if and for so long as the person in respect of

231

whose care the allowance [58 or payment] has been claimed remains in receipt of attendance allowance, [46 the care component of disability living allowance at the highest or middle rate prescribed in accordance with section 72(3) of the Benefits Act [52 or the care component of child disability payment at the highest or middle rate in accordance with regulation 11(5) of the DACYP Regulations]or the daily living component of personal independence payment at the standard or enhanced rate in accordance with section 78(3) of the 2012 Act [53 , the daily living component of adult disability payment at the standard or enhanced rate in accordance with regulation 5 of the [54 Disability Assistance for Working Age People (Scotland) Regulations 2022] [47 or armed forces independence payment]].

Pensioner premium where one member of a joint-claim couple has attained [40 the qualifying age for state pension credit]

3.498   **20E.**—The condition is that one member of a joint-claim couple has attained [40 the qualifying age for state pension credit]but not the age of 75.

Higher Pensioner Premium

3.499   **20F.**—(1) [33 Subject to sub-paragraph (5), the] condition is that one member of a joint claim couple—

(a)   has attained [40 the qualifying age for state pension credit] but not the age of 80, and either the additional conditions specified in paragraph 20H are satisfied in respect of him; or

(b)   has attained [40 the qualifying age for state pension credit] and—

   (i)   was entitled to or was treated as entitled to either income support or an income-based jobseeker's allowance and the disability premium was or, as the case may be, would have been applicable to him in respect of a benefit week within 8 weeks of [40 the date he attained the qualifying age for state pension credit] and he has, subject to sub-paragraph (2), remained continuously entitled to one of those benefits since attaining that age; or

   (ii)   was a member of a joint-claim couple who had been entitled to, or who had been treated as entitled to, a joint-claim jobseeker's allowance and the disability premium was or, as the case may be, would have been applicable to that couple in respect of a benefit week within 8 weeks of [40 the date either member of that couple attained the qualifying age for state pension credit] and the couple have, subject to that sub-paragraph (2), remained continuously entitled to a joint claim jobseeker's allowance since that member attained that age.

(2) For the purpose of this paragraph and paragraph 20H—

(a)   once the higher pensioner premium is applicable to a joint-claim couple, if that member then ceases, for a period of 8 weeks or less, to be entitled or treated as entitled to either income support or income-based jobseeker's allowance or that couple cease to be entitled to or treated as entitled to a joint-claim jobseeker's allowance, he shall or, as the case may be, that couple shall, on becoming re-entitled to any of those benefits, thereafter be treated as having been continuously entitled thereto;

(b)   in so far as sub-paragraph (1)(b)(i) or (ii) is concerned, if a member of a joint-claim couple ceases to be entitled or treated as entitled to either income support or an income-based jobseeker's allowance or that couple cease to be entitled to or treated as entitled to a joint-claim jobseeker's allowance for a period not exceeding 8 weeks which includes [40 the date either member of that couple attained the qualifying age for state pension credit], he shall or, as the case may be, the couple shall, on becoming re-entitled to either of those benefits, thereafter be treated as having been continuously entitled thereto.

(3) In this paragraph, where a member of a joint-claim couple is a welfare to work beneficiary, sub-paragraphs (1)(b)(i) and (2)(b) shall apply to him as if for the words "8 weeks" there were substituted the words "[32104 weeks]".

(4) For the purposes of this paragraph, a member of a joint-claim couple shall be treated as having been entitled to income support or to an income-based jobseeker's allowance or the couple of which he is a member shall be treated as having been entitled to a joint-claim jobseeker's allowance throughout any period which comprises only days on which a member was participating in an employment zone scheme and was not entitled to—

(a)   income support because, as a consequence of his participation in that scheme, he was engaged in remunerative work or had income in excess of the claimant's applicable amount as prescribed in Part IV of the Income Support Regulations; or

(b)   a jobseeker's allowance because, as a consequence of his participation in that scheme, he was engaged in remunerative work or failed to satisfy the condition specified in section 2(1)(c) or the couple of which he was a member failed to satisfy the condition in section 3A(1)(a).

[³³ (5) The condition is not satisfied if the member of the joint-claim couple to whom sub-paragraph (1) refers is a long-term patient.]

[³³ Disability Premium

20G.—(1) Subject to sub-paragraph (2), the condition is that a member of a joint-claim couple has not attained [⁴⁰ the qualifying age for state pension credit] and satisfies any one of the additional conditions specified in paragraph 20H.

3.500

(2) The condition is not satisfied if—

    (a) paragraph (1) only refers to one member of a joint-claim couple and that member is a long-term patient; or

    (b) paragraph (1) refers to both members of a joint-claim couple and both members of the couple are long-term patients.]

Additional conditions for Higher Pensioner and Disability Premium

20H.—(1) The additional conditions specified in this paragraph are that a member of a joint-claim couple—

3.501

    (a) is in receipt of [²⁶ the disability element or the severe disability element of working tax credit as specified in regulation 20(1)(b) and (f) of the Working Tax Credit (Entitlement and Maximum Rate) Regulations 2002] or mobility supplement;

    (b) is in receipt of severe disablement allowance;

    (c) is in receipt of attendance allowance or disability living allowance or is a person whose disability living allowance is payable, in whole or in part, to another in accordance with regulation 44 of the Claims and Payments Regulations (payment of disability living allowance on behalf of third party);

[⁴⁶ (ca) is in receipt of personal independence payment or is a person whose personal independence payment is payable, in whole or in part, to another in accordance with regulation 58(2) of the Universal Credit etc. Claims and Payments Regulations (payment to another person on the claimant's behalf);]

[⁵³ (caa) is in receipt of adult disability payment or is a person whose adult disability payment is payable, in whole or in part, to another in accordance with regulation 33 of the Disability Assistance for Working Age People (Scotland) Regulations 2022 (making payments);]

[⁴⁷ (cb) is in receipt of armed forces independence payment or is a person whose armed forces independence payment is payable, in whole or in part, to another in accordance with article 24D of the Armed Forces and Reserve Forces (Compensation Scheme) Order 2011;]

    (d) is in receipt of long-term incapacity benefit or is a person to whom section 30B(4) of the Benefits Act (long-term rate of incapacity benefit payable to those who are terminally ill) applies;

    (e) has been entitled to statutory sick pay, has been incapable of work or has been treated as incapable of work for a continuous period of not less than—

        (i) 196 days in the case of a member of a joint-claim couple who is terminally ill within the meaning of section 30B(4) of the Benefits Act; or

        (ii) 364 days in any other case,

and for these purposes, any two or more periods of entitlement or incapacity separated by a break of not more than 56 days shall be treated as one continuous period;

[³⁶ (ee) has had limited capability for work or has been treated as having limited capability for work for a continuous period of not less than—

        (i) 196 days in the case of a member of a joint-claim couple who is terminally ill within the meaning of regulation 2(1) of the Employment and Support Allowance Regulations; or

        (ii) 364 days in any other case,

and for these purposes any two or more periods of limited capability for work separated by a break of not more than 12 weeks is to be treated as one continuous period;]

    (f) has an invalid carriage or other vehicle provided to him by the Secretary of State under section 5(2)(a) of, and Schedule 2 to, the National Health Service Act 1977 or under section 46 of the National Health Service (Scotland) Act 1978 or provided by the Department of Health and Social Services for Northern Ireland under article 30(1) of the Health and Personal Social Services (Northern Ireland) Order 1972, or receives payments by way of grant from the Secretary of State under paragraph 2 of Schedule 2 to the Act of 1977 (additional provisions as to vehicles) or, in Scotland, under section 46 of the Act of 1978;

    (g) is a person who is entitled to the mobility component of disability living allowance but to whom the component is not payable in accordance with regulation 42 of the Claims and Payments Regulations (cases where disability living allowance not payable);

[⁴⁶ (ga) is a person who is entitled to the mobility component of personal independence payment but to whom the component is not payable in accordance with regulation 61 of the Universal Credit etc. Claims and Payments Regulations (cases where mobility component of personal independence payment not payable);]

[⁵³ (gb) is a person who is entitled to the mobility component of adult disability payment but to whom the component is not payable in accordance with regulation 34(6) of the Disability Assistance for Working Age People (Scotland) Regulations 2022 (amount and form of adult disability payment);]

    (h) was either—

        (i) in receipt of long-term incapacity benefit under section 30A(5) of the Benefits Act immediately before attaining pensionable age and he is still alive; or

        (ii) entitled to attendance allowance or disability living allowance but payment of that benefit was suspended in accordance with regulations under section 113(2) of the Benefits Act or otherwise abated as a consequence of either member of the joint-claim couple becoming a patient within the meaning of regulation 85(4) (special cases), [⁴⁶ [⁵³ . . .]

        (iii) entitled to personal independence payment but no amount is payable in accordance with regulations under section 86(1) (hospital in-patients) of the 2012 Act,] [⁵³ or

        (iv) entitled to adult disability payment but no amount is payable in accordance with regulation 28 (effect of admission to hospital on ongoing entitlement to Adult [⁵⁴ Disability Payment) of the Disability Assistance for Working Age People (Scotland) Regulations 2022,]

and [⁵³ in any of the cases described in paragraphs (i) to (iv)], the higher pensioner premium or disability premium had been applicable to the joint-claim couple; or

[⁴⁸ (l) is certified as severely sight impaired or blind by a consultant ophthalmologist.]

    (2) [⁴¹ . . . [³² . . .]]

[⁴⁸ (3) For the purposes of sub-paragraph (1)(i), a person who has ceased to be certified as severely sight impaired or blind on regaining his eyesight shall nevertheless be treated as severely sight impaired or blind, as the case may be, and as satisfying the additional condition set out in that sub-paragraph for a period of 28 weeks following the date on which he ceased to be so certified.]

Severe Disability Premium

3.502   20I.—(1) The condition is that—

    (a) a member of a joint-claim couple is in receipt of attendance allowance [⁴⁶ , the care component of disability living allowance at the highest or middle rate prescribed in accordance with section 72(3) of the Benefits Act [⁴⁷ , armed forces independence payment] [⁵³ ,] the daily living component of personal independence payment at the standard or enhanced rate in accordance with section 78(3) of the 2012 Act] [⁵³ , or the daily living component of adult disability payment at the standard or enhanced rate in accordance with regulation 5 of the Disability Assistance for Working Age People (Scotland) Regulations 2022]; and

    (b) the other member is also in receipt of such an allowance, or if he is a member of a polygamous marriage, all the partners of that marriage are in receipt of a qualifying benefit; and

    (c) subject to sub-paragraph (3), there is no non-dependant aged 18 or over normally residing with the joint-claim couple or with whom they are normally residing; and

    (d) either—

        (i) no person is entitled to, and in receipt of, [²⁴ a carer's allowance] [⁵⁸ or carer support payment] under section 70 of the Benefits Act [⁵⁰ or has an award of universal credit which includes the carer element] in respect of caring for either member or the couple or all the members of the polygamous marriage; or

        (ii) a person is engaged in caring for one member (but not both members) of the couple, or one or more but not all members of the polygamous marriage, and in consequence is entitled to [²⁴ a carer's allowance] under section 70 of the Benefits Act [⁵⁸ or carer support payment] [⁵⁰ or has an award of universal credit which includes the carer element].

(2) Where the other member does not satisfy the condition in sub-paragraph (1)(b), and that member is [48 severely sight impaired or blind or treated as severely sight impaired or blind] within the meaning of paragraph 20H(1)(i) and (2), that member shall be treated for the purposes of sub-paragraph (1) as if he were not a member of the couple.

(3) The following persons shall not be regarded as non-dependant for the purposes of sub-paragraph (1)(c)—

(a) a person in receipt of attendance allowance [46 , the care component of disability living allowance at the highest or middle rate prescribed in accordance with section 72(3) of the Benefits Act [47 , armed forces independence payment] [53 ,] the daily living component of personal independence payment at the standard or enhanced rate in accordance with section 78(3) of the 2012 Act] [53 , or the daily living component of adult disability payment at the standard or enhanced rate in accordance with regulation 5 of the Disability Assistance for Working Age People (Scotland) Regulations 2022];

(b) subject to sub-paragraph (5), a person who joins the joint-claim couple's household for the first time in order to care for a member of a joint claim couple and immediately before so joining, that member satisfied the condition in sub-paragraph (1);

(c) a person who is [48 severely sight impaired or blind or treated as severely sight impaired or blind] within the meaning of paragraph 20H(1)(i) and (2).

(4) For the purposes of sub-paragraph (1), a member of a joint-claim couple shall be treated—

(a) as being in receipt of attendance allowance, or the care component of disability living allowance at the highest or middle rate prescribed in accordance with section 72(3) of the Benefits Act if he would, but for his being a patient for a period exceeding 28 days, be so in receipt;

(b) as being entitled to and in receipt of [24 a carer's allowance] [58 or carer support payment] [50 or having an award of universal credit which includes the carer element] if he would, but for the person for whom he was caring being a patient in hospital for a period exceeding 28 days, be so entitled and in receipt [50 of carer's allowance [58 or carer support payment] or have such an award of universal credit].

[46 (c) as being in receipt of the daily living component of personal independence payment at the standard or enhanced rate in accordance with section 78 of the 2012 Act if he would, but for regulations made under section 86(1) (hospital in-patients) of the 2012 Act, be so in receipt.]

[53 (d) as being in receipt of the daily living component of adult disability payment at the standard or enhanced rate in accordance with regulation 5 of the [54 Disability Assistance for Working Age People (Scotland) Regulations 2022], if he would, but for regulation 28 (effect of admission to hospital on ongoing entitlement to Adult Disability Payment) of those Regulations, be so in receipt]

(5) Sub-paragraph (3)(b) shall apply only for the first 12 weeks following the date on which the person to whom that provision applies first joins the joint-claim couple's household.

(6) For the purposes of sub-paragraph (1)(d), no account shall be taken of an award of [24 carer's allowance] [58 or carer support payment] [50 or universal credit which includes the carer element] to the extent that payment of such an award is back-dated for a period before [34 the date on which the award is first paid].

[20(7) In sub-paragraph (1)(d), the reference to a person being in receipt of [24 a carer's allowance] [58 or carer support payment] [50 or as having an award of universal credit which includes the carer element] shall include a reference to a person who would have been in receipt of that allowance [58 or payment] [24 or had such an award] but for the application of a restriction under section [39 6B or] 7 of the Social Security Fraud Act 2001 (loss of benefit provisions).]

[50 (8) For the purposes of this paragraph, a person has an award of universal credit which includes the carer element if the person has an award of universal credit which includes an amount which is the carer element under regulation 29 of the Universal Credit Regulations 2013.]

[16 Enhanced disability premium

20IA.—[46 (1) Subject to sub-paragraph (2), the condition is that in respect of a member of a joint-claim couple who has not attained the qualifying age for state pension credit—

(a) the care component of disability living allowance is, or would, but for a suspension of benefit in accordance with regulations under section 113(2) of the Benefits Act or but for an abatement as a consequence of hospitalisation, be payable at the highest rate prescribed under section 72(3) of the Benefits Act; or

3.503

(b) the daily living component of personal independence payment is, or would, but for regulations made under section 86(1) (hospital in-patients) of the 2012 Act, be payable at the enhanced rate in accordance with section 78(2) of the 2012 Act [⁵³ , the daily living component of adult disability payment is, or would, but for regulation 28 (effect of admission to hospital on ongoing entitlement to Adult Disability Payment) of the [⁵⁴ Disability Assistance for Working Age People (Scotland) Regulations 2022], be payable at the enhanced rate under those Regulations,] [⁴⁷ or armed forces independence payment is payable].]

[³³ (2) The condition is not satisfied if—

(a) paragraph (1) only refers to one member of a joint-claim couple and that member is a long-term patient; or

(b) paragraph (1) refers to both members of a joint-claim couple and both members of the couple are long-term patients.]]

Carer Premium

3.504   **20J.**—(1) Subject to sub-paragraphs (3) and (4), the condition is that either or both members of a joint-claim couple are entitled to [²⁸ . . .] [²⁴ a carer's allowance] [⁵⁸ or carer support payment] under section 70 of the Benefits Act.

(2) [²⁸ . . .]

[²³ (3) Where a carer premium is awarded but—

(a) the person in respect of whose care the [²⁴ carer's allowance] [⁵⁸ or carer support payment] has been awarded dies: or

(b) in any other case the member of the joint-claim couple in respect of whom a carer premium has been awarded ceases to be entitled [²⁸ . . .] to [²⁴ a carer's allowance] [⁵⁸ or carer support payment],

the condition for the award of the premium shall be treated as satisfied for a period of eight weeks from the relevant date specified in sub-paragraph (3A) below.

(3A) The relevant date for the purposes of sub-paragraph (3) above shall be—

(a) [²⁸ where sub-paragraph (3)(a) applies,] the Sunday following the death of the person in respect of whose care [²⁴ a carer's allowance] [⁵⁸ or carer support payment] has been awarded or beginning with the date of death if the death occurred on a Sunday;

(b) [²⁸ . . .]

(c) in any other case, the date on which that member ceased to be entitled to [²⁴ a carer's allowance] [⁵⁸ or carer support payment].]

(4) Where a member of a joint-claim couple who has been entitled to [²⁴ a carer's allowance] [⁵⁸ or carer support payment] ceases to be entitled to that allowance [⁵⁸ or payment] and makes a claim for a jobseeker's allowance jointly with the other member of that couple, the condition for the award of the carer premium shall be treated as satisfied for a period of eight weeks from the date on which-

[²³(a) the person in respect of whose care [²⁴ carer's allowance] [⁵⁸ or carer support payment] has been awarded dies;

(b) [²⁸ . . .]

(c) [²⁸ in any other case, the person who has been entitled to a carer's allowance [⁵⁸ or carer support payment] ceased to be entitled to that allowance [⁵⁸ or payment].]]

Member of a joint-claim couple in receipt of concessionary payments

3.505   **20K.**—For the purpose of determining whether a premium is applicable to a joint-claim couple under paragraphs 20H to 20J, any concessionary payment made to compensate a person for the non-payment of any benefit mentioned in those paragraphs shall be treated as if it were a payment of that benefit.

Person in receipt of benefit

3.506   **20L.**—For the purposes of this Part of this Schedule, a member of a joint-claim couple shall be regarded as being in receipt of any benefit if, and only if, it is paid in respect of him and shall be so regarded only for any period in respect of which that benefit is paid.

PART IVB

Premium	Amount
20M.—	
(1) Pensioner premium where one member of a joint-claim couple [⁴⁰ has attained the qualifying age for state pension credit] and the condition in paragraph 20E is satisfied.	(1) [⁵⁷ £173.55].
(2) Higher Pensioner Premium where one member of a joint-claim couple satisfies the condition in paragraph 20F.	(2) [⁵⁷ £173.55].
(3) Disability Premium where one member of a joint-claim couple satisfies the condition in paragraph [³³ 20G(1)].	(3) [⁵⁷ £56.80].

(4) Severe Disability Premium where one member of a joint-claim couple satisfies the condition in paragraph 20I(1)—
   (i) if there is someone in receipt of [²⁴ a carer's allowance] [⁵⁸ or carer support payment] or if either member satisfies that condition only by virtue of paragraph [¹⁶ 20I(4)];
   (ii) if no-one is in receipt of such an allowance [⁵⁸ or payment].
	(4)
	
	   (i) [⁵⁷ £76.40];
	
	   (ii) [⁵⁷ £152.80].

(5) Carer Premium.	(5) [⁵⁷ £42.75] in respect of each person who satisfied the condition specified in paragraph 20J.]
[¹⁶ (6) Enhanced disability premium where the conditions specified in paragraph 20IA are satisfied.	(6) [⁵⁷ £27.90] where the conditions in paragraph 20IA are satisfied in respect of a member of a joint-claim couple.]

PART V

ROUNDING OF FRACTIONS

21.—Where an income-based jobseeker's allowance is awarded for a period which is not a complete benefit week and the applicable amount in respect of that period results in an amount which includes a fraction of one penny that fraction shall be treated as one penny."

3.508

AMENDMENTS

1. Jobseeker's Allowance (Amendment) Regulations 1996 (SI 1996/1516) reg.18 (October 7, 1996).
2. Jobseeker's Allowance (Amendment) Regulations 1996 (SI 1996/1516) reg.20 and Sch. (October 7, 1996).
3. Social Security and Child Support (Jobseeker's Allowance) (Miscellaneous Amendments) Regulations 1996 (SI 1996/2538) reg.2(11) (October 28, 1996).
4. Child Benefit, Child Support and Social Security (Miscellaneous Amendments) Regulations 1996 (SI 1996/1803) reg.44 (April 7, 1997).
5. Income-related Benefits and Jobseeker's Allowance (Personal Allowances for Children and Young Persons) (Amendment) Regulations 1996 (SI 1996/2545) reg.2 (April 7, 1997).
6. Income-related Benefits and Jobseeker's Allowance (Amendment) (No. 2) Regulations 1997 (SI 1997/2197) reg.7(5) and (6)(b) (October 6, 1997).

7. Social Security Amendment (Lone Parents) Regulations 1998 (SI 1998/766) reg.14 (April 6, 1998).

8. Social Security (Welfare to Work) Regulations 1998 (SI 1998/2231) reg.14(3) (October 5, 1998).

9. Social Security Amendment (Personal Allowances for Children and Young Persons) Regulations 1999 (SI 1999/2555) reg.2(1)(b) and (2) (April 10, 2000).

10. Social Security and Child Support (Tax Credits) Consequential Amendments Regulations 1999 (SI 1999/2566) reg.2(2) and Sch.2 Pt III (October 5, 1999).

11. Social Security (Miscellaneous Amendments) Regulations 2000 (SI 2000/681) reg.4(3) (April 3, 2000).

12. Social Security Amendment (Employment Zones) Regulations 2000 (SI 2000/724) reg.4 (April 3, 2000).

13. Social Security Amendment (Personal Allowances for Children) Regulations 2000 (SI 2000/1993) reg.2 (October 23, 2000).

14. Jobseeker's Allowance (Joint Claims) Regulations 2000 (SI 2000/1978) reg.2(5) and Sch.2 para.53 (March 19, 2001).

15. Social Security Amendment (Bereavement Benefits) Regulations 2000 (SI 2000/2239) reg.3(2) (April 9, 2001).

16. Social Security Amendment (Enhanced Disability Premium) Regulations 2000 (SI 2629) reg.5(c) (April 9, 2001).

17. Social Security Amendment (Joint Claims) Regulations 2001 (SI 2001/518) reg.2(7) (March 19, 2001).

18. Social Security Amendment (Bereavement Benefits) Regulations 2000 (SI 2000/2239) reg.3(2)(c) (April 9, 2001).

19. Social Security Amendment (Residential Care and Nursing Homes) Regulations 2001 (SI 2001/3767) reg.2 and Sch. Pt II para.18 (April 8, 2002).

20. Social Security (Loss of Benefit) (Consequential Amendments) Regulations 2002 (SI 2002/490) reg.2 (April 1, 2002).

21. Social Security Amendment (Residential Care and Nursing Homes) Regulations 2001 (SI 2001/3767) reg.2 and Sch. Pt II para.18 (as amended by Social Security Amendment (Residential Care and Nursing Homes) Regulations 2002 (SI 2002/398) reg.4(3)) (April 8, 2002).

22. Social Security Amendment (Personal Allowances for Children and Young Persons) Regulations 2002 (SI 2002/2019) reg.2 (October 14, 2002).

23. Social Security Amendment (Carer Premium) Regulations 2002 (SI 2002/2020) reg.3 (October 28, 2002).

24. Social Security (Miscellaneous Amendments) Regulations 2003 (SI 2003/511) reg.3(4) and (5) (April 1, 2003).

25. Social Security (Working Tax Credit and Child Tax Credit) (Consequential Amendments) Regulations 2003 (SI 2003/455) regs 1(9), 3 and Sch.2 para.20(b) (April 7, 2003).

26. Social Security (Working Tax Credit and Child Tax Credit) (Consequential Amendments) Regulations 2003 (SI 2003/455) regs 1(9), 3 and Sch.2 para.20(e) (April 7, 2003).

27. Social Security (Hospital In-Patients and Miscellaneous Amendments) Regulations 2003 (SI 2003/1195) reg.6 (May 21, 2003).

28. Social Security (Miscellaneous Amendments) (No. 2) Regulations 2003 (SI 2003/2279) reg.3(3) (October 1, 2003).

29. Social Security (Removal of Residential Allowance and Miscellaneous Amendments) Regulations 2003 (SI 2003/1121) reg.4 and Sch.2 para.9 (October 6, 2003).

30. Social Security (Working Tax Credit and Child Tax Credit) (Consequential Amendments) Regulations 2003 (SI 2003/455) reg.3 and Sch.2 para.20 (April 6, 2004, except in "transitional cases" and see further the note to regs 83 and to 17 of the Income Support Regulations).

31. Civil Partnership (Pensions, Social Security and Child Support) (Consequential, etc. Provisions) Order 2005 (SI 2005/2877) art.2(3) and Sch.3 para.26(11) (December 5, 2005).

32. Social Security (Miscellaneous Amendments) (No. 4) Regulations 2006 (SI 2006/2378) reg.13(10) (October 1, 2006).

33. Social Security (Miscellaneous Amendments) Regulations 2007 (SI 2007/719) reg.3(8) (April 9, 2007). As it relates to paras 15(2)(a) and 16, the amendment only affects "transitional cases". See further the note to reg.17 of the Income Support Regulations and the commentary below.

34. Social Security (Miscellaneous Amendments) (No. 5) Regulations 2007 (SI 2007/2618) reg.2 and Sch. (October 1, 2007).

35. Social Security (Miscellaneous Amendments) Regulations 2008 (SI 2008/698) reg.4(14) (April 14, 2008).

36. Employment and Support Allowance (Consequential Provisions) (No. 2) Regulations 2008 (SI 2008/1554) reg.3(1) and (24) (October 27, 2008).

37. Social Security (Miscellaneous Amendments) Regulations 2009 (SI 2009/583) reg.4(1) and (3) (April 6, 2009).

38. Social Security (Students and Miscellaneous Amendments) Regulations 2009 (SI 2009/1575) reg.3 (August 1, 2009).

39. Social Security (Loss of Benefit) Amendment Regulations 2010 (SI 2010/1160) reg.11(1) and (3) (April 1, 2010).

40. Social Security (Equalisation of State Pension Age) Regulations 2009 (SI 2009/1488) reg.13 (April 6, 2010).

41. Employment and Support Allowance (Transitional Provisions, Housing Benefit and Council Tax Benefit) (Existing Awards) (No. 2) Regulations 2010 (SI 2010/1907) reg.26(1) and Sch.4 para.1A(3) (as amended by the Employment and Support Allowance (Transitional Provisions, Housing Benefit and Council Tax Benefit) (Existing Awards) (No. 2) (Amendment) Regulations 2010 (SI 2010/2430) reg.15) (November 1, 2010).

42. Social Security (Miscellaneous Amendments) Regulations 2011 (SI 2011/674) reg.7(7) (April 11, 2011).

43. Social Security Benefits Up-rating Order 2012 (SI 2012/780) art.25(3) and Sch.13 (April 9, 2012).

44. Social Security Benefits Up-rating Order 2012 (SI 2012/780) art.25(5) and Sch.14 (April 9, 2012).

45. Social Security Benefits Up-rating Order 2012 (SI 2012/780) art.25(6) and Sch.15 (April 9, 2012).

46. Personal Independence Payment (Supplementary Provisions and Consequential Amendments) Regulations 2013 (SI 2013/388) reg.8 and Sch. para.16(1) and (7) (April 8, 2013).

47. Armed Forces and Reserve Forces Compensation Scheme (Consequential Provisions: Subordinate Legislation) Order 2013 (SI 2013/591) art.7 and Sch. para.10(1) and (7) (April 8, 2013).

48. Universal Credit and Miscellaneous Amendments (No. 2) Regulations 2014 (SI 2014/2888) reg.3(3) (November 26, 2014).

49. Welfare Benefits Up-rating Order 2015 (SI 2015/30) art.9 and Sch.3 (April 6, 2015).

50. Universal Credit and Miscellaneous Amendments Regulations 2015 (SI 2015/1754) reg.15 (October 28, 2015).

51. Universal Credit and Jobseeker's Allowance (Miscellaneous Amendments) Regulations 2018 (SI 2018/1129) reg.2 (November 28, 2018).

52. Social Security (Scotland) Act 2018 (Disability Assistance for Children and Young People) (Consequential Modifications) Order 2021 (SI 2021/786) Sch.3 paras 7–8 (July 26, 2021).

53. Social Security (Disability Assistance for Working Age People) (Consequential Amendments) Order 2022 (SI 2022/177) art.7 (March 21, 2022).

54. Social Security (Disability Assistance for Working Age People) (Consequential Amendments) (No. 2) Order 2022 (SI 2022/530) art.3(2) (June 6, 2022).

55. Social Security Benefits Up-rating Order 2023 (SI 2023/316) art.27(1) and (3)(a), and Sch.8 (April 10, 2023).

56. Social Security Benefits Up-rating Order 2023 (SI 2023/316) art.27(1) and (5), and Sch.9 (April 10, 2023).

57. Social Security Benefits Up-rating Order 2023 (SI 2023/316) art.27(1) and (6), and Sch.10 (April 10, 2023).

58. Carer's Assistance (Carer Support Payment) (Scotland) Regulations 2023 (Consequential Amendments) Order 2023 (SI 2023/1218), art.8 (November 19, 2023).

DEFINITIONS

"adult disability payment"—see reg.1(3).
"attendance allowance"—*ibid.*
"the Benefits Act"—see Jobseekers Act s.35(1).
"child"—*ibid.*
"child disability payment"—*ibid.*
"claimant"—*ibid.*
"couple"—see reg.1(3).
"DACYP Regulations"—*ibid.*
"disability living allowance"—*ibid.*
"family"—see Jobseekers Act s.35(1).
"invalid carriage or other vehicle"—see reg.1(3).
"lone parent"—*ibid.*
"mobility supplement"—*ibid.*
"non-dependent"—see reg.2.
"partner"—see reg.1(3).
"personal independence payment"—*ibid.*
"polygamous marriage"—*ibid.*
"preserved right"—*ibid.*
"single claimant"—*ibid.*
"welfare to work beneficiary"—*ibid.*
"young person"—see reg.76.
For the General Note to Sch.1, see Vol.V paras 3.509–3.518.

p.1120, *amendments to the Jobseeker's Allowance Regulations 1996 (SI 1996/207) Sch.2 para.17 (Non-dependant deductions)*

6.084   With effect from April 10, 2023, art.27 of the Social Security Benefits Up-rating Order 2023 (SI 2023/316) makes the following amendments to para.17 of Sch.2:

- in sub-para.(1)(a) for "£102.85" substitute "£115.75";
- in sub-para.(1)(b) for "£15.95" substitute "£18.10";
- in sub-para.(2)(a) for "£149.00" substitute "£162.00";
- in sub-para.(2)(b):
  (iv) for "£35.65" substitute "£41.60";
  (v) for "£149.00" substitute "£162.00"; and
  (vi) for "£217.00" substitute "£235.00";
- in sub-para.(2)(c):
  (iv) for "£50.30" substitute "£57.10";
  (v) for "£217.00" substitute "£235.00"; and
  (vi) for "£283.00" substitute "£308.00";
- in sub-para.(2)(d):
  (iv) for "£82.30" substitute "£93.40";
  (v) for "£283.00" substitute "£308.00"; and
  (vi) for "£377.00" substitute "£410.00"; and

- in sub-para.(2)(e):
  (iv) for "£93.70" substitute "£105.35";
  (v) for "£377.00" substitute "£410.00"; and
  (vi) for "£469.00" substitute "£511.00".

pp.1120–1122, *amendments to the Jobseeker's Allowance Regulations 1996 (SI 1996/207) Sch.2 para.17 (Housing costs—non-dependant deductions)*

With effect from July 26, 2021, Sch.3 para.9 of the Social Security   **6.085**
(Scotland) Act 2018 (Disability Assistance for Children and Young People)
(Consequential Modifications) Order 2021 (SI 2021/786) makes the
following amendments to Sch.2 para.17:

- in sub-para.(6)(b), at the end of para.(ii), insert "or (iia) the care
  component of child disability payment;"
- in sub-para.(8)(a), after "disability living allowance", insert ", child
  disability payment".

With effect from January 1, 2022, reg.3(6) of the Social Security (Income
and Capital Disregards) (Amendment) Regulations 2021 (SI 2021/1405)
inserts into para.17(8)(b), after "Grenfell Tower payment", ", child abuse
payment or Windrush payment".

With effect from March 21, 2022, art.5(8) of the Social Security
(Disability Assistance for Working Age People) (Consequential
Amendments) Order 2022 (SI 2022/177) makes the following amend-
ments to Sch.2 para.17:

- after para.17(6)(b)(iii) (non-dependant deductions), insert "(iiia)
  the daily living component of adult disability payment;");
- in para.17(8)(a):
  - after "armed forces independence payment" for "or" substitute ",";
  - after "personal independence payment" insert "or adult disabil-
    ity payment".

With effect from July 9, 2023, reg.3 of the Social Security (Income
and Capital Disregards) (Amendment) Regulations 2023 (SI 2023/640)
amends para.17 as follows:

- in paragraph 17(8)(b) (non-dependant deductions), for "or Windrush
  payment" insert ", Windrush payment or Post Office compensation
  payment".

p.1138, *amendment to the Jobseeker's Allowance Regulations 1996 (SI 1996/207) Sch.6 para.7(1) (Sums to be disregarded in the calculation of earn-ings)*

With effect from November 19, 2023, art.8(10) of the Carer's Assistance   **6.086**
(Carer Support Payment) (Scotland) Regulations 2023 (Consequential
Amendments) Order 2023 (SI 2023/1218) amended para.7(1) by inserting "or carer support payment" after "carer's allowance" in the first place
where that occurs. Carer support payment is newly defined in reg.1(3) by
reference to the Scottish legislation (see the entry for p.789 and Pt I of this
Supplement).

p.1144, *amendment to the Jobseeker's Allowance Regulations 1996 (SI 1996/207) Sch.6A para.2(1) (Sums to be disregarded in the calculation of earnings of members of joint-claim couples)*

6.087   With effect from November 19, 2023, art.8(11) of the Carer's Assistance (Carer Support Payment) (Scotland) Regulations 2023 (Consequential Amendments) Order 2023 (SI 2023/1218) amended para.2(1) by inserting "or carer support payment" after "carer's allowance" in the first place where that occurs. Carer support payment is newly defined in reg.1(3) by reference to the Scottish legislation (see the entry for p.789 and Pt I of this Supplement).

p.1146, *amendment to the Jobseeker's Allowance Regulations 1996 (SI 1996/207) Sch.7 para.7 (Sums to be disregarded in the calculation of income other than earnings—mobility component)*

6.088   With effect from March 21, 2022, art.5(9)(a) of the Social Security (Disability Assistance for Working Age People) (Consequential Amendments) Order 2022 (SI 2022/177) amended para.7 to read as follows (square brackets indicate only the present amendment, those indicating previous amendments having been omitted):

"**7.**—The mobility component of disability living allowance[,] the mobility component of personal independence payment [or the mobility component of adult disability payment]."

"Adult disability payment" is defined in reg.1(3) by reference to reg.2 of the Disability Assistance for Working Age People (Scotland) Regulations 2022 (SSI 2022/54) (see Vol.IV of this series).

p.1147, *amendment to the Jobseeker's Allowance Regulations 1996 (SI 1996/207) Sch.7 para.10 (Sums to be disregarded in the calculation of income other than earnings—attendance allowance, care component of DLA or daily living component)*

6.089   With effect from March 21, 2022, art.5(9)(b) of the Social Security (Disability Assistance for Working Age People) (Consequential Amendments) Order 2022 (SI 2022/177) amended para.10 to read as follows (square brackets indicate only the present amendment, those indicating previous amendments having been omitted):

"**10.**—Any attendance allowance, the care component of disability living allowance[,] the daily living component of personal independence payment [or the daily living component of adult disability payment]."

"Adult disability payment" is defined in reg.1(3) by reference to reg.2 of the Disability Assistance for Working Age People (Scotland) Regulations 2022 (SSI 2022/54) (see Vol.IV of this series).

p.1149, *amendment to the Jobseeker's Allowance Regulations 1996 (SI 1996/207) Sch.7 para.22(2) (Sums to be disregarded in the calculation of income other than earnings—income in kind)*

6.090   With effect from January 1, 2022, reg.3(7)(a) of the Social Security (Income and Capital Disregards) (Amendment) Regulations 2021 (SI

2021/1405) amended sub-para.(2) by inserting ", a child abuse payment or a Windrush payment" after "Grenfell Tower payment". All of those payments are defined in reg.1(3). See the entry for p.684 for discussion of the nature of child abuse and Windrush payments.

p.1151, *amendments to the Jobseeker's Allowance Regulations 1996 (SI 1996/207) Sch.7 para.28 (Sums to be disregarded in the calculation of income other than earnings—payments for persons temporarily in care of claimant)*

With effect from July 1, 2022, reg.10 of the Health and Care Act 2022 (Consequential and Related Amendments and Transitional Provisions) Regulations 2022 (SI 2022/634) amended para.28 by substituting the following for sub-para.(da):   **6.091**

"(da) an integrated care board established under Chapter A3 of Part 2 of the National Health Service Act 2006;"

Note that sub-para.(dzb) seems to be out of the proper order in the 2021/22 main volume.

With effect from November 6, 2023, reg.4 of the Health and Care Act 2022 (Further Consequential Amendments) (No.2) Regulations 2023 (SI 2023/1071) amended para.28(db) by substituting "NHS England" for "the National Health Service Commissioning Board".

p.1153, *amendments to the Jobseeker's Allowance Regulations 1996 (SI 1996/207) Sch.7 para.41 (Sums to be disregarded in the calculation of income other than earnings)*

With effect from January 1, 2022, reg.3(7)(b) of the Social Security (Income and Capital Disregards) (Amendment) Regulations 2021 (SI 2021/1405) amended para.41 by substituting the following for sub-para.(1A):   **6.092**

"(1A) Any—
(a)   Grenfell Tower payment;
(b)   child abuse payment;
(c)   Windrush payment."

In addition, reg.3(7)(c) amended sub-paras (2) to (6) by inserting ", a child abuse payment or a Windrush payment" after "Grenfell Tower payment" in each place where those words occur. All of those payments are defined in reg.1(3).

See the entry for p.684 (Income Support Regulations, Sch.10 (capital to be disregarded) para.22) for some technical problems arising from the date of effect of these amendments. Because all the payments so far made from the approved historic institutional child abuse compensation schemes and from the Windrush Compensation Scheme have been in the nature of capital, the question of disregarding income has not yet arisen.

With effect from July 9, 2023, reg.3(7) of the Social Security (Income and Capital Disregards) (Amendment) Regulations 2023 (SI 2023/640) amended para.41(1A) by adding the following after head (c):

"(d) Post Office compensation payment."

Such payments are newly defined in reg.1(3), where there is now also an expanded definition of Grenfell Tower payments (see head (a)). With effect from the same date, the words substituted in sub-paras (2) to (6) have been further amended by substituting ", a Windrush payment, a Post Office compensation payment or a vaccine damage payment" for "or a Windrush payment". "Vaccine damage payment" is also newly defined in reg.1(3). See the entry for pp.451–452 of Vol.II in this Supplement.

p.1156, *amendments to the Jobseeker's Allowance Regulations 1996 (SI 1996/207) Sch.7 (Sums to be disregarded in the calculation of income other than earnings)*

6.093   With effect from July 26, 2021, art.12(2) of the Social Security (Scotland) Act 2018 (Disability Assistance, Young Carer Grants, Short-term Assistance and Winter Heating Assistance) (Consequential Provision and Modifications) Order 2021 (SI 2021/886) inserted the following after para.81:

"**82.** Any disability assistance given in accordance with regulations made section 31 of the Social Security (Scotland) Act 2018."

The relevant regulations under s.31 of the 2018 Act so far are the Disability Assistance for Children and Young People (Scotland) Regulations 2021 (SSI 2021/174), also in effect from July 26, 2021, providing for the benefit known as a child disability payment. The regulations also authorise the payment of short-term assistance, to be disregarded under para.81.
    With effect from November 19, 2023, art.8(12) of the Carer's Assistance (Carer Support Payment) (Scotland) Regulations 2023 (Consequential Amendments) Order 2023 (SI 2023/1218) inserted the following after para.82:

"**83.** Any amount of carer support payment that is in excess of the amount the claimant would receive if they had an entitlement to carer's allowance under section 70 of the Benefits Act."

Carer support payment (CSP) is newly defined in reg.1(3) by reference to the Scottish legislation (see the entry for p.229 and Part I of this Supplement). Note that CSP in general counts as income and that the disregard is limited to any excess of the amount of the CSP over what the claimant would have been entitled to in carer's allowance under British legislation. That is in accordance with the Fiscal Framework Agreement governing the provision of devolved benefits in Scotland (see para.6.9 of the Explanatory Memorandum to SI 2023/1218). Initially, CSP is to be paid at the same rate as carer's allowance.

p.1165, *amendment to the Jobseeker's Allowance Regulations 1996 (SI 1996/207) Sch.8 para.12(1)(a) (Capital to be disregarded)*

6.094   With effect from July 26, 2021, art.12(3) of the Social Security (Scotland) Act 2018 (Disability Assistance, Young Carer Grants, Short-term Assistance and Winter Heating Assistance) (Consequential Provision and Modifications) Order 2021 (SI 2021/886) substituted "80, 81 or 82" for "80 or 81". See the entry for p.1156 for the new para.82 of Sch.7.

p.1166, *amendment to the Jobseeker's Allowance Regulations 1996 (SI 1996/207) Sch.8 para.12A (Capital to be disregarded—widowed parent's allowance)*

With effect from February 9, 2023, para.3(a) of the Schedule to the Bereavement Benefits (Remedial) Order 2023 (SI 2023/134) inserted the following after para.12:

6.095

> **"12A.** Any payment of a widowed parent's allowance made pursuant to section 39A of the Contributions and Benefits Act (widowed parent's allowance)—
> (a) to the survivor of a cohabiting partnership (within the meaning in section 39A(7) of the Contributions and Benefits Act) who is entitled to a widowed parent's allowance for a period before the Bereavement Benefits (Remedial) Order 2023 comes into force, and
> (b) in respect of any period of time during the period ending with the day before the survivor makes the claim for a widowed parent's allowance,
> but only for a period of 52 weeks from the date of receipt of the payment."

The legislation on widowed parent's allowance (WPA), and bereavement support payment (BSP) that replaced it for deaths after April 5, 2017, was declared incompatible with the ECHR by discriminating against children whose parents were cohabiting but not married to each other or in a civil partnership (see *Re McLaughlin's Application for Judicial Review* [2018] UKSC 48; [2018] 1 W.L.R. 4250 and *R. (Jackson) v Secretary of State for Work and Pensions* [2020] EWHC 183 (Admin); [2020] 1 W.L.R. 1441 in Vol.I of this series). The Remedial Order allows retrospective claims to be made for those benefits from August 30, 2018 onwards and accordingly for arrears of benefit to be paid if the conditions of entitlement are met. The new para.12A, and the amended para.65 on BSP, deal with the consequences of such payments on old style JSA entitlement, by providing for them to be disregarded as capital for 52 weeks from receipt. See the entry for p.682 on income support for the effect of the payment of arrears of WPA being in its nature a payment of income to be taken into account (subject to a £10 per week disregard under para.17(i) of Sch.7 to the JSA Regulations 1996) against entitlement in past periods (allowing revision and the creation of an overpayment) and the misleading state of para.7.15 of the Explanatory Memorandum to the Order.

pp.1167–1168, *amendments to the Jobseeker's Allowance Regulations 1996 (SI 1996/207) Sch.8 para.27 (Capital to be disregarded)*

With effect from January 1, 2022, reg.3(8)(a) of the Social Security (Income and Capital Disregards) (Amendment) Regulations 2021 (SI 2021/1405) amended sub-para.(1A) by inserting ", child abuse payment, Windrush payment" after "Grenfell Tower payment" and amended sub-paras (2) to (6) by inserting ", a child abuse payment or a Windrush payment" after "Grenfell Tower payment" in each place where those words occur. All of those payments are defined in reg.1(3).

6.096

See the entry for p.684 (Income Support Regulations Sch.10 (Capital to be disregarded) para.22) for some technical problems with the addition only with effect from January 1, 2022 of the disregards of payments from approved schemes providing compensation in respect of historic institutional child abuse in the UK and from the Windrush Compensation Scheme. All the schemes so far in existence provide payments in the nature of capital. That entry also contains information about the nature of the schemes involved, including the child abuse compensation schemes so far approved.

With effect from July 9, 2023, reg.3(8) of the Social Security (Income and Capital Disregards) (Amendment) Regulations 2023 (SI 2023/640) amended para.27(1A) by adding the following after "Windrush payment":

", Post Office compensation payment or vaccine damage payment."

Such payments are newly defined in reg.1(3), where there is now also an expanded definition of Grenfell Tower payments. With effect from the same date, the words substituted in sub-paras (2) to (6) have been further amended by substituting ", a Windrush payment, a Post Office compensation payment or a vaccine damage payment" for "or a Windrush payment". See the entry for pp.451–452 of Vol.II in this Supplement.

With effect from August 30, 2023, reg.2(1)(b) of the Social Security (Infected Blood Capital Disregard) (Amendment) Regulations 2023 (SI 2023/894) amended para.27 by inserting the following after sub-para.(5):

"(5A) Any payment out of the estate of a person, which derives from a payment to meet the recommendation of the Infected Blood Inquiry in its interim report published on 29th July 2022 made under or by the Scottish Infected Blood Support Scheme or an approved blood scheme to the estate of the person, where the payment is made to the person's son, daughter, step-son or step-daughter."

See the entry for pp.684–685 on income support for the background.

With effect from October 27, 2023, reg.4(3)(c) of the Social Security (Habitual Residence and Past Presence, and Capital Disregards) (Amendment) Regulations 2023 (SI 2023/1144) amended para.27(1) by inserting ", the Victims of Overseas Terrorism Compensation Scheme" after "the National Emergencies Trust". That scheme is newly defined in reg.1(3). See the entry for pp.684–685 on income support for the background.

p.1168, *amendment to the Jobseeker's Allowance Regulations 1996 (SI 1996/207) Sch.8 para.31 (Capital to be disregarded—payments in kind)*

6.097   With effect from January 1, 2022, reg.3(8)(b) of the Social Security (Income and Capital Disregards) (Amendment) Regulations 2021 (SI 2021/1405) amended para.31 by inserting ", a child abuse payment or a Windrush payment" after "Grenfell Tower payment". All of those payments are defined in reg.1(3). See also the entry for p.684.

p.1172, *amendment to the Jobseeker's Allowance Regulations 1996 (SI 1996/207) Sch.8 para.65 (Capital to be disregarded—bereavement support payment)*

6.098   With effect from February 9, 2023, para.3(b) of the Schedule to the Bereavement Benefits (Remedial) Order 2023 (SI 2023/134) amended para.65 by making the existing text sub-para.(1) and inserting the following:

"(2) Where bereavement support payment under section 30 of the Pensions Act 2014 is paid to the survivor of a cohabiting partnership (within the meaning in section 30(6B) of the Pensions Act 2014) in respect of a death occurring before the day the Bereavement Benefits (Remedial) Order 2023 comes into force, any amount of that payment which is—

(a) in respect of the rate set out in regulation 3(1) of the Bereavement Support Payment Regulations 2017, and

(b) paid as a lump sum for more than one monthly recurrence of the day of the month on which their cohabiting partner died,

but only for a period of 52 weeks from the date of receipt of the payment."

See the entry for p.682 on income support for the general background. The operation of this amendment is much more straightforward than that of the new para.12A on widowed parent's allowance. Although a payment of arrears of bereavement support payment (BSP) is in its nature a payment of income and attributable to the past period in respect of which it is due, the payment could not affect any entitlement to old style JSA in that past period because it would be disregarded entirely as income (Sch.7 para.76). The amount of the arrears would thus immediately metamorphose into capital, which would then be disregarded under para.65(2) subject to the 52 week limit.

p.1177, *annotation to the Jobseeker's Allowance Regulations 1996 (SI 1996/207) Sch.8 (Capital to be disregarded)*

With effect from June 28, 2022 "Cost of living payments" under the Social Security (Additional Payments) Act 2022, both those to recipients of specified means-tested benefits and "disability" payments are not to be taken into account for any old style JSA purposes by virtue of s.8(b) of the Act. The same effect was achieved with effect from March 23, 2023 in relation to payments under the Social Security (Additional Payments) Act 2023 (s.8(b) of that Act). See Pt I of Vol.II for the text of both Acts. **6.099**

p.1184, *annotation to the Jobseeker's Allowance (Schemes for Assisting Persons to Obtain Employment) Regulations 2013 (SI 2013/276)*

Note the doubts expressed in the note to reg.3 in the 2021/22 main volume about the validity of the prescription of the Work and Health Programme in reg.3(8C) and in the entry below for p.1187 about the validity of the prescription of the Restart Scheme in reg.3(8D). **6.100**

p.1187, *amendment to the Jobseeker's Allowance (Schemes for Assisting Persons to Obtain Employment) Regulations 2013 (SI 2013/276) reg.3 (Schemes for assisting persons to obtain employment)*

With effect from March 14, 2022, reg.2(3) of the Jobseeker's Allowance (Schemes for Assisting Persons to Obtain Employment) (Amendment) Regulations 2022 (SI 2022/154) amended reg.3 by omitting para.(8) and by inserting the following after para.(8C): **6.101**

"(8D) The Restart Scheme is a scheme which provides support for a period of up to 12 months for claimants who have been unemployed for 9 months or more and reside in England and Wales."

The Explanatory Memorandum to SI 2022/154 (note that a revised Memorandum, not labelled as such in its heading but with an additional "001" in the version online, was issued on April 13, 2022) explains that the Work Programme no longer exists. There is therefore no controversy about the removal of para.(8), which described that scheme.

However, the introduction of the new para.(8D) is of very doubtful validity. That is because s.17A(1) of the old style Jobseekers Act 1995 only allows claimants to be required to participate in schemes designed to assist them to obtain employment that are of a "prescribed description". The Supreme Court in *R. (Reilly and Wilson) v Secretary of State for Work and Pensions* [2013] UKSC 68; [2014] 1 A.C. 453 held that the Jobseeker's Allowance (Employment, Skills and Enterprise Scheme) Regulations 2011 (SI 2011/917) reg.2 did not satisfy that test because it did not add anything to the description of the schemes in the Act itself, which was necessary for the requirement for a prescribed description to have any point. Regulation 2 had provided that the Employment, Skills and Enterprise Scheme (ESES) meant a scheme of that name within s.17A and provided pursuant to arrangements by the Secretary of State that was designed to assist claimants to obtain employment or self-employment and which might include for any individual work-related activity, including work experience or job search. The Supreme Court must therefore have regarded the reference to the possible inclusion of work-related activity as too vague to constitute any kind of description of what the scheme involved. The Court agreed that it was not necessary in the case of the ESES to explore how much detail needed to be included in the regulations to comply with s.17A(1), as no description at all was given.

The amendment contained in SI 2022/154 may therefore not be on all fours with the ESES Regulations reg.2, because the new para.(8D) could be said to contain *some* description of the Restart Scheme, in identifying the categories of claimants who could be directed to the Restart Scheme, the maximum length of the scheme and that it would provide support (although arguably that word, in conjunction with the other specified elements, is also so vague as not to constitute any meaningful description at all). If it is accepted that there is *some* description, the question then, as in *R. (Smith) v Secretary of State for Work and Pensions* [2015] EWCA Civ 229 on the Jobseeker's Allowance (Mandatory Work Activity Scheme) Regulations 2011 (SI 2021/688), would be whether there is sufficient description for the purposes of s.17A(1). In *Smith*, Underhill LJ suggested at para.25 that the natural reading of "prescribed description" connoted "no more than an indication of the character of the scheme provided for, such as a scheme in which the claimant was required to undergo training or education or to work with a mentor, or—as here—to do work or work-related activity". So the CA held that the mention of work or work-related activity, with the specification of maximum weekly hours and length of participation, was enough for the MWAS Regulations to be valid. Although the present amendment specifies which claimants fall into the scope of the Restart Scheme and the maximum length, it says nothing worthwhile about the nature of the scheme. All it says is that it "provides support", nothing about what kind of support or who it will be provided by. Equally, if not more, important, it says nothing about what a claimant is to be expected to do by way of participation. What does it mean to have "support" thrust on a claimant? The argument that the new para.(8D) provides an insufficient description seems very strong. It might be thought that the Explanatory Memorandum betrays the faulty approach in paras 7.8 and 7.9, where it is said that the current legislation "lists" the employment schemes claimants can be required to participate in and that the amendment adds the Restart Scheme to the list. To be valid, and to carry the requirement to participate backed by sanctions, a regulation must not merely "list" a scheme, but must describe it.

The Explanatory Memorandum records that the Restart Scheme was already in existence through 12 providers in England and Wales, initially for universal credit claimants who had spent 12 to 18 months uninterrupted time in the Intensive Work Search Regime (i.e. subject to all work-related requirements), but now with the time reduced to nine months. Because of improved labour market conditions the opportunity arose to widen the eligibility criteria to provide intensive employment support for old style JSA claimants that had previously only been available to limited groups. The Scheme is still only available in England and Wales. The emphasis is said to be on positive engagement with the claimant to encourage participation, with the requirement to participate being "used as a backstop where reasonable attempts at engagement fail without good reason" (para.6.7). However, it is stated that claimants who fail to comply with the requirement to participate in compulsory activities may be issued with a low-level sanction (para.6.6). It is far from clear that "compulsory activities" are adequately described by the term "support" in para.(8D).

The policy paper *How the Restart Scheme will work* (January 18, 2022, updated April 26, 2022, available on the gov.uk website) states:

> "Through regular contact with all participants, providers will develop a strong understanding of individuals' employment history, skills, aspirations and support needs to develop the right package of support to help each participant succeed.
>
> For some this might be bespoke training to take advantage of opportunities in a growth sector or to succeed in a major recruitment exercise, for others it might be support to get the right certificate to take up a job in a different industry such as construction or transport or to update skills such as IT."

That document thus gets to a description of the scheme, but as there is no reference to it in para.(8D) there can be no reliance on its description merely by use of the label "Restart Scheme".

Providers will be given letters of empowerment under reg.17 authorising them to exercise the functions of the Secretary of State to issue notices requiring participation (reg.5) or that that requirement has ceased (reg.6(3)(a)) (Explanatory Memorandum, para.6.3). It is understood that providers and employees will not be designated as "employment officers" under s.35 of the old style Jobseekers Act 1995, so that they will have no power to issue jobseeker's directions under s.19A(2)(c).

p.1188, *annotation to the Jobseeker's Allowance (Schemes for Assisting Persons to Obtain Employment) Regulations 2013 (SI 2013/276) reg.3 (Schemes for assisting persons to obtain employment)*

Note, in addition to the points made in the entry for p.1187, that in the last paragraph of the existing note the reference to s.19(2)(c) should be to s.19A(2)(c).

6.102

PART IV

OLD STYLE EMPLOYMENT AND SUPPORT ALLOWANCE REGULATIONS

p.1209, *amendments to the Employment and Support Allowance Regulations 2008 (SI 2008/794) reg.2 (Interpretation)*

6.103   With effect from January 1, 2022, reg.7(2) of the Social Security (Income and Capital Disregards) (Amendment) Regulations 2021 (SI 2021/1405) inserts the following definitions:

"child abuse payment" means a payment from a scheme established or approved by the Secretary of State for the purpose of providing compensation in respect of historic institutional child abuse in the United Kingdom;"
    "Windrush payment" means a payment made under the Windrush Compensation Scheme (Expenditure) Act 2020;"

With effect from January 1, 2022, reg.7(2) of the Social Security (Income and Capital Disregards) (Amendment) Regulations 2021 (SI 2021/1405) inserts ", a child abuse payment or a Windrush payment" into the definition of "qualifying person", after "Grenfell Tower payment".
    With effect from July 26, 2021, Sch.9 para.2 of the Social Security (Scotland) Act 2018 (Disability Assistance for Children and Young People) (Consequential Modifications) Order 2021 (SI 2021/786) adds the following definitions:

"child disability payment" has the meaning given in regulation 2 of the DACYP Regulations;
    "the DACYP Regulations" means the Disability Assistance for Children and Young People (Scotland) Regulations 2021;

With effect from March 21, 2022, art.11 of the Social Security (Disability Assistance for Working Age People) (Consequential Amendments) Order 2022 (SI 2022/177) adds the following definition:

"adult disability payment" has the meaning given in regulation 2 of the Disability Assistance for Working Age People (Scotland) Regulations 2022;

With effect from April 4, 2022, reg.2(1) of the Universal Credit and Employment and Support Allowance (Terminal Illness) (Amendment) Regulations 2022 (SI 2022/260) amends the definition of "terminally ill" by substituting for "6 months", "12 months".

p.1214, *amendment to the Employment and Support Allowance Regulations 2008 (SI 2008/794) reg.1 (Interpretation)*

6.104   With effect from July 9, 2023, reg.7(2)(a) of the Social Security (Income and Capital Disregards) (Amendment) Regulations 2023 (SI 2023/640) substituted for the definition of "Grenfell Tower payment" the following new definition:

""Grenfell Tower payment" means a payment made for the purpose of providing compensation or support in respect of the fire on 14th June 2017 at Grenfell Tower;".

pp.1214, 1218 and 1221, *amendments to the Employment and Support Allowance Regulations 2008 (SI 2008/794) reg.1 (Interpretation)*

With effect from July 9, 2023, reg.7(2)(b) of the Social Security (Income and Capital Disregards) (Amendment) Regulations 2023 (SI 2023/640) inserted at the appropriate places the following new definitions:

6.105

""the Horizon system" means any version of the computer system used by the Post Office known as Horizon, Horizon Legacy, Horizon Online or HNG-X;";"

""the Post Office" means Post Office Limited (registered number 02154540);";"

""Post Office compensation payment" means a payment made by the Post Office or the Secretary of State for the purpose of providing compensation or support which is—
(a) in connection with the failings of the Horizon system; or
(b) otherwise payable following the judgment in *Bates and Others v Post Office Ltd* ((No. 3) "Common Issues");";"

""vaccine damage payment" means a payment made under the Vaccine Damage Payments Act 1979;".

p.1219, *amendment to the Employment and Support Allowance Regulations 2008 (SI 2008/794) reg.1 (Interpretation)*

With effect from July 9, 2023, reg.7(2)(c) of the Social Security (Income and Capital Disregards) (Amendment) Regulations 2023 (SI 2023/640) substituted ", a Windrush payment, a Post Office compensation payment or a vaccine damage payment" for "or a Windrush payment" in the definition of "qualifying person".

6.106

p.1230, *revocation of the Employment and Support Allowance Regulations 2008 (SI 2008/794) reg.6 (The assessment phase—a claimants appealing against a decision)*

Strictly speaking, reg.6 was *revoked* by reg.9(5) of the Social Security (Miscellaneous Amendments) (No. 3) Regulations 2010/840 (rather than *omitted* by the annotator).

6.107

pp.1238–1239, *amendment of the Employment and Support Allowance Regulations 2008 (SI 2008/794) reg.18 (Circumstances in which the condition that the claimant is not receiving education does not apply)*

Regulation 18 now reads, as amended, as follows:

6.108

"Paragraph 6(1)(g) of Schedule 1 to the Act does not apply where the claimant is entitled to a disability living allowance [³, child disability payment] [², armed forces independence payment] [⁴,] [¹ personal independence payment] [⁴ or adult disability payment]."

In addition, the following notes should be added to the list of

AMENDMENTS:

3. Social Security (Scotland) Act 2018 (Disability Assistance for Children and Young People) (Consequential Modifications) Order 2021 (SI 2021/786) Sch.9 para.3 (July 26, 2021).

4. Social Security (Disability Assistance for Working Age People) (Consequential Amendments) Order 2022 (SI 2022/177) art.11(3) (March 21, 2022).

p.1250, *amendment to the Employment and Support Allowance Regulations 2008 (SI 2008/794) reg.21 (Information required for determining capability for work)*

6.109   With effect from July 1, 2022, reg.4(2) of the Social Security (Medical Evidence) and Statutory Sick Pay (Medical Evidence) (Amendment) (No. 2) Regulations 2022 (SI 2022/630) omitted the words "a doctor's" between "form of" and "statement".

p.1260, *annotation to the Employment and Support Allowance Regulations 2008 (SI 2008/794) reg.24 (Matters to be taken into account in determining good cause in relation to regs 22 or 23)*

6.110   See, however, the successful application for a new inquest in *Dove v HM Assistant Coroner for Teesside and Hartlepool, Rahman and SSWP* [2023] EWCA Civ 289. Mrs Dove's daughter, Jodey, had died of an overdose shortly after her ESA award had been stopped. Jodey, who had been in receipt of ESA for several years, had a history of mental health problems, suicidal ideation and overdoses, as well as physical ill-health. In 2016, on a periodic review, she asked the DWP for a home visit. The DWP neglected to deal with that request and required her to attend an HCP assessment, which she failed to do. The DWP decided that Jodey had shown neither good cause for the failure to attend nor that she had limited capability for work. Jodey's ESA was duly stopped on February 7, 2017, and she died a fortnight later. Mrs Dove believed that the withdrawal of benefit had created extra stress and contributed to her daughter's death. The coroner ruled that questioning the DWP's decisions was beyond her remit under the Coroners and Justice Act 2009.

Mrs Dove applied to the High Court under the Coroners Act 1988 s.13, seeking two remedies: (a) to quash the coroner's suicide verdict; and (b) to order a new inquest covering the circumstances surrounding her daughter's death. Mrs Dove submitted that (1) the coroner's inquiry was insufficient in scope and should have covered the DWP's failings; (2) those failings meant that the state was in breach of ECHR art.2, so requiring a wider inquiry; (3) fresh evidence (in the form of an expert psychiatrist's report, obtained after the inquest, which concluded it was likely that Jodey's mental state would have been substantially affected by the decision to stop her benefits and an ICE report on a complaint about the DWP's handling of Jodey's claim) showed that a new inquest was necessary. At first instance the Divisional Court ([2021] EWHC 2511 (Admin); Warbey LJ, Farbey J and HH Judge Teague QC) dismissed the application on all three grounds.

However, the Court of Appeal allowed Mrs Dove's appeal and directed a fresh inquest ([2023] EWCA Civ 289: Lewis LJ, William Davis LJ and Whipple LJ). The Court ruled that the psychiatrist's report (but not the ICE report) was fresh evidence making it desirable in the interests of justice to hold a fresh inquest (*R v HM Coroner for North Humberside and Scunthorpe Ex p. Jamieson* [1995] Q.B. 1). Thus, "it is in the interests of justice that Mrs Dove and her family should have the opportunity to invite a coroner, at a fresh inquest, to make a finding of fact that the Department's actions contributed to Jodey's deteriorating mental health and, if that finding is made, to invite the coroner to include reference to that finding in the conclusion on how Jodey came by her death" (per Whipple LJ at [72]). One of the reasons for the Court reaching this conclusion was that "there is a public interest in a coroner considering the wider issue of causation raised on this appeal. If Jodey's death was connected with the abrupt cessation of benefits by the Department, the public has a legitimate interest in knowing that. After all, the Department deals with very many people who are vulnerable and dependent on benefits to survive, and the consequences of terminating benefit payments to such people should be examined in public, where it can be followed and reported on by others who might be interested in it."

p.1302, *annotation to the Employment and Support Allowance Regulations 2008 (SI 2008/794) reg.35 (Certain claimants to be treated as having limited capability for work-related activity)*

For further examples of the need for sufficient fact-finding and adequate reasons in appeals where reg.35 is in issue, see *MH v SSWP (ESA)* [2021] UKUT 90 (AAC) and *CT v SSWP (ESA)* [2021] UKUT 131 (AAC). On the importance of tribunals in universal credit appeals (that turn on the equivalent provision to reg.35 in Sch.9 para.4) ensuring they have been provided with an accurate list of work-related activities, see *KS v SSWP (UC)* [2021] UKUT 132 (AAC). Secretary of State appeal responses on such appeals may not have included accurate lists of work-related activities until after July 2020.

6.111

pp.1334–1335, *amendment of the Employment and Support Allowance Regulations 2008 (SI 2008/794) reg.64D (The amount of a hardship payment)*

The text in the main volume at para.4.174 should be replaced with the following:

6.112

"[1 The amount of a hardship payment

64D.—[2 (1) A hardship payment is either—
(a) 80% of the prescribed amount for a single claimant as set out in paragraph (1)(a) of Part 1 of Schedule 4 where—
   (i) the claimant has an award of employment and support allowance which does not include entitlement to a work-related activity component under section 4(2)(b) of the Welfare Reform Act 2007 as in force immediately before 3rd April 2017; and
   (ii) the claimant or any other member of their family is either pregnant or seriously ill; or
(b) 60% of the prescribed amount for a single claimant as set out in paragraph (1)(a) of Part 1 of Schedule 4 in any other case.]
(2) A payment calculated in accordance with paragraph (1) shall, if it is not a multiple of 5p, be rounded to the nearest such multiple or, if it is a multiple of 2.5p but not of 5p, to the next lower multiple of 5p.]"

AMENDMENTS

1. Employment and Support Allowance (Sanctions) (Amendment) Regulations 2012 (SI 2012/2756) reg.6 (December 3, 2012).

2. Employment and Support Allowance (Exempt Work Hardship Amounts) (Amendment) Regulations 2017 (SI 2017/205) reg.5 (April 3, 2017).

p.1336, *annotation to the Employment and Support Allowance Regulations 2008 (SI 2008/794) reg.67 (Prescribed amounts)*

6.113   On the lawfulness of not uplifting the amounts paid in IS, JSA and ESA by £20 per week (as was done with UC for 18 months during the coronavirus pandemic), see the annotation to the Income Support (General) Regulations 1987 (SI 1987/1967) reg.17 (Applicable amounts), above.

pp.1341–1342, *amendment to the Employment and Support Allowance Regulations 2008 (SI 2008/794) reg.70 (Special cases: supplemental—persons from abroad)*

6.114   The text in the main volume at para.4.187 should be replaced with the following:

"Special cases: supplemental—persons from abroad

70.—(1) "Person from abroad" means, subject to the following provisions of this regulation, a claimant who is not habitually resident in the United Kingdom, the Channel Islands, the Isle of Man or the Republic of Ireland.

(2) A claimant must not be treated as habitually resident in the United Kingdom, the Channel Islands, the Isle of Man or the Republic of Ireland unless the claimant has a right to reside in (as the case may be) the United Kingdom, the Channel Islands, the Isle of Man or the Republic of Ireland other than a right to reside which falls within paragraph (3) [8 or (3A)].

(3) A right to reside falls within this paragraph if it is one which exists by virtue of, or in accordance with, one or more of the following—

   (a) regulation 13 of the [8 Immigration (European Economic Area) Regulations 2016];
   (b) regulation 14 of those Regulations, but only in a case where the right exists under that regulation because the claimant is—
      (i) a jobseeker for the purpose of the definition of "qualified person" in regulation 6(1) of those Regulations; or
      (ii) a family member (within the meaning of regulation 7 of those Regulations) of such a jobseeker; [10 or]
[4[8(bb) regulation 16 of those Regulations, but only in a case where the right exists under that regulation because the claimant satisfies the criteria in paragraph (5) of that regulation;]]
   (c) [10 . . .]
   (d) [10 . . .]
   (e) [10 . . .]
[8 (3A) A right to reside falls within this paragraph if it exists by virtue of a claimant having been granted limited leave to enter, or remain in, the United Kingdom under the Immigration Act 1971 by virtue of—

(a) Appendix EU to the immigration rules made under section 3(2) of that Act; [^{11} . . .];

(b) being a person with a Zambrano right to reside as defined in Annex 1 of Appendix EU to the immigration rules made under section 3(2) of that Act.] [^{11}; or

(c) having arrived in the United Kingdom with an entry clearance that was granted under Appendix EU (Family Permit) to the immigration rules made under section 3(2) of that Act.]

[^{9} (3B) Paragraph (3A)(a) does not apply to a person who—

(a) has a right to reside granted by virtue of being a family member of a relevant person of Northern Ireland; and

(b) would have a right to reside under the Immigration (European Economic Area) Regulations 2016 if the relevant person of Northern Ireland were an EEA national, provided that the right to reside does not fall within paragraph (3).]

(4) A claimant is not a person from abroad if the claimant is—

[^{12}(zza) a person granted leave in accordance with the immigration rules made under section 3(2) of the Immigration Act 1971, where such leave is granted by virtue of—

    (i) the Afghan Relocations and Assistance Policy; or

    (ii) the previous scheme for locally-employed staff in Afghanistan (sometimes referred to as the ex-gratia scheme);

(zzb) a person in Great Britain not coming within sub-paragraph (zza) or [^{13} (h)] who left Afghanistan in connection with the collapse of the Afghan government that took place on 15th August 2021;]

[^{13}(zzc) a person in Great Britain who was residing in Ukraine immediately before 1st January 2022, left Ukraine in connection with the Russian invasion which took place on 24th February 2022 and—

    (i) has been granted leave in accordance with immigration rules made under section 3(2) of the Immigration Act 1971; [^{14} . . .]

    (ii) has a right of abode in the United Kingdom within the meaning given in section 2 of that Act;] [^{14} or

    (iii) does not require leave to enter or remain in the United Kingdom in accordance with section 3ZA of that Act;]

[^{15}(zzd) a person who was residing in Sudan before 15th April 2023, left Sudan in connection with the violence which rapidly escalated on 15th April 2023 in Khartoum and across Sudan and—

    (i) has been granted leave in accordance with immigration rules made under section 3(2) of the Immigration Act 1971;

    (ii) has a right of abode in the United Kingdom within the meaning given in section 2 of that Act; or

    (iii) does not require leave to enter or remain in the United Kingdom in accordance with section 3ZA of that Act;]

[^{16}(zze) a person who was residing in Israel, the West Bank, the Gaza Strip, East Jerusalem, the Golan Heights or Lebanon immediately before 7th October 2023, who left Israel, the West Bank, the Gaza Strip, East Jerusalem, the Golan Heights or Lebanon in connection with the Hamas terrorist attack in Israel on 7th October 2023 or the violence which rapidly escalated in the region following the attack and—

    (i) has been granted leave in accordance with immigration rules made under section 3(2) of the Immigration Act 1971;

       (ii) has a right of abode in the United Kingdom within the meaning given in section 2 of that Act; or

      (iii) does not require leave to enter or remain in the United Kingdom in accordance with section 3ZA of that Act;]

[⁷(za) a qualified person for the purposes of regulation 6 of the [⁸ Immigration (European Economic Area) Regulations 2016] as a worker or a self-employed person;

  (zb) a family member of a person referred to in sub-paragraph (za) [⁹ . . .];

  (zc) a person who has a right to reside permanently in the United Kingdom by virtue of regulation 15(1)(c), (d) or (e) of those Regulations;]

[⁹(zd) a family member of a relevant person of Northern Ireland, with a right to reside which falls within paragraph (3A)(a), provided that the relevant person of Northern Ireland falls within sub-paragraph (za), or would do so but for the fact that they are not an EEA national;]

[¹⁰(ze) a frontier worker within the meaning of regulation 3 of the Citizens' Rights (Frontier Workers) (EU Exit) Regulations 2020;

  (zf) a family member of a person referred to in sub-paragraph (ze), who has been granted limited leave to enter, or remain in, the United Kingdom by virtue of Appendix EU to the immigration rules made under section 3(2) of the Immigration Act 1971;]

   (g) a refugee within the definition in Article 1 of the Convention relating to the Status of Refugees done at Geneva on 28th July 1951, as extended by Article 1(2) of the Protocol relating to the Status of Refugees done at New York on 31st January 1967;

[⁶(h) a person who has been granted leave or who is deemed to have been granted leave outside the rules made under section 3(2) of the Immigration Act 1971 [¹³ . . .]

   (i) a person who has humanitarian protection granted under those rules; [⁶ or]

   (j) a person who is not a person subject to immigration control within the meaning of section 115(9) of the Immigration and Asylum Act and who is in the United Kingdom as a result of deportation, expulsion or other removal by compulsion of law from another country to the United Kingdom; [¹ . . .]

  (k) [⁶ . . .]

  (l) [¹ [⁶ . . .]]]

[⁹ (5) In this regulation—

"EEA national" has the meaning given in regulation 2(1) of the Immigration (European Economic Area) Regulations 2016;

"family member" has the meaning given in regulation 7(1)(a), (b) or (c) of the Immigration (European Economic Area) Regulations 2016 except that regulation 7(4) of those Regulations does not apply for the purposes of paragraphs (3B) and (4)(zd);

"relevant person of Northern Ireland" has the meaning given in Annex 1 of Appendix EU to the immigration rules made under section 3(2) of the Immigration Act 1971.]

[¹⁰ (6) References in this regulation to the Immigration (European Economic Area) Regulations 2016 are to be read with Schedule 4 to the Immigration and Social Security Co-ordination (EU Withdrawal) Act 2020(Consequential, Saving, Transitional and Transitory Provisions) Regulations 2020.]"

AMENDMENTS

1. Social Security (Habitual Residence) (Amendment) Regulations 2009 (SI 2009/362) reg.9 (March 18, 2009).
2. Social Security (Miscellaneous Amendments) (No. 3) Regulations 2011 (SI 2011/2425) reg.23(1) and (7) (October 31, 2011).
3. Treaty of Lisbon (Changes in Terminology or Numbering) Order 2012 (SI 2012/1809) art.3(1) and Sch.1 Pt.2 (August 1, 2012).
4. Social Security (Habitual Residence) (Amendment) Regulations 2012 (SI 2012/2587) reg.2 (November 8, 2012).
5. Social Security (Croatia) Amendment Regulations 2013 (SI 2013/1474) reg.7 (July 1, 2013).
6. Social Security (Miscellaneous Amendments) (No. 3) Regulations 2013 (SI 2013/2536) reg.13(1) and (24) (October 29, 2013).
7. Social Security (Habitual Residence) (Amendment) Regulations 2014 (SI 2014/902) reg.7 (May 31, 2014).
8. Social Security (Income-related Benefits) (Updating and Amendment) (EU Exit) Regulations 2019 (SI 2019/872) reg.7 (May 7, 2019).
9. Social Security (Income-Related Benefits) (Persons of Northern Ireland – Family Members) (Amendment) Regulations 2020 (SI 2020/638) reg.7 (August 24, 2020).
10. Immigration and Social Security Co-ordination (EU Withdrawal) Act 2020 (Consequential, Saving, Transitional and Transitory Provisions) (EU Exit) Regulations 2020 (SI 2020/1309) reg 73 (December 31, 2020 at 11.00 pm).
11. Immigration (Citizens' Rights etc.) (EU Exit) Regulations 2020 (SI 2020/1372) reg.23 (December 31, 2020 at 11.00 pm).
12. Social Security (Habitual Residence and Past Presence) (Amendment) Regulations 2021 (SI 2021/1034) reg.2 (September 15, 2021).
13. Social Security (Habitual Residence and Past Presence) (Amendment) Regulations 2022 (SI 2022/344) reg.2 (March 22, 2022).
14. Social Security (Habitual Residence and Past Presence) (Amendment) (No. 2) Regulations 2022 (SI 2022/990) reg.2 (October 18, 2022).
15. Social Security (Habitual Residence and Past Presence) (Amendment) Regulations 2023 (SI 2023/532) reg.2(1) and 2(2)(f) (May 15, 2023).
16. Social Security (Habitual Residence and Past Presence, and Capital Disregards) (Amendment) Regulations 2023, reg.2 (SI 2023/1144) (October 27, 2023).

MODIFICATION

Regulation 70 is modified by Sch.1 para.10A of the Employment and Support Allowance (Transitional Provisions, Housing Benefit and Council Tax Benefit) (Existing Awards) (No. 2) Regulations 2010 (SI 2010/1907) as amended for the purposes specified in reg.6(1) of those Regulations. For the details of the modification, pp.1410–1452 of Vol.I of the 2020/21 edition.

DEFINITION

"Immigration and Asylum Act"—reg.2(1).

p.1373, *amendment to the Employment and Support Allowance Regulations 2008 (SI 2008/794) reg.107(5A) (Notional income—exceptions)*

With effect from January 1, 2022, reg.7(3) of the Social Security (Income and Capital Disregards) (Amendment) Regulations 2021 (SI 2021/1405) amended para.(5A) by substituting the following for "a payment of income which is a Grenfell Tower payment":

6.115

"any of the following payments of income—
(a)   a Grenfell Tower payment;
(b)   a child abuse payment;
(c)   a Windrush payment."

All of those payments are defined in reg.2(1). See the entry for p.684 for discussion of the nature of child abuse and Windrush payments.

With effect from July 9, 2023, reg.7(3) of the Social Security (Income and Capital Disregards) (Amendment) Regulations 2023 (SI 2023/640) amended reg.107(5A) by inserting the following after sub-para.(c):

"(d)   a Post Office compensation payment."

Such payments are newly defined in reg.2(1), where there is now also an expanded definition of Grenfell Tower payments (see sub-para.(a)). See the entry for pp.541–452 of Vol.II in this Supplement.

p.1377, *annotation to the Employment and Support Allowance Regulations 2008 (SI 2008/794) reg.110 (Capital limit)*

6.116   In the Institute for Government and the Social Security Advisory Committee's 2021 joint report *Jobs and benefits: The Covid-19 challenge* it was noted that if the capital limit of £16,000 had risen in line with prices since 2006 it would be close to £23,500 (or £25,000: different figures are given) and recommended that the limit should be increased to £25,000 and subsequently automatically indexed to maintain its real value (pp.22 and 31). That recommendation was summarily rejected in the Government's response of March 22, 2022.

p.1378, *amendment to the Employment and Support Allowance Regulations 2008 (SI 2008/794) reg.112(8) (Income treated as capital—exceptions)*

6.117   With effect from January 1, 2022, reg.7(4) of the Social Security (Income and Capital Disregards) (Amendment) Regulations 2021 (SI 2021/1405) amended para.(8) by substituting the following for sub-para.(b):

"any—
(i)   Grenfell Tower payment;
(ii)   child abuse payment;
(iii)   Windrush payment."

All of those payments are defined in reg.2(1). See the entry for p.684 for discussion of the nature of child abuse and Windrush payments.

With effect from July 9, 2023, reg.7(4) of the Social Security (Income and Capital Disregards) (Amendment) Regulations 2023 (SI 2023/640) amended reg.112(8)(b) by inserting the following after head (iii):

"(iv)   Post Office compensation payment."

Such payments are newly defined in reg.2(1), where there is now also an expanded definition of Grenfell Tower payments (see head (a)). See the entry for pp.451–452 of Vol.II for the background.

With effect from October 27, 2023, reg.8(3)(a) of the Social Security (Habitual Residence and Past Presence, and Capital Disregards) (Amendment) Regulations 2023 (SI 2023/1144) amended reg.112(8)(a) by inserting ", the Victims of Overseas Terrorism Compensation Scheme" after "the National Emergencies Trust". That scheme is newly defined in reg.2(1). See the entry for pp.684–685 on income support for the background.

p.1382, *amendment to the Employment and Support Allowance Regulations 2008 (SI 2008/794) reg.115(5A) (Notional capital—exceptions)*

With effect from January 1, 2022, reg.7(5) of the Social Security (Income and Capital Disregards) (Amendment) Regulations 2021 (SI 2021/1405) amended para.(5A) by substituting the following for "a payment of capital which is a Grenfell Tower payment": 6.118

"any of the following payments of capital—
(a)   a Grenfell Tower payment;
(b)   a child abuse payment;
(c)   a Windrush payment."

All of those payments are defined in reg.2(1). See the entry for p.684 for discussion of the nature of child abuse and Windrush payments.

With effect from July 9, 2023, reg.7(5) of the Social Security (Income and Capital Disregards) (Amendment) Regulations 2023 (SI 2023/640) amended reg.115(5A) by inserting the following after sub-para.(c):

"(d)   a Post Office compensation payment;
(e)   a vaccine damage payment."

Such payments are newly defined in reg.2(1), where there is now also an expanded definition of Grenfell Tower payments (see sub-para.(a)). See the entry for pp.451–452 of Vol.II in this Supplement.

With effect from October 27, 2023, reg.8(3)(b) of the Social Security (Habitual Residence and Past Presence, and Capital Disregards) (Amendment) Regulations 2023 (SI 2023/1144) amended reg.115(5)(a) by inserting ", the Victims of Overseas Terrorism Compensation Scheme" after "the National Emergencies Trust". That scheme is newly defined in reg.2(1). See the entry for pp.684–685 on income support for the background.

pp.1406–1407, *annotation to the Employment and Support Allowance Regulations 2008 (SI 2008/794) reg.137(4) and (5) (Treatment of student loans and postgraduate loans)*

See the entry for p.539 on income support for details of the decision in *IB v Gravesham BC and SSWP (HB)* [2023] UKUT 193 (AAC); [2024] P.T.S.R. 130 on when a claimant cannot acquire a loan by taking reasonable steps to do so. 6.119

pp.1411, *amendment to the Employment and Support Allowance Regulations 2008 (SI 2008/794) reg.144 (Waiting days)*

With effect from November 19, 2023, art.19(4) of the Carer's Assistance (Carer Support Payment) (Scotland) Regulations 2023 (Consequential Amendments) Order 2023 (SI 2023/1218) amended reg.144(2)(a) by inserting ", carer support payment" after "carer's allowance". 6.120

p.1413, *annotation to the Employment and Support Allowance Regulations 2008 (SI 2008/794) reg.145 (Linking rules)*

6.121   For more detailed analysis see the commentary on SSCBA 1992 s.30C(1)(c) in Vol.I of the 2011/12 edition of this work (at paras 1.67–1.77).

pp.1431–1432, *amendments to the Employment and Support Allowance Regulations 2008 (SI 2008/794) reg.158 (Meaning of "person in hardship")*

6.122   With effect from July 26, 2021, Sch.9 para.4 of the Social Security (Scotland) Act 2018 (Disability Assistance for Children and Young People) (Consequential Modifications) Order 2021 (SI 2021/786) makes the following amendments to reg.158:

- In para.(3):
  - in sub-para.(c), after "disability living allowance", insert ", child disability payment";
  - in sub-para.(d)(ii), after "disability living allowance", insert ", child disability payment".
- For para.(7), substitute:
"(7) In this regulation, "care component" means—
(a) the care component of disability living allowance at the highest or middle rate prescribed under section 72(3) of the Contributions and Benefits Act; or
(b) the care component of child disability payment at the highest or middle rate provided for in regulation 11(5) of the DACYP Regulations.".

With effect from March 21, 2022, art.11(4) of the Social Security (Disability Assistance for Working Age People) (Consequential Amendments) Order 2022 (SI 2022/177) makes the following amendments to reg.158(3):

- in sub-para.(b):
  - after "armed forces independence payment" for "or" substitute ",";
  - after "daily living component" insert "or the daily living component of adult disability payment";
- in sub-para.(c):
  - after "armed forces independence payment" for "or" substitute ",";
  - after "personal independence payment", insert "or adult disability payment";
- in sub-para.(d):
  - in para.(i):
    - after "armed forces independence payment" for "or" substitute ",";
    - after "daily living component" insert "or the daily living component of adult disability payment";
  - in para.(ii):
    - after "armed forces independence payment" for "or" substitute ",";
    - after "personal independence payment", insert "or adult disability payment".

p.1437, *amendment to the Employment and Support Allowance Regulations 2008 (SI 2008/794) reg.165 (entitlement for less than a week—amount of an employment and support allowance payable)*

With effect from November 19, 2023, art.19 of the Carer's Assistance (Carer Support Payment) (Scotland) Regulations 2023 (Consequential Amendments) Order 2023 (SI 2023/1218) amends reg.165(3) as follows:

 6.123

after "carer's allowance" insert ", carer support payment".

p.1438, *amendment to the Employment and Support Allowance Regulations 2008 (SI 2008/794) reg.167 (modification in the calculation of income)*

With effect from November 19, 2023, art.19 of the Carer's Assistance (Carer Support Payment) (Scotland) Regulations 2023 (Consequential Amendments) Order 2023 (SI 2023/1218) amends reg.167(d) as follows:

 6.124

after "carer's allowance" insert ", carer support payment".

pp.1494–1496, *annotation to the Employment and Support Allowance Regulations 2008 (SI 2008/794) Sch.2 Activity 17 (Appropriateness of behaviour with other people, due to cognitive impairment or mental disorder)*

Consideration of Activity 17 may require the disclosure of Unacceptable Customer Behaviour (UCB) forms as provided in confidence by the DWP to HMCTS: *MH v SSWP (ESA)* [2021] UKUT 90 (AAC).

 6.125

pp.1507–1514, *amendments to the Employment and Support Allowance Regulations 2008 (SI 2008/794) Sch.4 (Amounts)*

Substitute the following for paras 4.420–4.429

 6.126

Regulations 67(1)(a) and (2) and 68(1)(a) and (b)

"SCHEDULE 4

AMOUNTS

PART 1

PRESCRIBED AMOUNTS

1. The weekly amounts specified in column (2) in respect of each person or couple specified in column (1) are the weekly amounts specified for the purposes of regulations 67(1) and 68 (prescribed amounts and polygamous marriages).

 4.420

(1) Person or Couple	(2) Amount
(1) *Single claimant*—	(1)
(a) who satisfies the conditions set out in section 2(2) [12 . . .] or 4(4) [12 . . .] of the Act [13 or who is a member of the work-related activity group];	(a) [15 £84.80];
(b) aged not less than 25	(b) [15 £84.80];
(c) aged less than 25.	(c) [15 £67.20];

(1) *Person or Couple*	(2) *Amount*
(2) Lone parent [⁶ or a person who has no partner and who is responsible for and a member of the same household as a young person]—	(2)
(a) who satisfies the conditions set out in section 4(4) [¹² ...] of the Act[¹³ or who is a member of the work-related activity group and satisfies the conditions set out in Part 2 of Schedule 1 to the Act];	(a) [¹⁵ £84.80];
(b) aged not less than 18;	(b) [¹⁵ £84.80];
(c) aged less than 18.	(c) [¹⁵ £67.20];
(3) Couple—	(3)
(a) where both members are aged not less than 18;	(a) [¹⁵ £133.30];
(b) where one member is aged not less than 18 and the other member is a person under 18 who—	(b) [¹⁵ £133.30];
(i) [³ if that other member had not been a member] of a couple, would satisfy the requirements for entitlement to income support other than the requirement to make a claim for it; or	
(ii) [³ if that other member had not been a member] of a couple, would satisfy the requirements for entitlement to an income-related allowance; or	
(iii) satisfies the requirements of section 3(1) (f)(iii) of the Jobseekers Act (prescribed circumstances for persons aged 16 but less than 18); or	(c) [¹⁵ £133.30];
(iv) is the subject of a direction under section 16 of that Act (persons under 18: severe hardship);	
(c) where the claimant satisfies the conditions set out in section 4(4) [¹² . . .] of the Act [¹³ or the claimant is a member of the work-related activity group and satisfies the conditions set out in Part 2 of Schedule 1 to the Act] and both members are aged less than 18 and—	
(i) at least one of them is treated as responsible for a child; or	
(ii) had they not been members of a couple, each would have qualified for an income-related allowance; or	
(iii) had they not been members of a couple the claimant's partner would satisfy the requirements for entitlement to income support other than the requirement to make a claim for it; or	
(iv) the claimant's partner satisfies the requirements of section 3(1)(f)(iii) of the Jobseekers Act (prescribed circumstances for persons aged 16 but less than 18); or	
(v) there is in force in respect of the claimant's partner a direction under section 16 of that Act (persons under 18: severe hardship);	
(d) where both members are aged less than 18 and—	(d) [¹⁵ £101.50];
(i) at least one of them is treated as responsible for a child; or	
(ii) had they not been members of a couple, each would have qualified for an income-related allowance; or	

(1) Person or Couple	(2) Amount
(iii) had they not been members of a couple the claimant's partner satisfies the requirements for entitlement to income support other than a requirement to make a claim for it; or	
(iv) the claimant's partner satisfies the requirements of section 3(1)(f)(iii) of the Jobseekers Act (prescribed circumstances for persons aged 16 but less than 18); or	
(v) there is in force in respect of the claimant's partner a direction under section 16 of that Act (persons under 18: severe hardship);	
(e) where the claimant is aged not less than 25 and the claimant's partner is a person under 18 who—	(e) [¹⁵ £84.80];
(i) would not qualify for an income-related allowance if the person were not a member of a couple;	
(ii) would not qualify for income support if the person were not a member of a couple;	
(iii) does not satisfy the requirements of section 3(1)(f)(iii) of the Jobseekers Act (prescribed circumstances for persons aged 16 but less than 18); and	
(iv) is not the subject of a direction under section 16 of that Act (persons under 18: severe hardship);	
(f) where the claimant satisfies the conditions set out in section 4(4) [¹² . . .] of the Act [¹³ or the claimant is a member of the work-related activity group and satisfies the conditions set out in Part 2 of Schedule 1 to the Act] and the claimant's partner is a person under 18 who—	(f) [¹⁵ £84.80];
(i) would not qualify for an income-related allowance if the person were not a member of a couple;	
(ii) would not qualify for income support if the person [¹ were] not a member of a couple;	
(iii) does not satisfy the requirements of section 3(1)(f)(iii) of the Jobseekers Act (prescribed circumstances for persons aged 16 but less than 18); and	
(iv) is not the subject of a direction under section 16 of that Act (persons under 18: severe hardship);	
(g) where the claimant satisfies the conditions set out in section 4(4) [¹² . . .] of the Act [¹³ or the claimant is a member of the work-related activity group and satisfies the conditions set out in Part 2 of Schedule 1 to the Act] and both members are aged less than 18 and paragraph (c) does not apply;	(g) [¹⁵ £84.80];
(h) where the claimant is aged not less than 18 but less than 25 and the claimant's partner is a person under 18 who—	(h) [¹⁵ £67.20];
(i) would not qualify for an income-related allowance if the person were not a member of a couple;	

(1) *Person or Couple*	(2) *Amount*

(ii) would not qualify for income support if the person
         were not a member of a couple;
    (iii) does not satisfy the requirements of section 3(1)(f)(iii)
         of the Jobseekers Act (prescribed circumstances for
         persons aged 16 but less than 18); and
    (iv) is not the subject of a direction under section 16 of
         that Act (persons under 18: severe hardship);
  (i) where both members are aged less than 18 and paragraph (d) does not apply.
	(i) [¹⁵ £67.20].

Regulations 67(1)(b) and 68(1)(c)

PART 2

PREMIUMS

4.421   **2.** Except as provided in paragraph 4, the weekly premiums specified in Part 3 of this Schedule are, for the purposes of regulation 67(1)(b) and 68(1)(c), to be applicable to a claimant who satisfies the condition specified in paragraphs 5 to 8 in respect of that premium.

3. An enhanced disability premium in respect of a person is not applicable in addition to a pensioner premium.

4.—(1) For the purposes of this Part of this Schedule, once a premium is applicable to a claimant under this Part, a person is to be treated as being in receipt of any benefit—

(a) in the case of a benefit to which the Social Security (Overlapping Benefits) Regulations 1979 applies, for any period during which, apart from the provisions of those Regulations, the person would be in receipt of that benefit; and

(b) for any period spent by a person in undertaking a course of training or instruction provided or approved by the Secretary of State under section 2 of the Employment and Training Act 1973, or by [³ Skills Development Scotland] or Highlands and Islands Enterprise under section 2 of the Enterprise and New Towns (Scotland) Act 1990, or for any period during which the person is in receipt of a training allowance]. [¹⁸ ; and

(c) in the case of carer support payment, for any period during which, apart from regulation 16 of the Carer's Assistance (Carer Support Payment) (Scotland) Regulations 2023, he would be in receipt of that benefit.]

[⁷ (2) For the purposes of the carer premium under paragraph 8, a person is to be treated as being in receipt of a carer's allowance by virtue of sub-paragraph (1)(a) [¹⁸ or carer support payment by virtue of sub-paragraph (1)(c)] only if and for so long as the person in respect of whose care the allowance [¹⁸ or payment] has been claimed

(a) attendance allowance;

(b) the care component of disability living allowance at the highest or middle rate prescribed in accordance with section 72(3) of the Contributions and Benefits Act; [⁸ . . .]

(c) the daily living component of personal independence payment at the standard or enhanced rate in accordance with section 78(3) of the 2012 Act [⁸ [¹⁴ . . .

(ca) the daily living component of adult disability payment at the standard or enhanced rate in accordance with regulation 5 of the Disability Assistance for Working Age People (Scotland) Regulations 2022; or]

(d) armed forces independence payment.]]

Pensioner premium

4.422   **5.** The condition is that the claimant or the claimant's partner has attained the qualifying age for state pension credit.

Severe disability premium

6.—(1) The condition is that the claimant is a severely disabled person.

(2) For the purposes of sub-paragraph (1), a claimant is to be treated as being a severely disabled person if, and only if—

4.423

    (a) in the case of a single claimant, a lone parent [⁶ , a person who has no partner and who is responsible for and a member of the same household as a young person] or a claimant who is treated as having no partner in consequence of subparagraph (3)—

          (i) the claimant is in receipt of the care component [⁷ , the daily living component] [¹⁴ , the daily living component of adult disability payment] [⁸ , armed forces independence payment] [⁵ or attendance allowance];

         (ii) subject to sub-paragraph (4), the claimant has no non-dependants aged 18 or over normally residing with the claimant or with whom the claimant is normally residing; and

        (iii) no person is entitled to, and in receipt of, [¹¹ a carer's allowance [¹⁸ or carer support payment] or has an award of universal credit which includes the carer element] in respect of caring for the claimant;

    (b) in the case of a claimant who has a partner

          (i) the claimant is in receipt of the care component [⁷ , the daily living component] [¹⁴ , the daily living component of adult disability payment] [⁸ , armed forces independence payment] [⁵ or attendance allowance];

         (ii) the claimant's partner is also in receipt of the care component [⁷ , the daily living component] [¹⁴ , the daily living component of adult disability payment] [⁸ , armed forces independence payment] or attendance allowance or, if the claimant is a member of a polygamous marriage, all the partners of that marriage are in receipt of the care component [⁷ , the daily living component] [¹⁴ , the daily living component of adult disability payment] [⁸ , armed forces independence payment] or attendance allowance; and

        (iii) subject to sub-paragraph (4), the claimant has no non-dependants aged 18 or over normally residing with the claimant or with whom the claimant is normally residing, and, either a person is entitled to, and in receipt of, a carer's allowance [¹⁸ or carer support payment] [¹¹ or has an award of universal credit which includes the carer element] in respect of caring for only one of the couple or, in the case of a polygamous marriage, for one or more but not all the partners of the marriage or, as the case may be, no person is entitled to, and in receipt of, such an allowance [¹⁸ or payment] [¹¹ or has such an award of universal credit] in respect of caring for either member of the couple or any partner of the polygamous marriage.

(3) Where a claimant has a partner who does not satisfy the condition in sub-paragraph (2)(b)(ii) and that partner is blind or severely sight impaired or is treated as blind or severely sight impaired that partner is to be treated for the purposes of sub-paragraph (2) as if the partner were not a partner of the claimant.

(4) For the purposes of sub-paragraph (2)(a)(ii) and (b)(iii) no account is to be taken of—

    (a) a person receiving attendance allowance, [⁷ the daily living component] [¹⁴ , the daily living component of adult disability payment] [⁸ , armed forces independence payment] or the care component;

    (b) subject to sub-paragraph (7), a person who joins the claimant's household for the first time in order to care for the claimant or the claimant's partner and immediately before so joining the claimant or the claimant's partner was treated as a severely disabled person; or

    (c) a person who is blind or severely sight impaired or is treated as blind or severely sight impaired.

(5) For the purposes of sub-paragraph (2)(b) a person is to be treated—

    (a) as being in receipt of attendance allowance or the care component if the person would, but for the person being a patient for a period exceeding 28 days, be so in receipt;

    (b) as being entitled to, and in receipt of, a carer's allowance [¹⁸ or carer support payment] [¹¹ or having an award of universal credit which includes the carer element] if the person would, but for the person for whom the person was caring being a patient in hospital for a period exceeding 28 days, be so entitled and in receipt [¹¹ of carer's allowance [¹⁸ or carer support payment] or have such an award of universal credit].

  [⁷(c) as being in entitled to, and in receipt of, the daily living component if the person would, but for regulations under section 86(1) (hospital in-patients) of the 2012 Act, be so entitled and in receipt.]

[14 (d)   as being in entitled to, and in receipt of, the daily living component of adult disability payment if the person would, but for regulation 28 (effect of admission to hospital on ongoing entitlement to Adult Disability Payment) of the Disability Assistance for Working Age People (Scotland) Regulations 2022, be so in receipt.]

(6) For the purposes of sub-paragraph (2)(a)(iii) and (b), no account is to be taken of an award of carer's allowance [18 or carer support payment] [11 or universal credit which includes the carer element] to the extent that payment of such an award is backdated for a period before the date on which the award is first paid.

(7) Sub-paragraph (4)(b) is to apply only for the first 12 weeks following the date on which the person to whom that provision applies first joins the claimant's household.

(8) In sub-paragraph (2)(a)(iii) and (b), references to a person being in receipt of a carer's allowance [11 or as having an award of universal credit which includes the carer element] are to include references to a person who would have been in receipt of that allowance [11 or had such an award] but for the application of a restriction under section [4 6B or] 7 of the Social Security Fraud Act 2001 (loss of benefit provisions).

(9) [11 (a)] In this paragraph—

[9 "blind or severely sight impaired" means certified as blind or severely sight impaired by a consultant ophthalmologist and a person who has ceased to be certified as blind or severely sight impaired where that person's eyesight has been regained is, nevertheless, to be treated as blind or severely sight impaired for a period of 28 weeks following the date on which the person ceased to be so certified;]

"the care component" means the care component of disability living allowance at the highest or middle rate prescribed in accordance with section 72(3) of the Contributions and Benefits Act.

[11 (b) A person has an award of universal credit which includes the carer element if the person has an award of universal credit which includes an amount which is the carer element under regulation 29 of the Universal Credit Regulations 2013.]

Enhanced disability premium

4.424

7.—(1) Subject to sub-paragraph (2), the condition is that—
  (a)   the claimant's applicable amount includes the support component; [7 . . .]
  (b)   the care component of disability living allowance is, or would, but for a suspension of benefit in accordance with regulations under section 113(2) of the Contributions and Benefits Act or, but for an abatement as a consequence of hospitalisation, be payable at the highest rate prescribed under section 72(3) of that Act in respect of—
        (i)   the claimant; or
        (ii) the claimant's partner (if any) who is aged less than the qualifying age for state pension credit [7 ; [8 . . .]
  (c)   the daily living component is, or would, but for regulations made under section 86(1) (hospital in-patients) of the 2012 Act, be payable at the enhanced rate under section 78(2) of that Act in respect of—
        (i)   the claimant; or
        (ii) the claimant's partner (if any) who is aged less than the qualifying age for state pension credit"]; [14 . . .
  (ca) the daily living component of adult disability payment is, or would, but for regulation 28 (effect of admission to hospital on ongoing entitlement to Adult Disability Payment) of the Disability Assistance for Working Age People (Scotland) Regulations 2022, be payable at the enhanced rate under section 78(2) of those Regulations in respect of—
        (i)   the claimant; or
        (ii) the claimant's partner (if any) who is aged less than the qualifying age for state pension credit; or]
  (d)   armed forces independence payment is payable in respect of—
        (i)   the claimant; or
        (ii) the claimant's partner (if any) who is aged less than the qualifying age for state pension credit.]

(2) An enhanced disability premium is not applicable in respect of—
  (a)   a claimant who—
        (i)   is not a member of a couple or a polygamous marriage; and
        (ii) is a patient within the meaning of regulation 69(2) and has been for a period of more than 52 weeks; or

(b) a member of a couple or a polygamous marriage where each member is a patient within the meaning of regulation 69(2) and has been for a period of more than 52 weeks.

Carer premium

8.—(1) Subject to sub-paragraphs (2) and (4), the condition is that the claimant or the claimant's partner is, or both of them are, entitled to a carer's allowance under section 70 of the Contributions and Benefits Act [18 or carer support payment].

    4.425

(2) Where a carer premium is awarded but—
  (a) the person in respect of whose care the carer's allowance [18 or carer support payment] has been awarded dies; or
  (b) in any other case the person in respect of whom a carer premium has been awarded ceases to be entitled to a carer's allowance [18 or carer support payment], the condition for the award of the premium is to be treated as satisfied for a period of 8 weeks from the relevant date specified in sub-paragraph (3).

(3) The relevant date for the purposes of sub-paragraph (2) is—
  (a) where sub-paragraph (2)(a) applies, the Sunday following the death of the person in respect of whose care a carer's allowance [18 or carer support payment] has been awarded or the date of death if the death occurred on a Sunday; or
  (b) in any other case, the date on which the person who has been entitled to a carer's allowance [18 or carer support payment] ceases to be entitled to that allowance [18 or payment].

(4) Where a person who has been entitled to a carer's allowance [18 or carer support payment] ceases to be entitled to that allowance and makes a claim for an income-related allowance, the condition for the award of the carer premium is to be treated as satisfied for a period of 8 weeks from the date on which—
  (a) the person in respect of whose care the carer's allowance [18 or carer support payment] has been awarded dies; or
  (b) in any other case, the person who has been entitled to a carer's allowance [18 or carer support payment] ceased to be entitled to that allowance [18 or payment].

Persons in receipt of concessionary payments

9. For the purpose of determining whether a premium is applicable to a person under paragraphs 6, 7 and 8, any concessionary payment made to compensate that person for the non-payment of any benefit mentioned in those paragraphs is to be treated as if it were a payment of that benefit.

    4.426

Persons in receipt of benefit

10. For the purposes of this Part of this Schedule, a person is to be regarded as being in receipt of any benefit if, and only if, it is paid in respect of the person and is to be so regarded only for any period in respect of which that benefit is paid.

    4.427

PART 3

WEEKLY AMOUNT OF PREMIUMS SPECIFIED IN PART 2

11.—

    4.428

Premium	Amount
(1) Pension premium for a person to whom paragraph 5 applies who—	(1)
(a) is a single claimant and—	(a)
(i) [12 . . .];	(i) [12 . . .];
(ii) is entitled to the support component; or	(ii) [16 £71.55];
[12(iii) is not entitled to the support component;]	(iii) [16 £116.25];
(b) is a member of a couple and—	
(i) [12 . . .]	(b)
(ii) is entitled to the support component; or	(i) [12];
[12 (iii) is not entitled to the support component;]	(ii) [16 £128.85];
	(iii) [16 £157.65];

Premium	Amount

(2) Severe disability premium—
   (a) where the claimant satisfies the condition in paragraph 6(2)(a);
   (b) where the claimant satisfies the condition in paragraph 6(2)(b)—
       (i) if there is someone in receipt of a carer's allowance [18 or carer support payment] or if the person or any partner satisfies that condition only by virtue of paragraph 6(5);
      (ii) if no-one is in receipt of such an allowance [18 or payment].
	(2)
	   (a) [16 £173.65];
	   (b)
	
	       (i) [16 £76.40];
	
	      (ii) [16 £152.80].

(3) Carer premium.	(3) [16 £42.75]; in respect of each person who satisfies the condition specified in [1 paragraph 8(1)].

(4) Enhanced disability premium where the conditions in paragraph 7 are satisfied.	(4)(a) [16 £19.55]; in respect of each person who is neither—
	      (i) a child or young person; nor
	     (ii) a member of a couple or a polygamous marriage, in respect of whom the conditions specified in paragraph 7 are satisfied;
	   (b) [16 £27.90]; where the claimant is a member of a couple or a polygamous marriage and the conditions specified in [1 paragraph 7] are satisfied in respect of a member of that couple or polygamous marriage.

Regulation 67(3)

PART 4

[12 THE COMPONENT]

4.429   **12.** [12 . . .].

    13. The amount of the support component is [17 £44.70]."

AMENDMENTS

    1. Employment and Support Allowance (Miscellaneous Amendments) Regulations 2008 (SI 2008/2428) reg.14 (October 27, 2008).

    2. Social Security (Miscellaneous Amendments) Regulations 2009 (SI 2009/583) reg.10(2) (April 6, 2009).

    3. Social Security (Miscellaneous Amendments) (No. 4) Regulations 2009 (SI 2009/2655) reg.11(1) and (16) (October 26, 2009).

    4. Social Security (Loss of Benefit) Amendment Regulations 2010 (SI 2010/1160) reg.12(1) and (3) (April 1, 2010).

5. Social Security (Miscellaneous Amendments) (No. 3) Regulations 2011 (SI 2011/2425) reg.23(14) (October 30, 2011).

6. Social Security (Work-focused Interviews for Lone Parents and Partners) (Amendment) Regulations 2011 (SI 2011/2428) reg.5(5) (October 30, 2011).

7. Personal Independence Payment (Supplementary Provisions and Consequential Amendments) Regulations 2013 (SI 2013/388) reg.8 and Sch. para.40(1) and (5) (April 8, 2013).

8. Armed Forces and Reserve Forces Compensation Scheme (Consequential Provisions: Subordinate Legislation) Order 2013 (SI 2013/591) art.7 and Sch. para.37(1) and (5) (April 8, 2013).

9. Universal Credit and Miscellaneous Amendments (No. 2) Regulations 2014 (SI 2014/2888) reg.3(7)(a) (November 26, 2014).

10. Welfare Benefits Up-rating Order 2015 (SI 2015/30) art.11(1) and Sch.4 (April 6, 2015).

11. Universal Credit and Miscellaneous Amendments Regulations 2015 (SI 2015/1754) reg.19 (November 4, 2015).

12. Employment and Support Allowance and Universal Credit (Miscellaneous Amendments and Transitional and Savings Provisions) Regulations 2017 (SI 2017/204) reg.2(1) and (4) (April 3, 2017).

13. Employment and Support Allowance (Miscellaneous Amendments and Transitional and Savings Provision) Regulations 2017 (SI 2017/581) reg.7(1) and (4) (June 23, 2017, subject to the transitional and savings provision in reg.10).

14. Social Security (Disability Assistance for Working Age People) (Consequential Amendments) Order 2022 (SI 2022/177) art.11(5) (March 21 2022).

15. Social Security Benefits Up-rating Order 2023 (SI 2023/316) art.31(1) and (2) and Sch.11 (April 10, 2023).

16. Social Security Benefits Up-rating Order 2023 (SI 2023/316) art.31(1) and (4) and Sch.12 (April 10, 2023).

17. Social Security Benefits Up-rating Order 2023 (SI 2023/316) art.21(6)(b) (April 10, 2023).

18. Carer's Assistance (Carer Support Payment) (Scotland) Regulations 2023 (Consequential Amendments) Order 2023 (SI 2023/1218), art.19 (November 19, 2023).

For the General Note to Sch.4, see Vol.V para.4.430.

pp.1525–1532, *amendments to the Employment and Support Allowance Regulations 2008 (SI 2008/794) Sch.6 (Housing costs)*

With effect from July 26, 2021, Sch.9 para.5 of the Social Security (Scotland) Act 2018 (Disability Assistance for Children and Young People) (Consequential Modifications) Order 2021 (SI 2021/786) makes the following amendments to Sch.6: **6.127**

- In para.15(11)(b) (linking rule), after "disability living allowance", insert ", child disability payment".
- In para.19(6)(b) (non-dependent deductions), after sub-para.(ii), insert "(iia) the care component of child disability payment;".

With effect from January 1, 2022, reg.7(6) of the Social Security (Income and Capital Disregards) (Amendment) Regulations 2021 (SI 2021/1405) inserts into para.19(8)(b), after "Grenfell Tower payment", ", child abuse payment or Windrush payment".

With effect from March 21, 2022, art.11(5) of the Social Security (Disability Assistance for Working Age People) (Consequential Amendments) Order 2022 (SI 2022/177) makes the following amendments to Sch.6:

- in para.15(11)(b) (linking rule):
  - after "armed forces independence payment" for "or" substitute ",";
  - after "personal independence payment", insert "or adult disability payment";
- in para.19(8)(a) (non-dependent deductions):
  - after "armed forces independence payment" for "or" substitute ",";
  - after "personal independence payment", insert "or adult disability payment";
- at the end of para.19(6)(b)(iii) omit "or";
- after para.19(6)(b)(iii) insert "(iiia) the daily living component of adult disability payment; or".

With effect from April 10, 2023, art.31 of the Social Security Benefits Up-rating Order 2023 (SI 2023/316) makes the following amendments to para.19 of Sch.6::

- in sub-para.(1)(a) for "£102.85" substitute "£115.75";
- in sub-para.(1)(b) for "£15.95" substitute "£18.10";
- in sub-para.(2)(a) for "£149.00" substitute "£162.00";
- in sub-para.(2)(b):
  (vii) for "£35.65" substitute "£41.60";
  (viii) for "£149.00" substitute "£162.00"; and
  (ix) for "£217.00" substitute "£235.00";
- in sub-para.(2)(c):
  (vii) for "£50.30" substitute "£57.10";
  (viii) for "£217.00" substitute "£235.00"; and
  (ix) for "£283.00" substitute "£308.00";
- in sub-para.(2)(d):
  (vii) for "£82.30" substitute "£93.40";
  (viii) for "£283.00" substitute "£308.00"; and
  (ix) for "£377.00" substitute "£410.00"; and
- in sub-para.(2)(e):
  (vii) for "£93.70" substitute "£105.35";
  (viii) for "£377.00" substitute "£410.00"; and
  (ix) for "£469.00" substitute "£511.00".

With effect from July 9, 2023, reg.7 of the Social Security (Income and Capital Disregards) (Amendment) Regulations 2023 (SI 2023/640) amends para.19 as follows:

- in paragraph 19(8)(b) (non-dependant deductions), for "or Windrush payment" insert ", Windrush payment or Post Office compensation payment".

p.1540, *amendments to the Employment and Support Allowance Regulations 2008 (SI 2008/794) Sch.8 paras 8 and 11 (Sums to be disregarded in the calculation of income other than earnings—mobility component and AA, care component and daily living component)*

6.128   With effect from March 21, 2022, art.11(7)(a) of the Social Security (Disability Assistance for Working Age People) (Consequential Amendments) Order 2022 (SI 2022/177) amended para.8 to read as follows (square brackets indicate only the present amendment, those indicating previous amendments having been omitted):

"**8.**—The mobility component of disability living allowance[,] the mobility component of personal independence payment [or the mobility component of adult disability payment]."

With effect from March 21, 2022, art.11(7)(b) of the same Order amended para.11 to read as follows (square brackets indicate only the present amendment, those indicating previous amendments having been omitted):

"**9.**—Any attendance allowance, the care component of disability living allowance[,] the daily living component of personal independence payment [or the daily living component of adult disability payment]."

"Adult disability payment" is defined in reg.2(1) by reference to reg.2 of the Disability Assistance for Working Age People (Scotland) Regulations 2022 (SSI 2022/54) (see Vol.IV of this series).

p.1542, *amendment to the Employment and Support Allowance Regulations 2008 (SI 2008/794) Sch.8 para.22(2) (Sums to be disregarded in the calculation of income other than earnings—income in kind)*

With effect from January 1, 2022, reg.7(7)(a) of the Social Security (Income and Capital Disregards) (Amendment) Regulations 2021 (SI 2021/1405) amended sub-para.(2) by inserting ", a child abuse payment or a Windrush payment" after "Grenfell Tower payment". All of those payments are defined in reg.2(1). See the entry for p.684 for discussion of the nature of child abuse and Windrush payments.

6.129

p.1544, *amendments to the Employment and Support Allowance Regulations 2008 (SI 2008/794) Sch.8 para.29 (Sums to be disregarded in the calculation of income other than earnings—payments for persons temporarily in care of claimant)*

With effect from July 1, 2022, reg.99 of and Sch. to the Health and Care Act 2022 (Consequential and Related Amendments and Transitional Provisions) Regulations 2022 (SI 2022/634) amended para.29(da) by substituting the following for the text after "(da)":

6.130

"an integrated care board established under Chapter A3 of Part 2 of the National Health Service Act 2006;"

With effect from November 6, 2023, reg.28 of the Health and Care Act 2022 (Further Consequential Amendments) (No.2) Regulations 2023 (SI 2023/1071) amended para.29(db) by substituting "NHS England" for "the National Health Service Commissioning Board".

p.1546, *amendments to the Employment and Support Allowance Regulations 2008 (SI 2008/794) Sch.8 para.41 (Sums to be disregarded in the calculation of income other than earnings)*

With effect from January 1, 2022, reg.7(7)(b) of the Social Security (Income and Capital Disregards) (Amendment) Regulations 2021 (SI 2021/1405) amended para.41 by substituting the following for sub-para.(1A):

6.131

"(1A) Any—
(a)   Grenfell Tower payment;
(b)   child abuse payment;
(c)   Windrush payment."

In addition, reg.7(7)(c) amended sub-paras (2) to (6) by inserting ", a child abuse payment or a Windrush payment" after "Grenfell Tower payment" in each place where those words occur. All of those payments are defined in reg.2(1).

See the entry for p.684 (Income Support Regulations Sch.10 (capital to be disregarded) para.22) for some technical problems arising from the date of effect of these amendments. Because all the payments so far made from the approved historic institutional child abuse compensation schemes and from the Windrush Compensation Scheme have been in the nature of capital, the question of disregarding income has not yet arisen.

With effect from July 9, 2023, reg.3(7) of the Social Security (Income and Capital Disregards) (Amendment) Regulations 2023 (SI 2023/640) amended para.41(1A) by adding the following after head (c):

"(d)   Post Office compensation payment."

Such payments are newly defined in reg.2(1), where there is now also an expanded definition of Grenfell Tower payments (see head (a)). With effect from the same date, the words substituted in sub-paras (2) to (6) have been further amended by substituting ", a Windrush payment, a Post Office compensation payment or a vaccine damage payment" for "or a Windrush payment". "Vaccine damage payment" is also newly defined in reg.2(1). See the entry for pp.451–452 of Vol.II in this Supplement.

p.1549, *amendments to the Employment and Support Allowance Regulations 2008 (SI 2008/794) Sch.8 (Sums to be disregarded in the calculation of income other than earnings)*

6.132   With effect from July 26, 2021, art.16(2) of the Social Security (Scotland) Act 2018 (Disability Assistance, Young Carer Grants, Short-term Assistance and Winter Heating Assistance) (Consequential Provision and Modifications) Order 2021 (SI 2021/886) inserted the following after para.73:

"**74.** Any disability assistance given in accordance with regulations made section 31 of the Social Security (Scotland) Act 2018."

The relevant regulations under s.31 of the 2018 Act so far are the Disability Assistance for Children and Young People (Scotland) Regulations 2021 (SSI 2021/174), also in effect from July 26, 2021, providing for the benefit known as a child disability payment. The regulations also authorise the payment of short-term assistance, to be disregarded under para.73.

With effect from November 19, 2023, art.19(8) of the Carer's Assistance (Carer Support Payment) (Scotland) Regulations 2023 (Consequential Amendments) Order 2023 (SI 2023/1218) inserted the following after para.74:

"**75.** Any amount of carer support payment that is in excess of the amount the claimant would receive if they had an entitlement to carer's allowance under section 70 of the Contributions and Benefits Act."

Carer support payment (CSP) is newly defined in reg.2(1) by reference to the Scottish legislation (see the entry for p.1211 and Pt I of this Supplement). Note that CSP in general counts as income and that the disregard is limited to any excess of the amount of the CSP over what the claimant would have been entitled to in carer's allowance under British legislation. That is in accordance with the Fiscal Framework Agreement governing the provision of devolved benefits in Scotland (see para.6.9 of the Explanatory Memorandum to SI 2023/1218). Initially, CSP is to be paid at the same rate as carer's allowance.

p.1556, *amendment to the Employment and Support Allowance Regulations 2008 (SI 2008/794) Sch.9 para.11(1)(a) (Capital to be disregarded)*

With effect from July 26, 2021, art.16(3) of the Social Security (Scotland) Act 2018 (Disability Assistance, Young Carer Grants, Short-term Assistance and Winter Heating Assistance) (Consequential Provision and Modifications) Order 2021 (SI 2021/886) substituted "72, 73 or 74" for "72 or 73". See the entry for p.1549 for the new para.74 of Sch.8.   **6.133**

p.1556, *amendment to the Employment and Support Allowance Regulations 2008 (SI 2008/794) Sch.9 para.11A (Capital to be disregarded—widowed parent's allowance)*

With effect from February 9, 2023, para.11(a) of the Schedule to the Bereavement Benefits (Remedial) Order 2023 (SI 2023/134) inserted the following after para.11:   **6.134**

"**11A.** Any payment of a widowed parent's allowance made pursuant to section 39A of the Contributions and Benefits Act (widowed parent's allowance)—

(a) to the survivor of a cohabiting partnership (within the meaning in section 39A(7) of the Contributions and Benefits Act) who is entitled to a widowed parent's allowance for a period before the Bereavement Benefits (Remedial) Order 2023 comes into force, and

(b) in respect of any period of time during the period ending with the day before the survivor makes the claim for a widowed parent's allowance,

but only for a period of 52 weeks from the date of receipt of the payment."

The legislation on widowed parent's allowance (WPA), and bereavement support payment (BSP) that replaced it for deaths after April 5, 2017, was declared incompatible with the ECHR by discriminating against children whose parents were cohabiting but not married to each other or in a civil partnership (see *Re McLaughlin's Application for Judicial Review* [2018] UKSC 48; [2018] 1 W.L.R. 4250 and *R. (Jackson) v Secretary of State for Work and Pensions* [2020] EWHC 183 (Admin); [2020] 1 W.L.R. 1441 in Vol.I of this series). The Remedial Order allows retrospective claims to be made for those benefits from August 30, 2018 onwards and accordingly for arrears of benefit to be paid if the conditions of entitlement are met. The new para.11A, and the amended para.60 on BSP, deal with the consequences of such payments on old style ESA entitlement, by providing for them to be disregarded as capital for 52 weeks from receipt. See the entry for p.682 on income support for the effect of the payment of arrears of WPA being in its nature a payment of income to be taken into account (subject to a £10 per week disregard under para.17(i) of Sch.8 to the ESA Regulations 2008) against entitlement in past periods (allowing revision and the creation of an overpayment) and the misleading state of para.7.15 of the Explanatory Memorandum to the Order.

pp.1558–1559, *amendments to the Employment and Support Allowance Regulations 2008 (SI 2008/794) Sch.9 para.27 (Capital to be disregarded)*

6.135   With effect from January 1, 2022, reg.7(8)(a) of the Social Security (Income and Capital Disregards) (Amendment) Regulations 2021 (SI 2021/1405) amended sub-para.(1A) by inserting ", child abuse payment, Windrush payment" after "Grenfell Tower payment" and amended sub-paras (2) to (6) by inserting ", a child abuse payment or a Windrush payment" after "Grenfell Tower payment" in each place where those words occur. All of those payments are defined in reg.2(1).

See the entry for p.684 (Income Support Regulations Sch.10 (Capital to be disregarded) para.22) for some technical problems with the addition only with effect from January 1, 2022 of the disregards of payments from approved schemes providing compensation in respect of historic institutional child abuse in the UK and from the Windrush Compensation Scheme. All the schemes so far in existence provide payments in the nature of capital. That entry also contains information about the nature of the schemes involved, including the child abuse compensation schemes so far approved.

With effect from July 9, 2023, reg.3(8) of the Social Security (Income and Capital Disregards) (Amendment) Regulations 2023 (SI 2023/640) amended para.27(1A) by adding the following after "Windrush payment":

", Post Office compensation payment or vaccine damage payment."

Such payments are newly defined in reg.2(1), where there is now also an expanded definition of Grenfell Tower payments. With effect from the same date, the words substituted in sub-paras (2) to (6) have been further amended by substituting ", a Windrush payment, a Post Office compensation payment or a vaccine damage payment" for "or a Windrush payment". See the entry for pp.451–452 of Vol.II in this Supplement.

With effect from August 30, 2023, reg.2(1)(f) of the Social Security (Infected Blood Capital Disregard) (Amendment) Regulations 2023 (SI 2023/894) amended para.27 by inserting the following after sub-para.(5):

"(5A) Any payment out of the estate of a person, which derives from a payment to meet the recommendation of the Infected Blood Inquiry in its interim report published on 29th July 2022 made under or by the Scottish Infected Blood Support Scheme or an approved blood scheme to the estate of the person, where the payment is made to the person's son, daughter, step-son or step-daughter."

See the entry for pp.684–685 on income support for the background.

With effect from October 27, 2023, reg.8(3)(c) of the Social Security (Habitual Residence and Past Presence, and Capital Disregards) (Amendment) Regulations 2023 (SI 2023/1144) amended para.27(1) and

(7) by inserting ", the Victims of Overseas Terrorism Compensation Scheme" after "the National Emergencies Trust" in both places. That scheme is newly defined in reg.2(1). See the entry for pp.684–685 on income support for the background.

p.1559, *amendment to the Employment and Support Allowance Regulations 2008 (SI 2008/794) Sch.9 para.31 (Capital to be disregarded—payments in kind)*

With effect from January 1, 2022, reg.7(8)(b) of the Social Security (Income and Capital Disregards) (Amendment) Regulations 2021 (SI 2021/1405) amended para.31 by inserting ", a child abuse payment or a Windrush payment" after "Grenfell Tower payment". All of those payments are defined in reg.2(1). See also the entry for p.684. 6.136

p.1563, *amendment to the Employment and Support Allowance Regulations 2008 (SI 2008/794) Sch.9 para.60 (Capital to be disregarded—bereavement support payment)*

With effect from February 9, 2023, para.11(b) of the Schedule to the Bereavement Benefits (Remedial) Order 2023 (SI 2023/134) amended para.60 by making the existing text sub-para.(1) and inserting the following: 6.137

"(2) Where bereavement support payment under section 30 of the Pensions Act 2014 is paid to the survivor of a cohabiting partnership (within the meaning in section 30(6B) of the Pensions Act 2014) in respect of a death occurring before the day the Bereavement Benefits (Remedial) Order 2023 comes into force, any amount of that payment which is—
(a) in respect of the rate set out in regulation 3(1) of the Bereavement Support Payment Regulations 2017, and
(b) paid as a lump sum for more than one monthly recurrence of the day of the month on which their cohabiting partner died,
but only for a period of 52 weeks from the date of receipt of the payment."

See the entry for p.682 on income support for the general background. The operation of this amendment is much more straightforward than that of the new para.111A on widowed parent's allowance. Although a payment of arrears of bereavement support payment (BSP) is in its nature a payment of income and attributable to the past period in respect of which it is due, the payment could not affect any entitlement to old style ESA in that past period because it would be disregarded entirely as income (Sch.8, para.68). The amount of the arrears would thus immediately metamorphose into capital, which would then be disregarded under para.60(2) subject to the 52 week limit.

pp.1565–1566, *annotation to the Employment and Support Allowance Regulations 2008 (SI 2008/794) Sch.9 (Capital to be disregarded)*

With effect from June 28, 2022 "Cost of living payments" under the Social Security (Additional Payments) Act 2022, both those to recipients of specified means-tested benefits and "disability" payments are not to be taken into account for any old style ESA purposes by virtue of s.8(b) of the Act. The same effect was achieved with effect from March 23, 2023 in 6.138

relation to payments under the Social Security (Additional Payments) Act 2023 (s.8(b) of that Act). See Pt I of Vol.II for the text of both Acts.

PART V

UNIVERSAL CREDIT COMMENCEMENT ORDERS

p.1613, *amendment of the Welfare Reform Act 2012 (Commencement No.9 and Transitional and Transitory Provisions and Commencement No.8 and Savings and Transitional Provisions (Amendment)) Order 2013 (SI 2013/983) art.5A (Transitional provision where Secretary of State determines that claims for universal credit may not be made: effect on claims for employment and support allowance and jobseeker's allowance)*

6.139   With effect from March 30, 2022, art.5 and Sch.1 para.1(2) of the Welfare Reform Act 2012 (Commencement No. 34 and Commencement No. 9, 21, 23, 31 and 32 and Transitional and Transitory Provisions (Amendment)) Order 2022 (SI 2022/302) omitted the phrase "or article 4(11) of the Welfare Reform Act 2012 (Commencement No. 32 and Savings and Transitional Provisions) Order 2019 (no claims for universal credit by frontier workers)" in art.5A(1). But note also the next entry.

p.1613, *revocation of the Welfare Reform Act 2012 (Commencement No.9 and Transitional and Transitory Provisions and Commencement No.8 and Savings and Transitional Provisions (Amendment)) Order 2013 (SI 2013/983) art.5A (Transitional provision where Secretary of State determines that claims for universal credit may not be made: effect on claims for employment and support allowance and jobseeker's allowance)*

6.140   With effect from July 25, 2022, reg.11 of, and Sch. para.2(2) to, the Universal Credit (Transitional Provisions) Amendment Regulations 2022 (SI 2022/752) revoked art.5A.

p.1615, *amendments to the Welfare Reform Act 2012 (Commencement No. 9 and Transitional and Transitory Provisions and Commencement No. 8 and Savings and Transitional Provisions (Amendment)) Order 2013 (SI 2013/983) art.6 (Transitional provision: where the abolition of income-related employment and support allowance and income-based jobseeker's allowance is treated as not applying)*

6.141   With effect from March 30, 2022, art.5 and Sch.1 para.1(3) of the Welfare Reform Act 2012 (Commencement No. 34 and Commencement No. 9, 21, 23, 31 and 32 and Transitional and Transitory Provisions (Amendment)) Order 2022 (SI 2022/302) omitted the phrase "or article 4(11) of the Welfare Reform Act 2012 (Commencement No. 32 and Savings and Transitional Provisions) Order 2019 (no claims for universal credit by frontier workers)" in art.6(1)(e)(ii).
    With effect from July 25, 2022, reg.11 of, and Sch. para.2(3) to, the Universal Credit (Transitional Provisions) Amendment Regulations 2022 (SI 2022/752) omitted para.(1)(e)(ii) in art.6 and the "or" preceding it.

pp.1663–1664, *annotation to the Welfare Reform Act 2012 (Commencement No.20 and Transitional and Transitory Provisions and Commencement No.9 and Transitional and Transitory Provisions (Amendment)) Order 2014 (SI 2014/3094)*

Article 6 of SI 2014/3094 (Transitory provision: claims for housing benefit, income support or a tax credit) was revoked with effect from July 25, 2022, by reg.11 of, and Sch. para.5 to, the Universal Credit (Transitional Provisions) Amendment Regulations 2022 (SI 2022/752).

6.142

pp.1670–1672, *amendment of the Welfare Reform Act 2012 (Commencement No.21 and Transitional and Transitory Provisions) Order 2015 (SI 2015/33) art.6 (Transitional provision: claims for housing benefit, income support or a tax credit)*

With effect from March 30, 2022, art.5 and Sch.1 para.2 of the Welfare Reform Act 2012 (Commencement No. 34 and Commencement No. 9, 21, 23, 31 and 32 and Transitional and Transitory Provisions (Amendment)) Order 2022 (SI 2022/302) omitted the phrase "or by virtue of article 4(11) of the Welfare Reform Act 2012 (Commencement No. 32 and Savings and Transitional Provisions) Order 2019" in art.6(11). But note also the next entry.

6.143

pp.1670–1672, *revocation of the Welfare Reform Act 2012 (Commencement No.21 and Transitional and Transitory Provisions) Order 2015 (SI 2015/33) art.6 (Transitional provision: claims for housing benefit, income support or a tax credit)*

With effect from July 25, 2022, reg.11 of, and Sch. para.3 to, the Universal Credit (Transitional Provisions) Amendment Regulations 2022 (SI 2022/752) revoked art.6.

6.144

p.1674, *annotation to the Welfare Reform Act 2012 (Commencement No.23 and Transitional and Transitory Provisions) Order 2015 (SI 2015/634) (General Note)*

Delete the letter "a" after "These" in line 3 of the General Note at para.5.116.

6.145

p.1681, *amendment of the Welfare Reform Act 2012 (Commencement No.23 and Transitional and Transitory Provisions) Order 2015 (SI 2015/634) art.7 (Transitional provision: claims for housing benefit, income support or a tax credit)*

With effect from March 30, 2022, art.5 and Sch.1 para.3 of the Welfare Reform Act 2012 (Commencement No. 34 and Commencement No. 9, 21, 23, 31 and 32 and Transitional and Transitory Provisions (Amendment)) Order 2022 (SI 2022/302) omitted the phrase "or by virtue of article 4(11) of the Welfare Reform Act 2012 (Commencement No. 32 and Savings and Transitional Provisions) Order 2019" in art.7(2). But note also the next entry.

6.146

pp.1681–1683, *revocation of the Welfare Reform Act 2012 (Commencement No. 23 and Transitional and Transitory Provisions) Order 2015 (SI 2015/634) art. 7 (Transitional provision: claims for housing benefit, income support or a tax credit)*

6.147   With effect from July 25, 2022, reg.11 of, and Sch. para.6 to, the Universal Credit (Transitional Provisions) Amendment Regulations 2022 (SI 2022/752) revoked art.7.

p.1732, *amendment to the Welfare Reform Act 2012 (Commencement No. 31 and Savings and Transitional Provisions and Commencement No. 21 and 23 and Transitional and Transitory Provisions (Amendment)) Order 2019 (SI 2019/37) art. 2 (Interpretation)*

6.148   With effect from July 25, 2022, reg.11 of, and Sch. para.4(2) to, the Universal Credit (Transitional Provisions) Amendment Regulations 2022 (SI 2022/752) omitted "and article 8(2)(b)" in art.2(3).

p.1734, *amendment to the Welfare Reform Act 2012 (Commencement No. 31 and Savings and Transitional Provisions and Commencement No. 21 and 23 and Transitional and Transitory Provisions (Amendment)) Order 2019 (SI 2019/37) art. 6 (Transitional provision: termination of awards of housing benefit)*

6.149   With effect from July 25, 2022, reg.11 of, and Sch. para.4(3) to, the Universal Credit (Transitional Provisions) Amendment Regulations 2022 (SI 2022/752) substituted "in regulation 2 of the Universal Credit (Transitional Provisions) Regulations 2014" for "respectively in sub-paragraphs (h) and (l) of article 7(11) of the No.23 Order" in art.6(4).

p.1734, *amendment to the Welfare Reform Act 2012 (Commencement No. 31 and Savings and Transitional Provisions and Commencement No. 21 and 23 and Transitional and Transitory Provisions (Amendment)) Order 2019 (SI 2019/37) art.7 (Transitional provision: application to housing benefit of the rules in universal credit for treatment of couples and polygamous marriages)*

6.150   With effect from July 25, 2022, reg.11 of, and Sch. para.4(4) to, the Universal Credit (Transitional Provisions) Amendment Regulations 2022 (SI 2022/752) substituted "regulation 6A of the Universal Credit (Transitional Provisions) Regulations 2014" for "article 6 of the No. 21 Order or article 7 of the No. 23 Order" in art.7(1)(a)(i).

p.1735, *amendment of the Welfare Reform Act 2012 (Commencement No. 31 and Savings and Transitional Provisions and Commencement No. 21 and 23 and Transitional and Transitory Provisions (Amendment)) Order 2019 (SI 2019/37) art.8 (Transitional provision: where restrictions on claims for universal credit are in place)*

6.151   With effect from March 30, 2022, art.5 and Sch.1 para.4 of the Welfare Reform Act 2012 (Commencement No. 34 and Commencement No. 9, 21, 23, 31 and 32 and Transitional and Transitory Provisions (Amendment)) Order 2022 (SI 2022/302) inserted "or" at the end of art.8(1)(a) and omitted both art.8(1)(c) and the "or" preceding it. But note also the next entry.

pp.1735–1736, *revocation of the Welfare Reform Act 2012 (Commencement No. 31 and Savings and Transitional Provisions and Commencement No. 21 and 23 and Transitional and Transitory Provisions (Amendment)) Order 2019 (SI 2019/37) art.8 (Transitional provision: where restrictions on claims for universal credit are in place)*

With effect from July 25, 2022, reg.11 of, and Sch. para.4(5) to, the Universal Credit (Transitional Provisions) Amendment Regulations 2022 (SI 2022/752) revoked art.8. 6.152

p.1738, *amendment of the Welfare Reform Act 2012 (Commencement No. 32 and Savings and Transitional Provisions) Order 2019 (SI 2019/167) art.1 (Citation and interpretation)*

With effect from March 30, 2022, art.4(3) of the Welfare Reform Act 2012 (Commencement No. 34 and Commencement No. 9, 21, 23, 31 and 32 and Transitional and Transitory Provisions (Amendment)) Order 2022 (SI 2022/302) omitted art.1(3). 6.153

p.1742, *amendment of the Welfare Reform Act 2012 (Commencement No. 32 and Savings and Transitional Provisions) Order 2019 (SI 2019/167) art.4 (Appointed day—coming into force of universal credit provisions and abolition of income-related employment and support allowance and income-based jobseeker's allowance: persons resident outside Great Britain)*

With effect from March 30, 2022, art.4(4) of the Welfare Reform Act 2012 (Commencement No. 34 and Commencement No. 9, 21, 23, 31 and 32 and Transitional and Transitory Provisions (Amendment)) Order 2022 (SI 2022/302) omitted art.4(11). 6.154

p.1745, *insertion of new Commencement Order at para.5.188 onwards.*

The Welfare Reform Act 2012 (Commencement No. 34 and Commencement No. 9, 21, 23, 31 and 32 and Transitional and Transitory Provisions (Amendment)) Order 2022

SI 2022/302 (c.12)

The Secretary of State makes the following Order in exercise of the powers conferred by section 150(3) and (4)(a), (b)(i) and (c) of the Welfare Reform Act 2012: 6.155

ARRANGEMENT OF ARTICLES

1. Citation
2. Interpretation
3. Full commencement of universal credit
4. Removal of restriction preventing frontier workers from claiming universal credit
5. Consequential amendments
Schedule: Consequential amendments

Citation

5.188   **1.** This Order may be cited as the Welfare Reform Act 2012 (Commencement No. 34 and Commencement No. 9, 21, 23, 31 and 32 and Transitional and Transitory Provisions (Amendment)) Order 2022.

Interpretation

5.189   **2.** In this Order—

"the No. 9 Order" means the Welfare Reform Act 2012 (Commencement No. 9 and Transitional and Transitory Provisions and Commencement No. 8 and Savings and Transitional Provisions (Amendment)) Order 2013;
"the No. 32 Order" means the Welfare Reform Act 2012 (Commencement No. 32 and Savings and Transitional Provisions) Order 2019.

Full commencement of universal credit

5.190   **3.** 30th March 2022 ("the appointed day") is the appointed day for the coming into force of the provisions of the Welfare Reform Act 2012 listed in Schedule 2 (universal credit provisions coming into force in relation to certain claims and awards) to the No. 9 Order, in so far as they are not already in force.

Removal of restriction preventing frontier workers from claiming universal credit

5.191   **4.**—(1) The amendments of the No. 32 Order set out in paragraphs (3) and (4) have effect from the appointed day.

(2) The No. 32 Order is amended as follows.

(3) In article 1 (citation and interpretation), omit paragraph (3).

(4) In article 4 (appointed day—coming into force of universal credit provisions and abolition of income-related employment and support allowance and income-based jobseeker's allowance: persons resident outside Great Britain), omit paragraph (11).

Consequential amendments

5.192   **5.** The consequential amendments set out in the Schedule have effect from the appointed day.

Article 5

SCHEDULE

CONSEQUENTIAL AMENDMENTS

5.193   **1.**—(1) The No. 9 Order is amended as follows.

(2) In article 5A (transitional provision where Secretary of State determines that claims for universal credit may not be made: effect on claims for employment and support allowance and jobseeker's allowance), in paragraph (1) omit "or article 4(11) of the Welfare Reform Act 2012 (Commencement No. 32 and Savings and Transitional Provisions) Order 2019 (no claims for universal credit by frontier workers)".

(3) In article 6 (transitional provision: where the abolition of income-related employment and support allowance and income-based jobseeker's allowance is treated as not applying), in

paragraph (1)(e)(ii) omit "or article 4(11) of the Welfare Reform Act 2012 (Commencement No. 32 and Savings and Transitional Provisions) Order 2019 (no claims for universal credit by frontier workers)".

2.—(1) The Welfare Reform Act 2012 (Commencement No. 21 and Transitional and Transitory Provisions) Order 2015 is amended as follows.

(2) In article 6 (transitional provision: claims for housing benefit, income support or a tax credit), in paragraph (11) omit "or by virtue of article 4(11) of the Welfare Reform Act 2012 (Commencement No. 32 and Savings and Transitional Provisions) Order 2019".

3.—(1) The Welfare Reform Act 2012 (Commencement No. 23 and Transitional and Transitory Provisions) Order 2015 is amended as follows.

(2) In article 7 (transitional provision: claims for housing benefit, income support or a tax credit), in paragraph (2) omit "or by virtue of article 4(11) of the Welfare Reform Act 2012 (Commencement No. 32 and Savings and Transitional Provisions) Order 2019".

4.—(1) The Welfare Reform Act 2012 (Commencement No. 31 and Savings and Transitional Provisions and Commencement No. 21 and 23 and Transitional and Transitory Provisions (Amendment)) Order 2019 is amended as follows.

(2) In article 8 (transitional provision: where restrictions on claims for universal credit are in place)—

    (a) at the end of paragraph (1)(a) insert "or"; and

    (b) omit subparagraph (1)(c) and the "or" preceding it.

PART VI

TRANSITIONAL, SAVINGS AND MODIFICATIONS PROVISIONS

PART VII

IMMIGRATION STATUS AND THE RIGHT TO RESIDE

p.1793, *annotation to the Immigration (European Economic Area) Regulations 2016 (SI 2016/1052) (General Note—EEA nationals and their family members with pre-settled status)*

In *R. (Fratila) v SSWP* [2021] UKSC 53; [2022] P.T.S.R. 448 the Supreme Court allowed the appeal by the Secretary of State against a decision of the Court of Appeal which had found reg.9(3)(c)(i) unlawfully discriminatory contrary to art.18 of the TFEU for treating EU nationals with pre-settled status differently to UK nationals. The judgment of the Court of Appeal had become unsustainable following the decision of the CJEU, in *CG v Department for Communities* (C-709/20) [2021] 1 W.L.R. 5919, that such a provision is not contrary to art.18 of the TFEU, or Directive 2004/38.

However, what the Supreme Court elected not to address (since it was a new point, which would have required new evidence) was the implications for the domestic Regulations of what had also been said in *CG* about the Charter of Fundamental Rights of the European Union (the Charter). The Court of Justice had stated:

"[93] . . . [Where] a Union citizen resides legally, on the basis of national law, in the territory of a Member State other than that of which he or she is a national, the national authorities empowered to grant social assistance are required to check that a refusal to grant such benefits based on that

    6.156

legislation does not expose that citizen, and the children for which he or she is responsible, to an actual and current risk of violation of their fundamental rights, as enshrined in Articles 1, 7 and 24 of the Charter. Where that citizen does not have any resources to provide for his or her own needs and those of his or her children and is isolated, those authorities must ensure that, in the event of a refusal to grant social assistance, that citizen may nevertheless live with his or her children in dignified conditions. In the context of that examination, those authorities may take into account all means of assistance provided for by national law, from which the citizen concerned and her children are actually entitled to benefit."

Important questions arising from *CG* are:

- whether the Charter has any ongoing application, since the end of the transition period in December 2020, for EU nationals resident in the UK on the basis of pre-settled status; and
- what if any substantive or procedural requirements are imposed on the Secretary of State by the obligation to 'check' that Charter rights will not be breached.

In *Secretary of State for Work and Pensions v AT (UC)* [2022] UKUT 330 (AAC) (December 12, 2022), a three-judge panel addressed those questions. It dismissed the Secretary of State's appeal against a decision that a destitute parent who was also a victim of domestic violence was entitled to UC. Though her only right of residence was on the basis of her pre-settled status, the refusal of UC would breach her Charter rights. The panel decided that by virtue of the Withdrawal Agreement, the Charter does indeed continue to apply following the end of the transition period where a person is residing in the UK with pre-settled status. It also decided that *CG* does indeed impose a requirement on the Secretary of State (and by extension the FTT) to check in individual cases that there is no breach of Charter rights. It gives guidance on how that check should be conducted. The Secretary of State appealed unsuccessfully to the Court of Appeal: [2023] EWCA Civ 1307 (November 8, 2023). On February 7, 2024 the Supreme Court refused the Secretary of State's further application for permission to appeal, so the decision of the Upper Tribunal is now final.

p.1798, *annotation to the Immigration (European Economic Area) Regulations 2016 (SI 2016/1052) (General Note—Overview)*

6.157   In *FN v SSWP (UC)* [2022] UKUT 77 (AAC), Judge Ward records an example of the evidential problems which can arise for claimants seeking to demonstrate a right of residence under these Regulations:

"[4] . . . On the (erroneous) basis that it was necessary to demonstrate that the husband was a 'qualified person', the claimant, by her social worker, had informed the DWP that she and her daughter had fled the family home due to domestic violence and that the claimant had obtained a non-molestation order against her husband. His name, date of birth, national insurance number and details of his then current and previous employers were provided to the DWP, who were asked to contact them, as although the social worker had had some contact with the husband, he had been uncooperative in providing the information necessary.

[5] On mandatory reconsideration, the DWP upheld the original decision saying that the Data Protection Act prevented them from providing the information relating to the husband that had been requested.
[6] On appeal, the DWP indicated they could provide information if in response to a tribunal or court order. The claimant's representatives emailed the FtT on 6 February 2020 explaining this and asking for an order to be made. The email did not on its face identify that the claimant and her husband were estranged due to domestic violence and that may have contributed to why the District Tribunal Judge (DTJ) refused the application, saying, put shortly, that the husband should get them and send them to the DWP and that the FtT would only become involved if the parties had exhausted their own efforts. This prompted a follow-up email on 16 March 2020 explaining the background of domestic abuse and providing a copy of the non-molestation order. The DTJ remained adamant, indicating that the order did not prevent the claimant from contacting her husband through solicitors and until there was evidence that an attempt had been made to do so and had been unsuccessful the decision remained unaltered. Subsequently, on 26 May 2020 a registrar did make an order for the evidence to be supplied by DWP but it was not, despite the representative sending a follow-up email. The case was then listed as a paper hearing, without further notification to the claimant or her representative, and decided [adversely to the claimant]."

As the facts of *FN* indicate, problems are particularly likely where a right of residence may derive from a family member from whom the claimant is estranged. A Tribunal's failure to exercise the FTT's inquisitorial duty to seek evidence of a right of residence, including by establishing details about a relative's identity and possible rights of residence, may constitute an error of law. See, e.g. *AS v SSWP (UC)* [2018] UKUT 260 (AAC); *ZB v SSWP* CIS/468/2017 unreported April 25, 2019 ([21]: "an award of benefit is not a prize rewarding only the most adept"), and *PM v SSWP (IS)* [2014] UKUT 474 (AAC). It is clear from those decisions that the Tribunal can direct the Secretary of State to provide information she holds about an estranged family member. Further, while the Secretary of State appears to consider that due to her data protection obligations she can provide information about such a third party only if ordered to do so by a court or tribunal, there is room for doubt about whether that view is in fact correct, as noted in *ZB* at [19].

pp.1826–1829, *annotation to the Immigration (European Economic Area) Regulations 2016 (SI 2016/1052) reg.4 ("Worker", "self-employed person", "self-sufficient person" and "student")*

Self-sufficient persons

In *VI v Commissioners for HMRC* (C–247/20 O) (September 30, 2021) at [56]–[64], AG Hogan's opinion described a "fundamental question" in that case as "probably" being whether free access to the NHS satisfies the requirement to have CSI, and lamented that the UK Government had not made any submissions about that issue. However, the AG did not express an opinion on the answer, and advised the Court not to do so either.

Surprisingly, the court's judgment ([2022] EUECJ C-247/20 [2022] 1 W.L.R. 2902) did give an answer, and the answer was that free access to the NHS does satisfy the CSI requirement:

6.158

"[68] In the present case, it is apparent from the documents before the Court that VI and her son were affiliated during the period in question, namely from 1 May 2006 to 20 August 2006, to the United Kingdom's public sickness insurance system offered free of charge by the National Health Service.

[69] In that regard, it must be recalled that, although the host Member State may, subject to compliance with the principle of proportionality, make affiliation to its public sickness insurance system of an economically inactive Union citizen, residing in its territory on the basis of Article 7(1)(b) of Directive 2004/38, subject to conditions intended to ensure that that citizen does not become an unreasonable burden on the public finances of that Member State, such as the conclusion or maintaining, by that citizen, of comprehensive private sickness insurance enabling the reimbursement to that Member State of the health expenses it has incurred for that citizen's benefit, or the payment, by that citizen, of a contribution to that Member State's public sickness insurance system (judgment of 15 July 2021, *A (Public health care)* (C–535/19) EU:C:2021:595 at [59]), the fact remains that, once a Union citizen is affiliated to such a public sickness insurance system in the host Member State, he or she has comprehensive sickness insurance within the meaning of Article 7(1)(b).

[70] Furthermore, in a situation, such as that in the main proceedings, in which the economically inactive Union citizen at issue is a child, one of whose parents, a third-country national, has worked and was subject to tax in the host State during the period at issue, it would be disproportionate to deny that child and the parent who is his or her primary carer a right of residence, under Article 7(1)(b) of Directive 2004/38, on the sole ground that, during that period, they were affiliated free of charge to the public sickness insurance system of that State. It cannot be considered that that affiliation free of charge constitutes, in such circumstances, an unreasonable burden on the public finances of that State."

That decision is obviously inconsistent with a long line of domestic authority, cited in the main volume commentary: for example *Ahmad v Secretary of State for the Home Department* [2014] EWCA Civ 988; *FK (Kenya) v Secretary of State for the Home Department* [2010] EWCA Civ 1302; *W (China) and X (China) v Secretary of State for the Home Department* [2006] EWCA Civ 1494 and *VP v SSWP (JSA)* [2014] UKUT 32 (AAC) and *SSWP v GS (PC) (European Union law: free movement)* [2016] UKUT 394 (AAC); [2017] AACR 7.

VI falls within the scope of art.89 of the Withdrawal Agreement (as a CJEU reference made before the end of the Transition Period). As such, it so far appears to be uncontentious that *VI* is directly binding, in relation to periods before December 31, 2020, and that the old domestic authorities should no longer be followed. See *WH v Powys County Council and SSWP* [2022] UKUT 203 (AAC), para.3.

In *SSWP v WV (UC)* [2023] UKUT 112 (AAC) the Upper Tribunal shows one way in which *VI* may have practical application for a person reliant on benefit income. A Belgian national was a carer for his disabled wife who received income-related ESA. The amount of social assistance decreased due to the claimant's presence in the household: the loss of some premiums, and the inclusion of carer's allowance (which is social security not social assistance), more than offset the increase to couple rates. UTJ Ward decided the claimant had a right to reside at that time as a self-sufficient person. Until *VI*, the claimant's argument would have foundered on the comprehensive sickness insurance requirement, but *VI* meant that the claimant met it. When the couple then claimed universal credit, the relatively modest additional cost which awarding that benefit to the couple rather than just awarding it to his UK national spouse as a single person (and only for the 23 months until the claimant qualified for settled status), along with the cost of similar such claims which would also now fall to be allowed, was not an "unreasonable burden" on the UK social assistance system. Consequently, the claimant did not lose his right to reside as a self-sufficient person, and was therefore entitled to a joint award of universal credit.

p.1889–1891, *modification to the Immigration (European Economic Area) Regulations 2016 reg.16 (SI 2016/1052) (Derivative right to reside)*

As explained in the main text, the 2016 Regulations continue to apply as saved and modified by the Immigration and Social Security Co-ordination (EU Withdrawal) Act 2020 (Consequential, Saving, Transitional and Transitory Provisions) (EU Exit) Regulations 2020 (SI 2020/1309).   6.159

With effect from February 2, 2023, by amending the 2020 Regulations, reg.5 of the Immigration (Restrictions on Employment etc.) (Amendment) (EU Exit) Regulations 2023 (SI 2023/12) makes additional modifications to the saved reg.16 of the 2016 Regulations:

- in paragraph (3)(b), after "a worker" insert "or a self-employed person";
- in paragraph (7), after sub-paragraph (c), insert— "(d) "self-employed person" does not include a person treated as a self-employed person under regulation 6(4);"

p.1890, *erratum—Immigration (European Economic Area) Regulations 2016 (SI 2016/1052), reg.16 (Derivative right to reside)*

There is an error in the first of the two parallel versions of reg.16(12) (i.e. the version stated as now applying to those with pre-settled status). The words "unless that decision" should be deleted from that version.   6.160

pp.1891–1892, *annotation to the Immigration (European Economic Area) Regulations 2016 (SI 2016/1052) reg.16 (Derivative right to reside)*

Primary carers of self-sufficient children
The main volume General Note discusses a pending reference to the CJEU in *Bajratari v Secretary of State for the Home Department* [2017] NICA 74. The Court's judgment (C-93/18) was delivered on October 2, 2019 ([2020] 1 W.L.R. 2327). It agreed with AG Szpunar and held (at [53]), that a Union citizen minor can meet the requirement to have sufficient resources not to become an unreasonable burden on the social assistance system of the host Member State during his period of residence, "despite his resources being derived from income obtained from the unlawful employment of his parent, a third-country national without a residence card and work permit".   6.161

pp.1892–1893, *annotation to the Immigration (European Economic Area) Regulations 2016 (SI 2016/1052) reg.16 (Derivative right to reside)*

Primary carer of children of migrant workers in education

6.162   The main volume General Note asserts: "Where primary carers are also jobseekers (in the EU sense of that term), they cannot be denied social assistance on the basis of the derogation in art.24(2) of the Citizenship Directive". There is now domestic authority for that proposition: *Sandwell MBC v KK and SSWP (HB)* [2022] UKUT 123 (AAC).

p.1893, *annotation to the Immigration (European Economic Area) Regulations 2016 reg.16 (SI 2016/1052) (Derivative right to reside)*

Primary carers of previously self-sufficient children with a right of permanent residence

6.163   Regulation 16(2) and reg.16(5) address the position of carers of *Chen* children and of *Zambrano* children respectively (*Zhu and Chen v Home Secretary* (C-200/02); *Zambrano v Office national de l'emploi (ONEm)* (C-34/09)). It might be thought that both groups are in essentially the same position, insofar as the carer's right of residence does not generate a right to reside triggering social security entitlement. However, the difference is that the *Chen* child may eventually acquire a right of permanent residence under Directive 2004/38 art.16. The situation of primary carers of *previously* self-sufficient children who *now* have a right of permanent residence is not recognised in domestic law. But in *FE v HMRC (CHB)* [2022] UKUT 4 (AAC) the Upper Tribunal decides that it is necessary to treat that category differently, and recognise their right of access to social assistance.

PART VII

FORTHCOMING CHANGES AND
UP-RATING OF BENEFITS

FORTHCOMING CHANGES

Universal credit: managed migration

The DWP's plans for the sequence for issuing UC migration notices have been confirmed in a letter to local authorities dated December 4, 2023. The DWP's aim is to issue migration notices to all those in receipt of only tax credits by the end of March 2024. The migration plans for 2024/25 include notifying the remaining applicable households of the need to move to UC during this period, which includes residual tax credits cases (including those on both Employment Support Allowance and tax credits and Housing Benefit), all cases on Income Support and Jobseeker's Allowance (Income Based) and those combined with Housing Benefit and Housing Benefit only cases (except those Housing Benefit only customers living in supported or temporary accommodation). The DWP plans to undertake the issuing of migration notices to working age benefit claimants sequentially starting with Income Support (April–June), Employment Support Allowance with Child Tax Credits (July–September) and Jobseeker's Allowance (September). If a Housing Benefit claimant is receiving one of these benefits, they will receive a migration notice. From April 2024 the DWP will also invite tax credits claimants with Housing Benefit and then Housing Benefit (only) claimants to move to UC.

7.001

Universal credit: minimum income floor

As and when the administrative changes announced on October 24, 2023 to the calculation of expected hours under reg.88 of the Universal Credit Regulations 2013 for responsible carers of children aged three to 12 begin to work through into an increased number of hours (see the entry in this Supplement for p.472 of Vol.II for the details), there will be an effect on the calculation of the level of earnings to constitute the minimum income floor under reg.62(2) and (3) for those in gainful self-employment. Those provisions adopt the levels of the individual or couple threshold (known as the conditionality earnings threshold) in reg.90. That effect was announced as a specific measure in para.5.34 of the *Autumn Statement 2023* (CP977, November 22, 2023), according to the Correction Note issued on December 1, 2023 to operate from January 2024 rather than April 2024 as originally indicated, but appears to be an inevitable knock-on effect of the October 2023 administrative changes.

7.002

Universal credit: transitional protection

The Universal Credit (Transitional Provisions) (Amendment) Regulations 2023 (SI 2023/1238), in force with effect from February 14, 2024, make further provision for transition to universal credit following the judgment of

7.003

Holgate J in *R. (on the application of) TP and AR (TP and AR No.3)* [2022] EWHC 123 Admin. The High Court concluded in *TP No.3* that there was an unjustifiable difference in treatment between severe disability premium recipients who naturally migrated from legacy benefits to universal credit, by virtue of making a claim to universal credit as a result of a change in their circumstances, and those who remain on legacy benefits. Accordingly, reg.2 inserts a new Sch.3 into the Universal Credit (Transitional Provisions) Regulations 2014 (SI 2014/1230). The Schedule provides for an additional amount of universal credit to be payable to certain claimants who were previously entitled to SDP or EDP in connection with their legacy benefits. See further *FL v SSWP (UC)* [2024] UKUT 6 (AAC) and the highly critical *Fifth Report* of the House of Lords' Secondary Legislation Scrutiny Committee, published on December 7, 2023.

Additional payments

7.004   The Social Security Additional Payments (Third Qualifying Day) Regulations 2023 (SI 2023/1352), in force with effect from January 15, 2024, specify the third qualifying day for the purpose of the means-tested additional payments under s.1 of the Social Security (Additional Payments) Act 2023 (c.7) as being December 12, 2023. As provided for by s.1(8) of the Act, and as an anti-abuse provision, this date falls before the day on which these Regulations come into force.

NEW BENEFIT RATES FROM APRIL 2024

NEW BENEFIT RATES FROM APRIL 2024

(Benefits covered in Volume I)

	April 2023 £ pw	April 2024 £ pw
Disability benefits		
Attendance allowance		
higher rate	101.75	108.55
lower rate	68.10	72.65
Disability living allowance		
Care Component		
highest rate	101.75	108.55
middle rate	68.10	72.65
lowest rate	26.90	28.70
Mobility Component		
higher rate	71.00	75.75
lower rate	26.90	28.70
Carer's allowance	76.75	81.90
Maternity allowance		
Standard rate	172.48	184.03
Bereavement benefits and retirement pensions		
Widowed parent's allowance or widowed mother's allowance	139.10	148.40
Widow's pension		
standard rate	139.10	148.40
Retirement pension		
Category A or Category B (higher)	156.20	169.50
Category B (lower), Category C or Category D	93.60	101.55
New state pension	203.85	221.20
Dependency increase for child		
The only, elder or eldest child for whom child benefit is being paid	8.00	8.00
Any other child	11.35	11.35

	April 2023 £ pw	April 2024 £ pw
Industrial injuries benefits		
Disablement benefit		
100%	207.60	221.50
90%	186.84	199.35
80%	166.08	177.20
70%	145.32	155.05
60%	124.56	132.90
50%	103.80	110.75
40%	83.04	88.60
30%	62.28	66.45
20%	41.52	44.30
Unemployability supplement		
Basic rate	128.40	137.00
Increase for adult dependant	76.75	81.90
Increase for child dependant	11.35	11.35
Increase for early incapacity-higher rate	26.60	28.40
Increase for early incapacity-middle rate	17.10	18.20
Increase for early incapacity-lower rate	8.55	9.10
constant attendance allowance		
exceptional rate	166.20	177.40
intermediate rate	124.65	133.05
normal maximum rate	83.10	88.70
part-time rate	41.55	44.35
exceptionally severe disablement allowance	83.10	88.70
reduced earnings allowance-maximum rate	83.04	88.60
retirement allowance-maximum rate	20.76	22.15
Death benefit		
Widow's pension (higher rate) or widower's pension	156.20	169.50
Widow's pension (lower rate)	46.86	50.85
"New-style" jobseeker's allowance		
Personal allowances		
aged under 25	67.20	71.70
aged 25 or over	84.80	90.50
"New-style" employment and support allowance		
Personal allowances		
assessment phase-*aged under 25*	67.20	71.70
aged 25 and over	84.80	90.50
main phase	84.80	90.50
work-related activity component	33.70	35.95
support component	44.70	47.70

NEW BENEFIT RATES FROM APRIL 2024

(Benefits covered in Volume II)

Universal credit	April 2023 £ pm	April 2024 £ pm
Standard allowances		
Single claimant-*aged under 25*	292.11	311.68
aged 25 or over	368.74	393.45
Joint claimants-*both aged under 25*	458.51	489.23
one or both aged 25 or over	578.82	627.60
Child element-*first child (if born before April 6, 2017)*	315.00	333.33
each other child	269.58	287.92
Disabled child addition-*lower rate*	146.31	156.11
higher rate	456.89	487.58
Limited capability for work element	146.31	156.11
Limited capability for work and work-related activity element	390.06	416.19
Carer element	185.86	198.31
Childcare element-*maximum for one child*	950.92	1014.63
-maximum for two or more children	1630.15	1739.37
Non-dependants' housing cost contributions	85.73	91.47
Work allowances		
Higher work allowance (no housing element)		
one or more children	631.00	673.00
limited capability for work	631.00	673.00
Lower work allowance		
one or more children	379.00	404.00
limited capability for work	379.00	404.00

Pension credit	£ pw	£ pw
Standard minimum guarantee		
Single person	201.05	218.15
Couple	306.85	332.95
Additional amount for child or qualifying young person		
first child (if both before April 6, 2017)	72.31	76.79
each other child	61.88	66.29
Additional amount for severe disability		
single person	76.40	81.50
couple (one qualifies)	76.40	81.50
couple (both qualify)	152.80	163.00
Additional amount for carers	42.75	45.60
Additional amount for additional spouse in a polygamous marriage	105.80	114.80
Savings credit threshold		
single person	174.49	189.80
couple	277.12	301.22
Maximum savings credit		
single person	15.94	17.01
couple	17.84	19.04

NEW BENEFIT RATES FROM APRIL 2024

(Benefits covered in Volume IV)

HMRC-administered payments	2022–23	2023–24
	£ pw	£ pw
Benefits in respect of children		
Child benefit		
only, elder or eldest child	24.00	25.60
each subsequent child	15.90	16.95
Guardian's allowance	20.40	21.75
Employer-paid benefits		
Standard rates		
Statutory sick pay	109.40	116.75
Statutory maternity pay	172.48	184.03
Statutory paternity pay	172.48	184.03
Statutory shared parental pay	172.48	184.03
Statutory parental bereavement pay	172.48	184.03
Statutory adoption pay	172.48	184.03
Income threshold	123.00	123.00

Tax credits	£ pa	£ pa
Working tax credit		
Basic element	2,280	2,435
Couple and lone parent element	2,340	2,500
30 hour element	950	1,015
Disabled worker element	3,685	3,935
Severe disability element	1,595	1,705
Child care element		
maximum eligible cost for one child	175 pw	175 pw
maximum eligible cost for two or more children	300 pw	300 pw
per cent of eligible costs covered	70%	70%
Child tax credit		
Family element	545	545
Child element	3,235	3,455
Disabled child element	3,905	4,170
Severely disabled child element	5,480	5,850
Tax credit income thresholds		
Income threshold	7,455	7,955
Income threshold for those entitled to child tax credit only	18,725	19,995

Scottish social security assistance	£ pw	£ pw
Adult disability payment		
Daily living component		
Enhanced rate	101.75	108.55
Standard rate	68.10	72.65

HMRC-administered payments	**2022–23**	**2023–24**
	£ pw	£ pw
Mobility component		
Enhanced rate	71.00	75.75
Standard rate	26.90	28.70
Child disability payment		
Care component		
Highest rate	101.75	108.55
Middle rate	68.10	72.65
Lowest rate	26.90	28.70
Mobility component		
Higher rate	71.00	75.75
Lower rate	26.90	28.70
Scottish child payment	25.00	26.70
	£	£
Best start grants		
Pregnancy and baby grant		
First child	707.25	754.65
Subsequent child and additional payment for twins etc	353.65	377.35
Early learning payment	294.70	314.45
School age payment	294.70	314.45
Funeral expense assistance		
Standard rate	1,178.75	1,257.75
Rate where the deceased has left in place a pre-paid funeral plan	143.85	153.50
Maximum rate for removal of an implanted Medical device by a person other than a registered medical practitioner	23.75	25.35
Young carer grant	359.65	383.75
Child winter heating assistance	235.70	251.50
Winter heating payment	55.05	58.75
Carer's allowance supplement (bi-annual)	270.50	288.60

NEW BENEFIT RATES FROM APRIL 2024

(Benefits covered in Volume V)

	April 2023 £ pw	April 2024 £ pw
Contribution-based jobseeker's allowance		
Personal rates-*aged under 25*	67.20	71.70
aged 25 or over	84.80	90.50
Contribution-based employment and support allowance		
Personal rates-assessment phase-*aged under 25*	67.20	71.70
aged 25 or over	84.80	90.50
main phase	84.80	90.50
Components		
work-related activity	33.70	35.95
support	44.70	47.70
Income support and income-based jobseeker's allowance		
Personal allowances		
Single person-aged under 25	67.20	71.70
aged 25 or over	84.80	90.50
lone parent-aged under 18	67.20	71.70
aged 18 or over	84.80	90.50
couple-both aged under 18	67.20	71.70
both aged under 18, with a child	101.50	108.30
one aged under 18, one aged under 25	67.20	71.70
one aged under 18, one aged 25 or over	84.80	90.50
both aged 18 or over	133.30	142.25
dependent child	77.78	83.24
Premiums		
Family-ordinary	18.53	19.15
lone parent	18.53	19.15
Pensioner-single person (JSA only)	116.25	127.65
couple	173.55	190.70
Disability-single person	39.85	42.50
couple	56.80	60.60
Enhanced disability-single person	19.55	20.85
couple	27.90	29.75
disabled child	30.17	32.20
Severe disability-single person	76.40	81.50
couple (one qualifies)	76.40	81.50
couple (both qualify)	152.80	163.00
Disabled child	74.69	80.01
Carer	42.75	45.60

	April 2023 £ pw	April 2024 £ pw
Income-related employment and support allowance		
Personal allowances		
Single person-aged under 25	67.20	71.70
aged 25 or over	84.80	90.50
lone parent-aged under 18	67.20	71.70
aged 18 or over	84.80	90.50
couple-both aged under 18	67.20	71.70
both aged under 18, with a child	101.50	108.30
both aged under 18 (main phase)	67.20	71.70
one aged under 18, one aged 18 or over	133.30	142.25
both aged 18 or over	133.30	142.25
Components		
work-related activity	33.70	35.95
support	44.70	47.70
Premiums		
Pensioner-single person with no component	116.25	127.65
couple with no component	173.55	190.70
Disability-single person	39.85	42.50
couple	56.80	60.60
Enhanced disability-single person	19.55	20.85
couple	27.90	29.75
Severe disability-single person	76.40	81.50
couple (one qualifies)	76.40	81.50
couple (both qualify)	152.80	163.00
Carer	42.75	45.60

JOURNAL OF SOCIAL SECURITY LAW

General Editors

Neville Harris Emeritus Professor of Law, University of Manchester

Gráinne McKeever Professor of Law and Social Justice, University of Ulster

The *Journal of Social Security Law* provides expert coverage and analysis of the latest developments in law, policy and practice across the field of social security law, covering the wide range of welfare benefits and tax credits in the UK and internationally.

To mark - and celebrate - the Journal's 30th anniversary the first two issues in 2024 have been designated as special issues. The articles in issue 1, comprise:

- Michael Adler Do Benefit Sanctions Have a Future?

- Terry Carney Automation and Conditionality: Towards "Virtual" Social Security?

- Jackie Gulland Age as a Condition of Entitlement to Social Security: Changing Ideas over Thirty Years

- Simon Halliday, Jed Meers and Joe Tomlinson Procedural Legitimacy Logics within the Digital Welfare State

- Amir Paz-Fuchs and Avishai Benish Privatizing Social Security

- Frans Pennings The Changing Perceptions on Benefit Recipients in Dutch Social Security Policy in the Past 30 Years

Available in print, as an eBook on ProView and online on Westlaw UK

CALL   0345 600 9355

EMAIL   TRLUKI.orders@thomsonreuters.com

VISIT   sweetandmaxwell.co.uk

Have you tried this publication as a **ProView** eBook?

For further information about ProView or to request a trial, please visit www.sweetandmaxwell. co.uk/proview

THOMSON REUTERS®